Margaret Hall

The Imperial Aircraft Flotilla

The Worldwide Fundraising Campaign for the
British Flying Services in the First World War

Margaret Hall

THE IMPERIAL AIRCRAFT FLOTILLA

The Worldwide Fundraising Campaign for the British
Flying Services in the First World War

ibidem-Verlag
Stuttgart

Bibliografische Information der Deutschen Nationalbibliothek
Die Deutsche Nationalbibliothek verzeichnet diese Publikation in der Deutschen Nationalbibliografie; detaillierte bibliografische Daten sind im Internet über http://dnb.d-nb.de abrufbar.

Bibliographic information published by the Deutsche Nationalbibliothek
Die Deutsche Nationalbibliothek lists this publication in the Deutsche Nationalbibliografie; detailed bibliographic data are available in the Internet at http://dnb.d-nb.de.

Cover design: Su Khoo.

Cover pictures: The Imperial Aircraft Flotilla appeal leaflet, late 1916/17. © The British Library Board.
Khoo Cheow Teong, co-donor of *Malaya XV*. Courtesy of Patrick Khoo.
Arthur Chapman, engineer at Shorts, in the cockpit of a replacement machine. Courtesy of David Payne.
Reprint with kind permission.

Gedruckt auf alterungsbeständigem, säurefreien Papier
Printed on acid-free paper

ISBN: 978-3-8382-1021-6

© *ibidem*-Verlag
Stuttgart 2017

Alle Rechte vorbehalten

Das Werk einschließlich aller seiner Teile ist urheberrechtlich geschützt. Jede Verwertung außerhalb der engen Grenzen des Urheberrechtsgesetzes ist ohne Zustimmung des Verlages unzulässig und strafbar. Dies gilt insbesondere für Vervielfältigungen, Übersetzungen, Mikroverfilmungen und elektronische Speicherformen sowie die Einspeicherung und Verarbeitung in elektronischen Systemen.

All rights reserved. No part of this publication may be reproduced, stored in or introduced into a retrieval system, or transmitted, in any form, or by any means (electronic, mechanical, photocopying, recording or otherwise) without the prior written permission of the publisher. Any person who does any unauthorized act in relation to this publication may be liable to criminal prosecution and civil claims for damages.

Printed in the EU

Table of Contents

List of Illustrations VII

Preface and Acknowledgments IX

Notes XI

Abbreviations XIII

Part I—How it began 1

Chapter 1: Introduction—Gifts for the Royal Navy, and the Patriotic League 3

Chapter 2: And for the Army, Vickers Gunbus *Dominica*, and a kite balloon … 17

Chapter 3: The Imperial Aircraft Flotilla Takes Off, 1915–1916 33

Part II—Case Studies: The campaign's spread and development … 53

Chapter 4: Press and personal networks: Canada and Newfoundland 55

Chapter 5: Sultan Seyyid Khalifa of Zanzibar and the Royal Naval Air Service 69

Chapter 6: Tropical Sugarcane Producers: Pacific, Indian Ocean, and Caribbean 83

Chapter 7: Eastern outposts—bankers and philanthropists of Hong Kong 101

Chapter 8: The Malaya Air Fleet Fund—the Straits Settlements and Malay states 115

Chapter 9: West Africa, and most particularly Gold Coast, and Hugh Clifford 135

Chapter 10: The Rhodesias—friends in high places, a Grey area? .. 153

Chapter 11: The Basuto nation, the British sovereign, and 25 Sopwith Camels 171

Chapter 12: Swaziland, Major Miller, the Union of South Africa, and Jan Smuts 187

Chapter 13: The Indian Empire: The sub-continent and Burma 201

Chapter 14: Birds of Ceylon—a very strange campaign indeed ... 215

Chapter 15: Furthest ripples of the Great War reach Abyssinia and Siam 231

Chapter 16: Big and small donors: The Shanghai Race Club and Argentine Britons 247

Chapter 17: Charles Alma Baker and the Australian Air Squadrons Fund 263

Part III—How it ended, and epilogue 283

Chapter 18: New Zealand and Britain's aeroplane gifts to the Dominions 285

Chapter 19: Cast list: minorities, colonials, 'subject peoples' and native rulers 303

Chapter 20: The orchestration of support—the British Empire's last curtain call? 317

Annexes 331

Annex I: The Overseas Club 332

Annex II: The Patriotic League of Britons Overseas 334

Annex III: The Imperial Air Fleet Committee 335

Annex IV: Procedural correspondence and instructions 336

Endnotes 339

Bibliography I—Primary Sources 367

Bibliography II—Secondary Sources 373

Index 387

List of Illustrations

Short 827 seaplane *Britons Overseas No. 6* in East African waters 16
Sopwith 1½ Strutter *Tientsin Britons No.1* 16
Sir (Henry) Hesketh Bell by Walter Stonemason, 1919 20
Picture of *Dominica* supplied by the Army Council, as reproduced on postcards ... 24
Lady Hylda des Voeux being taken for a flight in *Overseas No. 1* after the launch at Farnborough, May 1915 37
Queen Alexandra with Evelyn Wrench and Lieut. Gen. David Henderson at the naming ceremony for four aeroplanes from the empire, July 1915 37
The Imperial Aircraft Flotilla appeal leaflet late 1916/17 48–51
Albert Earl Grey, collotype 1910 59
The Sultan aboard Short 827 seaplane *Britons Overseas No. 4* 78
Sultan Seyyid Khalifa's seaplane trip, *Illustrated London News*, 6 January 1917 78
FE2b *Zanzibar No. 1* 82
FE2b *Zanzibar No. 7* in German hands, 1917 82
Bristol Fighter *Zanzibar No. 18* 82
Annette Kellerman in a still or publicity shot for 'A Daughter of the Gods' 94
Annette Kellerman appearing as '*Jamaica No. 1 Aeroplane*' at a benefit fancy dress ball in Kingston, The *Gleaner*, 1 March 1916 94
An appeal from the Overseas Club to the readership of the *West India Committee Circular* 97
FE2d *Mauritius No. 3* 100
BE2e *Trinidad and Tobago* 100
Sir (Francis) Henry May by Walter Stonemason, 1919 104
Studio photograph from Hong Kong published in the first issue of *Overseas* magazine under the motto 'The Partners of the Tai Yan Bank, Hong-Kong, who presented an airplane to our Flotilla' 107
Eu Tong Sen, undated photograph Singapore 119
Dr. Lim Boon Keng c. 1920, Lee Bros. Studio SIngapore 123
Khoo Cheow Teong: one of the joint donors of the first BE2c from Penang 127
Arthur Chapman in the cockpit of the misnamed *Malaya XV Cheon Teong, Ngoh Bee* .. 127
Studio portrait by Vandyk, April 1916, of Sultan Ibrahim of Johore posing in military uniform 131
The tank Eu Tong Sen presented in 1917 132

Joseph Ephraim Casely Hayford, undated photograph 143

Ofori Atta with entourage 145

Sir Hugh Clifford with family June 1915, including only son, who was to die at the Somme 150

Sir Hugh Clifford with his brother, Col. Henry Clifford, June 1915, also to fall at the Somme 151

Officers of the Jameson Raid, 1895/6, with L. S. Jameson and Lieut. Colonel Raleigh Grey 161

Colonel Sir Raleigh Grey in 1914 161

BE2c *Gatooma* 170

BE2c *Rhodesia No. 3* 170

Chief Griffith Lerotholi and delegation on arrival at Southampton, *Illustrated London News*, 25 October 1919 184

Sopwith Camel *Basutoland No. 2 Mokhachane* 186

Cartoon of Major Miller DSO 'the flying man' *Rand Daily Mail*, 11 December 1917 ... 194

Supplement to the *Times of Ceylon*, 21 January 1916 221

FE2b *Ceylon No. 3 Nightjar* 230

The SE5a presented by Addis Ababa flown by the Canadians in 1919 246

BE2c *British Residents in Siam* 246

FE2b *River Plate* after its crash, 1916 262

Front cover of the *Austral-Briton* special war edition, 16 September 1916 267

The opening of the NSW aviation school at Clarendon, The *Sydney Mail*, 6 September 1916 272

The first flight with the Governor's daughter, and staff and students, The *Sydney Mail*, 6 September 1916 273

Charles Alma Baker CBE in 1919 281

At Hendon, May 1913 289

Sir Joseph Ward climbs aboard *Britannia* 289

At the presentation of *City of Hull* to Australia in 1918 291

General Jan Smuts at the presentation of DH4 *South Africa* by the London Chamber of Commerce in 1917 291

Hardit Singh Malik with *Manchester-India*, March 1918 292

The IAFC's 'red route' map 295

Preface and Acknowledgments

This study arose from a combination of chance, curiosity, and the sudden leisure afforded by retirement. Patrick Khoo unwittingly initiated it in 2008 by asking me to find out why his (Straits Chinese) grandfather had jointly donated a plane to the British flying services in 1916. Previously unaware of the empire's part in financing Britain's first air war, initial research discovered a comprehensive survey of 1914-18 presentation aircraft compiled from surviving Royal Flying Corps records.[1] Attributions suggested that although colonial governments had gifted some, the overseas public and local rulers had subscribed many more. Curiosity about the underlying reasons for such support led me to widen the scope of my enquiry beyond Malaya and the Straits Settlements, to wherever, and whomsoever, had happened to contribute substantially to the campaign.

Since aircraft were designated after the communities, areas or individuals presenting them, and subscribers put forward their own presentation names, I was drawn by what this might tell us about identities, and how they related to voluntary association with the 'imperial' war effort. The First World War, when viewed from a later British perspective, seemed to present a sort of hiatus, or terrible diversion, in the life of the British Empire—some four years of bloody involvement in a catastrophic and all-consuming continental conflict, lodged in between generally successful and profitable British global expansion and the beginnings of that empire's long decline (just as it attained its greatest geographical extent). I wondered what gaps in the wartime history of the British Empire an account of the overseas fundraising might fill, and why exactly efforts concentrated so much on aircraft?

Because the Imperial Aircraft Flotilla campaign of 1915-18 was above all a voluntary and press driven affair, material for the country case studies largely derived from the British Library's extensive newspaper holdings, supplemented (or replaced, where there was no local press coverage) by official papers held at the National Archives, Kew. That and other archival material—along with Evelyn Wrench's pub-

---

1   Raymond Vann and Colin Waugh, 'Presentation Aircraft 1914-1918', *Cross and Cockade GB Journal*, special issue, 14:2 (1983)

lished memoirs, also supplied the story from the London end. My primary debt is thus collectively due to the many librarians, research staff and archivists involved, especially those of the old Colindale Newspaper Library, my habitual haunt before its closure; but also those based at the main British Library, Imperial War Museum, and Royal Air Force Museum.

Former colleagues from the Research Department at the Foreign and Commonwealth Office (more recently known as Research and Analysis Department) also helped. Sally Healy bravely struggled through inchoate initial versions of early chapters, as well as casting an expert eye over the Abyssinia story; and I am additionally most grateful to David Howlett for the benefit of his helpful comments and suggestions on Empire and Commonwealth, Pacific and Antipodean matters. Any mistakes are, of course, my own.

I thank copyright holders for permission to reproduce images, and would particularly like to express my appreciation to David Payne for allowing me to include the splendid photograph of his grandfather in *Malaya XV* not only within the book, but also on the cover design. (For the photographic composition of which, my thanks to Su Khoo.) If in any instance I have failed to identify copyright material, despite my best endeavours, I would be glad of information that would allow me to credit ownership. In addition, I gratefully acknowledge the good advice on publishing given by Margaret Ling, and the unobtrusive support of Jakob Horstmann in the completion of the manuscript, and Valerie Lange's patient efficiency in shepherding me in the publication process.

Shaped by my own past as much as anyone, I offer this monograph to the memory of my father, who worked on aircraft in the Second World War, and that of Dr. T.H.R. (Dick) Cashmore, long-time head of the FCO's Africa Research Unit and my old mentor on British colonial history and administrative practice.

Margaret Hall
May 2017

Notes

Values: £. s. d. = Pounds, shillings and pence. There were twenty shillings to the pound, and twelve pence in a shilling. A ha'penny = a half penny. A 'guinea' was one pound and one shilling (£1 1s 0d) or twenty-one shillings.

Luckily for those of us with little facility for figures, during 1914–18 both the UK and the English-language overseas press habitually expressed subscriptions for aircraft in terms of the sterling production costs for reconnaissance or fighter aeroplanes. These were £1,500 or £2,250 respectively for roughly the first two years of the war, and subsequently £2,500–£2,700 for fighting scouts (equipped with guns but also used for reconnaissance) and fighters, or fighter-bombers. The cost of seaplanes was generally given as £3,500. I have relied on statements of cost and subscription totals expressed in sterling whenever possible.

Civilian Honours: The Order of St. Michael and St. George was designed for service to the crown overseas and was particularly associated with the Colonial Service. In ascending order the ranks are: companion (CMG), knight commander (KCMG), and knight grand cross (GCMG). It ranked in precedence between the two Indian orders—the Order of the Indian Empire (CIE; KCIE; GCIE) and the Star of India (CSI; KCSI; GCSI). The Most Excellent Order of the British Empire was established in 1917 by George V in order to reward civilian service in the war, and consists of member (MBE), officer (OBE), commander (CBE), knight commander (KBE), and knight grand cross (GBE).[2] The Royal Victorian Order is in the sovereign's gift—in descending order, knight grand cross (GCVO), knight (KCVO), commander (CVO), lieutenant (LVO) and member (MVO).

Names: I have used the version most commonly employed at the time by the English-language press and in British official papers, generally indicating variants and alternative spellings, or later changes, the first time that name occurs in the main body of the text. The exceptions to this general rule are those former place-names so well known to an English-speaking readership as to make clarification superfluous

---

2 Kirk-Greene, 'On Governorship and Governors in British Africa'

(country examples: Abyssinia; Ceylon; Burma; Siam; cities: Peking; Bombay; Calcutta; Madras). Johor in Malaysia was then usually rendered as 'Johore' in the press of the day and in Colonial Office papers dealing with the Malay states, and I have kept to this usage, although I well understand that it can invite confusion with that other Johore in India.

Abbreviations

AFC	Australian Flying Corps
AIF	Australian Imperial Force
ANC	African National Congress
ANZAC	Australian and New Zealand Army Corps
APC	African Pioneer Corps
ARPS	Aborigines' Rights Protection Society
BNC	Basutoland National Council
BEF	British Expeditionary Force
BSAC	British South Africa Company
BSAP	British South Africa Police
BWIR	British West Indies Regiment
CEF	Canadian Expeditionary Force
CMS	Church Missionary Society
CO	Colonial Office
DADAE	Deputy Assistant Director of Aircraft Equipment
DFC	Distinguished Flying Cross
DSO	Distinguished Service Order
EEF	Egyptian Expeditionary Force
FMS	Federated Malay States
FO	Foreign Office
FCO	Foreign and Commonwealth Office
GOC	General Officer Commanding
IAFC	Imperial Air Fleet Committee
IWM	Imperial War Museum
JP	Justice of the Peace
KAR	King's African Rifles
KRRC	King's Royal Rifle Corps
LIS	Lebombo Intelligence Scouts
MC	Military Cross
MP	Member of Parliament
NEI	Netherlands East Indies
NRP	Northern Rhodesia Police
NSW	New South Wales
OFS	Orange Free State
PEMS	Paris Evangelical Mission Society
PTS	Pali Text Society
RAF	Royal Air Force
RAFM	Royal Air Force Museum
RAS	Royal Asiatic Society
RCI	Royal Colonial Institute

RFC	Royal Flying Corps
RNAS	Royal Naval Air Service
RNR	Rhodesian Native Regiment
RNVR	Royal Naval Volunteer Reserve
ROSL	Royal Over-Seas League
RPI	Retail Price Index
SAAF	South African Air Force
SADF	South African Defence Force
SANLC	South African Native Labour Contingent
SANNC	South African Native National Congress
SCBA	Straits Chinese British Association
SEF	Siamese Expeditionary Force
SMC	Shanghai Municipal Council
STC	Straits Trading Company
TNA	The National Archives
US	United States
VC	Victoria Cross
WO	War Office
ZAR	Zanzibar African Rifles

(See bibliography for newspapers)

Part I—How it began

Chapter 1:
Introduction—Gifts for the Royal Navy, and the Patriotic League

A great wave of fundraising 'patriotic' associations followed in the wake of Britain's declaration of war on Germany on 4th August 1914, at home but also right across the empire. Quite apart from the Prince of Wales' Fund (its aim to alleviate economic hardships caused by war) and donations to the Red Cross and to Belgian relief, the public contributed towards funds to provide tobacco for the troops; hospital beds; motor ambulances; aid for the disabled and their dependents; and a myriad of other purposes. Crown Colony legislatures voted money and advanced loans to Great Britain in support of the war effort, according to their means, and more needy areas at least tried to send gifts in kind. In the self-governing Dominions (Australia, New Zealand, Canada, Newfoundland and South Africa) there were scattered initiatives to raise cash locally for war materiel, such as machine-guns to equip the national troop contingents that were formed.

As for subscriptions towards 'vehicles of war', the most successful public campaign of all was launched in London at the beginning of 1915. Known as the Imperial Aircraft Flotilla, its inspiration most probably derived from a vote of monies for fighter aircraft by the island of Dominica in the Caribbean (examined in the next chapter). The scheme aimed to attract similar contributions towards aircraft production costs from throughout the British Empire, and was approved by the Army Council in London. Any country, locality, or community that provided sufficient funds for an entire 'aeroplane' (as they were usually called at this period) could have it named after them. It was promised that when the machine crashed or was shot down, the name would be transferred to a new one of the same type—initially either reconnaissance or fighter—but quite possibly of later and improved model. In this way the names designated by subscribers and inscribed on 'their' aeroplane were to be perpetuated as long as the war itself lasted.

The scheme coincided with rapid developments in military aviation and proved widely popular. Presentation aircraft subscribed from the Dominions, Crown Colonies, and even Protectorates, as well as scattered British subjects resident in allied and neutral countries outside the empire, were randomly dispersed among British flying squadrons from the outset, so that no single 'imperial' air formation ever came into material being. But this did not diminish the appeal of the scheme to donors, beguiled by this flotilla of the imagination if not in fact. By war's end the production costs for more than five hundred and fifty aircraft (aeroplanes and seaplanes) had been gifted in this way from all over the British Empire and even beyond. This is the story of that scheme, how it developed and spread, and its particularities from place to place.

Contributions towards the imperial air war came from far and wide as case studies illustrate, and the motivations of those subscribing were many and various. Apart from British settlers, businessmen and colonial officials, subscribers were often, but not only, drawn from local elites, though they were certainly not exclusively empire loyalists and political conservatives. In places, the fundraising took on aspects of a popular grass-roots movement. It offered an opportunity to support a new arm of warfare that was proving unexpectedly useful in battle, and which right from the beginning of the conflict played a defensive as well as offensive role. For aeroplanes were seen as providing a form of protection against enemy artillery, and thus the campaign appealed to those with kin at the Front, as well as those seeking a vicarious part in the fighting. Of course, they were often one and the same.

The story of the many fundraising efforts in their respective locations throughout the world also casts an incidental light on how the British colonies were run—or ran themselves—at this period of cataclysm which had engulfed Europe, when the imperial shelves were particularly bare. To a large degree, the administration of Britain's colonial empire marked time from 1914 to 1918, its ranks depleted of colonial cadre of military age who had enlisted in the forces and were fighting at the Front, its local garrisons depleted of regular troops, and often replaced by Volunteers; while in almost, but not quite all British Crown Colonies, public works schemes were held in abeyance until the war was over.

Very many of the British Colonial Governors, and other senior administrators and their wives left at post, had friends and sons and brothers in the war, some of whom were killed or wounded, and they shared the strains and grief of families back home. Some of those officials themselves over military age saw the local fundraising campaign for British aircraft as an indirect opportunity to contribute to the war effort, inasmuch as they were able from afar. At the same time, the name of 'their' patch of the empire literally made its mark in a way that was normally acknowledged in British newspapers and by Whitehall.

However, we beg the patience of the readership and start our narrative with an apparent digression, about the pre-war gift of a warship—a Dreadnought—from a Protectorate under British indirect rule. HMS *Malaya* provided a precedent for gifting vehicles of war from the far corners of empire. It also served as an example that stimulated the launch of a new association in autumn 1914, the Patriotic League of Britons Overseas. The League's aim was to collect for another warship, but this time from overseas Britons, and when that fund failed, it turned to raising money for seaplanes instead.

For in the naval arms race with Germany that had preceded the First World War, it was not to Protectorates like the Malay states, or even Crown Colonies under direct British rule, but on the contrary to the self-governing white Dominions that Great Britain had looked for practical support and burden sharing, especially Australia, Canada, and New Zealand. These first two countries had sent forces in support of imperial campaigns before—to Sudan in 1884–85, to China (the Boxer Rebellion, 1900) and to South Africa during the Boer War of 1899–1902 in which New Zealanders also took part.

There was no formal constitutional decision-making mechanism in existence to link Britain with the white settler Dominions however, and suggestions of a federal arrangement between them and the Mother Country (such as an overarching parliament, or deliberative joint council) had made no progress. The most that existed were periodic Colonial Conferences after 1887 that provided a flexible forum for the exchange of views, but within the context of ultimate British responsibility for external affairs and defence.

Nor did Great Britain have any desire to be constrained by the interests of the self-governing colonies in matters of imperial defence policy, but there was scope for greater consultation, and clear self-interest on the British part in the practical aspects of cooperation: The new Dreadnoughts—fast, big gun battleships—were very costly to build, initially almost £2 million apiece, and Britain's concerns increasingly centred on defence of northern waters and containing the ambitious German challenge, as well as on maintaining its dominance of the trade routes of empire. Naturally, however, this was only how matters appeared from a British perspective, as First Lord of the Admiralty Winston Churchill had conceded in a speech presenting the country's last pre-war Naval Estimates to the House of Commons in March 1914:

> Two things have to be considered: First, that our diplomacy depends in great part for its effectiveness upon our naval position ... Second, we are not a young people with a blank record and a scant inheritance. We have won for ourselves, in times when other powerful nations were paralysed by barbarism or internal war, an exceptional, disproportionate share of the wealth and traffic of the world.
> We have got all we want in territory, but our claim to be left in undisputed enjoyment of vast and splendid possessions, largely acquired by war and largely maintained by force, is one which often seems less reasonable to others than to us ... [and] we are witnessing this year increases of expenditure by Continental Powers in armaments beyond all previous experience.[1]

The King launched the first British Dreadnought in early 1906. By the end of 1912 Britain had built nineteen in all, with another twelve under construction. (The German total was thirteen Dreadnoughts built with another ten under way).[2] These capital ships grew ever larger and more expensive, with bigger and more powerful guns. The Naval Estimates rose year by year, so that in the six years culminating in those of 1912–13 Government expenditure, or appropriations for the Royal Navy had attained the dizzying sum of £229 million.[3]

New Zealand responded to Britain's appeal for support with an outright gift to the Royal Navy of HMS *New Zealand*, while *Australia* became the flag-ship of that nation's own naval unit, formed for both home and empire engagement. In Canada, however, an imperial naval contribution became a party political issue. At British instigation, Robert Borden, Canadian premier since 1911, proposed that Canada meet the cost of three new Dreadnoughts for the Royal Navy. The proposal divided English- and French-Canadians,[4] and his policy, announced to the Canadian parliament in December 1912, met with strong opposition. Nonetheless, in May 1913 his Navy Bill passed its third reading in the Canadian House of Commons. Borden addressed a crowd of more than 10,000 in Toronto—the country's biggest-ever political demonstration—beneath the motto 'One flag, one fleet, One Empire', while a huge model Dreadnought hung in mid-air, flashed electric lights, fired guns, and blew sirens when he rose to speak.[5] All to no avail: the Canadian Navy Bill was struck down in the Senate at its first reading.

Meanwhile, aid for the British Admiralty had come from a wholly unexpected direction: the promise of a Dreadnought by the Federated Malay States (FMS)—an Eastern Protectorate, and not even a Crown Colony directly ruled by Britain, let alone a self-governing Dominion. In November 1912, the FMS Federal Council unanimously passed a resolution introduced by Sultan Idris Shah of Perak, the Malay state with the richest tin deposits, and most of the tin mines which had contributed so much to economic growth and the swelling budgetary surplus. The resolution offered Great Britain £2.5 million from FMS funds for a first-class armoured ship, spread over five years. This was a quite breathtaking sum from the four federated Malay sultanates of the FMS, whose populations at the 1911 census together numbered only 1,037,000:[6] a century later it would have a value of about £200 million.[7]

The Council that had voted the gift was not an elected body. Along with the Sultan of Perak, it comprised the three Sultans (or their representatives) of Selangor, Negri Sembilan, and Pahang. All of them recognised Sultan Idris as the senior-most amongst them by virtue of age, experience, and ability. The remaining members of the Federal Council were the British High Commissioner to the FMS (and Governor of the Straits Settlements Colony, resident at Singapore), Sir Arthur Young; other senior British officials; and 'unofficials' as they were then known, nominated by the High Commissioner. The three European non-official members were each selected to represent planting, mining, and commercial interests, and the one Chinese member to represent the general interests of those Chinese resident in the FMS. This was the Perak millionaire Eu Tong Sen (of whom more later in this story, in relation to the personal gift not only of an aircraft, but of a tank).

In London, Parliament greeted the formal announcement of this extraordinary offer of £2.5 million with enthusiastic cheers.[8] As *The Times* of London remarked, even though payments were to be by yearly instalments over a five-year term, this sum represented half a single year's revenue for the FMS as a whole, and was a generous gift indeed from dependencies of such moderate size and recent development. Yet, although as members of the Federal Council the four Malay Sultans concerned took part in discussing the FMS budget, and in passing the necessary legislation to bring it into effect, unlike—say—

the Indian princes, they did not control their own state revenues; and they were obliged under treaty to accept the advice of their respective British Residents in all matters, except those pertaining to Malay custom and religion. When it was tacitly admitted that a senior official—Colonial Secretary E. L. Brockman—had suggested the gift of a Dreadnought to Sultan Idris in the first instance, the status of the 'gift' came to look more dubious.[9] (A newspaper columnist in Singapore had reportedly proposed the warship idea as a worthy destination for excess FMS funds some years before, planting the idea in the Colonial Secretary's mind).[10]

Ever since the American Revolution had popularised the demand for no taxation without representation, Great Britain had refrained from exacting a direct financial contribution towards defence from her Crown Colonies, save where there was a garrison of imperial troops, or where fortifications had been constructed at the expense of the Royal Exchequer. Patently, this was not the case of the FMS, a mere Protectorate. Its flourishing exports, however, did rely on the port facilities of the Straits Settlements (a Crown Colony) at Singapore and Penang; just before the offer was made Sir Arthur Young had accompanied Sultan Idris on a tour of the Singapore Docks.[11] The British Royal Navy, it was emphasised in those days, stood guardian over the safety of the seas and of free trade. This argument had some weight in the FMS, which had seen a diminution in piracy on account of the British naval presence in the Straits of Malacca.

In the House of Commons Churchill was asked for assurance that none of the money voted by the FMS should be spent until the House had had the opportunity to debate the matter. He retorted that the offer had been accepted, the contract had been settled, and construction would begin shortly. What lay behind this rather churlish question regarding a patriotic offer, he asked rhetorically: each nation was in reality a sum of its traditions and, if all nations were merged, the result would be a vast and colourless community—the end towards which they would all drift were Britain to curb patriotism either within her borders or on the part of her vast dominions overseas.[12] Secretary of State for the Colonies, Lewis Harcourt, maintained that the offer had been spontaneous, and had come as a complete surprise to the Colonial Office.

This was the heyday of indirect rule. British colonial expansion across large areas of the globe in the late nineteenth century had made it all the more expedient for its officials to cultivate the cooperation of local rulers, in the interests of cost-effective and peaceful governance. Lord Frederick Lugard, one of the grandees of Britain's Colonial Service, later theorised his own co-option of the Emirs of Northern Nigeria and their native administrations, into what was to become British colonial doctrine.[13] But other colonial administrators had been following a similar path elsewhere—out of instinct and pragmatic adaptation. Some British administrators were cultivated in their turn by local rulers, and some also found themselves beguiled by the lands in which they lived and worked. In addition, memories of 'pacification' campaigns remained in the recent background, to remind rulers of Britain's long military reach, thanks to her effective navy.

Friendships occasionally developed between colonial administrator and native ruler in which it is difficult to separate sentiment and mutual self-interest. Sir Frank Swettenham, who rose to become British Governor of the Straits Settlements 1901–1904,[14] wrote of Sultan Idris Shah of Perak as 'standing for all that is best in the Malay ruling class, able, energetic, just and high-principled, with great charm of manner and fluency of speech. A very earnest Moslem, without a trace of bigotry, and regarded as a high authority on questions of muslim law and religion.'[15] They first met in the context of a punitive expedition that followed on the assassination of the first British Resident in Perak, J. W. W. Birch, back in November 1875. Swettenham acted as deputy commissioner for the advancing British forces shipped in from India and China. Raja Idris, as he then was, was the Malay judge who tried and convicted the three men implicated in Birch's murder, Swettenham conducting the prosecution against them.[16]

In 1889 Frank Swettenham himself became British Resident of Perak and settled in a house at Kuala Kangsar (Perak's royal capital) near to Sultan Idris, a close friend now for many years, who had succeeded to the sultanate two years' previously: 'During the next ten years our friendship grew ever stronger, and whilst His Highness's Authority in Perak was unquestioned, he had great influence in other Western States, and he always used it wisely.'[17] Over time, Sultan Idris Shah had become close to the British authorities, and he was awarded the GCMG during the Prince of Wales's visit to Singapore in 1901. It would not have been difficult to persuade him to add his weight to ratifying Malaya's gift of a Dreadnought in 1912—a gift that drew the attention of London, if not the world, to this economically successful and helpful corner of the empire, which was by now producing more than fifty per cent of the world's tin, and nearly half its rubber. In 1913 he was awarded a rare British honour, the GCVO, which was in the gift of the British monarchy.

When war came in 1914, Sir Frank Swettenham was living in retirement in England on the directorships of several rubber companies. He was appointed initially assistant director, then in 1915 joint director, of the Press Bureau in London (operating wartime British 'news management'). Meanwhile, Sultan Idris continued to take a keen interest in the progress of HMS *Malaya*, and was privately informed of its completion before his death in January 1916.[18] It was one of five new 'Queen Elizabeth'-class fast and powerful Dreadnought battleships completed since the outbreak of hostilities. At the end of May, HMS *Malaya* took part in the Battle of Jutland, suffering sixty killed in action and many more injured.

As it turned out, it was to be British seaplanes and aeroplanes that were to become the objects of worldwide private and public generosity in the Great War (as the First World War was known at the time). It was not ships, although in the autumn of 1914 HMS *Malaya* provided the inspiration for the launch in London of the Patriotic League of Britons Overseas, with as its avowed aim to present a battle cruiser to the Royal Navy. This time, it was British communities resident in foreign countries *outside* the formal British Empire—from Argentina to the Treaty Ports of China—and estimated to number some three million people, who were expected to dig into their pockets.

The aim was to finance a modern warship (but not a mighty Dreadnought, which would have been too ambitious by far) for what was at first expected to be Great Britain's decisive battle against Germany on the high seas. But the fundraising campaign did not progress as planned, just as the larger matter of the Great War itself quickly turned into something much more unfamiliar and unwelcome for Britain than the naval dominance and limited imperial army campaigns to which they had become accustomed.[19] In a twist of fate, the Patriotic League was to become the main private benefactor for the Navy's branch of the British flying services instead.

The initiative for the Patriotic League of Britons Overseas had come from F. W. Hayne, an Englishman who had spent much of his life in Chile.[20] An impressive Home Committee was formed in London, chaired by Lord William Waldegrave Palmer Selborne, and the King lent his name as Patron of the League. Lord Selborne had been in turn Under Secretary of State for the Colonies 1895–1900; First Lord of the Admiralty; then High Commissioner in South Africa and Governor of

Transvaal and the Orange River Colony in the period from 1905 until establishment of the Union of South Africa in 1910. As First Lord of the Admiralty (1900–1905) he had overseen important changes in the Royal Navy, and pushed through plans to meet the threat of the new German navy, including those for the first British Dreadnought.[21] Lord Aldenham, whose family mercantile house of Antony Gibbs & Sons had made its fortune in South America trade, had been a business partner of F. W. Hayne in Chile, and acted as vice-chairman and treasurer. He approached the Admiralty with the League's plans to recruit 'patriotic' Britons worldwide to subscribe to a fund for a warship of some kind.

In his letter of approval Churchill set out the Navy's desired shopping list according to the monies that could be raised—upward of £300,000 for a light cruiser, £380,000 for a 'Town'-class cruiser, £150,000 for a destroyer.[22] Sir Edward Grey, who was British Foreign Secretary from 1905 until 1916, lent the campaign the support of those networks at his command, both formal and informal. Albert Earl Grey, his third cousin, was president of the Royal Colonial Institute (RCI), established in 1869 and the oldest of the imperial propaganda societies,[23] and the Foreign Secretary supplied the League with lists of the RCI's members abroad, to enlist their help. More importantly, a dispatch went out under his name to all British foreign missions enclosing packets (520 of them) of the Patriotic League's publicity material. They were accompanied by a Consular Circular of 17 December 1914 enjoining the British Consular Service to seek out Britons with local influence willing to found a branch of the League and to collect subscriptions for the warship.[24]

Faced with this directive from on high, those who felt unable to comply with the Circular hastened to explain themselves: British consular representatives in Russia, that it was actually illegal, under a Russian law of 1906 that prohibited organisations with political aims which were controlled by institutions or persons abroad. Excuses rolled in, all of them good. The Consul General in Rotterdam thought it 'inadvisable' on his part to take any action in support of the League because of the nearness of hostilities, the delicacy of the situation in the Netherlands, and because the Germans would make capital of it, accusing him of trying to break Dutch neutrality. The Vice Consul in Kansas City wrote personally to Lord Selborne, explaining that local opinion was influenced by the large number of people of German or Austrian extraction there, and was opposed to war armaments. More bluntly, a British Consul in Mexico (in the throws of continuing revolution) informed the Foreign Office that local Britons lacked not patriotism, but money. Given the dire economic situation, and the destitution of many, there was no point in his trying to canvass support for the League, or its aims.

Nevertheless, branches of the Patriotic League were formed in China, which was then a new Republic still in turmoil following the nationalist revolt that ended imperial Manchu rule in 1912. Branches were established in Manchuria; in foreign Treaty Ports like Canton and Swatow; and in the former Manchu capital of Peking; even in Tengyuah (Tengyue), in the remote south-west of China, where the British Assistant-in-Charge of the local Chinese Customs Service (still run by British officials) summoned a meeting of all eight adult male British subjects of the town, and managed to collect £38 for the warship. Shanghai in particular formed a large, active, and financially generous branch of the Patriotic League, headed by the Consul General, Sir Everard Fraser KCMG, as its president; and it continued to gift money throughout the First World War.

Branches were also formed, and respectable sums of money (£500–£1,000) collected in areas of British settlement in Chile and Argentina, and in big cities like Havana and Rio de Janeiro. But progress was hard in some parts of Latin America, where German investment and trade had begun to penetrate regions that had previously been a British preserve. The League's literature envisaged that its branches would persist after the end of the war, forming a network of 'patriotic' Britons across the globe. Quite possibly there was a longer-term aim implicit in this, to capture German trade, or recoup British trade from German companies. The Consul General in Quito hinted as much when he advised the Foreign Office that it was less a question of capturing German trade with a country where pro-German feeling ran high, than of holding on to Britain's own trade: 'There are none of the Great English West Coast Firms ... with which the Lord Aldenham is connected and acquainted with, the import trade is largely in the hands of Bremen and Hamburg firms and their agents.'[25]

Despite support from the extensive network of British Consular Officers abroad, by May 1915 the League had managed to collect only £22,000—nowhere near their initial target of £380,000. To his credit, Lord Selborne helped resolve this embarrassing situation by easing the League towards cooperation with John Evelyn Wrench, a newspaperman whose fundraising campaign for aircraft for the Army's branch of the flying services had met with considerable recent success. Selborne was acquainted already with Wrench's Overseas Club, and was a speaker at the inaugural launch of its new London premises in May 1914.[26] Additionally, Albert Earl Grey—the Fourth Earl of Grey, former Governor General of Canada, third cousin and friend to Sir Edward Grey, and the RCI's president—may well have commended Wrench, whom he had known well and favoured for a number of years, to Lord Selborne, his in-law.

In June 1915 Wrench became Honorary Secretary of the League, at Lord Selborne's invitation, and thereon effectively ran it from the Overseas Club, along with his own fundraising campaign. By the time Lord Aldenham wrote to the Foreign Office again on 27 July 1915, to advise them of the results obtained since the issue of their Consular Circular in December, the League had clearly concluded that even the smallest sum of £150,000 needed for a destroyer was unattainable:

> I have very great pleasure in informing you that ... no less than 105 Branches of the League have already been established in foreign countries and a sum of £35,000 has been handed to the First Lord of the Admiralty for the purchase of a squadron of ten large seaplanes of the latest and most approved type as a first gift to the Navy from our fellow subjects abroad.[27]

Ten large seaplanes constituted a useful face-saver. The first aeroplane flight from a British warship had taken place at the beginning of 1912: King George V, the ex-naval officer and Patron of the Patriotic League, took a keen interest in naval aviation and had observed the Fleet's first manoeuvres accompanied by aircraft in May that same year.[28] And George V's interest was not limited to naval aviation—in January 1914 the British aviator Gustav Hamel staged a 'Command' flying exhibition before the King and Queen Mary in Windsor private grounds.[29] For some years Winston Churchill, First Lord of the Admiralty from October 1911 until May 1915, had been a notable enthusiast for naval aeronautics, and underwent pilot tuition on every flight he made.[30]

The Patriotic League's July 1915 gift of £35,000 to the Navy—£22,800 of it subscribed by the fourteen branches of the League in China—paid for ten Short 827 seaplanes with 150 hp. engines:[31] a gift duly acknowledged on behalf of the Admiralty by its new First Lord, Arthur Balfour (replacing Churchill in the wake of the Gallipoli debacle).[32] Certainly the gift of ten seaplanes was a useful addition to the existing inventory, for the Royal Naval Air Service (RNAS) had no more than thirty-nine aeroplanes and fifty-two seaplanes when war was declared in August 1914.[33] Indeed, one estimate has placed the serviceable number initially available at mobilisation at only half that.[34] Moreover, those planes that the RNAS already possessed had proved their worth. While it was an arm of the Navy, under the authority of the Admiralty, and flew in support of naval operations, the RNAS had adopted an aggressive attack policy from early in the war (as part of the Navy's remit for the coastal defence of Britain).

A bombing raid on 13 October 1914 had successfully destroyed a Zeppelin in its shed at Düsseldorf; although another carried out on 21 November on the Zeppelin factory at Friedrichshafen on the shores of Lake Constance was of more limited effectiveness in those early days of aircraft design and engine power.[35] On Christmas Day 1914, RNAS seaplanes also made their first seaborne assault from a warship, against Zeppelin sheds at Cuxhaven. Just a few weeks later, the RNAS went into action off Africa. Three out of the League's presentation Short 827 seaplanes were in fact used in the East Africa campaign; two of them (*Britons Overseas Nos. 4 and 5*) being flown by HMS *Manica* at Zanzibar (see chapter five).

Yet *the* key attribute of both aeroplanes and seaplanes for donors back then was affordability, perhaps even trumping all other considerations. Essentially an engine encased in a lightweight wooden fuselage, with a wooden propeller, and with wings of treated canvas stretched over a wooden framework, in 1915–16 a biplane with gun cost £2,250 to produce, and without gun, £1,500. Seaplanes had floats instead of wheels, and more powerful engines than aeroplanes in order to aid take-off from water, and these entailed extra costs that brought them up to £3,500 each. But of whatever type, aircraft were a tiny fraction of the cost of any kind of warship: even the cheapest, a destroyer at £150,000 (as against £3,500 for a seaplane), cost the equivalent in today's terms of more than £10 million.[36]

Contributions towards the League's Warship Fund continued to trickle in from abroad, and were also quietly diverted to aircraft for the RNAS. A small sum in Italian *lire* was gathered by the Maltese community in Tripoli, at their own initiative, and remitted in November 1915 by the British Consul General; he explained that the community was a poor one, comprising mainly fishermen and labourers.[37] In July 1916 the Colonial Office in London was bemused to receive money from the Tonga branch of the Patriotic League of Britons Overseas— of which they had never previously heard—with the request that it be paid over to the Warship Fund. Noting dryly that the collection of £113 18s 2d from Tonga would not go far towards buying a Dreadnought, they consulted the Admiralty, who replied citing the squadron of seaplanes already received in order to reassure that the fund was genuine and not a scam, and expressing their entire approval of the League and its Honorary Secretary, John Evelyn Wrench.[38]

Support for the League was also beginning to permeate beyond the resident British community to some of their Chinese middlemen and interpreters in the Treaty Ports of China. By May 1916 the Patriotic League had handed a further £21,000 to the Admiralty for the purchase of naval aircraft.[39] It included 'a further generous contribution' from a number of Chinese British subjects at Swatow, who—it may be surmised—found it advisable to make a display of loyalty towards their British employers at a Treaty Port where the German business community was also strongly represented. Clearly, they were well aware of the League's British Establishment credentials. Their accompanying memorandum in part read:

> Now, Gentlemen, the British Government is at present involved in the greatest war in history. The loyal and patriotic Statesmen and Aristocrats of England, supported by His Majesty, the King, have deemed it proper to link us up with all the other British communities scattered throughout the globe in the interests of the British Empire. It is our duty [to do] all in our power to promote the interest and welfare of the Patriotic League of Britons Overseas ... If the Empire falls, God forbid it, where shall we all be?[40]

A further £10,000, subscribed by Britons and British subjects in the United States (US), China, Brazil, Abyssinia, and elsewhere outside the British Empire, and to be spent on seaplanes, was made over to the Admiralty on 21 October 1916: 'by way of celebrating Trafalgar Day' according to *Flight* magazine.[41] That same year, the League also transmitted £3,000 to the Secretary of State for War. It was destined for aeroplanes for the British Army's own flying service, the Royal Flying Corps (RFC).[42] In all, the League presented some fifty seaplanes and aeroplanes during its separate existence before it was formally amalgamated with the Overseas Club on the 31st March 1918,[43] the very day before a new British air service came into being uniting the flying arms of the Army and Navy respectively: the Royal Air Force (RAF).

One of the Patriotic Front's 10 seaplanes presented to the Admiralty in July 1915, Short 827 3098 *Britons Overseas No. 6* being manhandled in East African waters, courtesy of the National Museum of the Royal Navy

Sopwith 1½ Strutter 9395 *Tientsin Britons No. 1* gifted by one of the Patriotic League's branches in China, flown by 5 Naval Squadron in France 1917, courtesy of the National Museum of the Royal Navy

Chapter 2:
And for the Army, Vickers Gunbus *Dominica*, and a kite balloon …

Neither Anglo-German naval rivalry in the period before the outbreak of war, nor the Patriotic League's subsequent efforts at fundraising for a battle cruiser, indicated any lack of interest in aviation on the part of the British public. It was quite the contrary, given the 'Zeppelin factor' in popular perceptions of threats to the nation. *War in the Air* by H. G. Wells was published in 1908; in this the West's major cities, including London, were destroyed by airships. Press articles in Lord Northcliffe's newspapers, the *Daily Mail* and *The Times*, drew attention to the allegedly paltry resources devoted to aeronautics from 1909 onwards; and in that same year an Aerial League of the British Empire was also formed (and continued with propaganda activities throughout the Great War).[1] Then in 1913, the peak year for 'air agitation',[2] public disquiet over Britain's new vulnerability from the skies was fanned by reported sightings of German Zeppelins over England (denied by Germany).

For a good eighteen months before the outbreak of the Great War, therefore, pressure had been building for more spending. Great Britain, it was claimed, was lagging behind France and Germany in both government funding and voluntary fund-raising. At a meeting of the Aeronautical Society, then Brigadier General David Henderson stated that the reason the War Office had ordered so few aeroplanes, and none at all between September 1912 and January 1913, was down to lack of money.[3] His interest lay in maximising funding for the RFC. Henderson qualified for his pilot's certificate at the advanced age of forty-nine in 1911, and as Director of Military Training he exercised oversight of pilot instruction from the RFC's very beginnings. When in August 1913 the War Office created a Directorate of Military Aeronautics, Henderson was put in charge, and retained this responsibility, one way or another,[4] until replaced by Sir John Salmond in the autumn of 1917. Henderson was to play the key role on the service side in nurturing the Imperial Aircraft Flotilla campaign during its early stages.

While a Parliamentary Aerial Defence Committee (established in 1909 by Lord Montagu of Beaulieu and others) pressed the Government for greater public spending,[5] a number of private money-raising schemes had already been floated. In 1913 Captain Walter Faber MP proposed a voluntary scheme along the lines of the French *Avions Départementeaux*, which had raised the equivalent of £150,000 and provided the French Army with ninety-four military aircraft and training for seventy-five pilots in preparation for military service.[6] On the naval side, a large meeting was called in London under the auspices of the Imperial Maritime League to draw attention to the 'new peril of the air'. Held at the City's Baltic Exchange in April 1913, it appealed to Government to take the necessary steps to increase the numbers of both Dreadnoughts and naval aircraft.[7] In May, a short-lived National Aeronautical Defence Association launched at a meeting at Mansion House presided over by the Lord Mayor of London, its aim to bring together the various existing pressure groups.[8] In Liverpool, three thousand people attended a meeting convened by the Lord Mayor to call for the city's very own dedicated flying corps to defend it; a message from the Secretary of State for War, Colonel Seely, explained why that was undesirable and invited a contribution of £40,000 from Liverpool to equip an RFC squadron instead.[9]

The Great War was upon Britain before any of these initiatives bore fruit. However, in August 1914 Britain's first aeroplane gift of the conflict was indeed forthcoming from a Liverpool businessman under the Imperial Air Fleet scheme (outlined in chapter eighteen). The donor, William E. Cain, requested that it should ultimately go to the Commonwealth of Australia, in recognition of all the support that country was giving to Britain in the war.[10] It was handed over in formal ceremony at Farnborough; the Australian High Commissioner's wife broke a small bottle of champagne on the propeller to christen it *Liverpool* and Australia thereupon lent it to the British War Office to hold in trust.[11] A theoretically Australian-owned *Liverpool* was then allotted to the British Expeditionary Force (BEF) in France at the end of 1914.[12] It was a Blériot Experimental 2c model (BE2c), a reconnaissance biplane and the first aircraft to be manufactured in substantial numbers for the RFC.

The second and third aircraft to be presented in the war came from much further afield—or, rather, the funds for them did—from the island of Dominica in the Caribbean. Dominica was an atypical British

Caribbean island in many respects. It possessed relatively few landless labourers working on large estates, and had a much smaller planter aristocracy than was commonplace in the West Indies. Green and mountainous, with an area of little more than 300 square miles, most of the population of about 35,000 comprised an independent peasantry speaking a French *patois*, and owning plots of land of sufficient size to grow their own food and raise small cash crops of cocoa and limes. Dominica had its own resident British Administrator, but was under the supervision and control of the Leeward Islands' Governor based in Antigua.[13]

This was Sir Henry Hesketh Bell during 1912–16. Elegant, whimsically humorous, inventive and vain, Bell was nonetheless no mere lightweight. Born in the West Indies of French extraction, Bell had started out as a lowly 3rd class clerk in the office of the Governor of Barbados and the Windward Islands, and worked up from there. As well as winning the backing of one of the foremost British politicians of the age, Joseph Chamberlain, his talents impressed the mandarins of the Colonial Office.[14] As Governor of Uganda (1905–1909) he had rolled back a most deadly epidemic of sleeping sickness through the temporary evacuation of designated tsetse fly-infested zones around Lake Victoria, guided by an interest in entomology and his observation that few cases were found more than two miles from open water.[15] It was a pioneering and effective measure.

The Governor had a special interest in Dominica, where he had made quite an impact as Administrator from 1899 until his Uganda posting. During his term of office a new road across the island begun by his predecessor (entitled the Imperial Road) had opened up the interior to estate cultivation. He encouraged settlers from Britain to come to Dominica and invest in lime and cocoa estates run along modern lines, on lots carved out from Crown land; he also devised an accompanying scheme to provide insurance cover against hurricane damage to property in the West Indies.[16] Again, his scientific curiosity had been in evidence. He made a study of hurricane activity that persuaded Lloyds of London that the venture was worthwhile. Bell was full of ideas, not all of which came to fruition, like his scheme to bring 3,000 Boer War prisoners from South Africa to settle in the interior. (Volcanic eruptions on nearby Martinique warned off the British authorities, which after the scandal of the concentration camps in South Africa probably wanted no more bad publicity over the treatment of Boer captives.)

Sir (Henry) Hesketh Bell by Walter Stonemason, 1919
© National Portrait Gallery, London

Bell had exercised his charm on those in a position to further his plans; wooed the press; sent letters and articles to British newspapers and magazines publicising the attractions of the island; written recruitment pamphlets and a guidebook; and established his own experimental plantation off the Imperial Road ('Sylvania'), where prospective settlers could see tropical products being scientifically grown.[17] All this was in accordance with the imperial policies of Hesketh Bell's patron, Secretary of State for the Colonies Joseph Chamberlain, who looked to the advancement of the more economically backward corners of the British Empire through the agency of a British planter class, assisted by modern scientific agricultural methods and the provision of improved communications. Chamberlain had viewed Dominica as a test case, and advanced Colonial Office grants for the island's development.[18]

Hesketh Bell retained a soft spot for Dominica generally. He wrote of '99 per cent' of its population: 'These people live simple, quiet lives and are considerably under the good influence of the Roman Catholic Church. In complexion the peasantry and working classes vary from almost pure black to a very light shade of yellow.'[19] However, it was the one per cent constituting 'Society' that formed his immediate world. During Bell's period as Administrator, Government House in the island capital, Roseau, had become the heart of social life for its members, whether newcomers or old established families. 'Society' comprised the principal officials, planters, professionals, and heads of the main commercial houses. Most were of purely European descent, according to Bell, but the proportion of well-to-do people of light colour and good education was steadily increasing.[20] He was a fine dancer, held balls, waltzed with future writer Jean Rhys, then fourteen years old, at a children's fancy dress dance.[21]

During his term as Administrator some thirty to forty British settlers and their families were attracted to try their hand at planting on Dominica;[22] and the number of Europeans on the island increased from just a handful to almost four hundred between 1891 and 1911. One amongst them was Robin Hughes Chamberlain. Born at Greytown, Natal, in 1887, his father had fought in the British Army in the Zulu Wars, and later settled down as a Justice of the Peace (JP), with as part of his remit to combat gun-running in the vicinity. Initially taught at home by a governess, Robin was dispatched at the age of eight to continue his schooling in England and France. In 1907, he moved to Dominica to learn plantation management at the invitation of a resident, a solicitor to whom he had been introduced in England. After one year he settled down on his own lime and cocoa estate at Wotton Waven outside Roseau.

Already fascinated by aviation (and an avid reader of novels by such writers as Jules Verne and H. G. Wells), it was while on holiday in England at the very beginning of 1914 that Robin Hughes Chamberlain paid his two guineas for his very first short passenger flight, at a flying display at Hendon aerodrome.[23] Back once more in Dominica, the Great War broke out. In January 1915 he returned to England bearing letters of introduction from the then Administrator, Edward Drayton, and Leeward Islands Governor Hesketh Bell, with the intention to train as a pilot and serve on the Western Front. Three or four days after his interview at the War Office he was undergoing instruction at Brooklands.

Pilot training in the initial stages of the war usually implied a private income, for potential recruits had to qualify for a Royal Aero Club certificate for which they paid £75 upfront (it was generally refunded later if they were commissioned into the RFC as flying officers). In the

British Caribbean islands, as throughout the whole of the empire, British expatriates and residents of British descent and military age made their own way to England after war was declared, usually at their own expense, to join the army as volunteers. Robin Hughes Chamberlain was Dominica's only pilot.

Dominica had twenty-nine volunteers fighting on the Western Front at the time—most likely all drawn from the ranks of 'Society' and especially from the ranks of recent British settlers of military age. One amongst them, who had been studying at McGill University, joined the Canadian Royal Horse Artillery. With the formation of the British West Indies Regiment (BWIR) in October 1915, ordinary Dominicans—labourers, mechanics, and sons of small peasant proprietors—were enabled to volunteer. By mid-1917 there were 139 men from Dominica serving in BWIR ranks. They were employed on the Eastern Front (Egypt, the canal zone, Sinai and the borders of Palestine) on guarding the lines of communication and patrolling railway and pipelines, rather than frontline fighting.[24]

Dominica's aeroplane gift came about as follows: On 26 September 1914—when Robin Hughes Chamberlain was once more in Dominica and before he returned to Britain to join up—the island's Legislative Council introduced a resolution approving a grant of £4,000 from Dominica's financial surplus, to be offered to the British Government as a contribution to the RFC. Though the relevant official papers of the period do not actually mention the name of Hughes Chamberlain,[25] the gift, intended specifically for the RFC, was surely connected in some way with his intention to proceed to England for pilot training, reflecting local pride in one of their number, even if he was a comparative newcomer to the island:

> Mr. Rolle and Dr. Nicholls spoke also in support of the Resolution. Both members suggested that the Home Government might be asked to devote, if agreeable, the amount voted to the purchase of an armoured aeroplane to be called 'DOMINICA', and His Honour the Administrator promised that in his dispatch he would certainly mention this.[26]

Thus recorded the island's principal newspaper.

The Colonial Office subsequently directed that any monetary contribution to the imperial war effort on Dominica's part should go to the Prince of Wales' Fund (for the relief of dependents of those fighting at the Front, and others suffering economic effects of the war). But Administrator Drayton argued that he could not, at that late stage, have changed the published proposal, which was warmly supported by public opinion; however he had managed to modify the terms of the resolution so that it no longer specified an armoured aeroplane, but rather that the grant should, if possible, go to the war expenses of the RFC, or be expended on any other war purpose His Majesty's Government saw fit.

Governor Bell forwarded Drayton's dispatch to the Colonial Office with his endorsement of the Administrator's action.[27] The island's correspondent for the London-based West India Committee later reported that despite a cable from the Secretary of State for the Colonies, Dominica's Legislative Council had persisted in their desire to present the money for some war purpose, preferably to the benefit of the RFC, and Lewis Harcourt had gone along with this.[28] Dominica's Legislative Council (made up of six officials and six nominated 'unofficial' local members) passed the modified resolution unanimously on 7 October 1914.

The Admiralty then wrote to the Colonial Office to claim their share for the RNAS:

> The £4,000 voted by the Legislative Council of Dominica should be equally divided between the Naval and Military Wings. ... It would appear appropriate that the money available—£2,000 in each case—should be allocated for the construction of the aeroplane for the use of the particular Wing. The machine could have a plate fixed to their chassis recording the name of the donors etc., and the donors could be kept informed of any good work done by these machine. ... Should the cost of the Naval machine exceed the £2,000, the balance would be borne by Navy Votes, while any small saving would be credited to the Vote for aeroplane construction.[29]

This letter must have been cleared with the War Office, for the Army Council wrote in identical terms, save that excess costs were to be borne by the Army Vote.[30]

The War Office later forwarded to the Government of Dominica a photograph of the 100 hp. Gnome Vickers Gun Biplane presented to the RFC with its half share of the £4,000. The photograph was put on exhibit at the Free Library in Roseau in April, and reproduced on postcards placed on general sale for three pence apiece. (An enterprising retailer in Roseau also advertised *Dominica* Aeroplane Souvenirs in the form of 'pendants and brooches for the Ladies and Gentlemen and spoons for the table'.)

H.M. BIPLANE "DOMINICA"—THE GIFT OF THE ISLAND OF THAT NAME.

Picture of *Dominica* supplied by the Army Council, as reproduced on postcards
Courtesy of the West India Committee, London

The promise to keep donors informed of 'good work' done by *Dominica*, and the forwarding of a photograph, set a precedent for future presentation machines from elsewhere. However, the Army Council later specified that the photographs supplied of aeroplanes presented were *not* for publication.

Unlike the FMS in 1912, there were no local journalistic critics to query the monies voted by the Legislative Council. Then was peacetime, this was wartime. But it was in part due to the nature of the main newspaper in Dominica. Like those of other British dependencies, the *Dominica Chronicle* carried news of the war issued by the Press Bureau in Britain (some of the larger circulation papers in bigger British colonies also carried *Reuters* reports). But the *Dominica Chronicle* was also a Roman Catholic newspaper, with a circulation of about 450 in an overwhelmingly Christian, and largely Catholic, population of only some 35,000. Moreover, Belgian priests had run it ever since the paper's establishment in 1909 by Bishop Schelfhaut of the Redemptorist Order.[31] It had its own special flavour of war reportage, and published the occasional letter from Catholic priests in Europe, including those of chaplains on the Western Front. It can be surmised that their accounts were also read from pulpits to those in the countryside who did not read the *Chronicle*.

One particularly gripping report was sent right at the start of the war in the form of a letter to the Bishop of Roseau from the Rev. Father Vermeiren in Antwerp. Father Vermeiren, Superior of the Redemptorist Fathers at St. Thomas in the Virgin Islands,[32] just over 300 miles from Dominica and part of Schelfhaut's Diocese, had been visiting his native land of Belgium when the German army invaded. He wrote forcefully from Antwerp in August 1914:

> It appears that Germany is also determined to seize Holland, Switzerland and the Grand Duchy of Luxembourg. The Franciscan Fathers and the Jesuits have put their fathers, brothers, nay their very houses at the disposal of the Government. I suppose we (Redemptorists) will soon do the same. I will try to make myself useful among the English-speaking soldiers.

His account of the siege of Liège relates an exciting, but entirely false, legend about the renowned French pilot Roland Garros (who was not present, and not killed):

> The famous aviator Garros succeeded also in destroying a 'Zeppelin' occupied by 26 German officers. All were killed on the spot. Unfortunately, Garros himself underwent the same fate, his aeroplane dropping down like a stone after his glorious feat.[33]

Yet despite its factual inaccuracies, his letter demonstrates the emotional filter through which war news reached Dominica, and the influence of Belgian Catholic sensibilities. This was not a pacifist Church, and this was holy war.

The RFC's initial establishment in 1912 was as a unitary body to serve both Army and Navy. But the Senior Service was jealous to exercise complete control over naval air operations, including pilot training and aircraft procurement policy. On the eve of war, in July 1914, the RNAS gained official recognition, so that the RFC entered the Great War as the flying arm of the British Army, and the RNAS that of the Royal Navy. No one was then quite sure what precise role in warfare aviation might come to play, but the expectation was that it would centre on reconnaissance, over land or water respectively (in particular, without the aid of sonar in those days, spotting submarines was easier from the air than from a ship).

When war began, Brigadier General David Henderson decided to lead the RFC, leaving the War Office and taking almost all the aeroplanes the RFC then possessed off to France with him. Henderson's professional army background had been in field intelligence and reconnaissance, on which he had published two handbooks, and the new BE2c biplane, manufactured from a design developed at the Royal Aircraft Factory, Farnborough, was specifically made for this very purpose, as a stable platform with a good view of the ground. Advanced enough for the blueprints to be the object of pre-war freelance industrial espionage for sale to American firms,[34] the BE2c was not equipped with a powerful engine, and was unable to carry heavy machine guns. With the development of air fighting, it was soon realised that purpose-built gun-mounted fighting machines were urgently needed.[35] By the beginning of 1915, they had left the design stage and were in British production ready for dispatch to the Western Front; and Henderson himself handed over command of the RFC in France to then Brigadier General Hugh Trenchard in August 1915 to return full-time as Director General of Aeronautics at the War Office.

In those early days, the greater part of the RFC's aeroplanes in France were reconnaissance craft, and from early 1915 especially the ubiquitous BE2c. After the introduction in mid-1915 of the faster, and more manoeuvrable German Fokker E-type monoplane, equipped with a synchroniser gear that allowed repeated forward machine-gun fire between the blades of the moving propeller, the BE2c proved fatally vulnerable. It also had structural inadequacies. The observer who sat in front of the pilot had a very limited view, and, although he had a gun for defence, could not fire forward at all because of the propeller, while backwards fire was severely hindered by wires, struts, and the tail plane.[36] The 'Fokker Scourge', as it was known, lasted from July 1915 until early-mid 1916. However, because of production runs, and because inexperienced pilots thrown hastily into battle were often unable to handle faster, more manoeuvrable, but less stable aircraft, the BE2c biplane continued in use in Europe into 1917.[37] (It also developed a new role as a night flyer, employed in Home Defence of England against Zeppelin and air raid attack—one for which its stability proved ideal, and where speed and manoeuvrability were unimportant.)[38]

The Vickers FB5 biplane, nicknamed the 'Vickers Gunbus', entered service in February 1915. Its engine was situated at the back of the aeroplane instead of the front, giving the machine gunner a clear range of fire ahead. Tasked with protecting the slow and defenceless BE2c, and taking on the Fokkers, it could itself only manage 70 mph.[39] On 25 July 1915, Robin Hughes Chamberlain arrived at St. Omer in France with 11 squadron, the first RFC fighter squadron to be fully equipped with the 2-seater fighter, but he apparently never in fact flew Vickers Gunbus *Dominica* presented by the island; for neither the original, nor any of its later replacements seem to have flown with any squadron with which he was associated.[40] He wrote back of one experience in September 1915:

> On the 23rd I was sent off on a long reconnaissance into German territory, going over the trenches we were shelled. A Fokker Monoplane at about 1,500 feet started to climb at me and I kept my machine climbing but he soon caught us up. I slipped into a cloud, turned round and nose-dived on straight at the German. My observers turned the machine gun on him letting off some 60 rounds, whereupon the Fokker dived to earth leaving us master of the situation. On the 26th I was hit in four places—and we ended up by landing in the dark, a difficult job but on this occasion successful.[41]

Though in 1916 the average life expectancy of a new RFC pilot in France was barely three weeks,[42] Robin Hughes Chamberlain survived the whole of the remaining war years—even the build-up to, and opening weeks of, the Battle of the Somme, which he described as his busiest period as a pilot, trying to prevent German air reconnaissance of British positions. The more experienced the pilot, the better his survival prospects, and he had been flying since early 1915. However, he was badly wounded in the foot in August 1916 and only returned to action after an extended period in hospital. By this stage, he was with 24 squadron flying a newer aeroplane, the De Havilland 5 (DH5) scout, which he considered a match for the Fokker in terms of manoeuvrability, but still too slow.

Then he was made an instructor: from November 1917 until February 1918, to the Australian 71st squadron RFC, newly equipped with state-of-the-art, but unstable and difficult to pilot, Sopwith Camels; and from March 1918 with 65 Training Squadron at Dover. Commissioned initially as a 2nd Lieutenant, he was appointed RFC Flight Commander in December 1915, and later became a Major in the newly formed RAF.

When the war ended Robin Hughes Chamberlain was offered, but declined, the post of British Air Attaché in Paris, returning instead to the plantation in Dominica. However the estate suffered neglect during the war years, and the limes had deteriorated. In 1929 he sold up and settled in UK, finding employment in an RAF liaison role with a company that manufactured aircraft gun turrets.[43] He was not alone. Most British settlers on Dominica had abandoned their estates for various reasons within a few years, not least the Great War, but also on account of diseases, pest infestations and crop failures. The few still cultivating were resigned to making little profit.[44] Many in any case saw their identity primarily as part of the wider British Empire and had not had time to put down deeper Dominican roots: to that extent the planters were 'transnational' Britons.

One of the reasons the Imperial Road had taken its specific, and not always completely logical, path was to reach the estate of a planter from Ceylon who had made major investments in Dominica. Its maintenance was difficult to sustain and its economic rationale questionable. Hesketh Bell later admitted that his agricultural scheme for opening up Dominica's interior had been a failure, blaming poor road maintenance and transport difficulties, serious outbreaks of a disease that afflicted the lime trees, and a 'ruinous fall' in the price of cocoa: 'One by one they gave up the struggle, and there are few who were not obliged either to abandon their plantations or sell them for a song.'[45]

The small island of Dominica had proved generous in many ways during 1914–18. Throughout the conflict, the larger estates and companies supplied consignments of limes for the wounded at Netley Hospital, near Southampton; and the Dominica Agricultural and Commercial Society organised their shipment through the mail steamer. Belgian relief funds also benefitted. The very same meeting of the Legislative Council that had voted £4,000 for the RFC in October 1914 also voted £1,000 towards the Belgian National Relief Fund, a grant described as the crowning act of the noble efforts of the Rev. Bourchier, Rector of the Anglican Church at Roseau (later a chaplain at the Somme in France) whose private Belgian Relief Fund had already raised £235. By July 1917, the island had given just over £2,000 for Belgian relief, half from Government funds, and half by private donation. At one stage, the Cardinal of the Belgian town of Mechelen wrote expressing his 'heartfelt thanks' for all the help forthcoming from Dominica.[46] At the official level, Dominica provided £10,000 to the British Government through raising an export tax of one shilling per barrel of green limes.[47]

As well as dropping coins into the collection boxes for Belgian relief, islanders wishing to donate to war charities, but able to afford only very small amounts, could contribute to the Tobacco Fund through local organiser Alfred Peter Charles, harbour master at Portsmouth in the north of the island. Dominica's 1914 Christmas present to troops on the Western Front consisted of 50 cigarettes, a quarter of a pound of tobacco and a box of matches.[48] Indeed in terms of the sheer numbers of people involved across the empire, the Tobacco Fund was perhaps the most successful of the many 'patriotic' funds that right from the very beginning of the Great War were springing up like mushrooms. It began in September 1914. John Evelyn Wrench, founder of the Overseas Club in London, and Director of the Paris office of Lord Northcliffe's *Daily Mail*, was approached by Walter Martin, proprietor of a tobacco firm in Piccadilly—a man, Wrench later wrote, with a prolific mind for salesmanship, who devised a leaflet fit to draw blood from a stone:

> In moving language was set forth Tommy's longing for cigarettes. Each collecting list had a space for 50 names. Every donor of a shilling or upwards entered his name and address. In each packet of cigarettes was enclosed an addressed postcard to the donor. All Tommy had to do was to write a few lines of thanks to his unknown friend.[49]

The costs of the scheme were borne by the organisers. Walter Martin can hardly be said to have been a disinterested party; nonetheless, he did not get rich on the proceeds, so not too many questions were raised. The scheme was enormously successful, thanks in part to the support and coverage of *The Times* weekly and the overseas edition of the *Daily Mail*, and, in part, because it was immaterial how small the donation. Each contributor could feel they were helping in some tangible way to ameliorate life in the trenches. Wrench used his press connections to mobilise newspapers throughout the British Empire as local agents for the fund. By early 1916 the Tobacco Fund had received donations from almost 255,000 people outside Britain, and before the war was over, from several millions of donors worldwide. On 24th May 1915 (Empire Day), over £10,000 was collected in pennies from children; in 1916, nearly three million children donated, and postcards of thanks went directly from the trenches to the schools.[50] By May 1918, the Tobacco Fund had collected more than £300,000 from donors worldwide.[51]

Moving forward from organising a fund that had caught on like wildfire, Wrench's mind turned to aviation. While the Tobacco Fund was the 'patriotic' scheme with a human face, designed to establish contact between the soldier at the Front and residents of the empire, this had a more political dimension:

> The provision of smokes was all very well, but we were engaged in a life-and-death struggle. Our society must seek to link up residents overseas with the Empire's war effort on the battlefield. Aviation was more or less in its infancy oversea ... The idea suddenly occurred to me that nothing would make some of the smaller or more isolated sections of the Empire feel so linked up with the great events in Europe and in the East as aircraft named after their districts. Australia had her super-Dreadnought. Why should not Ceylon and St. Kitts have their aircraft?[52]

Surely the idea must have suggested itself from learning of Vickers Gunbus *Dominica*, and the other aircraft (type unknown) that benefitted the RNAS, although Wrench's memoirs record it as a brainwave coming to him out of the blue. Perhaps in late 1914 he was even informed of Dominica's £4,000 war gift by the island's Tobacco Fund organiser, harbour master Alfred Peter Charles. The timing would fit.

By such contagion of ideas was the notion of an Imperial Aircraft Flotilla born. Wrench duly approached the War Office with his brainwave, and at the beginning of 1915 the Army Council gave its formal approval for his fundraising campaign, supplying photographs of the two types of aeroplane then in current production—the brand new 100 hp. Gnome Vickers Gun Biplane, or FB5, at £2,250 (like *Dominica*) and the 70 hp. Renault engine BE2c reconnaissance craft at £1,500. Propagated by its author, John Evelyn Wrench, a hyperactive newspaperman with a scattergun approach, it overtook, and eventually subsumed, the Patriotic League's fundraising efforts aided by the Foreign Office, to spread swiftly across the 'British' world. Its early success is the topic of the next chapter.

A spoof joint appeal launched by kite balloon officers in France, Lieutenants Francis Bryan Berkeley Shand of Dominica, and Stanley Standford Stone of Trinidad rounds off the Dominica story. They issued the following plea in May 1917:

> Well then, old pals of palmier days, will you foot the bill of a *Dominica* and a *Trinidad* balloon, just as you did for *Dominica I*, *Dominica II*, and presentation exactly as was done in the case of the planes. £800 per balloon will do the trick. Only, buck up, or the war may be over before

the goods are delivered ... Anyhow, seriously, come up to scratch, as you did before, and don't let two of your fellow-citizens appeal to you in vain for such a cause.[53]

The job of kite balloon officer on the Western Front was principally to spot and direct artillery fire, and was dangerous in the extreme, though unlike RFC aircrew, they at least had the use of parachutes. The basket-carrying kite balloons were tethered over the lines, sometimes for ten or more hours at a time, at about 3,000 feet. Thus suspended 'beneath 28,000 cu. ft. of highly flammable hydrogen in what amounted to a wickerwork laundry hamper that swung wildly in windy conditions', they were targets for enemy aircraft and at risk from allied anti-aircraft guns attempting to ward off such attacks.[54]

'Jauntiness', 'pranks', and the somewhat desperate gaiety evidenced in the memoirs of First World War pilots were evidently common to kite balloon officers too, presumably a coping mechanism for the nerve-shredding quality of their daily working lives. Lieutenant Stanley Stone, newly qualified as a solicitor at Port of Spain just before his enlistment in 1914, had been seriously wounded in France by machine-gun bullets in the spring of 1916.[55] Here he was in 1917, poking fun at fundraising efforts for presentation aeroplanes to the benefit of RFC flying service colleagues. (Maybe his nerve gave way eventually, for in December 1917 he was declared unfit for further overseas service, and transferred to a Home establishment Balloon Training Wing.)[56] Lieutenant Shand was a barrister-at-law who left his practice in Roseau to join the Royal Naval Volunteer Reserve (RNVR) at the end of 1914.[57] He served with the balloon ship HMS *Manica* in the Dardanelles, and had manned observation balloons in France since September 1916.[58]

Over in Roseau, tiny capital of Dominica, Mrs. Elfreda Shand was apparently taken in by the practical joke and sent the *Dominica Chronicle* an extract from a letter or notebook that her husband purported to have found on a German prisoner at Beaumont in France, in the hope, she said, that it would speed up subscriptions for 'A Dominica Balloon'. The extract read:

> Their airmen are constantly over our lines, discover our batteries so that they may be peppered, and are always attacking our captive balloons, which is the same thing as putting our eyes out. Meanwhile the sky is black with captive balloons and hostile airmen—but of that I will say nothing, it would merely be pouring water into the Rhine. Solely

the English artillery, the English Flying Corps and their balloon observation, have given them the success they have obtained.[59]

More than six months later, just £40 had been subscribed towards a presentation kite balloon in Dominica. The newspaper eventually saw the funny side and handed the £40 over to the Overseas Club Aircraft Fund—towards yet another machine for the Imperial Aircraft Flotilla and the aviators of the RFC.[60]

The RFC of course also targeted enemy kite balloons, and in 1918 the island's presentation aeroplane was the vehicle. For in one of its later incarnations as Bristol Fighter serial number B1122, *Dominica* accounted for a majority of the eleven kills claimed by Thomas Colvill-Jones of Buenos Aires. He had been one amongst the many 'colonials' persuaded to transfer to the RFC from British army units in the wake of 'Bloody April' 1917, with encouragement from his brother in the infantry ('You get about 28/- a day with all allowances when qualified, compared to our 10/-.... you get topping billets behind the line and when you finish flying you finish for the day...'). New RFC officer cadets were urgently needed to fill the many pilot vacancies on the Western Front created by superior German aircraft (namely the Albatros Scout).

Arriving in France on 30th September, newly commissioned 2nd Lieutenant Colvill-Jones joined 20 Squadron. By this time the RFC in France were flying fighter models to match, or even better, the performance of the German aircraft. Allocated Bristol Fighter B1122 to pilot, with the name *Dominica* painted along its side in large white letters, his six victories (five against Albatros) culminated in the destruction of a German kite balloon on 4th February. The Argentine 'ace' was to down a further five German aircraft, but no longer in *Dominica* and flying with the rank of Captain with 48 Squadron, before being himself shot down and taken prisoner in May 1918.[61]

Country	Approx. population	Number of planes
Dominica	c. 35, 000	2

Chapter 3:
The Imperial Aircraft Flotilla Takes Off, 1915–1916

Evelyn Wrench, as he preferred to be known, owed his introduction to aviation to Lord Northcliffe. As early as 1906, the press magnate sought to stimulate its development in Britain through the medium of the *Daily Mail* by offering a £10,000 prize for the first flight between London and Manchester, followed by a smaller prize for a successful flight across the Channel.[1] In 1909, Wilbur and Orville Wright were his private guests at Pau in the Pyrenees for a flying exhibition before an invited audience that included King Edward VII.[2] Wrench later wrote of this, the first occasion he had ever even seen an aeroplane in flight, that Wilbur Wright predicted to him then that the first role of aircraft in war would be found in military scouting, acting as the 'eyes' of the army: if war came, there would be undreamt of development of the flying arm. Yet he believed that neither Wilbur Wright nor his brother could possibly have foreseen the phenomenal expansion of military and naval aviation in the Great War.[3]

Nor could they have foreseen the static nature of trench warfare that developed across northern France and Belgium in late 1914, and rendered the time-honoured practice of scouting by cavalry no match for surveillance from the air. The RFC's first operational use of aerial photography for reconnaissance was in mid-September 1914, as the Marne campaign was concluding, and movement on the Western Front was about to solidify into semi-subterranean siege warfare for the next four years.[4] In the new heavy mechanised warfare, artillery spotting from the air and aerial mapping became critically important, as was attempting to prevent the enemy from doing the same over your lines, and air fighting led to the development of faster and more manoeuvrable gun-mounted aeroplanes. As Lloyd George commented, in his sonorous manner:

> To the infant invention of aviation, the War proved to be a forcing-house of tropical intensity ... and as in the West the deadlock of trench warfare on the ground developed, we came to devote increasing attention to a battlefield where no trenches could be dug, no minefields sown.[5]

On 5 January 1915 Evelyn Wrench sought the Army Council's approval for a public campaign aimed at getting each and every section of the British Empire to present an aeroplane to the RFC, to be named after the district that provided it: an offer the Army Council in reply 'gladly accepted'.[6] The appeal launched in the 30th January overseas edition of the newspaper, with a photograph of the FB5 (the Vickers Gunbus) at £2,250. It invited contributions from all parts of the empire for the fighter, or alternatively the BE2c reconnaissance plane at £1,500. Every donation from a reader would be acknowledged in its columns, it was initially promised—before the scheme grew too large. At that stage, the appeal's success was a far from foregone conclusion. Wrench's hopes were to collect enough money for at least one aeroplane, though he did not anticipate anything like the popular response to the Tobacco Fund.

King George V gave the all-important royal seal of approval by becoming Patron of the Overseas Club in February. By Easter Sunday, £350 had been collected, and in mid-May, 1915, Wrench and Lieutenant General Sir David Henderson met to arrange the presentation of a cheque for the first aeroplane, *Overseas No. 1*, at a cost of £1,500. Wrench also went to see Lord Selborne, to talk over the position of his Patriotic League of Britons Overseas, which was getting nowhere fast with its plans to buy a warship for the Admiralty. Before the month was out three developments placed the Imperial Aircraft Flotilla campaign on its upward trajectory. Firstly, *Overseas No. 1* was launched at the Royal Aircraft Factory, Farnborough, with funds for another on the way. Wrench, in receipt of 'a very nice letter' from Secretary of State for War, Field Marshal Lord Kitchener, and also one from Lord Stamfordham (George V's private secretary) with a message from the King, decided to keep the fund open until further notice and to embark on a mass leafleting campaign.

Second, a Committee meeting of Lord Selborne's Patriotic League of Britons Overseas unanimously elected Wrench joint Honorary Secretary and invited him to run the whole outfit from the Overseas Club office. As he explained in a letter to his parents, this placed him in a very strong position with respect to patriotic organisations abroad, and would ultimately mean absorption of the League by the Overseas Club.[7] It incidentally also avoided the potential problem of rivalry as between the two organisations and between the RFC and the RNAS over the respective appeals: Amounts subscribed for the RFC were handled by the special Overseas Club account for the Aircraft Fund at

Coutts Bank and were paid over to the Army Council, while money collected through the League's auspices for the RNAS went to the Admiralty through the Bank of England, and Wrench—Janus-headed—dealt with both. The third event was the arrival of a fat cheque from Hong Kong.

Evelyn Wrench's intention in launching the Imperial Aircraft Flotilla scheme had been essentially political—to give British communities in all parts of the empire a sense of involvement in the war; and he considered himself uniquely fitted to do so through his Ulster background, which he believed equipped him with a greater rapport with citizens of the Dominions, and with British settlers in the Colonies, than 'the hundred per-cent Englishman'. Certainly, he was successful in persuading a number of senior Dominion politicians to sign up as Vice Presidents of the Overseas Club, as well as current and former British Governors General.

Moreover, his conception of the empire was not that of an exclusively British-run enterprise:

> I knew from first-hand knowledge that there was a gigantic task to be performed in bringing together Englishmen and Irishmen, French and British Canadians, Dutch and British South Africans; apart from the even greater task of giving a conscious sense of citizenship to the millions living under the Union Jack. The Empire was too widely scattered and too varied in origin to be run by a handful of people who hailed from two small islands in the northern seas.[8]

By the standards of the age, his racial attitudes were also liberal, though reflecting the contemporary assumption that unlike those of the white Dominions, 'subject peoples' were as yet unprepared for self-government. Noting that the white population of the British Empire constituted just one-sixth of the whole, he held that 'old-fashioned doctrines of white predominance must go by the board. Equal rights for every civilised man was the only logical goal. We must take all these nations into partnership when they were ready for political advancement.'[9]

His fundraising campaign was launched with each and every part of the empire in his sights: he simply fired off leaflets and subscription forms to all Colonies and Protectorates, as well as to press contacts and Overseas Club branches abroad and to influential figures on his mailing lists in the Dominions. At the outset, however, it is doubtful that he expected cash to come in from communities other than British by blood descent. He was soon to get used to the idea. On 30 May 1915, he wrote to his parents:

> I was tremendously bucked by Hong Kong's donation of £4,500 to our Aircraft Fund. Just think, casually coming upon a cheque for this amount in the morning's mail! I had another very nice letter from Lord Stamfordham expressing the King's thanks.
> This week we are paying a cheque for £6,000 to the War Office for aeroplanes.

By June 1915 the Overseas Club had sent out 100,000 appeal leaflets that incorporated the messages of support from the King and from Lord Kitchener.[10] The Flotilla by this stage was described as consisting of *Overseas No. 1*, paid for by general subscription; *Gibraltar*, a 100-hp. Vickers FB5 gun-mounted biplane donated to the RFC by the people of Gibraltar through the Colonial Office; *Victoria-Hong Kong 1*; *Victoria-Hong Kong 2*; *Tai Yan Bank Hong Kong*; and *British West Indies*. (The order of listing later changed.) All except *Gibraltar* were BE2cs. *Tai Yan Bank Hong Kong* carried parallel inscriptions in English and in Chinese characters, at the request of the donors.[11]

Evelyn Wrench's cousin and helper at the Overseas Club, Lady Hylda des Voeux, had launched *Overseas No. 1* in May. On 3rd July, however, Alexandra of Denmark, the Queen Mother, performed the naming ceremony for four more presentation aeroplanes at the RFC Headquarters, Farnborough, which left immediately for the Front. *South Africa* was one of those launched, along with all three presented by Hong Kong. Wrench was subsequently able to insert a photograph of Queen Alexandra at the naming ceremony into the Imperial Aircraft Flotilla campaign leaflet, which was periodically updated to incorporate new messages of support and include details of new aircraft provided under the scheme. He recorded the interest Alexandra had shown on that occasion, and a teatime conversation at which her daughter, Princess Victoria, spoke of their meeting with Count Zeppelin during a stay in Copenhagen—she declared herself relatively unimpressed with his airship invention. Victoria, he wrote, declined the strawberries on account of her gout.[12]

Lady Hylda des Voeux being taken for a flight in *Overseas No. 1* after the launch at Farnborough, May 1915 (John Evelyn Wrench, *Struggle*)

Queen Alexandra with Evelyn Wrench (left) and Lieut. Gen. David Henderson (far left) at the naming ceremony for four aeroplanes from the empire, July 1915 (John Evelyn Wrench, *Struggle*)

Others also set up new overseas funds. Aircraft listed at Nos. 7, 8 and 9 in the Imperial Aircraft Flotilla were all presented through an entirely separate Malaya Air Fleet Fund established by one Charles Alma Baker. This is described in a later chapter, but it is worth pointing out at this juncture that the donor of the first of those aeroplanes from Malaya, Eu Tong Sen, was the Chinese member of the FMS Federal Council involved alongside the Malay Sultans in the voting of funds for HMS *Malaya* in 1912. With the appearance of new funds (one of them begun by the Lieutenant Governor of Nova Scotia) Wrench appealed for information about units provided directly to the RFC, rather than through the Overseas Club, so as to keep accurate consolidated listings.[13] In the case of Malaya, this task was facilitated by the incorporation of Sir Ernest Birch KCMG, an old friend of Charles Alma Baker, onto the Central Committee of the Overseas Club as FMS representative; Birch under his other hat acted as Alma Baker's London liaison with the Army Council.

The recently appointed Secretary of State for the Colonies, Andrew Bonar Law, accepted the position of Overseas Club Vice President in August 1915.[14] Even then, the Colonial Office did not seek to emulate the degree of official support the Foreign Office had afforded to Lord Selborne's Patriotic League (perhaps learning from the Warship Fund's lack of progress). It did not issue an official circular, or offer to act as postman. Instead, Wrench dispatched publicity material and subscription forms direct to Governors and Administrators throughout the British Empire. It was left to individual officials to respond, or not, as they felt fit. Wrench, however, sent periodic updates of aeroplanes presented to the Colonial Office, and the Colonial Office in turn informed the Overseas Club of those gifted through Governors and Administrators abroad. The Colonial Office was also the channel for communicating consolidated lists supplied by the Overseas Club to the British press; save, that is, for any notice of gift aeroplanes from India, which fell within the remit of the India Office.[15]

Lord Hardinge of Penshurst, GCB, GCMG, Viceroy of India, joined the increasingly grand list of Overseas Club Vice Presidents in 1916, which now also included Lord Selborne.[16] However, it must also be said that one of the Vice Presidents was Will Crooks MP, a Labour Party activist and Poor Law reformer (he had spent years of his youth in Poplar workhouse), who was of quite different stripe, but a significant figure during the Great War. An active supporter of the recruitment campaigns during 1914–15 and the Military Service Bills of

1916, he represented Woolwich, which included the Royal Arsenal, chief munitions manufacturer in Britain. In the Shell Crisis driven by Northcliffe's newspapers that brought down the Liberal government in May 1915 (and brought Lloyd George to the fore as Minister of Munitions in the Coalition Government that resulted), Will Crooks played a prominent part on behalf of his constituents in highlighting munitions shortages, and he was tireless at the time in pursuing the issue in parliament.[17]

For British colonial officials abroad, the King's patronage, and the array of leading Establishment figures who allowed their names to be associated with the Overseas Club as Vice Presidents, provided assurance that this was an entirely reputable fund, and no scam, while endorsement of the Imperial Aircraft Flotilla movement by Kitchener and the Army Council provided solid proof of its utility in the war. In addition, Lieutenant General Sir David Henderson at the Aeronautics Directorate appears to have looked very favourably on the scheme as a useful tool in the RFC's expansion programme, in view of the future aerial support requirements of a BEF swollen with the arrival of Kitchener's volunteers to a mass army approaching those of France and Germany.

There was a long way to go: at the beginning of March 1915 the RFC in France comprised just eighty-one aeroplanes divided into three wings (with another eighteen machines on charge in the Aircraft Park)—only twenty-one more than had been flown there at the outset of the war.[18] Henderson later noted his appreciation of Wrench's campaign in a letter to the Parliamentary Under-Secretary at the Colonial Office: 'it matters very little to us through what channel money comes to buy aeroplanes with, but I am all in favour of the Over-seas Club and will be glad to help them if I get a chance.'[19]

Crucially for the continuing appeal of the scheme to donors, Henderson and the Army Council undertook in autumn 1915 that if the original aeroplane presented was destroyed by enemy action or by flying accident ('struck off RFC charge'), it would be replaced by a new unit of the same name, often of improved type. This was important, since not only was wastage very severe, but the Great War saw rapid developments in aircraft function, design, and engine power, and aeroplane models soon became outdated. It was surely no coincidence that this pledge was made shortly after Henderson returned from France to his desk at the Aeronautics Directorate in London.

By mid-October 1915 the Overseas Club had provided 35 aeroplanes to the RFC—or £60,000 in cash—with several more promised. However Henderson's undertakings to Evelyn Wrench and the Overseas Club were to prove onerous for the RFC over time, as the Imperial Aircraft Flotilla scheme mushroomed throughout the British world. As well as naming a replacement for any presentation aircraft struck off charge, the Army Council also promised to send a photograph of 'their' aircraft to each donor or group of donors. These promises were incorporated in Overseas Club literature and were undoubtedly an attraction for potential contributors, as the name they chose was assured of being perpetuated throughout the length of the war. They continued to be honoured by the RFC and Army Council, of which Henderson was himself made a full member in spring 1916.

For each donation of £1,500–£2,250 (after mid-1916, £2,500–£2,700 as aircraft were equipped with guns, cameras, and other paraphernalia as a matter of course) the name selected by the donors was inscribed onto a relevant aeroplane model. During 1915–16 this was largely either the BE2c or the Farman Experimental 2b (FE2b) fighting scout (the latter progressively replacing the slower and soon outdated Vickers Gunbus). The first presentation aircraft had the name painted along the fuselage in the largest lettering possible, but this provided a tempting extra target for enemy gunners. Later, the lettering shrank and could be located anywhere from the aeroplane's nose to the rear fuselage area, sometimes inscribed on a brass plaque.

In October 1915 it had been agreed that the task of transferring the name of any presentation plane struck off charge should be carried out in England, rather than fall to the RFC in the field.[20] Aircraft depots received regular lists of names specified by donors for inscription on types of aeroplane (reconnaissance or fighter, according to the amount subscribed) as they came off the production line. Their serial numbers were then sent to RFC headquarters, and Brigade or Wing headquarters checked squadron weekly aircraft returns and daily aircraft casualty lists, and prepared a monthly presentation aircraft 'struck off charge' listing. This was returned to the UK, where the list was divided into aircraft types, and replacement machines ordered from the relevant depot.[21] In the process of transfer, it was not unknown for some of the more exotic presentation names to become garbled. Thus *Malaya No. 1 Eu Tong Sen* of early 1915 could morph into 'Eu-Tung-Sen' and eventually complete its transformation into 'Eu San Tongo' in RFC/RAF listings.

Given a time lag of up to two months in the process of name transfer, a replacement machine usually went to the next unit that required that type of aeroplane, rather than to the very one that had reported the loss. Thus there was no continuity of aviator or even squadron for a named presentation aircraft. Put another way, a label like *Newfoundland No. 1* for which subscribers had contributed a total of £2,250, could be painted on any RFC fighter aeroplane coming off the production line, and sent to any RFC squadron that needed one; similarly for its replacements. (There was an Australian exception to this general rule later in the war, covered in chapter seventeen.) Thus there was no 'imperial' aircraft unit or formation, as such, in existence at any stage, and the Imperial Aircraft Flotilla was a purely notional construct that never took on material form—an air flotilla of the imagination rather than in fact. However, it proved to be a persuasively attractive fundraising idea, which in some parts of the empire really touched a popular chord.

When Wrench took over the running of the Patriotic League's fundraising efforts for the RNAS, lines between that and his own Imperial Aircraft Flotilla scheme tended to become blurred, and the division of effort—so to speak—began to dissolve between British communities in foreign countries outside the empire, raising money for the Admiralty and RNAS, and within it, raising money for the Army Council and RFC. Some presentation aircraft named after localities in the Americas, for instance, were donated to the RFC rather than the RNAS. The initial attraction of Wrench's scheme over that of the Patriotic League was probably twofold: RFC aeroplanes cost less than seaplanes, and contributors were promised that any complete aircraft subscribed would carry the name of their choice, and it would be perpetuated for the length of the war, no matter how many replacements were destroyed.

The ten seaplanes initially presented by the League to the RNAS in July 1915 (in lieu of a warship) were ready for active service by early November. They had been anonymously labeled *Britons Overseas Nos. 1-10*. Evidently, however, Wrench later managed to reach a similar arrangement with the Admiralty to that vouchsafed by Sir David Henderson for gifts to the RFC. For in 1916 the Patriotic League's fund—by now called the 'Seaplane Fund'—emulated that of the Overseas Club in promising that any town or district providing £3,500 was to have the honour of having a seaplane named after it. In May, Wrench was able to report a total of sixty-eight biplanes presented to date through the Overseas Club, while the Patriotic League of Britons Overseas had presented twelve large seaplanes and fourteen aeroplanes to the Royal Navy.[22] RNAS paperwork on five presentation aircraft supplied subsequently by the League (in September 1916) shows that they were processed and inscribed in like fashion to those of the RFC.[23]

It remains to gauge the contribution in money terms. Out of the 1,680 aeroplanes delivered to RFC units during 1915, 710 of them were BE2c reconnaissance craft.[24] In rough measure of the significance of overseas donations at this stage in the First World War, we can take the total production costs of all BE2cs for the year as £1,065,000 (710 x £1,500). Allowing for six to eight weeks between the remittance of the money to London and the allocation of a presentation name to an individual aircraft coming off the production line, the quantity of named BE2cs recorded as 'presented' to the RFC between February 1915 and the close of January 1916 should give an approximate measure (with the *caveat* that the estimate is based on a variety of published sources, and is only a very rough approximation). About forty-three BE2cs were so presented in this period: an overall contribution of £64,000, or about 6 per cent of the total for BE2c production for that year.

Around thirty-three fighter aircraft were also presented in the same period at a cost of £2,250 each. They were FB5s or the later FE2b scout, a faster plane that superseded the Vickers Gunbus and was additionally equipped with an aerial camera for reconnaissance.[25] That makes a further £74,250 for fighters. The Imperial Aircraft Flotilla scheme, including national spin-offs like the Malaya Air Fleet Fund, thus contributed an estimated £138,250 towards aircraft production costs for the RFC in the twelve months from its launch in January 1915—for roughly seventy-six aeroplanes (excluding the prior gift of *Dominica*) as shown in Table 1. Around forty-three were reconnaissance craft (at £1,500 each) and thirty-three, fighters or fighting scouts (at production costs of £2,250 apiece).

Table I – Presentation planes Jan. 1915-Jan. 1916 (RFC only)

Argentina:	3	Australia:	2	British Guiana:	1
British West Indies:	1	Burma:	3	Canada:	7
Ceylon:	4	China:	2	Gibraltar:	1
Gold Coast:	5	Hong Kong:	5	India:	6
Jamaica:	1	Malaya & Singapore:	10	Newfoundland:	5
New Zealand:	1	Nigeria:	2	'Overseas' general:	1
Rhodesia:	4	Sierra Leone:	1	South Africa:	6
Trinidad:	1	Zanzibar:	4		
		Grand total:	76		

NB—This table omits all gifts to the RNAS for lack of a sufficient and comprehensive record

The War Office initially promised to keep contributors informed of 'good work' done by their presentation aeroplane, but this undertaking was 'regretfully' (but understandably) dropped in late 1916 due, it was explained, to pressure of work in the field (in the wake of the Battle of the Somme!)[26] However, a handful of short letters from RFC pilots about the satisfactory performance of the presentation aircraft they flew did reach columns in the overseas press before the practice was ended. The most fulsome of them all was sent to the organiser of the Malaya Air Fleet Fund, Charles Alma Baker. It was penned by 2nd Lieutenant Hazelton R. Nicholl of No. 8 Squadron RFC, BEF France (who is to reappear at several further points in this story) and dated 14th October 1915, the very day after a directive went out from the Aeronautics Directorate in London to RFC units in France, requiring reports of 'interesting actions' by presentation aircraft for the benefit of donors.[27]

What makes Hazleton Nicholl's letter particularly interesting is that he was related to Sir David Henderson (a cousin most likely).[28] He joined the RFC in April 1915 at thirty-three years old, having previously served in the London Scottish Volunteers, and then as a trooper (1903–4) with the Southern Rhodesia Volunteers. Although he proved equal to younger airmen—and eventually attained the position of Air Vice Marshal in the RAF—he owed his initial entry into the flying service at his comparatively advanced age to his influential relative.[29] Hazelton Nicholl's letter was widely reproduced in newspapers in the FMS and Straits Settlements:

> 14 October 1915
> No. 8 Squadron, RFC,
> BEF France
>
> Dear Mr. Baker,
>
> I feel sure you will be interested to know that a machine has come to this squadron bearing the inscription 'Malaya No. 3 presented by C. Alma Baker, Esq., Kinta'. Curiously enough it was my privilege to take 'Victoria Hong-Kong No. 1' for its trip over the lines and I have now given 'Malaya No. 3' its baptism of fire and a real good 'wetting' we got. I had a rather tedious job to do and was under continuous fire from the German Anti-Aircraft guns for 2 hours and 5 minutes—without a break, but the machine was good: beautifully trued up, and the engine good, and curiously enough I came back without a single hit on the machine, and that is by way of being an unusual thing, for one of our machines: as the German gunners are wonderfully good.
>
> The machine is of the BE2C type of Biplane, and the first I have seen turned out by Ruston Proctor & Co. of Lincoln a well finished and sound machine. I can assure you that the fellows in this Squadron in particular and the Flying Corps in general are immensely pleased and proud when they see machines rolling up, marked from the far places of the Empire. It is such a very practical way of showing how much the thoughts of our ain folk are with us in these strenuous days, and as one who has been some 13 years in S. Africa perhaps I feel it a little more than the fellows who have not been to the Colonies. The little dorp of Gatooma, Rhodesia, where I was engaged in mining, have started an aeroplane fund which has reached just on £1,000 so I hope to see 'Gatooma No. 1' out here soon to help us go and chase the Boches off the sky, and keep up the standard that the good fellows, who came out here at the start, set us to follow.
>
> Any details of our work of course I am not allowed to tell you—much as I feel it would interest you, and we rather pride ourselves upon keeping pretty quiet.
>
> Yours truly,
> Hazelton R. Nicholl
> 2nd Lt. No. 8 Squadron

While the timing of his letter could simply have been dictated by the RFC's receipt of the new directive, it seems somewhat quick off the mark. It may be significant that it was addressed to Charles Alma

Baker just when his motivation for starting the Malaya Air Fleet Fund was being publicly questioned in the Straits Settlements Legislative Council, and provided useful positive publicity locally for his case.[30] There is a distinct possibility (but no direct evidence) that Henderson stimulated Lieutenant Hazelton Robson Nicholl to write, to this very end. He may very well have been alerted to the verbal attack on Alma Baker and his Malaya Air Fleet Fund at Singapore, since Henderson was certainly personally known to, and in contact with, Sir Ernest Birch, Alma Baker's old friend and liaison in London with the War Office and Army Council.

Examples of internal RFC reporting, however, appear innocent of any similar extraneous factors and mainly concentrate, as instructed, on the performance of the machine.[31] Reports such as those from which the following extracts were taken formed the basis for brief accounts sent out by the War Office, via the Overseas Club, for benefit of donors; and a few of those accounts duly found their way into the overseas press. They illustrate the short life expectancy of aircraft (as well as aircrew) and the consequent importance to donors of the commitment to transfer presentation names onto replacement machines:

> BE2c No. 1698 Victoria Hong Kong:
> This machine was personally presented ... by H. M. Queen Alexandra on July 3rd 1915 ... and was flown direct to France ... and allotted to No. 4 Squadron. It proved fast and reliable, and was used at first chiefly for cooperation with artillery, and afterwards for reconnaissances. On July 26th, it was attacked by two German machines over the enemy's territory, both of which were driven off, but the engine ... was hit by a bullet and stopped, and the pilot had to land behind German lines under heavy fire. The pilot and observer managed to burn the machine and were taken prisoners.
>
> Vickers FB5 No. 1616 Dominica:
> This aeroplane had a most successful career. Four times it was engaged in fights with enemy machines. ... On the 5th May VICKERS 1616 brought down its first victim [...] On the 6th June VICKERS 1616 was engaged in another successful fight ... The German machine was last seen falling into a wood just behind the German trenches. After this action and while returning home the machine was very badly damaged by the enemy's

anti-aircraft guns ... After repair ... she did excellent work fighting combats in the air on at least six occasions and receiving numerous holes in her planes as honourable wounds. These and other wear and tear made a complete overhauling and repairing necessary [in July]. ... she returned to work but after ten more patrols a shell from an anti-aircraft gun destroyed her undercarriage and the subsequent landing naturally made her a total wreck. But both pilot and observer escaped unhurt.

BE2c No. 1701 British West Indies:
This machine was taken over by No. 4 Squadron on July 5th 1915, and was used for bomb dropping, reconnaissance, and cooperation with artillery ... On one occasion on September 23rd, it returned safely to the aerodrome after a bomb dropping raid, carrying pilot and observer, with over 100 holes in the planes and fuselage ... On another occasion, a big-end bearing in the engine seized while over the German lines, and the machine just succeeded in gliding back, making a forced landing in a small field close behind the French lines.

BE2c 2682 Reid Newfoundland:
On 8th December [while] doing a Tactical Reconnaissance... the BE2c was struck by one shell, and another exploded immediately below her, several pieces penetrating the fuselage. The Pilot was wounded in the leg; the engine stopped and the machine dived down for about 3000 feet. The Observer endeavoured to assist the pilot, who became faint and stated that the controls were shot away, which necessitated immediate landing. After effort had been made to locate the cause of the engine failure, it fortunately started again enabling the machine to be brought across the line of the trenches, though subjected to heavy rifle and machine gun fire and to land near ARMENTIERS, when the Pilot was brought into Hospital. The reconnaissance was successfully carried out. The Machine was not seriously damaged and will shortly again be available for work.

It was the early gifts that made the greatest proportional difference to the numbers of aircraft available to the RFC. The Overseas Club Aircraft Fund listed its most significant source of subscriptions by mid-September 1915 as follows:[32]

1) Newfoundland	£10,500
2) Canada	£9,750
3) Hong Kong	£4,500
4) Bombay	£4,500
5) South Africa 'including Rhodesia'	£4,500

(NB. This list excludes Malaya, which had contributed more than £10,000 by that date, but channeled through a separate national fund, as well as Argentina, whose £5,250 from the British community there was also presented independently of the Overseas Club.)

By the first quarter of 1916, the Overseas Club Aircraft Fund alone had taken £100,000 in subscriptions (and the Tobacco Fund £118,000);[33] and by Empire Day 1918, the Overseas Club and Patriotic League had altogether presented 150 seaplanes and aeroplanes to the Royal Navy and RFC, at a total cost of £250,000.[34] Additional machines were presented separately by national aircraft funds, like those of Malaya and Australia, so that from the inception of the scheme in early 1915 up until the Armistice, hundreds more presentation aeroplanes and seaplanes were subscribed from abroad. Some funds remitted their money directly to the War Office or the Colonial Office through the medium of British officials abroad, or else the Crown Agents; some transmitted it via the Overseas Club or other associations or agencies; many used the good offices of overseas branches of British or Dominion banks. While, however, the overall symbolic value to Britain of such voluntary overseas support as this remained high, the relative significance of the financial contribution shrank in proportion to the large increase in direct British Government funding of domestic aircraft production during 1917–18.

The Imperial Aircraft Flotilla campaign appeal leaflet
late 1916/17
© The British Library Board

THE OVER-SEAS CLUB

Patron: HIS MAJESTY THE KING.
Vice-Patron: H.R.H. THE DUKE OF CONNAUGHT, K.G.

President: LORD NORTHCLIFFE.

Vice-Presidents:

EARL GREY, G.C.B., G.C.M.G.
EARL OF LIVERPOOL, K.C.M.G.,
 Governor of New Zealand.
EARL OF MEATH, K.P.
EARL SELBORNE, K.G., G.C.M.G.
VISCOUNT GLADSTONE, G.C.M.G.
LORD HARDINGE OF PENSHURST, G.C.B.
VISCOUNT BRYCE, O.M.
LORD DENMAN, G.C.M.G.
Sir R. MUNRO FERGUSON, G.C.M.G.,
 Governor-General of Australia.
VISCOUNT BUXTON, G.C.M.G.,
 Governor-General of the Union of South Africa.
LORD ISLINGTON, G.C.M.G., D.S.O.

Rt. Hon. A. BONAR LAW,
 Secretary of State for the Colonies.
Rt. Hon. LEWIS HARCOURT, M.P.,
 Ex-Secretary of State for the Colonies.
Rt. Hon. Sir GEORGE REID, M.P.
Rt. Hon. Sir ROBERT R. L. BORDEN, K.C.M.G.,
 Prime Minister of Canada.
Rt. Hon. W. M. HUGHES,
 Prime Minister of Australia.
Rt. Hon. ANDREW FISHER,
 High Commissioner for Australia.
Rt. Hon. W. F. MASSEY,
 Prime Minister of New Zealand.
Sir STARR JAMESON.

Sir OWEN PHILIPPS, K.C.M.G.
Lt.-General Sir BEVAN EDWARDS.
Lt.-General Sir ROBERT BADEN-POWELL, K.C.B., *Chief Scout.*
Sir T. VANSITTART BOWATER.
General BOOTH.
Rev. and Hon. EDWARD LYTTELTON.
GEORGE R. PARKIN, Esq., C.M.G., *Secretary, Rhodes Trustees.*
KENNAWAY JONES, Esq.
Sir JOHN KIRK.
WILL CROOKS, Esq., M.P.

Central Committee:

W. A. BULKELEY-EVANS (Chairman).
ALGERNON ASPINALL, Esq.
Sir ERNEST BIRCH, K.C.M.G.
RALPH S. BOND, Esq.
HARRY E. BRITTAIN, Esq.
GEORGE McL. BROWN.
PERCY C. BURTON, Esq.
Colonel FRANK BUTLER.
HOWARD D'EGVILLE, Esq.

Sir FREDERICK DES VOEUX, Bart.
FRANCIS DEVEREUX, Esq.
G. D. ODDWELL.
Rev. R. L. GWYNNE.
F. W. HAYES, Esq.
A. E. HORSFALL, Esq., D.S.O.
GORDON INGLIS, Esq.
RICHARD JEBB, Esq.
W. MAXWELL LYTE, Esq.

E. R. PEACOCK, Esq.
Sir EDWARD ROSLING.
EARL STANHOPE.
MURRAY STEWART, Esq.
Sir JOHN TAVERNER, K.C.M.G.
C. F. TRUESITY, Esq., *Hon. Treasurer.*
EVELYN WRENCH, Esq., *Hon. Organiser.*
E. LAYTON BENNETT, Esq., F.C.I., *Hon. Auditor.*

The Over-Seas Club is a non-party society of British subjects residing in all parts of the world. Its underlying motive is to promote the unity of British Subjects. Its four chief objects are:—

1. To help one another.
2. To render individual service to our Empire.
3. To maintain our Empire's supremacy upon the seas and in the air.
4. To draw together in the bond of comradeship British people the world over.

British subjects in all parts of the world are proud of the splendid achievements of the British Royal Flying Corps. Indeed, one of the outstanding features of the war has been the daring of the British airmen. Residents overseas are now afforded a further opportunity of expressing their admiration of our brave airmen in a practical manner, and above all, of assisting in maintaining British supremacy in the air. Thanks to the generosity of friends overseas, over 80 aeroplanes had already been provided by November, 1916. But the need for aeroplanes and yet more aeroplanes requires no emphasis. In the words of the General commanding the Royal Flying Corps "any assistance that can be given to us to provide the very large number of aeroplanes required to replace casualties, and to augment our air force, will be much appreciated. Some thousands of aeroplanes are necessary to meet our requirements, and at the present stage I should hesitate to suggest any definite limit to the expansion which may be required for this War." We appeal therefore with the utmost confidence to residents overseas to assist the British Government by providing the funds to purchase a further 100 aeroplanes for presentation to the Royal Flying Corps.

Queen Alexandra performing the naming ceremony of four of the Overseas Flotilla, at the headquarters of the Royal Flying Corps.

The late LORD KITCHENER wrote as follows to the Central Committee of the Over-Seas Club. It will be seen that Lord Kitchener hoped that every section of the Empire would be represented.

WAR OFFICE, WHITEHALL, S.W.
17th May, 1915.

DEAR SIR,

I am gratified to hear of the prompt response to the appeal issued by the Over-Seas Club to its members and friends in all parts of His Majesty's Dominions overseas, which has already permitted the presentation of an aeroplane to the Royal Flying Corps.

I was interested to learn that the aeroplane in question had been paid for by the generous donations of several thousands of British subjects overseas, and, as I understand that you are hoping to obtain the gift of an aeroplane from each part of the Empire, I sincerely wish you success in your efforts.

The Honorary Secretary,
 The Over-Seas Club,
  General Buildings, Aldwych. W.C.

Yours very truly,
(Signed) KITCHENER.

Hong-Kong's Third Aeroplane.

Each district or group of individuals overseas which provides £2,250 or £1,500 can have an aeroplane called by a name signifying the district from which the gift comes.

These aeroplanes are the latest word in aircraft, are manufactured under the direct supervision of the Royal Flying Corps, and can be obtained for *immediate delivery*.

The following letter from Mr. Lloyd George (Secretary of State for War) expresses the hope that the Imperial Aircraft Flotilla will reach a total of 100 units. It is for Britons overseas to supply the answer.

WAR OFFICE, WHITEHALL, S.W.
August, 1916.

DEAR SIR,

I should like to take this opportunity of congratulating the Over-Seas Club on the formation of the Imperial Aircraft Flotilla. I understand that to date—thanks to the splendid generosity of the subscribers overseas—you have been able to present to the Royal Flying Corps seventy-four aeroplanes, with promises of a number more.

I hope that your ambition of an Imperial Air Fleet of 100 units will be realised.

It is very gratifying to note that our kinsmen overseas are taking such a deep interest in our Air Service.

Yours very truly,
(Signed) D. LLOYD GEORGE.

The scheme has aroused the liveliest interest everywhere, and among those who have expressed their approval are H.R.H. the Duke of Connaught, the High Commissioner for South Africa, and most of the governors of the different sections of the Empire.

The 85 aeroplanes already presented represent almost every section of the world—Canada, Australia, New Zealand, South Africa, Newfoundland, India, Hong-Kong, Ceylon, Gibraltar, British West Indies, Rhodesia, Nigeria, Gold Coast, and from British residents in China, United States, South America, and elsewhere. But there are still many districts not represented.

The greater the response, the greater the number of aeroplanes which we shall be able to furnish. *No subscription will be too small*, and we invite every British subject to contribute to the Fund. The Over-Seas Club has already collected £120,000 for the provision of aircraft. We confidently appeal to the patriotism of British subjects beyond the seas to enable us to double this amount. It is only by straining every nerve that we shall defeat our foe. Will you help us by subscribing yourself and asking your friends to do the same?

Captain Winfield-Smith, Pilot of the first unit of the Imperial Aircraft Flotilla.

Please start collecting to-day and return us this collecting sheet as soon as possible. *The fund will be kept open while the war lasts.* Every contributor can have the satisfaction of knowing that although prevented through circumstances from taking his place in the field, that he or she is indirectly helping to repel the German invader.

All communications and donations should be addressed to the Hon. Organiser, The Over-Seas Club, General Buildings, Aldwych, London, W.C. All remittances will be acknowledged by return.

Overseas No. 50.

Contributors to the
IMPERIAL AIRCRAFT FLOTILLA

N.B.—Please write clearly.

The Over-Seas Club has paid over to the War Office £120,000 for the purchase of Aircraft. Nearly every week we forward a large cheque to the Secretary of State. Will you help us to keep these gifts up?

NAME	FULL POSTAL ADDRESS	COUNTRY	£	s.	d.
		TOTAL - £			

To EVELYN WRENCH, Esq., Hon. Secretary, The Over-Seas Club, General Buildings, Aldwych, London, W.C., England.

Herewith I enclose Cheque/Draft value £_____ being the amount I have collected for the Imperial Aircraft Flotilla.

Name_____

Address_____

All Subscriptions will be acknowledged by return mail. Remittances should be made payable to the Imperial Aircraft Flotilla Fund, crossed "Messrs. Coutts & Co.," and marked "not negotiable."

A PERMANENT LINK WITH ROYAL FLYING CORPS.

SIR DAVID HENDERSON, the Commander of the Royal Flying Corps, has kindly promised that every district providing an aeroplane in our Imperial Flotilla shall have the satisfaction of knowing that a unit in the Royal Flying Corps will be permanently called after that district. This is an important point, as the wastage in aeroplanes is, of course, very heavy. For instance, should the machine provided by the Shanghai Britons come to an untimely end, a new aeroplane will at once be christened "Shanghai Britons" to take its place. In this way subscribers overseas will have a permanent link with the Royal Flying Corps.

PHOTOGRAPHS OF MACHINES.—Every group of individuals providing for the purchase of a machine will receive a letter of thanks from the War Office and a photograph of their machine.

Part II—Case Studies: The campaign's spread and development

Chapter 4:
Press and personal networks: Canada and Newfoundland

Voluntary associations were hardly new in the life of Great Britain, or its empire, and were a feature of the Victorian age. There were fundraising campaigns for various purposes during the Boer War, 1899–1902. But the whole effort was magnified in 1914–18 by the sheer scale of the Great War itself and the numbers involved in it. In addition, a British newspaper with a mass circulation actively propagated the Imperial Aircraft Flotilla scheme. It had channels of communication to the main colonial newspapers, which were able to pick up the campaign locally and run with it. The central character in its worldwide dissemination was its author, the founder of the Overseas Club, Evelyn Wrench. In establishing the Club in 1910, and its Aircraft Fund in 1915, Wrench used his connections with two influential figures, both of which had strong links with Canada. To fully appreciate the extent of the press networks and networks of personal influence that he was able to tap into and exploit, it is necessary to go back a few years.

Evelyn Wrench was the protégé of Alfred Harmsworth, Lord Northcliffe, who recruited him to his press empire in 1904.[1] Wrench's picture postcard business, established when he was just eighteen, failed after three years, but Northcliffe had been impressed by his character and entrepreneurship; Wrench by all accounts also possessed an 'almost manic' energy that must also have commended itself.[2] The press magnate established the *Daily Mail* in 1896 as the first truly mass circulation daily newspaper, and in November 1904 started an overseas edition, printed on lightweight paper to minimise postal charges. This was aimed especially at Canada, which Northcliffe viewed as too much the recipient of information from the US; it was also designed to provide an imperial perspective for readerships in India and Australia, which in his opinion were fed an excessively parochial diet of local news. He appointed the 21-year old as editor. Wrench was to remain in Northcliffe's employ for another twelve years, though gradually moving over to the managerial and business side of his press empire.³

Both Northcliffe and Wrench were imperial-minded admirers of the expansionist policies of Cecil Rhodes and enthusiasts for pan-British ('Anglo-Saxon') empire unity, although the youthful Evelyn Wrench was the more extreme in his views, later describing them in his memoirs in quasi-religious terms.⁴ Northcliffe took a strong but more practical interest in imperial issues and often visited Canada, and also Newfoundland (then a separate self-governing Dominion) where he had established a pulp and paper-mill for the *Daily Mail*. The enterprise was on a heroic scale with a vast area of woodland under lease. Construction of the mill began in June 1907 under the auspices of his Anglo-Newfoundland Development Company, and on 22 December 1909 the first shipments of paper were sent from Grand Falls to London.⁵

In 1906 Northcliffe despatched Wrench to the US and Canada, to look into their respective newspaper operations. At Ottawa, he stayed for three days with the Governor General, Albert Earl Grey (the Fourth Earl of Grey), who thereupon became one of Wrench's avowed imperial heroes, ranking alongside Cecil Rhodes, Lord Milner, and Lord Curzon of India. Earl Grey had been one of the original Directors of Rhodes' Chartered Company, the British South Africa Co. (BSAC), and a close personal friend of Cecil Rhodes; he was Administrator of Southern Rhodesia for a couple of years, and BSAC Vice-President for a further six before his period as Governor General of Canada (1904–11).⁶ 'To meet him is to become enthusiastic about him', wrote Wrench in a letter to his parents.⁷

Portrayed as a light-hearted and charming man, with many friends and admirers,⁸ Albert Earl Grey has also been described, less kindly, as a consummate networker.⁹ He certainly had the right connections. Leaving aside the useful aristocratic linkages through his wife, and the marriages of his sisters into prominent City families, his grandfather was a former British Prime Minister, his father had been private secretary to Prince Albert, and later Queen Victoria, and an uncle had held the post of Secretary of State for War and the Colonies. He counted Sir Edward Grey, British Foreign Secretary, amongst his cousins, and his son, Lord Howick, was married to the only daughter of Lord Selborne.

Though better known in Canada today as the donor of the Grey Cup to the Canadian Football League, the name of Earl Grey used to be more closely associated with another league, of which he was a founder in 1884: The Imperial Federation League promoted the idea of an overarching federal structure to link the self-governing Dominions constitutionally with the Mother Country. Similar federal notions had been around since at least the late nineteenth century, indeed, in one form or another from much earlier,[10] and were expressed most concretely and prominently in the call by Joseph Chamberlain for a preferential British Empire trade area (an imperial customs union) accompanied by a political federation of the self-governing Dominions and Great Britain, with a single, shared imperial council to coordinate defence, diplomacy, and tariff issues.

Canada had been a key source of inspiration. Speaking in Toronto at the end of 1887, Chamberlain called the Canadian federation 'a lamp lighting our path to the federation of the British Empire. If it is a dream—it may be only the imagination of an enthusiast—it is a grand idea...'[11] Immediately upon becoming Governor General of Canada in 1904, Earl Grey sought the endorsement of Canada's Premier for Chamberlain's Tariff Reform policy, though unsuccessfully.[12] The League's own political proposals, however, had been vague and woolly, although by omitting the economic element, they thereby also avoided a choice between the long established British policy of international free trade and the Tariff Reforms that Chamberlain stood for (and which were in the end decisively defeated by the Liberals in their 1906 landslide electoral victory).

While the Imperial Federation League was a failure, however, and had been dissolved by 1894, Lord Milner's Round Table continued the federal crusade. As a political notion, Imperial Federation, drawing upon what was then known as 'race patriotism'—or solidarity between those of British descent in Britain and in the Dominions—did not peter out entirely until after the end of the First World War.

During his stay in Ottawa in 1906, Earl Grey carried Evelyn Wrench along on a wave of imperial fervour during lengthy discussions at Government House. As Wrench expressed it 'the more one sees of Lord Grey, the more one likes him and he fires one with enthusiasm'. Grey, a Rhodes' Trustee, showed Wrench a copy of 'Reflexions on Imperialism', written by Cecil Rhodes on the South African *veldt* at the age of twenty-two, with its proposal for a secret society to further the expansion and interests of the British Empire.[13] Wrench swore that he was so inspired by Rhodes' vision as to determine to devote his life to trying to give it substance—save, that is, for his good newspaperman's *caveat* that he perceived in it no necessity for secrecy. Wrench later credited Cecil Rhodes with inception of the Overseas Club idea, Lord Northcliffe with nurturing it by placing the *Daily Mail* at the disposal of the movement, and Earl Grey with recruiting most of its prominent members in Canada.[14] Indeed, he recorded that in the Club's early days, when associates were charged just a shilling, Earl Gray enrolled hundreds of leading Canadians:

> Though I fear some of them signed on without a clear idea of what they were joining! He cabled me for 4,000 badges. The idea of a great brotherhood, recognising no class distinctions, appealed to him. His valet was one of our most attractive recruits.[15]

Now, Evelyn Wrench was not one to be overawed by title. He was quite at home with it despite personal populist leanings. He had been born into an influential Anglo-Irish family in County Fermanagh in 1882, and in his youth acted as pageboy to the wife of the Lord Lieutenant (viceroy) of Ireland; he was educated at Eton. If, in Earl Grey, Wrench had discovered another figure of influence to admire, alongside the press baron, Lord Northcliffe, it was the imperial sweep of Grey's vision that did the trick, rather than the aristocratic pedigree. His discussions with Earl Grey, he declared, left him 'charged with inexhaustible supplies of energy for the Imperial cause. Every time I passed a fluttering Canadian flag the blood coursed more quickly through my veins!'[16] They clearly had much in common as personalities, Wrench once being led to observe that Earl Grey was a man of many enthusiasms:

> Equally ready to plunge into Empire unity, Canadian Nationalism, Public-house Reform, Co-Partnership, Proportional Representation, Garden Cities or Anglo-American friendship. I sometimes wished he had not had so many...[17]

Albert Grey, 4th Earl Grey, by the Autotype Company after
John Singer Sargent, collotype 1910
© The National Portrait Gallery, London

Following his return from his US and Canada trip, Wrench corresponded with Earl Grey over a couple of years, setting out his ideas for an Empire Society to campaign for better transport links and improved cable services; state-aided emigration; imperial defence contributions from the Dominions; annual or biannual imperial conferences, and so on.[18] All in all, Earl Grey probably answered to Wrench's own networking instinct, in pursuit of his newly discovered mission in life—to build an empire-wide association. Meanwhile, however, Wrench's press links with the Dominions grew, as an important cog in Northcliffe's organisation and editor of the *Overseas Daily Mail* (or *Daily Mail Over-seas Edition*—the paper vacillated in the early days in what it chose to call itself).

The key event was the Imperial Press Conference that opened in London on 5 June 1909, of which Northcliffe was an Executive Committee member and acted as Honorary Treasurer. A prime aim of this gathering of more than fifty overseas editors and newspaper proprietors was apparently to rally empire support for the Mother Country in a time of anticipated future war.[19] Delegates to the Conference came from Canada, Newfoundland, Australia, New Zealand, South Africa, Burma, Ceylon, the Straits Settlements, and India. (All from the white 'Anglo-Saxon' press world, save for one French-Canadian, two from the Afrikaans-language South African media, and, from India, Surendranath Banerjee of *The Bengalee*, a member of the Indian National Congress and the lone non-European.)[20] Wrench, one of the dozen or so British pressmen in attendance, was again enthused.

Ostensibly an event staged by the press, for the press, it would be surprising if there were no backstage official British guiding hand. It arose out of informal conversations in Winnipeg with Canadian pressmen in autumn 1907. The foremost organiser of the London Conference was Sir Harry Brittain, journalist and Tory politician,[21] but it is interesting that Earl Grey was apparently involved in the deliberations at an early stage.[22] Conference participants attended formal discussions at the Foreign Office chaired by leading British statesmen, politicians, and military; they were present at an Army field day at Aldershot; and, in the evident hope of impressing these opinion-formers of empire, were shown 'a massive naval review at Spithead, where an eighteen-mile display of battleships, cruisers, destroyers, scouts, and submarines was arrayed for the edification of the delegates.'[23] (Perhaps the very Singapore newspaper columnist who reportedly first suggested the gift of a Dreadnought by the FMS had been one of the Conference delegates?[24] If so, the Imperial Press Conference will have been worth every penny.)

The pressmen themselves also benefitted from the opportunity to network, and as a result, Harry Brittain was able to found the Empire Press Union (later the Commonwealth Press Union) to improve the cable distribution of news, and provide a permanent organisation in London for representatives of overseas newspapers; Northcliffe, who had added *The Times* to his own press empire just the previous year, was made Honorary Treasurer.[25]

Tracing the germ of the idea back to his discussion with Earl Grey in 1906, Wrench founded the Overseas Club in August 1910. He launched it with an article in the overseas edition of the *Daily Mail*, and ran it out of Carmelite House (the paper's headquarters), initially as a non-subscription organisation. Its first public meeting on 27 June 1911 was held to coincide with the coronation of George V and take advantage of the presence of many important Dominion figures in London. Lord Northcliffe shared the platform with, amongst others, the Premier of Alberta and the Lieutenant Governor of Ontario,[26] as well as the parliamentarian, imperialist, and future advocate of air power, Leo Amery.[27]

Earl Grey (who seems to have had a liking for secrecy) helped recruit the Canadian section of the Overseas Club, and approached a large range of important figures but stressed that his involvement be kept confidential, so as not to raise suspicions that Government House was behind it. (He later accepted the position of Overseas Club Vice President, but after his period as Governor General of Canada had ended.) The close association with Lord Northcliffe was a problem. Earl Grey's influence on Evelyn Wrench apparently operated in tension with that of the press baron ('the Chief'), at least until 1917, when Earl Grey died. Grey wrote urging Wrench to separate the organisation from the *Overseas Daily Mail*, since many in Canada regarded it as a publicity stunt, designed to sell Northcliffe's newspaper. His views naturally carried weight, for he was instrumental in persuading 'half the Canadian Cabinet and frontbench members of the Opposition, and the premiers of New Brunswick, Ontario, Manitoba, Alberta, and British Columbia' to join the Overseas Club as members.[28]

Yet Carmelite House provided an important organisational base for Wrench, and one that gave his Club free publicity. It made sense to distance the Overseas Club from Northcliffe's newspaper operations, but not to break away entirely. In 1912 Wrench took leave of absence and set off with his sister Winifrede on an Empire tour that aimed to counter rumours, and establish new Overseas Club branches. It took in Canada, New Zealand, Australia and South Africa, with stopovers or side trips *en route* to Ceylon, to Fiji and other South Sea Islands, and to Southern Rhodesia. With intervals, the trip lasted eighteen months.

He was favoured on the Canadian leg of the journey (May–July 1912) by letters of introduction to prominent Canadians supplied by Earl Grey, who also suggested that he should try to enrol a hundred members of the RCI to the Overseas Club during his travels, and Wrench records that he succeeded in so doing.[29] Wrench found the less class-obsessed and more democratic nature of society in the Dominions refreshing. Ironically, Earl Grey had helped open doors, especially in Canada; to a lesser extent, Wrench also benefitted from the patronage of Liberal peer Lord Islington, Governor of New Zealand (and, incidentally, brother-in-law of Brigadier General David Henderson) during that leg of his tour.[30]

While in Pretoria, news came in that Northcliffe had issued orders to circularise all on the Club's membership list inviting them to subscribe to the *Overseas Daily Mail*. Since that risked sabotaging the tour's entire object—to establish that the Overseas Club was not Northcliffe's tool—it sent Wrench rushing back to London, to retrieve the situation.[31] He arrived back in 1913 'alive in every fibre of my being with enthusiasm for Imperial unity and with the knowledge that destiny had linked me up with the self-governing Dominions as few Englishmen had been linked before.'[32] Wrench knew that in order to maintain credibility he had to put the Overseas Club on a more independent financial footing, with a properly constituted Central Committee.[33]

He secured Club premises in Aldwych opposite those of the Australian Commonwealth; but it was still Northcliffe that underwrote the rent under its first seven-year lease.[34] A New York banker friend, multi-millionaire Alexander Smith Cochran, made a donation that enabled him to furnish the new headquarters. Further donations made the latter the Club's largest benefactor overall (£3–4,000), but Northcliffe had also given generously, to the tune of £2,400.[35] The Lord Mayor of London performed the formal opening ceremony on Empire Day (24th May) 1914. The Overseas Club was imbued by Wrench with an ethos of service to the British Empire from the beginning: he described it as a kind of grown-up Boy Scouts,[36] and indeed got Sir Robert Baden-Powell on board as one of the Club's Vice Presidents. But it was the outbreak of war in August 1914 that gave it a real sense of purpose, providing a welcome London venue for soldiers over from the Dominions, and campaigning hard in support of the war effort.

When war came, Wrench was sent to run Northcliffe's Paris office, a role he continued to fill until 1916. Pared down to just four pages, the *Continental Daily Mail* became virtually the official newssheet for the British forces in France at the start of the war, with ten thousand copies delivered to the Front daily by military vehicle.[37] The job was complicated by the fact that the paper's private telephone line to London had been taken over by Government, so a daily courier service had to be organised to ferry the latest news to and from Carmelite House.[38] Although at first it had to be combined with frequent visits to Paris, Wrench also worked flat-out organising fundraising campaigns, aided by his devoted first cousin and unpaid helper at the Overseas Club, Lady Hylda des Voeux.[39] But by early 1915 differences had arisen with Northcliffe over Wrench's perceived desire to prioritise his Overseas Club activities over the interests of the newspaper.

Nonetheless, the overseas edition of the *Daily Mail* continued to devote a full page to news of the Overseas Club and its activities each week, while the name of Lord Northcliffe remained prominently associated with it as Overseas Club President. Though Wrench ceased to be employed by the press baron in 1916, the newspaper's coverage of Overseas Club news did not begin to diminish until well into the final year of the war. Its campaigns included the frantically busy and successful Tobacco Fund, and, from early in 1915, Wrench's Imperial Aircraft Flotilla scheme which handled funding for 350 aeroplanes during the course of the war (this included collections from a number of 'spin-off' funds, organised on a national basis).

While Wrench's aim for the aeroplane appeal had been primarily political, to encourage empire unity, he was better informed than many civilians about the setbacks and stalemates of the war's early stages, both through Lord Northcliffe, and from his own observations of motor ambulances and trains evacuating British casualties on his frequent journeys to and from Paris. Wrench also knew from personal contacts that the RFC in France was outclassed by superior German aircraft (the Fokker E-type) and incurring terribly heavy losses in both men and machines, and was aware also of the existing rivalry between Army and Navy over aircraft supply—especially aero engines.[40] Overseas Club literature dropped hints to the readership of a scale of losses that military censors would not like to see published.

Though Wrench was called up in March 1917 and joined the RFC, the authorities placed him in jobs that allowed him to pursue his Overseas Club activities in his spare time. Initially recruiting for the RFC in Scotland, he later occupied desk jobs in London, first as private secretary to Lord Rothermere, Northcliffe's brother, at the newly established Air Ministry, and subsequently as head of the British Empire section of the Ministry of Information, under another press baron, the Canadian, Lord Beaverbrook. Never a combatant, he ended up with the RAF rank of Major.

There is little doubt that at the outset Wrench expected his aeroplane appeal to attract its most vigorous support from the white self-governing Dominions, and, secondly, from amongst scattered British settler communities in the Colonies and elsewhere. After all, the white Dominions had mobilised large armies with astonishing readiness to come to the aid of the Mother Country following King George V's declaration of war—and even though the King had declared war on behalf of the whole British Empire, it had been left to each Dominion to decide what form their involvement would take. As it turned out, the global response to a voluntary fund for presentation aircraft deviated quite significantly from that expected. Since the campaign eventually ran across the great, scattered, and largely non-'Anglo-Saxon' extent of the British Empire, it is perhaps not to be wondered at that the movement's success rested on more than just the generosity of donors in the Dominions. However, we will begin the story of the Imperial Aircraft Flotilla campaign proper with Canada, which fully met Wrench's expectations, then focus on Newfoundland, Canada's poorer island neighbour, where early fundraising surpassed anything that could have been envisaged.

To recap: under the Imperial Aircraft Flotilla scheme, subscribers who singly or collectively contributed £1,500 or £2,250 during 1915–16, according to the type of machine, could have an aeroplane named after their home country, city, or district (from about the middle of 1916 the cost of fighting scouts and fighters increased to £2,500–£2,700). Thus, initially, £1,500 underwrote the production costs of a BE2c reconnaissance aircraft, and in early 1915, £2,250 'bought' a Gnome Vickers Gun Biplane complete with gun, just like *Dominica*, and later, the FE2b scout. By September 1915, the Dominion of Canada had provided the RFC with five aeroplanes through the Overseas Club—two BE2cs and three Vickers Gunbus FE5s at a total cost of £9,750: *Ontario Canada* and *Nova Scotia* were subscribed by residents of those respective provinces, while the money for *St. Catherines, Ontario* was donated by a single individual and *Montreal No. 1* likewise, with the British Empire Grain Company putting up the money for *Montreal No. 2*.

Following Canada's gifting of its first presentation aeroplanes to the RFC through the Overseas Club, Lieutenant General David Henderson wrote to Wrench from the Military Aeronautics Directorate on 30 September 1915:

> The calls on the services of the Royal Flying Corps are continually increasing, and as the work increases so also does the wastage due to wear and to breakages. Any assistance that can be given to us to provide the very large number of aeroplanes required to replace casualties, and to augment our air force, will be much appreciated. Some thousands of aeroplanes are necessary to meet our requirements, and at the present stage I should hesitate to suggest any definite limit to

the expansion which may be required for this war. There is only one condition attached to the acceptance of any assistance towards the purchase of aeroplanes for war purposes. It is essential that the selection of types of aeroplanes to be purchased, and the inspection of the machines, should be left to the Royal Flying Corps.

We are already indebted to the generosity of Canada for several aeroplanes, which are now in action at the Front, and to Canada also we owe some of the most efficient officers. Any further assistance which the Dominion can give will be warmly welcomed.[41]

Within a month, the Montreal Board of Trade had met the bill for two more fighter planes (*Montreal Nos. 3 and 4*). Canada was to provide fifteen presentation aeroplanes in all by the end of the war. Its pilot contribution also continued to grow, until by the later stages of the conflict Canadians constituted almost a quarter of British airmen,[42] many the product of the RFC's own training establishment in Canada, where recruitment for flying cadets began in February 1917.

Taking into account its small population, Newfoundland's contribution to the Overseas Club Aircraft Fund during 1915 was proportionately greater than Canada's: four fighters and one reconnaissance aeroplane were presented to the RFC at a total cost of £10,500. This was surprising. Newfoundland was then a completely separate self-governing Dominion within the British Empire. Its population stood at under a quarter of a million at the time, and, with little manufacturing or industry, most workers were engaged in fisheries. The remainder worked in mining or forestry—many involved in some capacity with Lord Northcliffe's pulp and paper-mill at Grand Falls. The capital, St. John's, was the only town of any size (32,000 people). Public finances were precarious. Indeed, there were already doubts in London about Newfoundland's viability as a self-governing entity on economic grounds, doubts that were shared by the British Governor himself, Sir Walter E. Davidson.

Newfoundland politics were also unstable and fractious, with parties divided along both class and confessional (Anglican, Catholic, and Nonconformist) lines, reflecting English, Irish, or Scots ancestry. Nonetheless, after Great Britain's declaration of war against Germany on 4 August 1914, the Newfoundland government immediately pledged its support, and thousands came out onto the streets of St. John's singing patriotic songs. Local newspapers swiftly tapped the surge of enthusiasm in an unofficial propaganda campaign in support of the empire's war effort.[43] On 12 August 1914 Governor Davidson held a public meeting to announce his intention to raise a Newfoundland contingent, initially of five hundred men, as the most appropriate contribution of a territory 'poor in money, vocal [but] rich in men.'[44] With the agreement of Newfoundland Prime Minister Edward Morris, the British Governor, and not the elected government, exercised overall control of Newfoundland's war effort: a state of affairs lasting until formation of a coalition government in 1917.

An appointed Patriotic Association responsible for recruiting, equipping, and shipping Newfoundland troops for the imperial war effort aided the Governor. It was drawn largely from the upper echelons of St. John's society, with the addition of several trade union leaders, and had an Executive Committee carefully balanced denominationally, with four Anglicans, four Methodists, and four Roman Catholics. No difficulty was encountered in raising the first five hundred men, so Governor Davidson and the Patriotic Association decided to expand the unit to a full infantry battalion of over a thousand. The Newfoundland legislature had to raise a loan to equip and maintain the Regiment, but left its administration to the Patriotic Association and the Governor. The government loan, however, was insufficient to furnish them with machine guns. So in January 1915 one of the owners of the cross-island railway, W. D. Reid, donated two Vickers machine guns, and the Patriotic Association turned to public donation to buy the rest, setting up a Machine Gun Fund that raised $53,000 by summer 1915.[45]

So encouraging was the public response to the Machine Gun Fund that an Aeroplane Committee was set up as a sub-committee of the Patriotic Association to fundraise for Wrench's Imperial Aircraft Flotilla scheme. Indeed, Wrench later expressed especial thanks to the Patriotic Association of Newfoundland for giving an early lead for other Patriotic Societies to follow.[46] The Committee canvassed support from businesses, societies, and labour unions in St. John's, and sent out circulars and posters to outlying settlements. Two newspaper editors, J. A. Robinson (of the *Daily News*) and W. F. Lloyd, were among its members. Lloyd's newspaper, the *Evening Telegram*, ran almost daily updates on Aeroplane Fund donations. These bore witness to widespread popular support, especially from employees in both public and private sectors in St. John's and at Grand Falls, with donations to the fund typically $1–2 per contributor.

The initial fundraising appeal referred to the aeroplane's reconnaissance role as the army's 'eagle eye', able to spot enemy troop movements, the underlying message being that local donations—even if destined for imperial aircraft production in Great Britain—would help protect the Newfoundland contingent at the Front from enemy attack. By August 1915, the Committee had remitted £3,750 to London for one FB5 and one BE2c—the latter a personal gift of the Reid brothers, co-owners of the Newfoundland railway. The balance was set aside for machine guns.

Informed by London that the Newfoundland Regiment was already fully equipped with these, however, the Grand Falls Committee diverted their cash towards aircraft subscriptions instead, and Sir Edgar Bowring, head of the Newfoundland-based Bowring Brothers Group (shipping and insurance) followed suit. So yet more was remitted to the Overseas Club in London for the purchase of no less than three further FB5 fighters for the RFC. Newfoundland thus became, for a short while at least, the largest single contributor to the Imperial Aircraft Flotilla.[47] Although the War Office forbade publication of photographs supplied to donors, the *Daily News* managed to publish illicit snapshots of two of the *Newfoundland* planes taken surreptitiously at an airfield in England.[48]

Newfoundland's actual sacrifice in blood during the First World War dwarfed the fundraising. In the autumn of 1915, the First Newfoundland Regiment took part in the later stages of the unsuccessful Gallipoli campaign. Subsequently, it was moved to the Western Front. On the first day of the Battle of the Somme, 1st July 1916, the Regiment met with disaster at Beaumont Hamel. In just forty minutes it suffered more than 90 per cent (720) casualties, about a quarter of them fatalities. The Regiment suffered further serious casualties during 1916–17. Of the 5,046 volunteers that went overseas, most of them from St. John's, 1,281 were killed.[49] Lloyd George later recorded that casualties had wiped out the Newfoundland Regiment twice over.[50] With a population of only some 32,000, St. John's must have experienced as much concentrated grief as anywhere in the Great War.

Newfoundland shipping also suffered heavy losses, a number of Bowring vessels (which included sealers and fishing, as well as passenger, boats) being sunk by German U-boats. The worst disaster, though, was not war damage but the loss of the passenger liner *Florizel* on rocks in February 1918 with only 44 survivors out of the 137 souls on board. It was one of Bowring's Red Cross Line ships linking New York, Newfoundland and Halifax, Nova Scotia. (The dead included Sir Edgar Bowring's adopted son and granddaughter.) The

Florizel had previously been employed as a troop transporter for the men of the Newfoundland Regiment.

Newfoundland's engagement in the war had been billed as a way to promote the country's position within the British Empire in whatever scheme for Imperial Federation might be developed when the war ended. The outcome was ironic: there was no scheme for Imperial Federation, but there was a crippling increase in Newfoundland's public debt due to the cost of the war effort, which included an estimated more than $16 million for the Newfoundland Regiment alone. This was the main factor behind Newfoundland's loss of self-government and Britain's resumption of direct rule in 1934.[51]

At the end of the Second World War Newfoundland narrowly voted against renewed self-government to join the Canadian confederation.[52] However, back in 1915, presentation aeroplanes bearing the name *Newfoundland* had been a mark of local pride, even for such prominent supporters of confederation with Canada as W. D. Reid of the Newfoundland Railway. In interview in 1915, he dismissed the planned manufacture of military aeroplanes for the imperial war effort on the part of their big neighbour Canada as 'in imitation' of contributions towards the air war already made by Newfoundland citizens.[53]

Country	Approx. population	Number of planes
Canada	c. 8 million	15
Newfoundland	Less than 250, 000	5

Chapter 5:
Sultan Seyyid Khalifa of Zanzibar and the Royal Naval Air Service

The only example of a government voting money for presentation aeroplanes under Wrench's scheme each and every year of the war since its inception was that of the island of Zanzibar in the Indian Ocean. The *Zanzibar* series of aircraft were all gun-mounted, and cost £2,250–£2,700 apiece: from FE2b fighting scouts presented in 1915–16; through the multipurpose Reconnaissance Experimental 8s (RE8s) in 1917; and then Bristol Fighters and Scouting Experimental 5as (SE5as) in 1918; spanning aircraft models ever more advanced. On the face of it, this all seems very odd. However, Zanzibar was heavily involved in the East Africa campaign, and RNAS pilots and aircraft were stationed there. Moreover, Zanzibar was a British Protectorate. Like other Protectorates, its government was based on a native administration under varying degrees of British guidance and hidden or overt control. In Zanzibar's case, the native administration was personified in one man—the Sultan—and he had his own reasons for Zanzibar's energetic engagement in support of the British forces.

The Zanzibar Protectorate was indeed one of the lesser-known protagonists of the First World War. A thriving port, and one of the world's largest exporters of cloves, the island of Zanzibar commanded the East African coast; and it linked Aden to Durban on Britain's underwater telegraphic cable network. The ruling Arab elite had settled from Oman, from which Zanzibar had been a separate and independent political entity since the mid-nineteenth century, but the Sultan's subjects were of predominantly African origin. At the most recent census, the population of Zanzibar island itself was 114,000, of whom some 32,000 lived in Stone Town, on the west coast, and there were a further 83,000 people on the island of Pemba.[1]

Zanzibar had been the base for Livingstone's expeditions, and became the fulcrum of British anti-slavery activities in the Indian Ocean during the latter part of the nineteenth century, and headquarters for the Royal Navy's anti-slaving patrols. Livingstone's companion, the surgeon and naturalist Sir John Kirk, was successively resident British Vice Consul for Zanzibar (1866–73), Consul General (1873–80), and British Political Agent (1880–87). It was he that convinced Sultan Barghash (1870–88), to close down Zanzibar's slave market. Living in retirement by the First World War, Sir John Kirk was persuaded to add his august name to the long list of eminent Overseas Club Vice Presidents.

Over the course of the Great War, the Government of Zanzibar was to present no less than twenty-four aeroplanes to the RFC. The association of Sir John Kirk's name with Evelyn Wrench's Overseas Club may well have been a contributory factor, but for the full explanation for this generosity, it is necessary to delve a little more into the contemporary geopolitics, as well as the historical background. For in addition to the islands of Zanzibar and Pemba, the Sultan of Zanzibar's possessions included Mombasa Island and an adjacent fifty two-mile long and ten-mile wide coastal strip on the mainland, leased since the close of the nineteenth century to the British East African Protectorate (later, Kenya) with its headquarters at Nairobi. Another section of the Sultan's coastal strip had been absorbed—under duress—into German East Africa.

Even before a British Protectorate was declared in 1890, Zanzibar had been subject to a form of indirect control. Amenable Sultans received British support against rivals, while difficult ones learnt all about gunboat diplomacy. It was not just the British, however, that had practiced gunboat diplomacy towards Zanzibar. In August of 1885, five German warships entered the lagoon facing Sultan Barghash's palace, and ran out their guns. They were carrying on board the Sultan's sister, Frau Emily Ruete, who had been banished from Zanzibar following an affair with a German trader—the pair later married and lived in Germany. Despite her banishment order, the former Zanzibari princess promenaded about the harbour for several days protected by German officers. Since the challenge to his authority could not be ignored indefinitely, Sultan Barghash finally acted, but took the prudent path, putting his signature to a letter accepting a German protectorate over a part of the mainland that included a slice of his coastal possessions. The German warships then sailed away, Frau Ruete with them.

Great Britain, which was preparing a deal with Germany under which East Africa was to be partitioned into their separate 'spheres of influence', did not intervene; and, indeed, Sir John Kirk counselled the Sultan to accept the new political reality.[2] (Colonel H. H. Kitchener, incidentally, being the British member of the Zanzibar Boundary Commission of 1885–86 that deliberated on the extent of the Sultan's coastal possessions.)[3] As Frau Ruete later put it: 'everyone familiar with Zanzibar is fully aware that the Sultan rules but in small things, whereas the British consul-general manages the rest. His very enemies admit him to be an accomplished diplomat.'[4]

However, a further event more than ten years later, in August 1896, installed Anglo-German rivalries at the heart of Zanzibari dynastic intrigues. The then ruling Sultan—Hamid-bin-Thuwaini—died suddenly, after just three years on the throne, most probably poisoned. Before his successor could be named his twenty-five-year-old cousin, Seyyid Khalid—son of the old Sultan Barghash—seized the Palace with the aid of more than a thousand of the late Sultan's troops, as well as seizing a frigate in the harbour that had been a gift from Britain and constituted the entire Zanzibar naval marine. Two days later, after the expiry of an ultimatum, Royal Navy warships bombarded the wooden palace complex, causing carnage amongst those crammed into the buildings and narrow alleyways. This went on for some forty minutes, until it was ablaze and about five hundred lay dead.[5]

Meanwhile, the failed *coup*-maker, Seyyid Khalid-bin-Barghash, and some of his followers found refuge in the German Consulate. At the beginning of October, Khalid and his entourage were smuggled by boat to asylum in German East Africa, where they so stayed, providing a focus for many plots and intrigues. When the new British-backed Sultan of Zanzibar, Hamoud-bin-Mahomed, suffered a stroke and died in 1902, his son, Ali-bin-Hamoud, was a pupil at Harrow boarding school in England (his father had insisted on a public-school education). During his minority the former British Vice Consul of the East African Protectorate transacted affairs of state as Regent of Zanzibar.[6]

Ali-bin-Hamoud attained his majority in 1905, and proved a disastrous Sultan. Personally dissolute, the young Sultan more damagingly professed open contempt for Zanzibar and his subjects; popular rumour even had it that he had forgotten the Swahili language, and needed an interpreter to converse with his family.[7] In any case, whatever the extent of their own contribution to his demons, the British considered him utterly unfit to rule. In 1911 they bought his agreement to abdicate with an undertaking to pay him an allowance for life, and clear his gambling debts.[8] It appears to have been neatly arranged. On 7 May 1911, Sultan Ali-bin-Hamoud and his brother-in-law, prince Seyyid Khalifa, left Zanzibar *en route* for London to attend the coronation of George V. The former went on to Paris, where he announced his intention to abdicate, leaving Seyyid Khalifa to represent Zanzibar at the ceremony.

On return home, Seyyid Khalifa was approached by the British to accept the sultanate, and ascended to the throne on 9 December 1911. He possessed the qualities that his predecessor so patently lacked—a 'graceful demeanour, the calm serenity and smiling courtesy of the perfect Arab gentleman.' To British approval, he even wore traditional Arab robes in preference to European dress.

Yet he was no stranger to danger and intrigue, having experienced many 'alarums and excursions' during his childhood back in Muscat, Oman. These, the British Resident on Zanzibar wrote, had made him an expert horseman at an age before most children had left the nursery. Summoned at the age of thirteen to join his uncle, Hamid-bin-Thuwaini, when he became Sultan, Seyyid Khalifa had experienced the 1896 British naval bombardment up close, after his uncle so suddenly died. He was caught between the British naval guns and their intended target, in apartments situated immediately above a basement gunpowder store, and next to another in which was stored paraffin oil for lamps. Making his escape, he found the house guard lying outside the gate, disemboweled by a fragment of shell.[9]

This was the dynastic and personal backdrop against which, on the outbreak of the Great War, Sultan Seyyid Khalifa-bin-Harub decided to hoist his banner to that of the protecting power (Great Britain). He issued a decree declaring war on Germany on 5 August 1914, and another a few days later that declared war on Austria-Hungary.[10] The British administrative dispensation on Zanzibar was quite new at the time, responsibility for the island protectorate having passed formally from the Foreign Office to the Colonial Office in early 1914. The dispensation included the recently arrived British Resident, who replaced the former British Consul General. Like his predecessor, the new Resident was to act as the Sultan's First Minister. This was Major F. B. Pearce, an energetic and decisive man, in contrast to his nominal superior based in the East African Protectorate, the dilatory and ineffectual Governor, Sir Henry Conway Belfield, who was also High Commissioner for Zanzibar.

The Sultan certainly stuck his neck out to be helpful. When Great Britain declared war on Turkey and the Ottoman Empire on 5 November 1914, it also mounted an immediate propaganda campaign to placate Islamic opinion worldwide, and sought messages of support from Muslim leaders. The Sultan obliged by convening a meeting of Muslim representatives at his palace the very next day; they passed a unanimous resolution that denounced Turkey's current stance and confirmed their wish for Germany's downfall.[11] The text of Seyyid Khalifa's further letter of advice to coastal Muslim leaders on the East African mainland was widely circulated as an effective piece of propaganda. Even by the end of 1916 the Colonial Office was still calling for a further fifty copies for circulation, only to be advised that just two were then still available, the type having already been broken up.[12] The following extracts from the letter are taken from a full text version published in a Rangoon newspaper:

The Weekly Rangoon Times and Overland Summary, 1 May 1915:

GREETINGS.
To Salim [Liwali of Mombasa] etc., and all true friends and Mahomedans in my mainland dominions of Merima.
I have thought it well to write this letter to tell you my wish that at this time you and all true Mahomedans remain steadfastly loyal to the British Government. Let no consideration or promises from Germans prevail upon you to change your allegiance from the mighty Empire of England. [...] Let me warn you against believing lies coming from Germans. Remember how the Germans behaved during the reigns of Seyyid Majid and Seyyid Barghash respectively. The amount of outrages and violation of the local Government's rights and forced intervention in our religious concern ... even entering the mosques with their shoes on, not even regarding the sacred rights of the mosques. [...] The seizing of the dominions on Mainland ... was no less despotism and open enmity, without deserving any right thereto. The hanging of many Arabs and confiscating their properties and the tyrannical acts committed at that time have no limit. [...] Do not be led away by German tales concerning Turkey. Do not let you hearts be disquieted because Turkey is fighting with the Germans. I learn from Stamboul itself that the Turkish people do not wish to fight the English, their friends, but the Germans have forced the Turks to fight. The Germans have taken charge of Constantinople and will verily bring to destruction the Turkish Empire and our holy places to suit their own ends.
I received a letter from the Sultan of Muskat, in which he declares his extreme allegiance and loyalty to the Government of Great Britain, and he further declares his readiness at short notice to render any assistance whenever asked for, [...] and remembers the sincerity of the British Government during the past years in safeguarding the integrity of his Sultanate both military and financially. ... Remember that all Mahomedans in India and in Egypt, in Tunis and in Algeria, in Malaya and in Africa, have announced publicly their intention in this war to remain faithful to the English cause, and they have publicly denounced the action of Turkey in siding with the Germans. Seventy thousand Mahomedan soldiers from India are now fighting with the British forces against the Germans. Listen what the great Sheikh Seyyid El-Morghani, a direct descendant of our glorious prophet, says from Egypt. He condemns the actions of the Turkish Government, and says that Turkey is being sacrificed to German ambition, that those in authority at Constantinople by placing themselves under German evil influence have lost the sympathies of Mahomedans throughout the world ... and thus have spoken the heads of all Moslem communities throughout the world.
I commend this letter to your consideration so that the truth may be known. Let it be read by every true Moslem in Africa.

In contrast to Belfield's Nairobi, censorship of civilian mail and apprehension and execution of spies on Zanzibar began right from the start of hostilities;[13] and it included a public hanging on 6 December 1914, under Martial Law, of an Arab who had sent intelligence reports to German East Africa via fishing boat.[14] There was an identity of interest in such matters between the British Resident and the Sultan, who had quite a lot riding on an Allied victory, for the alternative German power on Zanzibar would have threatened both his throne and his life. Outright subversives on Zanzibar having been dealt with at the start of hostilities, Pearce reported that by 1916 leading Arab families still remained divided in their loyalties, and many continued to regard the exiled Khaled as the rightful heir to the Zanzibar throne, while others waited and watched to see how the tides of war would flow.[15]

At the outbreak of the Great War, imperial and allied forces moved to seize German colonies worldwide. In general, this was swiftly accomplished, within the first few weeks or months. In West Africa, German Togoland lasted just three weeks, although fighting went on for more than a year in Cameroon. But the East African theatre, in which the Zanzibar Protectorate found itself, was a different matter entirely. British imperial forces experienced initial serious setbacks (especially at Tanga in November 1914) and made no progress in 1915, save for neutralising Germany's naval threat in the region. Thus until 1916 the prospect of a German victory must have seemed at least a strong possibility from the standpoint of contemporary Zanzibar. British imperial reinforcements eventually arrived in East Africa at the beginning of that year under the command of General Jan Smuts, many of them from the Union of South Africa, and managed to occupy key areas of German East Africa, including the ports and railways.

Lieutenant Colonel (later Lieutenant General) von Lettow-Vorbeck thereupon embarked, however, on a mobile campaign employing African troops that tied down large numbers of Allied soldiers until the end of the Great War (indeed, von Lettow-Vorbeck's force did not lay down its arms until after the Armistice). Because of the prevalence of tsetse fly, pack animals soon became sick and died, so that the imperial campaign in East Africa came to rely on human porters instead, and more than 100,000 out of over 700,000 of those Africans from both East and West Africa recruited or impressed for service as carriers perished, through privation, exhaustion, and disease.[16] (The official death rate for Nigerian carriers in East Africa was over 20 per cent.)[17]

Thousands from Zanzibar served in the island's port and other naval facilities, or on the East African mainland under the Sultan's Native Carriers Recruitment Decree of 1916.[18] Many more of the Sultan's subjects were enlisted in the King's African Rifles (KAR) as combatants. The KAR included troops from East Africa, Nyasaland (later Malawi), Somaliland, and Zanzibar; British naval officers knew the unit based on Zanzibar Island as the Zanzibar African Rifles (ZAR), regarded them as the Sultan's men, and used them in amphibious operations against German held coastal settlements.

The naval war came right to Zanzibar's front door in the early stages of the conflict, when the light cruiser SMS *Königsberg* sank HMS *Pegasus* in Zanzibar waters on 20 September 1914. The German cruiser then hid in the Rufiji River delta on the coast of German East Africa—a swampland maze thirty miles wide. In one of the best-known episodes of the East Africa campaign, the Royal Navy was dispatched to smoke out and destroy the *Königsberg*, deemed a threat to shipping. The cruiser was spotted at the end of October, but the only way to get at it was through shallow-draught vessels (which did not arrive in the area until June 1915) and aerial reconnaissance. The ship meanwhile tied down a large blockading British fleet, there to prevent its exit.

In January 1915 the Admiralty in London tasked Flight Lieutenants Cull and Watkins of No. 4 Squadron RNAS with locating and—if possible—destroying the *Königsberg* with bombs (the early seaplanes could only fly with a very light bomb-load, and then only at low altitude in tropical conditions). They initially flew reconnaissance from a secret base about 100 miles south of Zanzibar at Niororo (or Nyororo) Island, provided to them courtesy of the Sultan. Then the British capture of Mafia Island in the Zanzibar archipelago (once part of the Sultan's dominions, but subsequently incorporated into German East Africa) allowed the Navy to use it as a base, and the RNAS to construct a new aerodrome closer to the Rufiji delta.[19] Cull's party had also been joined in June by a further 15 RNAS personnel under a Squadron Commander Gordon; they were accompanied by four aeroplanes (Henry Farmans and Caudrons) of which two were quickly lost.[20]

It took until 11 July 1915 to finally eradicate the *Königsberg*, which was bombarded, eventually set on fire; and finally sunk by her captain, but only after he had salvaged artillery pieces that then joined the German land campaign.[21] The destruction of the cruiser was only accomplished at that time thanks to RNAS seaplanes, which were able to accurately locate the vessel and keep her under sustained surveillance.[22] It was also the first naval operation in which aircraft had been used to spot the fall shots from battleships.[23] Lieutenant Cull (later Wing Commander J. T. Cull, DSO, RAF) has left us an account of his role in the sinking of the *Königsberg*.[24] He managed to secure aerial photographs of the cruiser on 25 April 1915, which had been camouflaged by tree trunks laid across the deck, although he had to fly low through anti-aircraft fire to do so. Flying one of the Farmans, on 6th and again on 11th July Cull dropped bombs on the *Königsberg*, initially causing little damage, again the target of the German guns. He was hit several times, and nearly drowned once.[25]

Cull's account throws incidental light on the relationship of the RNAS with their host: Sultan Seyyid Khalifa threw a reception at his palace in honour of the British victory at which 'everyone wore their best clothes and consumed large quantities of sherbet, ices, cigars and cigarettes.' Subsequently the Admiralty offered the RNAS aeroplanes flown by Cull's party to the Army, in support of the inland military campaign, while Gordon and others left by sea to join the campaign in Mesopotamia. These aircraft were involved in the battle of Salaita Hill of February–March 1916, alongside the newly arrived South African Squadron of the RFC equipped with twelve BE2cs.[26]

Cull returned from upcountry operations in May 1916, to find a number of RNAS personnel who had arrived at Zanzibar some weeks earlier housed in comfort at Chukwani, six or seven miles outside Stone Town. They were accommodated in the disused palace of a former Sultan, set 'amongst cocoanuts and other palms on top of a small cliff overlooking the sea.' The palace's overgrown gardens, he recalled, were full of fruit-bearing trees—oranges; mangoes; passion fruit; bananas, and custard apples—and a first floor veranda provided cooling breezes and views of the sea. The stores were located in the old Turkish baths attached to the palace. Despite its drawbacks (damp, bats, and the occasional scorpion) it was a location described by their RNAS storekeeper as 'most picturesque' with 'walls ... about 3 feet thick and the interior ... something of a maze. In the centre underneath a dome is a marble fountain imported from Marseilles ... it must have been extremely pleasant ... in the days of its glory.'[27]

No. 8 Squadron RNAS at Chukwani was there to support the British naval blockade of the East African coast. With Cull as Acting Commander, they flew reconnaissance over Tanga and Dar-es-Salaam and carried out aerial photography; they spotted for enemy warships; and bombed military installations and encampments.[28] Two days before Cull and his party set sail for England in August 1916, the Sultan made an official visit and was given a flying display and a tour of the machines, followed by a talk and the opportunity to fire a Lewis gun. Even though officially vetoed by higher authority, they found a way to accede to his expressed wish for a 'joyride':

> [The Sultan] was taken for a 'taxi' in a Short seaplane, which 'taxied' so fast that it got off the water and was actually in the air for some 100 yards at a height of a few feet. This he enjoyed immensely, being in those days probably one of the first, if not the first Sultan to have flown in a seaplane.

Everyone, Cull wrote, had been most impressed by his keen interest and quick grasp. He wrote the RNAS party a 'very nice' letter of thanks in Arabic, in which:

> He expressed his pleasure at the honour and cheerful affability with which he was received and commented on the explanation given to him of the science and skill of flying and the art of gliding in the air at will, which discovers the enemy's hiding place and lays them open to heavy destructive bombs as well as deadly balls of fire. He mentioned how he enjoyed his flight in a seaplane which took him to a great height and brought him back in perfect safety.[29]

The triumph over the *Königsberg* in 1915 had involved balloon-ship HMS *Manica*. The same warship subsequently took part in further British coastal amphibious operations in German East Africa, but was now fitted out to carry a seaplane as well as the observation balloon, with other aircraft carried on auxiliary cruisers.[30] (For while the Zanzibar-based Short 827 seaplanes had the ability to patrol the approaches to the island itself and the coast immediately opposite, more extensive coastal coverage required support ships.)[31] Three of the ten Short 827 seaplanes presented to the Royal Navy by the Patriotic League in July 1915 took part in these operations. Inscribed *Britons Overseas Nos. 4-6*, two of them (Nos. 4 and 5) were flown by HMS *Manica* based at Zanzibar; so also was another Patriotic League Short 827 gift, *Shanghai Britons No.3*.[32] Sultan Seyyid Khalifa will therefore have been well acquainted with their naval role in the East Africa campaign.

The Sultan aboard Short 827 *Britons Overseas No. 4* for his 'joyride' in 1916, courtesy of Cross & Cockade International Archive

Sultan Seyyid Khalifa's seaplane trip, passing his capital; and the Sultan alighting from the plane, with his RNAS pilot to his immediate right, *Illustrated London News*, 6 January 1917 © Mary Evans

Overlapping with the departure of Cull's RNAS unit from Zanzibar in August 1916, a British naval force commanded by Rear Admiral Edward Charlton was beginning operations along the coast of German East Africa with ZAR assistance. On 1st August a landing party from two of HM ships supported by a fifty-strong ZAR contingent took the port of Saadani, while seaplanes and a kite balloon kept the whole coast under surveillance. An attack on Bagamoyo—the old slaving port, from whence armed caravans had once set off for the African interior—was carried out on 15 August by marines, seamen from HMS *Vengeance* and HMS *Challenger*, and a party of fifty-four ZAR. After defeating the German defenders, they carried off one of the ten 4-inch guns that had been salvaged from the *Königsberg*. (German forces later used another artillery piece from the cruiser—dragged inland by more than a hundred native carriers—to force the retreat of a 1,500-strong Portuguese military incursion across the Rovuma River and back into Portuguese territory.)[33]

The captured gun was paraded in triumph through Stone Town in a procession that included the Sultan of Zanzibar's brass band led by the British Colour Sergeant from HMS *Pegasus* (sunk by the *Königsberg* in September 1914). There were reportedly 130 ZAR and 100 seamen from two of the British warships in the parade; with just offshore, the flagship HMS *Vengeance*, followed by HMS *Manica* flying her kite balloon, followed by a seaplane. Somewhere in the procession through the town was a baby hippo that the navy had brought back from Bagamoyo as a gift to the Sultan. (The Sultan wrote thanking 'My dear Friend Admiral Charlton' for his news of the successful participation of the ZAR in the capture of Bagamoyo, and for the gift of the young hippopotamus; his letter also thanked him 'from the very bottom of my heart in freeing us from the barbarism of our common enemy.')[34]

By the end of 1916, virtually all of coastal German East Africa had fallen under imperial control, including Dar-es-Salaam, which was surrendered in early September. Remaining RNAS units then served inland in pursuit of von Lettow-Vorbeck's mobile forces.[35] Seyyid Khalid, the Sultan's rival, surrendered unconditionally to British forces in 1917,[36] and was exiled, to St. Helena and the Seychelles. (Eventually allowed to return to Mombasa in 1925, he died there two years later.) These imperial military successes had done much to lighten Sultan Seyyid Khalifa's mood. During 1915 he had found relief in the fairly frequent appearances of a Royal Navy cruiser or two, according to Major Pearce; in addition, 'one of the seaplanes gave a flying exhibition a few weeks ago, and it created a tremendous effect'.[37] Further on in time, a visit by High Commissioner Belfield in September 1916 discovered the Sultan by then in excellent health and spirits, all anxieties banished: 'It was clear that the progress of the War and the successful local operations of our Naval and Military forces had removed from his mind all apprehension of personal trouble or inconvenience.'[38]

The Zanzibar Protectorate Council had been instituted in 1914, before the outbreak of war. It comprised as official members the Sultan as President; the Resident, Major Pearce; and three other British colonial officials. In addition, three nominated unofficial members were there to represent the interests of different sections of the community—a Parsee barrister for the resident Indian traders, an Arab, and a European (but no Africans, who formed the majority of the population). In reality, however, the three 'unofficials' had little voice or influence. The Council possessed no legislative authority, and was to meet as and when convened by the British Resident to 'advise' the Sultan on questions brought before it.[39]

In June 1915 the Protectorate Council, at the instigation of Major Pearce, passed a unanimous resolution offering the Imperial Government £10,000 from that year's budgetary surplus towards war expenses.[40] This sum, it was suggested, might be devoted to aircraft purchase, thus adding to 'the interest with which the inhabitants of all the Communities of Zanzibar would regard this contribution.'[41] London accordingly announced that it had been decided to 'appropriate' this gift towards the provision of four fighter planes named *Zanzibar Nos. 1-4*.[42]

Each year of the war followed the selfsame pattern. Zanzibar's clove exports were flourishing, and each year the Protectorate Council voted part of the budgetary surplus to the Imperial authorities for war expenditure—£20,000 in 1916, 1917, and 1918 respectively: £70,000 in total for the whole period of the First World War, transmitted through the Crown Agents.[43] Each successive year the sum was devoted to aeroplanes, at the request of the Government of Zanzibar (essentially Sultan Seyyid Khalifa and Major Pearce); in addition, £245,000 was invested in war loans and £19,500 subscribed by the public for the British Red Cross.[44]

All the aeroplanes so presented—*Zanzibar Nos. 1-24*—went to the RFC (not the RNAS) and none were used in East Africa. Most seem to have been directed to the Western Front or employed in British Home Defence. Of the 1918 crop, a photograph of *Zanzibar No. 17, presented by the Government of Zanzibar* was selected for transmission to the donors, as showing a typical inscription.[45] Curiously, the Bristol Fighter that last carried this inscription was sent to Canada at the end of the war, its name changed to *Huddersfield-Canada*.[46] But probably all this was irrelevant to Sultan Seyyid Khalifa, whose prime motive in devoting the annual budget surplus from the sale of cloves to presentation aeroplanes was to cultivate goodwill, especially among British military and naval officers on the spot, as well as the protecting power in London.

The Sultan—whose chances of a long reign did not always look terribly bright—had made a successful wager on the victors of the First World War. After all, his life probably depended on it, and his throne certainly. Already the recipient of an honorary KCMG in early 1914, he was awarded a KBE in recognition of his wartime service and the 'valuable assistance continuously given by the exercise of his influence not only in Zanzibar but on the Mainland of Africa from Uganda to Nyasaland.'[47] He reigned from 1911 until his death in 1960 aged eighty-one, attended the coronations of George V, George VI, and Queen Elizabeth II, and was decorated with three British orders of knighthood: the GBE (1935), the GCMG (1936), and the GCB (1956).[48]

In May 1918, he had awarded Vice Admiral Edward Charlton the Brilliant Star of Zanzibar of the First Class. After the war the Vice Admiral presided over the Allied Naval Armistice Committee, one of the advisory committees to the Paris Peace Conference that formulated the Treaty of Versailles. On 23 July 1920 he wrote to his wife:

> We took a holiday yesterday afternoon and spent it on the Wann See. The day before, without any warning to us, the Military took a holiday on account of Belgian National Day, so I gave our people one on account of the Sultan of Zanzibar's birthday which comes any day of the year one likes to fix it.[49]

Yet, unbeknown to the Vice Admiral, it was not an entirely appropriate birthday celebration. The new order of post-war national self-determination inaugurated by the Paris Peace Conference created an unkind political environment for the Zanzibar sultanate over time. Though Sultan Seyyid Khalifa did not live to see it, the Zanzibar Protectorate became independent from Britain in December 1963. Within weeks the sultanate government was overthrown in a revolution in which the African population of Zanzibar took political power. The last Sultan of Zanzibar went into exile in England, and many of Zanzibar's Arabs fled or were killed. In April 1964, Zanzibar joined in political union with independent Tanganyika, the ex-League of Nations mandated territory that had once been German East Africa. (The new nation was named the United Republic of Tanzania in October 1964.)

Country	Approx. population	Number of planes
Zanzibar	c. 200, 000	24
East African Protectorate	Over 2 million	1

The first in the series, presented in 1915, FE2b 6341 *Zanzibar No. 1*, courtesy of Cross & Cockade International Archive

FE2b 7714 *Zanzibar No. 7* in German hands, 1917, courtesy of Cross & Cockade International Archive

Bristol Fighter D8061 *Zanzibar No. 18*, photographed with name and serial number on temporary fabric strips—an official concession to hard-pressed aircraft depots in UK in August 1918, but supposedly just for presentations by UK towns and army units not overseas donors, courtesy of the National Museum of the Royal Navy

Chapter 6:
Tropical Sugarcane Producers: Pacific, Indian Ocean, and Caribbean

On 20 February 1916, No. 25 Squadron RFC flew to St. Omer to take up duties as a long-range reconnaissance and fighter unit. They were newly equipped with their operational aircraft, the FE2b fighting scout (along with several Bristol Scouts), the majority of them presentation aeroplanes. These bore the names *Zanzibar Nos. 1-4*; *South Australia*; *Montreal No. 3* and *Members of the Trinidad Chamber of Commerce*. The German Fokker E-type tripled the casualty rate mid-year, but the squadron's strength was increased from twelve to eighteen machines, twenty pilots, and eighteen observers; and they all gained a reflected fame on the evening of 18 June 1916 when Lieutenant McCubbin (a South African pilot) and Corporal Waller shot down the German 'ace' Max Immelmann.[1] Further new presentation FE fighting scouts that came the way of No. 25 Squadron during 1916/early 1917 included *Johore Nos. 8 and 13*; *Colony of Mauritius No. 1*; *Australia Nos. 2 and 10*; and *Zanzibar Nos. 8 and 10*.[2]

It was not just 25 Squadron that was being hastily equipped with the new FE2b between January and April 1916, but a number of other squadrons too, while the faster FE2b was also replacing 11 Squadron's now outclassed Vickers Gunbus. There is little doubt, therefore, that aeroplanes subscribed by the Colonies, Dominions and Protectorates answered to a real need at this stage in the war. But how were they financed? Why did some countries subscribe heavily and others not? The Zanzibar Protectorate financed its gifts from its surplus balance from the clove harvest: What about the others? Why did most of them offer money at all if it was not compulsory? And what was the role of British officialdom in each case?

During the First World War years the British Government generally accepted loans and gifts voted by colonial legislatures, even if they were not strictly prudent financially. They were taken as earnests of a desire to share in the burdens of the war, in however small a way. Nevertheless British colonies were expected to be self-supporting in as far as possible, and to balance their books without financial support from London: local circumstances could not be ignored entirely. There were instances of the Colonial Office vetoing gifts conceived in a fit of 'patriotic' enthusiasm by smaller and poorer Colonies that simply could not afford them. Depending on the principal export, some areas fared better than others. Tropical sugar growers benefitted from a world sugar shortage during 1914–18 as the normally beet-growing fields of Flanders were pounded by artillery and mined by trenches. Tin and rubber producers also prospered from an increase in demand due directly to the war, while territories dependent on the export of fruit or of cotton experienced hardship.[3]

As for contributions towards 'patriotic' causes (as the term was then used, to signify support for the imperial war effort) presentation aeroplanes under Wrench's scheme fell into a grey area. A donation could be purely private, raised through a press campaign and channeled through a commercial bank, and there was no more to be said; but where the disposition of the public revenue of a Colony was concerned, the Colonial Office in London felt it had the right to intervene, especially where the suggestion appeared to come from a British official. For instance, the Gilbert and Ellice Islands (a Protectorate 1892–1915, then a Crown Colony—now Kiribati and Tuvalu) enjoyed a quiet prosperity during the war based on a steady demand for Ocean Island phosphates. The islanders were generous contributors to the Prince of Wales' Fund; and some of the local police volunteered for war service with Maori troops (but were still in New Zealand at the time of the Armistice).[4]

When, however, the Resident Commissioner enquired from his headquarters at Ocean Island (Banaba, where the phosphate was being mined commercially) if £1,500 from surplus funds could be put to a biplane for presentation to the RFC, the Colonial Office quickly slapped him down:

> The Natives of the other Islands (to whom the Protectorate surplus morally belongs as it consists of the Island Funds handed over to Prot. Govt. on understanding that they would be spent for their benefit) are in effect contributing to the war, as the cost of the Volunteers from Ocean Is. will cause a deficit in their Estimates which will have to come out of Surplus ... I see no reason why this expenditure should be sanctioned. (The suggestion comes from an unofficial Circular which the Overseas Club seems to have sent direct to all Colonies & Prots.)—
> ? Reply through HC that S of S is not prepared to sanction this expenditure. (We refused a similar war offering from Solomons.)[5]

The High Commissioner for the Western Pacific, based at Suva in Fiji, accordingly vetoed his initiative.

There was, in contrast, no objection when the chiefs and people of Rewa Province, Fiji, wished to gift £1,500 for a reconnaissance aircraft for the RFC (two other Fijian Provinces were providing motor ambulances).[6] The Sydney–based Colonial Sugar Refining Company virtually financed the Colony, and was doing very well, producing Fiji sugarcane with Indian imported labour, but that was not the reason. The Provincial Council of Rewa that was making the gift was part of the native administration of Fiji, and the monies provided were regarded as a community matter. The Fijian population, some 62 per cent of the total,[7] viewed the cession of the islands to Queen Victoria in 1874 as almost a personal bond of allegiance and reciprocal protection and this loyalty was sharpened by contrasting themselves with the incoming Indians.

The capital, Suva, had been the launching pad for the mainly New Zealand force that captured German Samoa in August 1914, and there was a sense of engagement in the war and repeated attempts by Fijian Chiefs to supply combatants. But the War Office in London did not view Fijians as potential British troops despite their 'martial' traditions: One of Fiji's elder statesmen, Ratu Sir Lala Sukuna, exemplified the dilemma; unable to join British forces he joined the French Foreign Legion in January 1915 and fought on the Western Front for about a year before returning home wounded. By 1917, however, the British authorities had accepted a Fijian Labour Corps for the Western Front.[8] It was one of the many 'native' labour contingents shipped to France to compensate for the BEF's manpower losses in 1916 military offensives, and Ratu Sukuna returned with them to France once again.

Country	Approx. population	Number of planes
Fiji	c. 150,000 – Fijians c. 88,000	1

Mauritius was one of the world's largest sugar-producers. Its finances blossomed from 1914 until 1920 as a direct consequence of the world sugar shortage occasioned by the war. Strategically situated in the Indian Ocean, Mauritius had been seized from the French in the Napoleonic Wars, and was formally ceded by France in 1814. The terms of the 1810 surrender permitted French settlers (many of them aristocratic fugitives from the French Revolution) to retain the official use of their language on par with English, and preserve the privileged position of the Roman Catholic Church. They also preserved their property, and with the abolition of slavery in 1835, were paid generous compensation. Most ex-slaves, of mainly African and Malagasy origin, voted with their feet and left the cane-fields to become fishermen or dockworkers, and large-scale importation of indentured Indian labour followed, to replace them (and to undercut the wage demands of those who remained).

Throughout these social and demographic changes, the Franco-Mauritians retained their economic dominance as proprietors of the larger estates and the sugar mills. They were politically dominant too, through control of a majority of seats on the legislature, the Council of Government, which comprised the Governor and senior colonial officials, a number of nominated 'unofficials' and ten elected members. In 1914 Franco-Mauritians held some of the 'unofficial' nominated seats, and all the elected ones under a Constitution unchanged since 1885. They had been elected on a highly qualified property franchise by an (all-male) electorate of 6,186 out of a total Mauritian population of 368,791. Their leader was the Hon. Henri Leclezio, opponent of self-government and extension of the franchise on overt grounds of class and racial arithmetic (white Mauritians and lighter skinned, educated, Creoles were too few, and working-class Creoles, blacks, and Indians, too many).[9] He was president of the Chamber of Agriculture, owner of one of the largest sugar estates and sugar mills, and chairman or director of a number of Mauritian companies.

By February 1916, private subscriptions to a Mauritius Aircraft Fund had provided three fighters to the RFC, inscribed *Mauritius Nos. 1-3, Presented by the People of Mauritius*.[10] Yet it was the arrival of a new British Governor in May 1916 that galvanised a significant extra financial contribution. This was Sir Henry Hesketh Bell, KCMG, previously of the Leeward Islands, which, it will be remembered, had set the ball rolling when the legislature of Dominica voted £4,000 for fighter aircraft in late 1914. He arrived on a charm offensive that targeted the only section of Mauritian society that really counted in those days: the Franco-Mauritian elite. They were soon to devote significant sums to presentation aircraft. Bell (who recalled that his first sight of an aeroplane had been at Rheims in 1909)[11] could well have been behind it.

In his first public speech (delivered half in fluent French) he expressed himself fortunate 'in entering my duties at a time when the public finances are in a satisfactory condition and the staple industries are flourishing', praised the 'handsome gifts' made towards the war effort 'both in money and in kind' and 'the increasing numbers of brave young Mauritians who have joined the colours', and declared his understanding of how dear to Mauritians were the influence and traditions of '*la belle France*'. The new Governor emphasised that in the Great War in Europe, France and Great Britain stood shoulder to shoulder. He certainly hit the right note: never, it was vouched, had a British Governor on his landing so rapidly conquered Mauritian sympathies.[12]

Like other Crown Colonies with a healthy treasury, the Government of Mauritius contributed to the British war effort through generous donations and loans. In its war coverage, a Mauritian press catering for the tastes and interests of a Franco-Mauritian and upper-class Creole readership devoted as much space to coverage of French military action as British—particularly the heroic defence at Verdun which lasted almost the length of 1916.[13] Even news of the massive British offensive at the Somme in July did not displace the focus on Verdun entirely. A public meeting of some two and half thousand people to commemorate the second anniversary of the Great War was held on 4th August at the racecourse—the aptly named Champs-de-Mars. It ended with the singing of the Marseillaise 'by the whole public' then God Save the King 'led by the Harbour Master and Collector of Customs'.[14]

In Canada, where volunteering for military service became a statement of British identity and Protestant conscience, proportionately over ten times more English-speakers joined the Canadian Expeditionary Force (CEF) on the Western Front than French-speakers.[15] (It was similar in Australia, where those of Irish Catholic descent were under-represented in the Australian forces.) This was far from true of the small, privileged, French elite in the Crown Colony of Mauritius. Mauritians who served with British forces on the Western Front during the Great War numbered 521, and although this included a handful of British settlers (a small minority of the white population), the great majority were Franco-Mauritians, drawn from a community just some 10,000 strong; besides these, an unknown number fought as volunteers with the French forces. In addition, the island dispatched a 1,700-man Mauritius Labour Battalion to Mesopotamia comprising

Creole and Indian Mauritians officered by white Franco-Mauritians and British regulars.[16]

In Mauritius as in Europe, fighter pilots were the popular press heroes of the First World War.[17] Against the sombre background of events in France, Bell's charm offensive combined with the contemporary glamour of aviation to produce a large financial gesture on the part of the big sugar planters. In October 1916, Henri Leclezio called a meeting of the Chamber of Agriculture and moved a resolution to gift half a million rupees from the Planters of Mauritius to the Imperial Government, the money to be devoted to the acquisition of an airship or a flotilla of aeroplanes.[18] In his guise as leader of the so-called 'Oligarchs' who dominated the legislature, he followed up with a further motion in the Council of Government offering one million rupees for the imperial Air Service, half to be given by the Planters and half to come out of the surplus balance of the Public Treasury. Thus it transpired that fifteen FE2b fighters inscribed *Mauritius Nos. 1-15 Presented by the Colony of Mauritius* went to the RFC in 1916–17, and an equal number went to the RNAS.

The total cost of this gift of thirty planes from the Colony (the three gifted earlier by subscription through the Mauritius Aircraft Fund not included) was nearly £67,000.[19] The Planters, however, were amply recompensed at war's end. Up until the First World War they had been satisfied with sugar prices ranging from £12–£15 a ton. But in 1919 there was an extreme scarcity of sugar throughout the world and Mauritius was the only remaining large source. The British Sugar Commission was obliged to agree a rate of £90 a ton for the 240,000 tons that they were able to supply, and Governor Bell arranged the disbursement of no less a sum than £23 million among a comparatively small number of people; great fortunes were made, although they disappeared over the next twenty years.[20] Bell stayed on as Governor of Mauritius until his retirement in 1924 to the French Riviera, where he frequented the gaming tables at Monte Carlo, trying to perfect a winning system.[21] He spent the Second World War years in the Bahamas.

Country	Approx. population	Number of planes
Mauritius	c. 370,000	33

Jamaica's situation was quite different. It was a poor Colony, reliant also on crops other than sugar. Its public finances were precarious at the best of times. In September 1914 the Legislative Assembly nonetheless voted to give sugar to the value of £50,000 towards the imperial war effort, and from the beginning of the war taxes were increased and public spending cut. There was not a great deal of money to spare during the war years, and most donations were in any case funnelled into two large war funds: the Central War Fund of which the Governor, Sir William Manning, was Patron, and the *Daily Gleaner*'s Jamaican War Relief Fund. Hurricane damage in 1915, and even more serious hurricane damage in 1916, destroyed virtually the whole banana crop, and much of the cocoa and coconuts on the trees. Sugar, however, escaped almost entirely.

As elsewhere, men of British descent and military age made their own way to England to join the British forces. There was a strong local movement to raise a Jamaican Contingent as part of a larger West Indies force to fight in France, but it ran against a resistance in British military circles to employing black troops in a combat role on the Western Front. It was a touchy subject on the island—believed due to reluctance to arm them against Europeans (probably accurately). It was not until October 1915 that King George V made his appeal to the empire to send more volunteers, although he was thought to have supported the raising of troops from the Caribbean for some time.

Publication of the King's appeal almost coincided with the announcement of the creation of the BWIR. The effect on an island with deep loyalties to the British Crown, linked to a popular perception that Queen Victoria had delivered emancipation from slavery, was described as electrifying by the editor of the *Daily Gleaner*.[22] The BWIR was able to enlist almost 10,300 men from Jamaica out of an eventual 16,000 from the West Indies overall. To pay for the cost of Jamaica's BWIR Contingent heavy export taxes were levied on sugar, rum, logwood and some other items. Food prices rose by a third between 1914 and 1918.[23] Nine of the twelve BWIR battalions were deployed as labour units in Europe, but three eventually saw front-line action in Palestine and the Jordan valley, while a small detachment was employed in the East Africa campaign.[24]

There were volunteers from the island in RFC ranks. Two brown-skinned Jamaicans even managed to get in, despite the RFC's pervasive colour bar on recruitment,[25] though not as commissioned officers: they were Flight Sergeants Lancelot McIntosh, an aerial observer, and W. 'Robbie' Clarke, an aerial photographer. A snapshot of both was published in the *Daily Gleaner*.[26]

A solicitor's clerk in civilian life, it was the sponsorship of his former employer, T. R. McMillan, that had enabled Lancelot McIntosh to join the RFC. On 27 May 1916 he wrote to let him know that he had been wounded and taken to a field dressing station:

> Well it's now three month since I've been out here and the many narrow escapes I have had are marvelous. The many instantaneous deaths I have witnessed caused by anti-aircraft gun fire, bullets from German Fokkers, Albatross, Aviatiks etc. and only 20 or 30 yards from me, I sometimes sit and wonder how on earth (or rather in the air) I managed to escape.
>
> Well to the point, I was detailed last Monday 22nd inst. to find out the movements of troops, trains etc. at ------------, over the German lines ... Having completed our journey successfully the homeward journey was commenced, when at about 3 miles over (we had trespassed 8) and at a height of 8,000 feet THE HUNS SPIED US from the ground and got their anti-aircraft on us (archies). Of course this is an everyday affair. We got away from their fire and after commenting to the Pilot over their inaccuracy, we got right over another of their batteries. Their aim was better this time, and our main tank was pierced ... The Pilot (a very good one) managed with the aid of his service tank, to plane down to within 150 yds. of terra firma when he lost control of the machine (no petrol left in service tank) and crashed to earth the heavy ... engine covering me under ... [They came down over British lines but in a thick wood.] The Pilot after using sticks to jack the engine up managed to extricate me [and next morning attracted the attention of a British plane passing overhead with a smoke fire of leaves and lubricating oil; after three hours stretcher-bearers arrived.] My leg was pronounced broken at first, but the doctor after careful examination said it wasn't.
>
> (*Daily Gleaner*, 14 June 1916)

Flight Sergeant Robbie Clarke was seriously injured 5,000 feet above Ypres in July 1917, just two days after completing his first year's service with the RFC. The *Gleaner* published extracts from his several letters home:

> [Date indecipherable] I had a bit of an accident the day before yesterday, but will soon be all right again so do not worry. I was doing some photographing a few miles the other side, when about five Hun scouts came down upon me, and before I could get away, I got a bullet through the spine. I managed to pilot the machine nearly back to the aerodrome, but had to put her down, as I was too weak to fly anymore, and she was damaged on the landing, as it was bad ground. ...My observer escaped without any injury. I am writing this in hospital in France; but expect to be back in Blighty in a few days. Don't suppose I will do any more flying for some time.
>
> [Early August] I suppose you are somewhat anxious to know how I am faring. Well, I am very much alive and kicking, though it was a near thing, and on the safe side now ... and in the American Hospital. They are ever so nice and look after me well, though there are so many patients they can't spend much time on anyone in particular. I was X-rayed yesterday morning. I do not think I will have to undergo an operation now. I feel much improved since yesterday though very sore. The bullet passed through my spine and came out under the arm ...
>
> [August 12th] I am once again in Blighty. I am getting on splendidly, felt almost fit today [...] Things were very hot when I left France. Oh! The suffering the fellows have to bear: It is indescribable. I got my 'packet' over the Ypres front about five miles on the German side. [Photography finished for the day] I ... was looking for a nice place to give Fritz a couple of pills (bombs) ... We were so taken up looking for a good target, that we forgot to look out for enemy scouts. The first thing I knew was hearing the rat-tat-tat of his machine guns, and glancing back saw about five of them diving for me, and I could not get away in time. I was hit almost at the start of the scrap. The machine was riddled. ... When I was hit, I was about 5,000 feet up.
>
> (*Daily Gleaner*, 7 September 1917)

A Jamaica Aeroplane Fund had launched in February 1915, in immediate answer to Wrench's Overseas Club appeal. Given the island's straightened circumstances, its ambitions were modest: to collect Jamaica's offering towards a 'West Indies' aeroplane. It succeeded in raising £300, and then the fund languished and in mid-1915 was closed down. But following publicity about Queen Alexandra's launch of four aeroplanes from the British Empire in July, Adolph Levy, general merchant of Kingston, picked up the cause. Adolph Levy's aims were more ambitious—to raise sufficient money to present Jamaica's very own aircraft to the RFC. He targeted the wealthy, formed an Aeroplane Committee of prominent citizens, and called his campaign the Alexandra Aeroplane Fund.

The Victoria Mutual Building Society and the Jamaica Mutual Life Assurance Co. each gave £500, and the *Gleaner* and the Jamaica Cooperative Fire Insurance Co. donated another £250 respectively; the Aeroplane Fund also benefitted to the tune of over £200 from American banker and property-owner in Jamaica, Mr. J. F. Thompson. The money for *Jamaica No. 1* (£2,250 for a fighter) was telegraphed to England on 28 October 1915 and—in a piece of strategic timing—came shortly after the King's appeal for men from the empire and announcement of the BWIR's creation.[27] Queen Alexandra acknowledged the gift personally in a message of 'sympathetic appreciation' for Jamaica's 'generous and patriotic help'.[28]

Meanwhile, the Aeroplane Committee had secured the fund-raising assistance of the Fox Film Company (later, Twentieth Century Fox), which was in Jamaica to film the first million-dollar movie, *A Daughter of the Gods*. It was already causing much excitement on the island, not least by hiring local extras for its aquatic extravaganza at a time of economic depression, with bonus rates for strong swimmers.[29] *A Daughter of the Gods* featured Australian swimming star of the silent movies, Annette Kellerman, who had created a sensation in America some years earlier with her revolutionary own design 'one-piece' swimming costume (in which she was once arrested for indecency). In this film she appeared in one scene fully nude, tastefully framed by a waterfall—a first in commercial cinema by a well-known actress and positively scandalous then. (But not a whisper of any of this appeared in the Jamaican press.)

The film's director was an Englishman, Herbert Brenon. With the consent of the proprietor, William Fox, he lent the whole acting company for a sold-out entertainment in aid of the Aeroplane Fund at

Kingston's Palace Theatre on 4 November 1915 (shortly before the Jamaican Contingent embarked to join the rest of the BWIR—an event caught on newsreel by the company). The stage had to be enlarged to accommodate the entire troupe. The *Daily Gleaner* heralded the benefit performance and its object in the following terms:

> A winged messenger in the shape of a huge biplane driven by a hundred horse-power Gnome engine and carrying a quick firing machine gun has already blazed a trail from Jamaica to the front—a trail that will soon be followed by the Jamaica Contingent.
> We all earnestly hope that when the brave men who are leaving these shores reach the firing line, Fate who governs us all will make it possible for the Jamaica aeroplane to 'do its bit' for them ... [30]

The event was a pioneering example of the twentieth century entertainment industry fundraising for a war charity—but it was also an American acting troupe raising money for a war in which the US was not yet directly involved. The spectacle included a patriotic *ensemble* with Fox's actresses appearing as 'Britannia', 'Belgium', and 'France'; as well as Annette Kellerman herself featuring in a ballet fantasy entitled 'the Swan'. It realised more than £700 through ticket sales and sale of 'aeroplane' badges by members of the cast. In his closing address Herbert Brenon told the audience (which included the Governor, Sir William Manning):

> He felt sure that if Mr. Fox, whom he represented, was present, he would feel as he did. These efforts were made because they were a duty and that was always easy to do. He did not want them to think that this effort was merely a tribute from British to British. It stood for something more because most of the members of the organisation were Americans. Those who had commented on the Americans not entering the war before should mark this occasion as an example of the feeling of the people of America towards England. ... Every member of the company had assisted in getting up the performance and thanks were most due to the thirty-three girls he had brought down from New York.[31]

Annette Kellerman was presented from the audience with an aeroplane built of flowers and marked 'Jamaica'.

Annette Kellerman in a still or publicity shot for 'A Daughter of the Gods' Fox Pictures, January 1916 (public domain), Wikimedia Commons

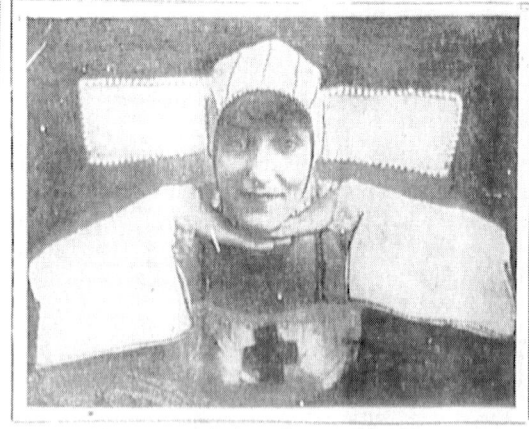

Annette Kellerman appearing as 'Jamaica No. 1 Aeroplane' at a benefit fancy dress ball in Kingston, courtesy of The *Gleaner*

Despite the fact that the campaign relied primarily on the pockets of the wealthy, the *Gleaner* took pains to list all the small donations to the Fund. In an issue commemorating the imminent departure of the First Jamaican Contingent to join the BWIR, the names of every single labourer that had contributed any amount, however small, to a collection on the Caymanas sugar estate was duly recorded and published.[32] This inclusiveness was taken a step further in December 1915 when Aeroplane Committee member Mr. Lewis Ashenheim developed a War Stamp League, inspired by a scheme he had witnessed in the US for collecting money in small amounts from the wider public. A special stamp with the face value of one ha'penny, used in addition to normal postage, was sold in all post offices on the island, with the proceeds going to war charities. The scheme raised nearly £900 by March 1917, and benefitted the Red Cross, the Aeroplane Fund, the Fund for the Relief of Polish Jews, and the Jamaica Contingent Sufferers' Fund.[33]

In early 1916, *Jamaica No. 2* (a second fighter) was presented to the RFC. Fundraising had included a diving and swimming exhibition by Annette Kellerman, and benefit flying exhibitions by the visiting American Fred de Kor, who 'looped the loop' at Knutsford racecourse in two flying displays.[34] Later, nearly £500 was sent to the Overseas Club to assist in buying a third machine, then the fund was closed, but subsequently reopened towards the end of 1916 following Wrench's appeal for five more aircraft from the West Indies to complete a 'flotilla' of twelve. Finally, in May 1918, Jamaica's last contribution of just under £650 was remitted to the Overseas Club. The fundraising had entailed ingenuity and quite a bit of American-style razzmatazz, with raffles, badge days with processions of ladies ('badgers') in flower-bedecked cars, and a fancy dress ball in which Annette Kellerman appeared as *Jamaica No. 1* aeroplane.[35]

The press campaign in aid of the Fund had been stamped with an assertive local pride, conveying the impression that this was seen as a small island's opportunity to make its mark on a big world:

> The importance of the aeroplane is only just being properly realised. Its speed and its immense range of action at so small a cost make it one of the most valuable arms of modern warfare. ... And how extraordinary that we in Jamaica should be participating in this tremendous struggle raging five thousand miles away. When, within a few days we

are able to cable the amount of £2,250 to London the Aeroplane *Jamaica I* will be started and in a few short weeks will be taking the name of our beautiful island right into the German lines.[36]

Moreover:

> Have you reflected that *Jamaica I* the biplane mounting a gun, which we shall be able to order within the next day or two, will be the first piece of fighting material identified with the name of the island, ever seen in Europe? Many sons of Jamaica have crossed the seas to fight—some have been wounded and some have died. They have each been absorbed into different regiments, and have therefore lost their onward identity as Jamaicans. But our biplane will always be associated with this island ... so also will *Jamaica II*, when we get it, and then *Jamaica III*, which we may hope to get.[37]

An appeal by the Fund's Honorary Secretary, John Henry Cargill, a Kingston solicitor and commander of a company of the Jamaica Reserve Regiment (who was to receive the OBE in 1918 for his fundraising),[38] was even more direct:

> A *quattie* a head for all Jamaica would give us three planes—not any baby thing, but full-blown biplanes, each carrying a gun. We expect to hear that the word 'Jamaica' is painted on each, and we hope it will be big enough for the Germans to see it.[39]

The Trinidad story was not dissimilar to that of Jamaica, although lacking assistance with fundraising from a visiting American film company. In September 1914 the island voted to send Great Britain cocoa to the value of £40,000 as its contribution to the war effort. By February 1915, there were at least sixty-one Trinidadians serving at the Front in Europe, many of them with the Canadian First Division, and when the BWIR was formed, Trinidad supplied a contingent. The local Chamber of Commerce pledged £2,250 for a fighter in October 1915, noting that Colonies including British Guiana and Jamaica had already presented twenty-one aeroplanes.[40]

A number of men from Trinidad served in the RFC—as mechanics, as well as pilots or observers. In the summer of 1916, Air Mechanic Alfred Horne reported from France that 'a chum' had alerted him to the presence of a very large plane bearing the inscription *Presented by the Trades and Commerce Chamber of Trinidad*, since he knew he was from 'that far away isle'; he later wrote to let those back home know that he had been notified that he would be going 'up the line' as an observer.[41]

PLEASE PIN THIS UP AND SHOW IT TO YOUR FRIENDS

TO READERS OF THE WEST INDIA COMMITTEE CIRCULAR

THE inhabitants of the British West Indies have given such frequent proof of their generosity that we hesitate to make yet a further appeal.

From time to time gifts of aircraft have been received on behalf of various of His Majesty's West Indian possessions for presentation to the Royal Flying Corps. The following are the gifts to date, as far as we are aware, to the Imperial Aircraft Flotilla organised by the Overseas Club:—

(1) £1,500, "British West Indies."—Presented by general subscriptions from residents in the British West Indies.

(2) £2,250, "Jamaica No. 1."—Presented by the people of Jamaica, through the Jamaica Aeroplane Committee.

(3) £2,250, "British Guiana."—Presented by the people of British Guiana.

(4) £2,250, "Jamaica No. 2."—Presented by the people of Jamaica, through the Jamaica Aeroplane Committee.

Presented direct to the Colonial Office:

(5) £2,000, "Dominica I."—Presented by the residents of Dominica. This was the first aeroplane presented to the Royal Flying Corps from overseas.

(6) £2,000, "Dominica II."—This was the first aeroplane presented to the Royal Naval Air Service from overseas.

(7) £2,250, "Trinidad."—Presented by the Chamber of Commerce, Trinidad, through the West India Committee.

It will be seen, therefore, that the residents of the British West Indies have presented seven aeroplanes to date.

We are very anxious that a complete flotilla of twelve machines should stand to the credit of the West Indies, and we are inviting the powerful assistance of readers of the West India Committee Circular to help in bringing this about.

We have recently received the sum of £500 through the West India Committee on behalf of Mrs. Perez, Fairview, St. Joseph, Trinidad, which sum, together with previous monies received from residents in Trinidad, makes a total of £680 16s. 1d. We are hoping for a further sum from Trinidad and Tobago to complete the cost of this Trinidad machine. If this sum is forthcoming, it will bring the total of the West Indian machines to eight, with only four more required to complete a flotilla.

Yours sincerely,

ALGERNON E. ASPINALL.
EVELYN WRENCH.

Overseas Club
General Buildings
Aldwych, London
W·C

An appeal from the Overseas Club to the readership of the *West India Committee Circular*

A further two aircraft were to be provided by Trinidad and Tobago. There had been instances of fraud in the islands' Tobacco Fund—with bogus collectors using genuine forms—so that when in early 1916 someone collecting for the Trinidad Aeroplane Fund began using a chain-letter system for distributing forms and netting in subscriptions, it appears to have set off alarm bells. Consequently, fund collectors were advised to remit their monies each week to Mrs. Mary Perez, wife of the Government Medical Officer, who had agreed to act as honorary treasurer and undertook to publish donors' names on a regular basis, along with the amount received from each.[42] By October 1916, Trinidad had remitted £680 to London. Mary Perez stressed a protective intention: 'Prevention is better than cure—let our airplane (as a watchful scout) save some of our gallant soldier-men in the trenches, from death and mutilation, by enemy shell-fire.'[43]

Mary Perez was an amateur dramatics enthusiast who produced a ragtime revue entitled 'Topsy-Turveydom' in late 1916, bringing together several amateur theatre companies at Prince's Building in Port of Spain. The performance combined fundraising for the Aeroplane Fund with the 'Society' function of welcoming Lady Chancellor, the wife of the new Governor. It was apparently a glittering event, with every reserved seat in the house taken, so that 'for the first time in history, Trinidad's dainty ladies found themselves in all their finery in the gods. All the cream of Trinidad's youth and beauty was on the stage.' The new US Consul in Trinidad, Henry D. Baker, declared the revue:

> The most charming and artistic amateur production I have ever seen ... The sentiment so delightfully expressed in the catchy song with the aeroplane dance—'Everybody is giving' and 'Tonight is the night'—really expresses in short words the spirit of Trinidad.[44]

A large-scale model of an aeroplane, made at the prison, was raffled in the theatre bar.[45] Thanks to two flag days, and the efforts of Trinidad's amateur dramatic societies and its prisoners, Trinidad was able to remit a further £819 to London. At the end of the war, Mrs. Mary Perez was awarded an MBE in recognition of her work in raising money for war charities.[46]

Over on the mainland, the people of British Guiana (later, Guyana) presented their first aeroplane to the RFC in October 1915. The war years were prosperous ones for the local sugar industry, but many workers were squeezed financially especially by food price inflation from 1915 onwards, and the campaign was broad-based, and not targeted particularly at the well heeled. But the British Guiana Aircraft Fund did manage to scrape together the £2,250 required for FE2b *British Guiana No. 1*. A third of this sum was raised on Aircraft Day (4 October 1915) when ladies sallied forth throughout the towns and districts presenting rosettes of their own confection to contributors. There were amateur benefit concerts and fundraising garden fêtes. Collections on sugar estates netted contributions of very many tiny sums, individually credited in the press.[47] Finally, *British Guiana No. 2*, a Sopwith Pup fighter plane, was a gift of Government presented in time for Empire Day 1917. (It was authorised from 'anticipated surplus of revenue over expenditure' or, in the event of no such surplus, from the revenue itself.)[48]

In the last year of the war, the St. Kitts' legislature voted the monies for a presentation SE5a, *St. Kitts Nevis*, rounding off what Dominica had begun in 1914. Its contribution formed part of a larger cheque for eight additional units for the Imperial Aircraft Flotilla ceremoniously handed over to William Weir, Secretary of State for the RAF, at the Overseas Club headquarters on Empire Day 1918.[49] By this stage, the symbolism of empire unity had come to surpass any practical contribution to the British air inventory—so much had official spending on aircraft production grown from mid-1917 onwards. Going on for 15,000 British aeroplanes were produced in 1917, and double that in 1918.[50] However wreckage and attrition reduced the actual number available on all fronts and in Home Defence to just 2,630 in June 1918.[51] St Kitts' single SE5a aircraft added very little in practical terms, but as part of a notional Imperial Air Flotilla it signified support in adversity from the far corners of the empire.

In addition to Dominica's pioneering gifts, the West Indies presented another nine aircraft:

Country	Approx. population	Number of planes
Jamaica	c. 880,000	2
Trinidad and Tobago	Less than 400,000	3
British Guiana	c. 300,000	2
St Kitts Nevis	Less than 40,000	1
British West Indies	-	1

FE2d A6364 *Presented by the Colony of Mauritius No. 3*; used in France 1917 then as a trainer in UK, courtesy of Cross & Cockade International Archive

The collection by Mary Perez for this presentation aircraft featured in the appeal for a 'flotilla' of West Indian machines shown on p. 97; BE2e A3096 *Trinidad and Tobago* was flown by the RFC in India, courtesy of Cross & Cockade International Archive

Chapter 7:
Eastern outposts—bankers and philanthropists of Hong Kong

On receipt of Evelyn Wrench's appeal, the Governor of Hong Kong, Sir (Francis) Henry May, passed it on to the newspapers. Referring to the recent Zeppelin bombing raid on Yarmouth, it cited an official German statement to the effect that there would be more of the same to come: in the light of this threat, every aeroplane that could be provided would be needed, with no subscription too small. Local contributions were to be sent to the Hong Kong and Shanghai Bank.[1] A message of support from Secretary of State for the Colonies, Lewis Harcourt wished every success to this 'excellent' proposal of the Overseas Club, although, he added, he hesitated to take part in any further fundraising appeal, the generosity of British subjects in all parts of the empire having been so 'striking and profuse'.

Harcourt's message would have had particular resonance in Hong Kong, and may indeed have been drafted with the example of Hong Kong in mind. For in a recent dispatch selected for printing for Parliament,[2] Henry May had drawn attention to the open-handedness of both local Chinese and resident Portuguese communities towards British war charities. Not only had a sum of £17,000 been remitted to London for the Prince of Wales' Fund in December 1914, but, as he pointed out, this had been in addition to support for existing Chinese charities in the Colony, which remained as generous as ever. Though the small Portuguese community (mostly clerks and security guards in British employ from nearby Macau) was far from wealthy, they deserved recognition for subscribing to many charitable lists 'owing to their inability to make single subscriptions of any large amount'.

His dispatch highlighted contributions by Robert Ho Tung, Hong Kong's richest man, who was to receive a British knighthood later in 1915. Amongst other helpful gestures, he had undertaken to import rice from Bangkok and Saigon and sell it in the Colony at cost price. His donations to war charities had included one of nearly £1,000 to the Prince of Wales' Fund.

Philanthropy was not a new phenomenon among the leading Chinese merchants of the Colony. Many of them were very wealthy in their own right, as well as acting as *compradors*—or middlemen and fixers—for British trading houses. They gave generously to relief funds for natural disasters in China, and some had been rewarded with Chinese Government honours (as well as acquiring Chinese titles by outright purchase). But Hong Kong's Chinese merchants had also proved the largest individual subscribers in the Colony for the Irish Famine Fund in 1879, responsible for more than half the sum collected, and they had contributed heavily to funds set up for dependents of British soldiers fighting in the Boer War.[3] Above all, the wealthy Chinese businessmen of Hong Kong provided money for the social and economic improvement of the Colony itself. Public respectability and social standing derived from 'good works', at home and abroad.

Leading Chinese merchants shared a mutual interest with the British colonialists in a strong trading economy, but Hong Kong was also a place of rigid segregation and parallel and separate European and Chinese social institutions. At the census of 1911, the total population was 456,739, comprising 444,664 Chinese and 12,075 non-Chinese: it could not be run without the cooperation of local Chinese elites. Yet it was not a British Protectorate with a 'native administration' to lean on. There existed the usual Crown Colony structures of the Legislative and Executive Councils (the latter comprising solely British officials), with two nominated Chinese representatives on the fourteen-man Legislative Council, but these did not suffice.[4] The practical solution that developed was to 'consult' wealthy and respectable Chinese businessmen.

Those figures that suggested themselves were the office-holders of key voluntary Chinese welfare associations and the like, especially the board of Hong Kong's Tung Wah Hospital, and the District Watch Committee—whose formal role was to superintend a volunteer force of 120 Chinese constables and detectives operating in Chinese areas of Hong Kong, financed by Chinese merchants. Officially recognised by the colonial government since the later nineteenth century, the fourteen-man District Watch Committee had transmuted from an informal police force management body to *de facto* shadow Chinese Executive Council of Hong Kong. Comprising the elite of Hong Kong Chinese society, its advice was sought on every issue of importance to the community.[5]

The Governor, Henry May, knew much about Hong Kong and its mirror police forces. He was an unusual kind of British Governor, and the first the Crown Colony ever had to have climbed the ranks from that of administrative cadet in 1881, all the way to the top. Son of a former Lord Chief Justice of Ireland, and educated at Trinity College Dublin, from 1891–93 he was private secretary to the Officer Administering the Government, Major General Digby Barker, whose daughter he married. As Captain Superintendent of Police 1893–1902, he was remembered as one who had determinedly purged the urban force of corrupt elements. Serving as Hong Kong's Colonial Secretary for eight years before being made Governor of Fiji in 1910, he returned to Hong Kong as Governor in 1912, against the background of a China in turmoil following the 1911 revolution.

The Hong Kong Legislative Council (or at least its European members) had petitioned the Colonial Office to bring back May with his close knowledge of the Colony and strong disciplinarian streak, in order to fill the vacant Governor slot and deal with the unrest.[6] Perhaps given the turbulence and uncertainties of the times, a hard Governor stronger on 'law and order' matters than the diplomatic skills was also deemed the safer appointment by the Colonial Office. The survivor of an assassination attempt at the beginning of his term of office (the bullet hit his wife's sedan chair), May was dour, taciturn, and boldly headstrong—perhaps even bone-headed at times—as well as tactless. May's car was stoned whenever he appeared in public.

There was unrest in the urban areas and attacks on police stations, not to mention attempts to release inmates of the overflowing prisons. May was certainly the man to deal with it all. With Hong Kong suffering the backwash of the upheavals and lawlessness next door, he retaliated violently against roaming bands of criminals from over the border, and nocturnal raids by pirates along the coast.

Sir (Francis) Henry May by Walter Stonemason, 1919
© National Portrait Gallery, London

Notwithstanding this dramatic backdrop, a feature of his administration during the Great War years was that public works schemes already underway were not shelved (possibly alone amongst British Crown Colonies) but were methodically pursued to their completion, including construction of a major dam in the years 1912–18 to double Hong Kong's water storage capacity. (This, even though China was 'convulsed in revolution and the world was at war'...)[7] He was just as single-minded in marshalling support for the RFC through his contacts in the Colony.

Just in time for Empire Day, 1915 (24th May and the late Queen Victoria's birthday), Hong Kong remitted the sum of £4,500 to London for two presentation fighter aeroplanes. This was the cheque that had so surprised Wrench when it landed on his desk, and further encouraged him to extend and expand the Imperial Aircraft Flotilla campaign. Governor May was in direct contact with the six partners of the Tai Yan Bank of Hong Kong, in parallel with the press appeal to the public, and they put up half this sum. He transmitted their special request to London that the name of the bank should be inscribed on their fighter aircraft in both English and Chinese characters.[8] The balance of £2,250 was raised by public subscription amongst both British and Chinese communities. For some reason, however, the War Office devoted the donation to three reconnaissance aeroplanes costing £1,500 each, instead of two fighters for the same money (possibly the BE2cs simply represented what was coming off the production line at the time). They were inscribed *Tai Yan Bank* and *Victoria—Hong Kong Nos. 1 and 2*.

As requested, the name of the Tai Yan Bank was rendered in parallel scripts, inscribed on an aluminium plate affixed to the presentation aircraft. The Governor's Office supplied details for the Chinese characters required, for the benefit of possibly puzzled, but presumably also game, workmen at the aircraft depot in England ('numbered as follows in the 1912 edition of Giles' Chinese Dictionary: Nos. 4256, 1245, 10470, 13376, 13253, 3884').[9] Wrench later wrote to Governor May to inform him that Queen Alexandra had been especially intrigued by the Chinese inscription on the first of Hong Kong's aeroplanes at the naming ceremony, and had expressed deep interest in the great generosity of the people of the Colony.[10]

The War Office sent a report on one of Hong Kong's presentation aeroplanes at the end of 1915:

> This machine has mainly been used for cooperation with artillery, but has also been out on reconnaissances. In July, when over the enemy's territory, it was attacked by 2 German machines, both of which were driven off. On 22nd October 1915, when on reconnaissance, at a height of 7,000 feet, a 2-seat Fokker type attacked. The enemy came from below and, in rear, firing from about 100 yards. The *Victoria, Hong Kong* was turned round, nose put downwards, so getting the enemy machine behind, and fire was opened half a drum being expended. The enemy lost ground in climbing, but was still in range. Attacking again, another half-drum was fired, and for the rest of the flight the German machine kept within moderate range. While the pilot of *Victoria, Hong Kong* completed the reconnaissance, the observer fired two or three rounds occasionally to prevent the enemy from closing.[11]

By this stage in the war, therefore, the RFC authorities were certainly still concerned to assure donors of the value of their gift by supplying detailed accounts of the aircraft's activities, and directives had gone out in recent months requiring the RFC in the field to provide them.[12]

However, such reports probably also played a defensive publicity role. For doubts were starting to be voiced—in the UK at least—about the performance of the RFC's aircraft and the vulnerability of its airmen to the German Fokker. An accompanying editorial in the *South China Morning Post* commented that the three Hong Kong machines had been amongst the pioneer aeroplanes presented when Great Britain was still short of the new weapon, and it was gratifying to know that the machine in question was 'not one of the comparatively useless type' but a unit to be seriously reckoned with in the contest for air supremacy. But all three Hong Kong aeroplanes were, in fact, examples of the very aircraft model (the BE2c) that was coming under most fire both literally and figuratively, though such detail was probably little known to a Hong Kong readership, and was certainly not dwelt on by journalists there.

A report submitted by the RFC in the field concerning another of Hong Kong's presentation aircraft, BE2c No.1699, the *Tai Yan Bank*, was not transmitted to subscribers—and fortunately so. It was probably suppressed by the RFC both because it was flippant, and because it reported a faulty engine rather than a successful combat. However the jokey tone, with the inherent casual racism of the times, also offensively evoked Japanese military tradition:

> Shortly after starting for its second reconnaissance the engine developed a serious defect. Finding itself unable to carry out the duty upon which it had started and distressed at the disgrace involved the engine followed the traditions of the East and completely disemboweled itself.
> The entrails of the engine having been strewn over the face of Flanders, the aeroplane was compelled to descend.
> In the ensuing forced landing in unfavourable ground the machine was totally wrecked, but pilot and observer escaped uninjured.[13]

The RFC officers on the Western Front who supplied that report were doubtless completely unaware of just how provocative to the donors those remarks would have been.

In its maiden publication at the end of 1915, the Overseas Club monthly magazine, *Overseas*, published a photograph of the six partners of the Tai Yan Bank.[14] All six were British subjects resident in Hong Kong.[15] All were also rich and successful businessmen heavily involved in welfare associations and public philanthropy. They were Robert Ho Tung (or Robert Hotung); his (half) brothers Ho Fook and Ho Kam Tong (or Ho Kom-tong); Lau Chu Pak; Chan Kai Ming; and Lo Cheung Shiu. A Eurasian, Robert Ho Tung stands out as the only one of the group of markedly non-oriental appearance, with his long, angular features, and reportedly deep blue eyes. (His father was a British subject of Dutch descent.) However, he defined himself as Chinese, chose to dress in Chinese fashion the great majority of the time, and although he lived with his family in the European enclave of the Peak, his children were brought up in a Confucian moral atmosphere, followed the Chinese lunar festivities, and practiced ancestor-veneration, though tracing descent through the female line.[16]

Studio photograph from Hong Kong published in the first issue of *Overseas* magazine under the motto 'The Partners of the Tai Yan Bank, Hong-Kong, who presented an airplane to our Flotilla'.
Left to right—Back row standing: Ho Fook, Chan Kai Ming, Lo Cheung Shiu; Front row seated: Lau Chu Pak, Robert Ho Tung, Ho Kam Tong (public domain), Wikimedia Commons

Nevertheless, miscegenation was not socially approved by either British or Chinese society in Hong Kong, and Eurasians were regarded with a certain degree of ambivalence that not even wealth could totally erase. Sir Robert Ho Tung's exotic appearance may have contributed to certain distinct character traits, notably a thin-skinned desire for status and recognition manifested in his collection of honours and decorations. Well-known as a philanthropist in both Hong Kong and China, Robert Ho Tung had administered Queen Victoria's Diamond Jubilee Fund and (at the time of the Boer War) the South African War Fund in the Colony.[17] He had started out as chief *comprador* to the British trading giant founded by Scots, Jardine Matheson, before creating his own business empire and considerable fortune around the turn of the century, with interests in finance and insurance, property, import-export, shipping, and trading in gold and silver.[18]

All three Ho brothers were graduates of Queen's College, an elite English school in Hong Kong, and all three were very major donors to the Tung Wah Hospital, of which they held long-term chairmanships. This carried considerable prestige. Moral authority attached to the provision of welfare to the community; and the greater the donation, the higher the reputation of the family concerned.[19] Robert Ho Tung's younger maternal half-brother, Ho Kam Tong, held the position of assistant *comprador* to Jardine Matheson, and he was even more prominent in public philanthropy, with many good works to his credit: distributing medicines during the plague of 1894; providing coffins to Chinese families otherwise too poor to buy them; establishing scholarships at local schools; raising money for the School of Tropical Medicine in London. Some of his charitable work had been war-related: During the Boxer Rebellion he chartered steamers to evacuate refugees; and subsequently provided help to the families of Japanese soldiers killed in the Russo-Japanese War of 1904–05. The third brother, Ho Fook, was assistant then head *comprador* at Jardine Matheson, and owned and managed a company in partnership with Lo Cheung Shiu that transported sugar between Hong Kong and Chinese ports. In 1917, Ho Fook succeeded to a nominated Chinese seat on the Legislative Council, joining his colleague Lau Chu Pak.

The virtuous roll-call of social respectability continues: Of the three partners of the Bank not of the immediate Ho family, Lau Chu Pak, *comprador* to A. S. Watson, was a close friend and old school colleague of Robert Ho Tung.[20] He co-founded the Chinese Chamber of Commerce in 1896; and was a director of the Tung Wah Hospital; Vice-Chairman of the Po Leung Kuk (an organisation to rescue women abducted or sold into prostitution), and a member of the District Watch Committee. Since 1914 he had occupied one of the two nominated Chinese seats on Hong Kong's Legislative Assembly; he chaired the Confucian Society of Hong Kong; and was a member of the Council and Court of Hong Kong University, as well as a founder member of the Ellis Kadoorie Chinese Schools Society along with the eponymous Baghdadi Jewish philanthropist. Chan Kai Ming, a member of Hong Kong's Sanitary Board, as well as the Court of Hong Kong University, was another director of the Tung Wah Hospital and a committee member of the Po Leung Kuk and the Chinese Chamber of Commerce. Lo Cheung Shiu held the position of Tung Wah Hospital Chairman for 1915.[21]

Their families were closely intertwined through arranged marriages. As well as being Ho Fook's business partner, Lo Cheung Shiu was his brother-in-law, while his two sons were married to two of Robert Ho Tung's daughters.[22] These six partners of the Tai Yan Bank, then (all of them JPs) were a close group, and amongst the top notch of Hong Kong's 'great and good'; and they were also doing very well in troubled and uncertain times. The Chinese banking sector in Hong Kong was flourishing, and three banks came into being during the war years (the first modern Chinese bank, the Bank of Canton, having been founded in 1912).[23] The Tai Yan Bank itself only started up in 1914, with a fully paid-up capital of HK$600,000.[24] It remained small over the years of its operation, and focused on syndicated loans in the Chinese mainland.[25]

Hong Kong's overall official financial contribution to the British war effort during 1914–18 was a substantial one: HK$10 million (a little under £1 million), roughly the size of total Government revenue for 1914. This total included HK$2 million raised by a 7 per cent special charge on rates paid by (mostly Chinese) property owners. But Hong Kong's local economy flourished during the war years. Following the surrender of the important German naval base at Tsingtao (Qingdao) in China to a Japanese force on 7 November 1914, and within a couple of days, the destruction by the Australian navy of the German commerce-raider, the *Emden*, at the Cocos Islands, Hong Kong was a safe harbour once more. At the same time, British vessels were directed away from Hong Kong and China in support of the war, creating opportunities for local Chinese business to expand into modern shipping.

Hong Kong's Chinese subscribers to the Overseas Club Aircraft Fund thus possessed long track records of philanthropic activity, some of it directed towards war related charities, and were operating commercially in an expansive environment. While Henry May emphatically lacked the persuasive charm of Governor Hesketh Bell, he was probably someone with whom they could do business. As Governor, May operated socially within the parameters of European society and actively sought to maintain those boundaries. Regulations forbade employees in the Public Works Department or prison service with Chinese or Eurasian wives from occupying government quarters, and May prided himself that no European police officer or prison officer married Chinese or Eurasians under his administration.[26] He was Commodore of the Hong Kong Yacht Club, a European preserve, and author of *Yachting in Hong Kong: A Retrospect, with some Hints on small Yacht Racing*, published in 1905.[27] But his wealthy and influential Hong Kong Chinese contacts inhabited a parallel world of status and privilege all their own.

Excluded from the all-European Hong Kong Club, Robert Ho Tung and his brother Ho Kam Tong were among the founders of the Chinese Club—a gentleman's club exclusively for Chinese. (In 1926 Ho Kam Tong was to become the first Chinese admitted to full membership of the Hong Kong Jockey Club.)[28] The Chinese Recreation Club of which Lau Chu Pak was a Committee member paralleled the all-white Hong Kong Cricket Club.[29] Despite the rigid social boundaries, there was nevertheless an important avenue of practical cooperation between Henry May and the leading Chinese merchants of the Colony in the form of the University of Hong Kong, of which May was Chancellor. The University building opened in 1912, coinciding with the beginnings of May's Governorship, and the first graduation ceremony was held in December 1916. The University—brainchild incidentally of the previous Governor, Frederick Lugard—had been established to take students from China (numbering some two hundred in 1916), and from overseas Chinese communities, as well as from Hong Kong itself.

Its establishment met with widespread support and approval, in the Colony and outside it. Sir Robert Ho Tung was one of the largest contributors to the University Endowment Fund, and in 1915 donated HK$50,000 for a Chair of Clinical Surgery, as well as pledging an annual subscription of $5,000 for ten years. His contributions were calculated to be worth HK110, 000—little short of £11,000—over the full ten-year period.[30] While over on a visit from Kuala Lumpur in 1915, the China-born FMS tin millionaire, Loke Yew, additionally promised an interest-free loan of HK$500,000 over a twenty-one year term; income from its investment was to be used to establish four scholarships in his name open to Chinese youths from the FMS and Straits Settlements.[31] In 1918 the University received a donation of HK$55,000 from Eu Tong Sen of the FMS.[32]

Apart from a joint interest in the good order and prosperity of the Colony, and in the future of the University, there was an apparent meeting of minds in another matter: attitudes towards Japan. The political situation in China was very disturbed at this time—and for the whole period of the Great War and well into the nineteen twenties. For many early nationalists in Asia and elsewhere, the rise of Japan, and its victory over Russia in the war of 1904–05 represented a source of pride, and an inspirational example of a non-European country modernising and arming itself, and challenging Western imperialism.[33] But not so in China in early 1915, when Japan made its own imperial ambitions manifest in its 'Twenty-one Demands' of the shaky new Republic, which, if complied with in full, would have made the country virtually a Japanese Protectorate.

In his communications with the Colonial Office May reflected local Chinese anger and hostility, and was given to anti-Japanese diatribes. His dispatch warning of a trade boycott in the offing employed some quite extraordinary terminology for an official communication:

> The feeling against the Japanese amongst the Chinese, who know their aggressors for a treacherous, unscrupulous people dominated by an aggressive militarism, is so strong that the situation created by Japan's unwarranted and far-reaching demands is fraught with much danger. A collision would be disastrous to China and to the trade of this Colony.

The Secretary of State, Lewis Harcourt, commented in manuscript of Governor May on another communication: 'I think I will not write. If he used foolish language publicly I should disavow him and make him withdraw.'[34]

It should be stressed that Japan was one of the Allies in the First World War. The biggest German overseas naval base at the beginning of the war was located at Tsingtao on the Shantung (Shandong) peninsula in China, acquired by Germany in 1897; Germany's East Asiatic Squadron was based there. However, Japan (with whom Britain had concluded an alliance in 1902) possessed a powerful navy, and Britain requested its assistance in protecting their merchantmen from German cruisers. The Japanese responded by submitting an ultimatum to Germany to hand over colonial possessions in China and ships in Chinese waters for the duration of the war.

Then Japan declared war on Germany on 23 August 1914. Britain contributed 2,800 men (including Indian troops) to the Japanese military force of 29,000 that finally obtained the surrender of the German garrison at Tsingtao in early November 1914, the Japanese navy taking the opportunity to seize the German Pacific islands north of the equator.[35] They already had their own air capacity, and besides flying reconnaissance over the German naval base, pilots of three Japanese aircraft claimed to have hit German vessels with hand-thrown bombs from a height of seven hundred metres, while a Japanese seaplane was reported to have bombed and demolished a portion of the fortifications.[36]

Although Japanese troops were not committed to any of the major European warfronts, Japanese ships ferried Australian and New Zealand (ANZAC) troops from the Pacific via the Indian Ocean to Aden between 1914 and 1918; and following German attacks on Japanese merchantmen in February 1917, thirteen Japanese ships joined the Allied anti-submarine effort in the Mediterranean. In August 1918 Japan intervened in Siberia and the Russian Far East, eventually committing 72,000 troops, and by the Paris Peace Conference of 1919 its involvement in the Great War had lifted it from a regional player to the ranks of the Great Powers.[37]

China, on the other hand, remained a neutral until it entered the war on the Allied side on 14 August 1917, subsequently supplying 96,000 workers for labour battalions in Europe, with the limited domestic objective to regain Shantung and Tsingtao and reassert sovereignty. This objective was thwarted by the bitterly resented decision of the Peace Conference to award Tsingtao and Shantung to Japan in 1919, and consequently China refused to sign the Paris Peace Treaty (though the area did in fact revert to China later, following a further international conference).[38]

Writing from Tsingtao in December 1915, where he had gone for his health, Sir Robert Ho Tung sent Governor May an order on his bankers for HK$50,000, with a request to apply it to whatsoever war related purpose the Governor deemed best. May chose to remit £3,000 to the Overseas Club for two further aeroplanes, and the remaining £1,921 to the Red Cross for motor ambulances 'either boat or wheeled' (both in desperate need for Indian casualties in Mesopotamia) and their upkeep.[39] The two additional presentation BE2c reconnaissance planes were respectively named the *Sir Robert Ho Tung Hong Kong* and the *Lady Ho Tung Hong Kong* at May's behest. Then in April 1917, spurred by another appeal from Evelyn Wrench, Ho Fook provided the Overseas Club (of which he had been made a life member) with the money for yet another reconnaissance aircraft. *Ho Fook Hong Kong* was the sixth from the Colony;[40] and some aspiring artist of the RFC fancifully decorated it with fiery dragon and other painted *chinoiserie*.[41]

Two more aircraft followed in 1917 by public subscription, one an RE8, improved replacement for the BE2c (though with an evil reputation for going down in flames), the other a DH5 scout. These will probably have drawn mainly or wholly on contributions from Hong Kong's British expatriates. Many had kin at the Front, since out of a male British population of 2,157, Hong Kong sent 579 volunteers abroad for military service,[42] including a contingent drawn from the Hong Kong Police. Fundraising events for the Overseas Club Aircraft Fund within the British community included a 'smoking concert' at Kowloon Masonic Hall in May 1917 (evidently no rival to parallel productions in Jamaica or Trinidad) with amateur performances of songs to piano or banjo accompaniment, step dancing, conjuring, and bird and animal imitations—winding up with the roar of the 'Peak Tiger'.[43]

On 24th May 1916, Northcliffe's other newspaper, *The Times,* published a special Empire Day supplement, in which Evelyn Wrench reviewed the work done over the year by the 'Imperial Patriotic Societies'.[44] He wrote of the 'magnificent response' to the appeal for funds for an Imperial Aircraft Flotilla, which had enabled the Overseas Club to present to the Government no fewer than 69 units since Empire Day 1915 (when Hong Kong's original cheque for £4,500 had just arrived on Wrench's desk). Over £100,000 had been received and paid over to the War Office by the Overseas Club Aircraft Fund by that stage. In addition, a large number of aeroplanes had been presented to the British Government direct.

A separate article from an unnamed correspondent, entitled 'A Chance for the Outer Peoples', called for a mobilisation of finance from Britons across the empire, and concluded:

> The appeal would have a subtle influence upon those other millions who share our Empire. There are great reservoirs of loyalty which we have not yet begun to tap. The Anglo-Indians in the Empire are not a wealthy class. Yet they are capable of real sacrifice. The wealthy Parsee community ought not to be overlooked. The large Chinese communities in Hong Kong, Singapore, Penang, Rangoon, and the Malay States are not only well off, but realise just as acutely as we do the advantages of political freedom and stability. I have met Arabs and very many black men in the depth of the tropics for whom the Empire has a meaning. There is in fact untapped wealth in the hands of coloured races all over the Empire—many hidden wells, too, of quiet loyalty. We should at least be able to devise methods of putting both of these to the test.

Although the writer is anonymous, the personal reminiscences contained elsewhere in the piece about Cecil Rhodes suggest that it might well have been Albert Earl Grey, former Governor General of Canada, Rhodes Trustee, and at that time chair of the RCI's Land Settlement Committee (for British soldiers and sailors at the end of the war).

Henry May's active governorship of Hong Kong did not outlast the Great War itself. His health had deteriorated. In November 1917 he took himself off on a grouse-shooting holiday to Corea (Korea—which had been under Japanese military administration since 1910) to recuperate. He found it necessary to send a reassuring message to a nervous Colonial Office (which had attempted to head him off) that the Japanese authorities had been fully apprised of, and understood, his intentions. On his return he declared himself 'much struck' with Corea's development in the matter of roads and railways, an opinion he had declared to the Japanese Civil Governor.[45]

However any recuperation was but temporary. Under considerable strain and pressure throughout his period as Governor, May's final months in office were marked by two catastrophes: During the annual race meeting at Happy Valley in February 1918 a stand collapsed and six hundred Chinese race-goers died in the resultant conflagration. At around the same time a grave epidemic of cerebral-spinal meningitis broke out amongst refugees from the civil strife in China, who were living crammed into fetid and rat-infested tenements on the northern shore of Hong Kong Island. A thousand died. In September 1918, May left on what was intended to be a short period of leave, but suffered a stroke while away.[46] He submitted his resignation in early 1919, and retired to Vancouver for health reasons. He died at Clare Priory, Suffolk, his wife's family home, in 1922.

Ironically, Sir Robert Ho Tung, who retired from active business around 1900 on health grounds, and spent frequent periods convalescing in either Tsingtao or Portuguese-ruled Macau, lived on into his mid-nineties. His insistent petitioning during the 1920s for a higher British honour has been detailed elsewhere.[47] For the whole period of the Second World War and the Japanese occupation of Hong Kong, he remained on Macau. During his sojourn, he presented a warplane to the Chinese Government, and two fighter-planes to the RAF, returning to Hong Kong with the British military governor after the Japanese surrender. He finally received his coveted KBE at the age of ninety-two, in 1955. In his old age, whilst his portrait was being painted, he asked to be seen wearing all twenty-two decorations acquired during his lifetime; the artist declined on aesthetic grounds, but compromised, and painted the decorations themselves in a separate picture, to be hung nearby in its own frame.[48]

Country	Approx. population	Number of planes
Hong Kong	c. 500, 000	8

Chapter 8:
The Malaya Air Fleet Fund—the Straits Settlements and Malay states

By Empire Day 1916 it was clearly beginning to dawn that financial support for Britain's war effort was to be found in communities outside the Dominions and the various white settler outposts strewn about the empire. In part this was due to Hong Kong, but even more so to the Straits Settlements and Malay states. The Battle of Jutland, in which the Dreadnought HMS *Malaya* was to play its part, was still a week away. But the Malaya Air Fleet Fund had featured in British newspapers for the past year. Launched in March 1915, by that September it had collected upwards of £10,000. Subscriptions in the FMS alone exceeded £25,000 by mid-1916, quite apart from contributions from the Straits Settlements and a recent gift of more than £31,000 made through the Governor by the Sultan of Johore (or Johor) for an entire squadron of fighters.[1]

The principal exports of the FMS were strategically important, and controlled during the Great War through the Rubber and Tin Exports Committee in London. Apart from a dip at the very beginning, prices climbed and then remained high throughout. At the outset, exports were threatened by the activities of Commander Müller and his light cruiser, the *Emden*, which detached from Germany's East Asiatic Squadron to raid Allied shipping in the Indian Ocean. On 15 October 1914 the *Emden* plundered and then sank a Blue-Funnel liner on her maiden voyage some way off Colombo, carrying valuable cargo that included tin and rubber from the Straits.[2] Then on 28th October Commander Müller launched a lightening raid on the harbour at Penang—one of the Straits Settlements and situated off the northwestern Malay coast—and sank a Russian cruiser at her moorings, and then a French destroyer off the northernmost point of Penang island. Like Hong Kong, destruction of the *Emden* by HMAS *Sydney* rendered the Straits Settlements safe for shipping for the rest of the war.

The hundreds of thousands of Chinese coolies working the tin mines of the FMS were not British subjects, and returned to southern China at the end of their contracts. There was, however, a substantial and relatively prosperous resident Chinese community centred on the

Straits Settlements of Singapore, Penang, and Malacca who were. They were known as the 'Peranakan' or 'Baba' or Straits Chinese. There had been overseas Chinese communities established in the Malay states long before the British founded the Straits Settlements Colony under East India Company rule in the early nineteenth century—in the case of Malacca, or rather the Malay sultanate of Melaka, since at least the mid fifteenth century. Language, culture and cuisine had absorbed local influences and included Malay elements, so that the Straits Chinese were distinct from the recent arrivals from China who came to work in the tin mines. At the time of the Great War, Straits Chinese were also vocally loyal to the British Empire.

The title of their political movement, the Straits Chinese British Association (SCBA), speaks for itself. But the SCBA urged greater democratic representation for those subjects of the empire literate in English, as well as equal opportunities and promotion on merit—in today's language, an end to racial discrimination. A leading figure of the SCBA, Dr. Lim Boon Keng, ran his own plebiscite in 1915 when a nominated Chinese seat on the Legislative Council of Singapore fell vacant, distributing voting forms inside copies of the *Malaya Tribune*, of which he was Chairman of the Board of Directors and one of the founders in 1913. The paper had as its expressed aim to give space to the views of the majority permanent population of Asiatic descent—Indian, Arab, Javanese and Malay as well as Chinese. He received 665 of the 796 'votes' cast via the newspaper.[3] It was to be his third time on the Legislative Council (the first appointment was in 1895 at the age of twenty-six, then again in 1901) and he would probably have been nominated anyway, but he had made his point.

In the late nineteenth century, it was possible, but rare, for a near penniless migrant from southern China to strike it rich for himself in the FMS tin fields through hard graft, shrewdness, and great good fortune. There were a handful of self-made tin millionaires who became British subjects too, and if not they themselves, then their children became educated in English-language schools, and moved closer to the existing society of the Straits-born. Eu Tong Sen occupied an intermediate position. His father migrated from southern China in 1876, and he spent his early years in China with his grandfather. After his father's death in 1891 he joined his stepmother (who had wealthy Straits Chinese family connections) in Penang, later moving to Gopeng, Perak, in the FMS. His stepmother, Man Vun Cheong, was a shrewd businesswoman in her own right who recognised the benefits of cultivating British officials (whom she entertained with lavish champagne dinners).[4] English-speaking herself, she groomed her stepson accordingly with a private English tutor. Eu Tong Sen also lived for two years with his father's business partner, R. Butler, not only becoming fluent in English but ostentatiously anglophile.

He restructured his father's crisis-ridden businesses and bought an apparently exhausted mining site from a bankrupt merchant that turned out to be very productive. After clearing his father's debts, he built up a business fortune based on tin mining, rubber planting, real estate, Chinese medicine, and transmitting remittances from Southeast Asia to southern China. He also remained close to the British. When in 1911 Eu Tong Sen came to Britain to attend the coronation of George V, old friends from the FMS entertained him, among them Sir Ernest Birch and Sir Frank Swettenham.[5] As at Hong Kong, the Great War brought opportunities for local Chinese banking and shipping interests. With the wartime disruption of Western banking in the area, Eu Tong Sen's remittance network also flourished. That network was based on his chain of shops selling traditional Chinese medicine around the tin mines of Perak and in the urban areas of the FMS and Straits Settlements, which eventually formed the basis for a pharmaceutical empire spread throughout Southeast Asia and the Far East that remains to this day.[6]

In March 1915 Charles Alma Baker, a planter from New Zealand who had grown very rich in the FMS, launched his aircraft campaign. He was born in 1857 to immigrant parents from London who ran a hotel in Oamaru, South Island. Tall and imposing, and evidently socially ambitious, as a young man he cultivated an 'aristocratic' British accent, affected a monocle, and added 'Alma' to his surname of Baker for more distinguished effect. After training as a surveyor he moved to Auckland, where he met and married the daughter of a leading New Zealand politician of the day, and the couple moved to Perak in the FMS in 1890. Charles Alma Baker left New Zealand soon after fathering a half Maori son while surveying in the Opotiki district of North Island; but if he was aware of his son's existence, he kept it a close secret throughout his lifetime, and there is no actual evidence that he left to avoid scandal. (The son, Pita Heretaunga Baker, joined the Maori Pioneer Corps—later, Battalion—in 1916, served in France in 1918, and in Düsseldorf after the Armistice but Alma Baker may not have known this.)[7]

Perak's Kinta Valley was then the richest tin-field in the world, and Alma Baker found work there as a contract surveyor. His contract was terminated five years later, but by that time he had acquired numerous mining concessions. One of them, Gunong Lanno, was worked by two Chinese brothers holding the sub-lease, the Chews, and turned out to be enormously profitable. It gave Alma Baker an annual income of at least $50,000 (roughly £6,000) a year. He invested his profits in rubber plantations in the FMS, and was a millionaire with an opulent lifestyle by the outbreak of the First World War.[8] His mining income alone between 1898 and the end of the Great War has been conservatively estimated at more than £100,000, after payment of all expenses.[9]

Convinced long before the war, he claimed, of the future military importance of aeroplanes, in February 1915 Alma Baker cabled his old friend Sir Ernest Birch (former British Resident of Perak, now in retirement in London) to approach the War Office for permission to establish an aircraft fund in Malaya and the Straits Settlements.[10] (This was presumably sparked by Wrench's original appeal, though it seems he never acknowledged this.) Approval gladly forthcoming, Alma Baker's campaign launched in a low key manner with a letter to the press referring to the rise in demand for tin pushing up prices and leading to the current 'wave of prosperity that is beginning to roll over the Kinta Valley'. Writing in support, a fellow resident appealed to 'the English, Irish, Scotch and Welsh of Selangor' in the following words: 'we talk a lot of our volunteer army. Let us be volunteer taxpayers, as we cannot place our bodies at the disposal of our country.'[11]

Subsequently deploying a more emotive campaigning style, Alma Baker went on to argue that those who could afford it had a moral duty to contribute to an arm of warfare that was proving exceptionally effective in the great conflict in Europe. His call, he said, was to those enjoying their lives 'in safety, commercial prosperity and comparative luxury, with no extra taxation, while the greatest war the world has seen is raging around us.' It aimed to supply a Malaya squadron that would form part of a Great Air Fleet 'ready to operate in the early summer with the large new Armies and other important movements on land and sea.' At a cost of little more than $10,000 apiece for these 'inexpensive and invaluable craft', there were scores of people in the Straits Settlements and FMS who could pay for an aeroplane 'out of their own pocket without being consciously poorer.'[12]

Eu Tong Sen, undated photograph Singapore (public domain), Wikimedia Commons

Alma Baker sought agreement from the FMS Chamber of Mines to pledge one aeroplane, but although individual mine owners were willing to subscribe, the Chamber of Mines as a body was not: an extraordinary general meeting later decided by thirteen votes to four against support which would deplete funds.[13] Eu Tong Sen donated the money for the first aircraft, a BE2c that bore his name.

The money was forwarded to a special account set up at the Bank of England to receive contributions for this and all subsequent presentation planes subscribed through the Malaya Air Fleet Fund, which were numbered consecutively, as well as named. Malaya No. 2 was *The Kinta*, subscribed by Alma Baker himself and his business associate at Gunong Lanno, Chew Boon Juan (putting in $1,000 apiece); mineowner Leong Eng Khean gave $2,000; Messrs. McAlister & Co., engineers and suppliers of mining equipment, provided $500; and five others with mining interests—Wong Fong, Ban Seng Leong, Leong Sin, Gan Ngoh Bee, and Chow Kai also donated $500 each.

From the beginning then, the Fund's larger donors in the FMS reflected the interlinked and interdependent nature of European and Chinese business enterprise in the tin-mining state of Perak at that period, also reflected in the mixed membership of the Chamber of

Mines.[14] There were collaborative arrangements based on the fact that Europeans found it easier to stake mining claims, but relied on Chinese imported labour, the supply of which was controlled by Chinese entrepreneurs. The latter had long exploited shallow alluvial tin seams in this way, paying royalties to the Malay owners of the land. But deeper workings required modern hydraulic dredgers, and such enterprising operators as Eu Tong Sen invested in new equipment and employed British managers and mining engineers, and there was a convergence of mining methods.[15]

However the smelting process was all under European ownership by this time. The London-registered Eastern Smelting Co., of which Sir Ernest Birch was chairman, processed ore in Penang, while the larger Singapore-based Straits Trading Co. (STC), was probably responsible for smelting about two-thirds of FMS output overall;[16] and by 1912 the FMS was responsible for more than half of all the world's tin. Established in 1887, the STC advanced working capital to Chinese miners at competitive rates in order to secure supplies of tin ore on a long-term basis.[17] While Scots were prominent among STC investors and the mining engineers, managers, and suppliers of mining equipment, British investment in tin-mining ventures in the FMS often derived from individuals with existing interests in the (declining) Cornish tin-mining industry. While in Britain for George V's coronation in 1911, Eu Tong Sen had paid a visit to Ireland but also took the opportunity to motor around both Scotland and Cornwall.[18]

Charles Alma Baker campaigned full time for over a year and met all of the administrative costs of the Malaya Air Fleet Fund himself—£7,000 until it was wound up at the end of the war—as well as contributing the cost of four aeroplanes personally (a further £7,000 plus).[19] The only source of opposition seems to have come from the British community of Singapore, who effectively boycotted the Fund from the beginning. The president of the Singapore Chamber of Commerce, C. W. Darbishire, insinuated in the Colony's Legislative Council (of which he was a nominated member) that Alma Baker acted out of a desire for self-publicity, and argued that the provision of warplanes rightly fell to the British War Chest. There were press hints at the time that Darbishire's attack was due to personal antagonism.

Alma Baker's rejoinder issued in the form of a letter circulated to the newspapers arguing that the financial burden of the war was crippling for Great Britain. Since the war had found the British Empire without any common unifying financial mechanism, the respective contributions from the Colonies could only depend on each citizen's sense of duty and on voluntary effort. While the War Office could draw on the British Treasury for the manufacture of whatsoever number of aeroplanes it deemed necessary, any contribution from abroad as a free gift, rather than an interest-bearing loan, relieved the burden on the Capital Account and the British taxpayer.[20]

If Evelyn Wrench had a mission in life to encourage empire-wide togetherness, Charles Alma Baker had a mission to evangelise the citizens of the empire about the pressing need to support military aviation, expressed first through the Malaya Air Fleet Fund, and later the Australian Air Squadrons Fund. Alma Baker firmly believed that only aircraft could break the deadlock on the Western Front. Some of his claims were very extravagant at the time, though perhaps visionary of future developments in air warfare:

> They can destroy military formations, throw big guns out of action, break down bridges, annihilate trenches, cut the lines of communication, destroy the manufacturing centres of munitions of war, and, in short, play havoc, section by section, and with little loss; make concerted action impossible, so that the armies must surrender to the Power who first rules the air.[21]

He wrote this when the Great War was not quite one year old and when flimsy wood and canvas contraptions were flying with no more than 100 hp. engines, for purposes of reconnaissance, artillery spotting, and aerial mapping (or, in the case of gun-mounted aircraft, in the defence of those so engaged).

Wherever possible, he proffered supporting evidence, though it never added up to all the claims, such as this letter from a former rubber estate manager in Perak describing the value of the flying service as perceived by a Captain in the firing line:

> Once in November when we were at Laventie I saw an aeroplane observing a French battery. The aeroplane came up heading for the target—a German battery which had already done a lot of damage to our front trenches. We were in reserve at the time. When the aeroplane reached a certain spot it dropped the 'Ready' signal and stopped the engine, then the gun fired and the engine was thrown in again; the aeroplane wheeled round to the rear and signaled how the shots had gone. It wheeled forward and the performance was repeated. This went on for an hour, then the aeroplane went home and the battery

left off firing. Later in the afternoon the German battery began to shell the front trenches heavily. After about 8 shells the French battery spoke; about 10 rounds simultaneously. The German battery never fired another round. It was most dramatic.[22]

As well as writing to the press, Alma Baker toured, and addressed public meetings, showing photographs of aeroplanes engaged in air fighting. FMS Chief Secretary, Sir Edward Brockman paid tribute to his fundraising style as demonstrating 'what may be done by a vigorous personal canvass by someone who is not only enthusiastic but can infuse some enthusiasm into others.'[23] On a visit to Penang in 1915, Alma Baker succeeded in enlisting the help of wealthy Malay merchant, Mohammed Ariff, an aviation enthusiast, who addressed a fundraising meeting on 'Aircraft and the Present War', tracing their construction history; the progress that had been made in aerial navigation; their current military role in Europe; and the aircraft strengths of the various belligerents.[24]

Although the president of the Singapore Chamber of Commerce, C. W. Darbishire, was hostile, the Chinese Chamber of Commerce of Singapore actively propagated Alma Baker's Air Fleet Fund. According to the *Straits Echo* (which was under Straits Chinese ownership though the editor was British) other Chinese Chambers of Commerce in Penang and Malacca were as much involved.[25]

Above all, the Malaya Air Fleet scheme received the active support of SCBA leader Dr. Lim Boon Keng, an Edinburgh University-educated medical doctor (and Singapore's first Queen's Scholar). He was also a social reformer, politician, writer, and banking and insurance entrepreneur. Dr. Lim Boon Keng promoted the Malaya Air Fleet Fund as the most useful and practical route available to support the war effort, and personally canvassed contributions from the Straits Chinese of Singapore and Malacca. No doubt his influence contributed to the fact that Chinese donors in the Straits Settlements and FMS largely or wholly provided a third of the thirty-six aeroplanes presented through the Fund, and made smaller contributions to several others.

The Fund received donations, too, from the small Armenian business community (comprising eighty-seven souls in all), which had first arrived in Penang and Singapore with the East India Company. Hoseb S. Arathoon presented a BE2c entitled *The Armenia* on 15 September 1915, just a few weeks after launching an Armenian Relief

Fund in Singapore that attracted generous support from several Chinese firms, his appeal speaking of the 'thousands ... deliberately massacred and tortured to death' by the Ottoman Turks and 'the large numbers left entirely destitute and homeless.' Other Armenians donating substantial amounts to Alma Baker's Fund included the Sarkies Brothers (owners of Eastern and Oriental Hotel in Penang and Raffles Hotel in Singapore) and the insurance and shipping business A. A. Anthony & Co.[26] Manasseh Meyer, a merchant and hotelier of Baghdadi Jewish origin who migrated to Singapore from Calcutta in his youth, also provided £2,250 for a fighter plane bearing his name; he was otherwise known as a generous public benefactor, especially to Singapore's Jewish community.[27]

Dr. Lim Boon Keng c. 1920, Lee Brothers Studio Collection, courtesy of National Archives of Singapore

Charles Alma Baker knew full well that no 'Imperial' RFC unit or squadron existed, let alone one that brought together the numbered and named planes subscribed through the Malaya Air Fleet Fund. Nonetheless, he also knew that the notion of such a unit appealed to donors, and he called insistently for subscriptions to complete a 'Malaya Air Squadron' of at least fourteen aircraft. (And when they were all subscribed, a 'Second Air Squadron from Malaya'.) On 16 March 1916 the *Straits Echo* of Singapore published a reader's letter, which asked indignantly:

> Four aeroplanes have come from Singapore, Nos. 4, 6, 7 and 8, but who are the donors? No. 4—Messrs. Tan Wi Yan, Sim Cheng Mea and Tan Kim Wah. No. 6—Messrs. Lee Choon Guan and Lim Peng Siang. No. 7—Mr. H. S. Arathoon, No. 8 (Fighter)—Mr. Manasseh Meyer. Chinese, an Armenian and a Jew. In addition to the individuals named above other Chinese donors are Mr. Eu Tong Sen—No. 1, and Messrs. Gan Ngoh Bee and Khoo Chong Teong [sic. Khoo Cheow Teong] of Penang—No. 15. Surely the British Europeans are not going to be put to shame in such a matter as this by Chinese, Armenians and Jews!

However, this was accompanied by an even worse shaming.

The Jaffna Tamils resident in the Malay states, most of whom were middle and lower-level clerks in British employ, especially government employ, had started collecting within their community for their very own presentation aeroplane and managed to put together £2,250 for a fighter—*Malaya No. 11, The Jaffna*. Reports of fundraising speeches within the community suggest that they were motivated by a desire for greater recognition and respect from the British. At a meeting held in the northern Malay state of Kedah in August 1915, for example, their image in British eyes was described as that of 'an indifferent community only.... known to them as a subject race, as a community of clerks only', but they could together demonstrate through their very own presentation aeroplane that although 'placed on the lowest ladder of the Government service though we are, we have not altogether lost our sense of duty'; moreover they would thereby show solidarity with 'poor and powerless Belgium'.[28] In remitting their offering to London at the end of 1915, Alma Baker made the point that this gift from a modestly off community of less than 2,000 Ceylon Tamils in the FMS marked a real spirit of self-sacrifice.[29] Secretary of State for the Colonies Andrew Bonar Law singled them out for commendation for their 'patriotic spirit' in subscribing for a fighter 'out of their comparatively small resources'.[30]

At the beginning of 1916 Bonar Law issued a communiqué welcoming the first ten presentation aircraft from the Malaya Air Fleet Fund and noting the Chinese contribution.[31] He reinforced this in April by officially acknowledging completion of Malaya's first 'squadron' of sixteen presentation aircraft through the Straits Settlements Governor and High Commissioner to the FMS, Sir Arthur Young. He also wrote personally to Alma Baker on 1 May to say that he had read the representative list of subscribers 'with much interest', and would be placing it in the Colonial Office Library as a record.[32] Emboldened to ignore opposition from within Singapore's Legislative Council by this clear endorsement from the Secretary of State for the Colonies, Sir Arthur Young came out publicly in support of Alma Baker's fundraising for the first time, declaring himself 'most anxious' to see the European population of Singapore respond as generously as the Chinese.[33] The *Straits Times* of Singapore immediately started a collection for a fighter aircraft. Within three weeks, the newspaper was able to report six fighter planes fully paid for.[34]

Yet an analysis of subscription lists does not suggest a sudden great upsurge of support from the British community of Singapore. The Governor and his wife headed the subscription lists for three of the planes, followed by other British subscribers. Yet Tan Jiak Kim—a founder member of the SCBA and a prominent Straits Chinese community leader in Singapore, who until his retirement had last held the Chinese seat on the Legislative Council now occupied by Lim Boon Keng—wholly paid for yet another one. Two were provided from Malacca rather than Singapore (one, the *Sime-Darby*, by the plantation company of the same name). Two further fighters presented through the *Straits Times* in July included *The Malacca Chinese No. 2*. The other was entitled *The Singapore*, but became alternatively known as *The Anzac*, since Australian and New Zealand expatriates had subscribed, as well as Straits Chinese Singaporeans; while staff of the Anglo-Petroleum Company based in Mini-Sarawak and Brunei had donated a good half of its cost.[35]

Quite why British residents of Singapore (unlike those of Penang, Malacca, and the FMS) should have been quite so resistant to contributing to Alma Baker's fund however remains unclear. Perhaps Lim Boon Keng's pre-war stand against the colour bar on senior civil service appointments, and his association with the Malaya Air Fleet Fund, was an allergenic, as well as Darbishire's dislike of Alma Baker.

The pattern of donation in Penang was even more ethnically diverse than Singapore. A free port like Singapore, but also a regional entrepôt serving the northern Malay states, northern Sumatra, and southern Siam and Burma, Penang had its own heterogeneous commercial society as well as a large Straits Chinese presence, and subscriptions reflected this fact.

The first purely Penang-subscribed craft, *Malaya No. 15*, was a BE2c presented on 4 March 1916 by two local Straits Chinese businessmen (neighbours in the capital, Georgetown) after whom it was named. Khoo Cheow Teong had spent most of his years trading at the mouth of the Asahan River in Sumatra, and was a founder of the Deli Bank at Medan, the commercial centre of Netherlands East Indies (NEI) tobacco production; but he settled back in Penang on retirement. Gan Ngoh Bee, son of a wealthy rice merchant of Saigon, French Indo-China, was the owner of a tin mine in Perak and large stakes in others, as well as extensive landholdings in Penang.[36] They were responding to a local newspaper appeal for Penang's very own presentation aeroplane.

The two other Penang planes were raised by public subscription. Donors included commercial and trading minorities, and those with shipping interests: *Penang No. 1* was subscribed by the Penang Chettiars (a community of South Indian origin engaged in money-lending); by several Straits Chinese businessmen; by Malay merchant Mohamed Ariff; K. M. Syed Abubaker; the Armenian Sarkies Brothers; ships' chandler K. Pachee (Indian Muslim); and the Penang Eurasian community.[37] *Penang No. 2* represented subscriptions from Straits Chinese businessmen and locally resident British donors and firms, as well as one Subadar Major Bhall Singh JP.

Khoo Cheow Teong: one of the joint donors of the BE2c from Penang presented in March 1916 and originally inscribed *Malaya 15 – The Khoo Cheow Teong-Gan Ngoh Bee*; courtesy of Patrick Khoo

Arthur Chapman, engineer at Shorts on the Isle of Sheppey before joining the RFC in November 1916, photographed in the cockpit of a replacement machine; this time inscribed *Malaya XV Cheon Teong, Ngoh Bee* it demonstrates the 'name creep' that often occurred with more exotic presentation names, courtesy of David Payne

Leading subscriber names in Malacca were British and Chinese, and involved in tapioca and rubber planting. In Perak, as we have seen, the larger donors were engaged in one way or another with tin mining, and some in estate production too: The Tamil planter Solomon Ramanathan contributed $1,000 towards the collection for the fighter plane *Kuala Kangsar* made by J. M. O'May of the Malay College (which catered for the education of the Malay elite), who personally gave $1,500.[38]

What then of the Malay states other than Perak, more dependent on agriculture than on tin, where a Malay peasantry existed largely outside the money economy? The FMS as a whole had given the British the whopping gift of HMS *Malaya*. In 1916 there were additional gifts of presentation aeroplanes from two Malay states outside the Federation. One was the northern Sultanate of Kedah, an agricultural—rice-producing—state. It had been a tributary of its northern neighbour, the independent kingdom of Siam, until 1909, when an Anglo-Siamese treaty transferred it into the British sphere; it was already closely linked to Penang commercially, which had indeed belonged to Kedah before East India Company rule. In March 1916, the Sultan of Kedah and his State Council sent £2,536 to the British War Office for a fighter aeroplane, *Kedah No.1*.[39] (*Kedah No. 2*, an RE8, was presented by the public within the state, and collected by a member of the British community).[40]

The other aeroplane gift came from Johore and was a very large one indeed. In 1911, Johore's total population stood at 180,412, of whom native Malays numbered only 71,315; there was also an overwhelmingly male Chinese population of more than 63,000, most of them labourers. The economy was based on tin and rubber; on gambier (used in betel wads) and pepper estates; and on the gambling casinos catering for the flood of Chinese weekend punters from Singapore. Indeed, much of Johore's revenue derived from the Chinese clan association holding the monopoly on running gambling establishments there.

The Sultan, Ibrahim II, had inherited a Malay state in 1895 that had guarded its independence from British interference as best it could, and was the only one with a purely Malay bureaucracy, but he had inherited his father's debts. A British Adviser was foisted on him in 1909, whom he habitually frustrated by deploying obstructionist tactics,[41] but financial crisis finally forced him to acquiesce in a tightened arrangement a few months before the outbreak of war, when a *de facto* British Resident was given power over the budget (still called a British Adviser, however, out of deference to local sensitivities).

Until the Great War, Ibrahim II had been regarded by the British as something of the black sheep amongst the Malay Sultans, with numerous scandals to his name, mainly revolving around women and racehorses. He was fond of the high life, and made frequent foreign trips to London and Paris. However, the somewhat censorious tone used by British officials in discussing his affairs changed sharply after the events of February 1915. For Sultan Ibrahim maintained and commanded a regular military force, consisting in December 1914 of 382 Malay Infantry, 98 Indian Artillery, and 81 Bandsmen. He habitually dressed in military uniform, and described himself first and foremost as 'Colonel Commandant, Johore Military and Volunteer Forces'.[42] On the outbreak of war in August 1914 he placed himself and his military force at the disposal of the General Officer Commanding (GOC) Straits Settlements, Brigadier General Dudley Ridout, based at Singapore.

By early 1915, the British Regiment defending Singapore had been withdrawn for service in France and replaced by units of the Indian Army. On 15 February 1915—Chinese New Year, a public holiday—the Rajput wing of the Fifth Light Infantry mutinied. The death toll was well over forty and included a Captain Cullimore who had drilled and trained the Sultan Ibrahim's Forces and was leading a small detachment on duty in Singapore at the time. The Sultan, on hearing the news, led the rest of his men in operations over two months to suppress the mutiny, both on Singapore island and in hunting down fugitives in Johore itself (he arrested four mutineers personally and extradited them to Singapore for trial). Thirty-six of the leading mutineers went before the firing squad,[43] while another sixty-four were sentenced to transportation for life and seventy-three to various terms of imprisonment.

More than 15,000 Singaporeans witnessed the public execution of a batch of more than twenty of the condemned men against the wall of the prison in March 1915.[44] Neither the Malay States Volunteer Rifles nor their commander had previous experience or guidance.[45] The operation was bungled, so that some were still loading while others had already fired, and a regular officer had to go along the line and blow each man's brains out with a revolver.[46] An Indian merchant living near the barracks, who had acted as channel of communication with plotters in India, was also separately hanged for treason. A leading Singapore lawyer involved in the preliminary Commission of Inquiry and the Court Martial wrote that a secret service to counter 'seditious activities' was subsequently established in Singapore under Dudley Ridout, assisted by trained officers sent by the Government of India.[47]

The Singapore Mutiny marked the transformation of Sultan Ibrahim's relationship with the British, and he received an honorary GCMG in the 1916 New Year's Honours List. In addition to his established pastimes of big-game hunting, racehorse training, and motoring, Ibrahim II was taking an increasing interest in aviation, and in January 1916 he made a personal gift of £3,000 for two aeroplanes for the RFC, both BE2cs. He gave a second gift on behalf of the Johore Government in June 1916: £31,500 for a further 14 fighter planes, no less, enough for a whole squadron of aircraft bearing the name 'Johore' had such a unit existed.

In fact, *Johore Nos. 1-14*, all of them FE2b fighting scouts, were dispersed around RFC squadrons in France. Although in autumn 1916 half of them were initially issued to 11 Squadron, several went to 22 and 25 Squadrons, and one to Home Defence in England.[48] (Luckily for the State Treasury, Johore enjoyed good prices for its exports during 1916 and 1917.) On 15 March 1918, King George V conferred on Ibrahim II an honorary KBE, and in 1919, in deference to his interests and self-image, this was changed to the Military Division of the KBE, instead of the Civil Division as previously bestowed.[49]

Studio portrait by Vandyk, April 1916, of Sultan Ibrahim of Johore
posing in military uniform
© The National Portrait Gallery, London

Charles Alma Baker moved his aeroplane crusade across to Australia in 1916. By now, the Malaya Air Fleet Fund had its own momentum, and was to present a grand total of thirty-six aircraft by the end of the war at a cost of more than £60,600. There was a short-lived rival in the FMS during 1917 in the form of the revolutionary new military land vehicle, the 'tank', which had appeared on the battlefields of Europe. Eu Tong Sen gave £6,000, and on 17 August FMS Chief Secretary, E. L. Brockman, wrote to let him know that:

> Dr. Addison, Minister of Munitions, had expressed personal appreciation of his generosity [and] proposed to have a brass plate riveted on the Tank with a suitable inscription, and to have painted on the Tank two eyes of the kind which Dr. Addison understands are, according to Chinese custom, painted on all ships and boats. The appropriate design was being selected with the assistance of Sir Frank Swettenham.[50]

In fact the tank in question, which took part in the Battle of Cambrai,[51] also sported a rather homely dragon motif (evidently from a Welsh regimental template) as well as a pair of eyes. The eyes were at the knowing suggestion of Sir Frank Swettenham, former British Resident in Perak, now at the Press Office in London. What Eu Tong Sen would have appreciated was the visual pun on the acronym for Eu Yan Sang—EYS—his chain of Chinese traditional medicine shops that also acted as service points for transmitting miners' remittances home.

Left side view of the tank Eu Tong Sen presented in 1917
© Tank Museum, Bovington

A campaign for a second tank from the FMS failed to reach its target, and with the agreement of the subscribers—mainly young Chinese from Ipoh—their money was transferred into the Malaya Air Fleet Fund for No. 35, an SE5a, given the title *The Chinese Loyalty* (tin magnate Loke Yew topped up their subscriptions to the necessary for the plane). The final aircraft in the series, *Malaya No. 36*, was the gift in January 1918 of J. A. Russell, founder of the family firm of the same name. 'Archie' Russell had built up the firm's tin-mining interests in cooperation with several Chinese mining entrepreneurs, including Loke Yew. The company later branched out into rubber; finance; construction; property (coming to own almost a third of the town of Ipoh); and coal-mining; and post-Great War also went into match manufacture and tea production.[52]

Other prominent European donors to the Malaya Air Fleet Fund (apart from Alma Baker himself) included E. T. C. Garland, partner in the engineering firm of Aylesbury & Garland (and along with Eu Tong Sen, one of Kinta's two most prominent motoring aficionados); A. N. Kenion, outspoken unofficial member of the FMS Federal Council and senior partner in a leading Ipoh law firm that managed estates on behalf of the Malay royalty and nobility;[53] and finally H. Ashworth Hope, amateur composer, and sole partner in another Ipoh law practice.

If the sixteen planes from Johore and two from Kedah are included, the Malay states and Straits Settlements together provided money for an impressive fifty-four presentation aircraft—in sterling terms, around £111,000. Contributions towards British war expenditure had also been larger than from any other part of Britain's colonial empire.[54] As the press commented with respect to the FMS: 'The presentation of a Dreadnought to the British Navy, a cash gift which may ultimately reach the best part of two million pounds, and a loan of thirty million dollars with more to go, is no mean help rendered by these small States with a population of little more than a million.'[55]

Country	Approx. population	Number of planes
FMS + Straits Settlements	Straits Settlements - 715,000; FMS - 1m.	36
Johore	c. 200,000	16
Kedah	c. 300,000	2

Table II: Official contributions during 1914–18 amounted to the following:

The Straits Settlements Government:

War loans		£8,280,000
Government investments in Imperial Loans		£5,278,744
Gifts		£1,921,946
	Grand total	£15,480,690

The FMS Government:

War loans and Saving Certificates		£2,925,532
Government investments in Imperial Loans		£7,616,609
Gifts		£2,863,660
	Grand total	£13,405,801

Johore:

Gifts. Aeroplanes		£31,500
Gifts. The King's Fund for Disabled Soldiers		£30,000
	Grand total	£61,500

Kedah:

Gifts. Aeroplanes		£2,356
Gifts. The King's Fund for Disabled Soldiers		£20,000
	Grand total	£22,356

(Adapted from Sir Charles Lucas, *The Empire at War*, Vol. 2, pp. 396–7)

Chapter 9: West Africa, and most particularly Gold Coast, and Hugh Clifford

At the close of 1914, a Lagos newspaper questioned how far the British approach towards its subject dependencies in West Africa would alter, in view of the 'deep loyalty manifested towards the King Emperor which has allowed Great Britain to crush Germany, her most formidable rival, seize all her Colonies and thus create a favourable opportunity for the world-wide extension of Anglo-Saxon civilisation.' It continued that albeit optimists had predicted more sympathetic treatment, there had been no discernible change in attitude since the British captured the port of Duala from the Germans in September; but concluded that it was still too soon to tell, since the neighbouring colony of Cameroon as a whole remained in a state of war.[1]

Apart from demonstrating how differently the Great War appeared in its initial stages from a West African perspective, focused as it was on military campaigns in nearby German colonies, these words reveal a widespread African hope for British concessions in return for wartime support. (An attitude, incidentally, also common to black elites in South Africa, despite all avenues for constitutional change there having been virtually closed to them.)[2] By this time, Gambia had already contributed £10,000 to the Prince of Wales' Fund; the Sierra Leone legislature £5,000 to the imperial war effort; and the Emirs of Northern Nigeria £38,000 towards the Nigerian Government's military expenditure on the Cameroon campaign. Finally, the legislature of the Gold Coast (later Ghana, and the richest British West African dependency at that time) voted £60,000 to meet all expenses of their military expedition to German Togoland in August 1914, and promised £80,000 or more for Britain's war expenses during 1915 and to defray the costs of Togoland's administration.[3]

British rule over large areas of West Africa was then quite recent. Until the European 'Scramble' for Africa at the end of the nineteenth century, the British presence was confined to coastal enclaves. In those enclaves, western influence was centuries' old. Educated, and largely Christian, Africans were represented from very early days as nominated members on legislative bodies; and they participated in a legal system based on that of Britain, with juries, a separate judiciary and a bar.[4] With the extension of British rule inland over vast new areas after 1884, however, colonial administrators faced with establishing control over entirely new subject peoples relied on indirect rule through existing emirs, kings and chiefs, and local forms of African customary law and land tenure.

The degree of compulsion entailed in establishing British control varied widely. Some West African kingdoms were strong enough to require outright British military conquest—most notably Ashanti (or Asante), in the forests of Gold Coast, and Benin, on the Gulf of Guinea—and their vanquished rulers were exiled. Nonetheless, where it was possible to co-opt, and work with and through existing indigenous political leadership without undue violence (and expensive military campaigns), British colonial officials did so. There was no attempt to extend the system that had developed over centuries at the coast.

This process of co-opting traditional notables worked to marginalise the once important westernised coastal elite—a tendency also reinforced by the growth of racism in Britain in the late nineteenth century, as well as medical advances (for example, in the control of malaria) which made it possible to discriminate in favour of European cadres in colonial government employ.[5] By 1914, the westernised African elite at the coast had political ambitions still limited to advancement within the British constitutional order and Empire. The African press expressed loyalty throughout the war, in particular carrying articles comparing the nature of German colonial rule unfavourably with British practice.

The following two examples of press comment come from Gold Coast, next door to Togoland where notions of racial superiority were enforced more harshly and sometimes brutally:[6]

> It is true that we are subject races, that we labour under great disadvantages under the present condition of government of subject races in the British Empire. England has faults and does us wrong in many things, but she has been the source of the little light we have seen and known ... and we would not exchange her for any other European master.[7]

Yet it was more than a case of 'better the devil you know':

> The struggle that is convulsing the whole world has a most vital interest for us. If by any unlikely chance, Germany should get the upper

hand, we may be sure that in terms of settlement a small tropical country like ours would change flags, and we should experience for ourselves, the miseries that were inflicted upon our Togoland brethren.[8]

The two newspapers from which these quotations were taken were respectively associated with leading journalist and political activist, Joseph Ephraim Casely Hayford, and with the Aborigines' Rights Protection Society (ARPS) to which he belonged, political organisation of the Colony's coastal intellectuals. The ARPS had originally been established in 1897 as a local branch of the Aborigines' Protection Society of London, and it is likely that these views also reflected that Society's wartime propaganda highlighting the alleged iniquities of German colonial rule.[9]

In 1915, Wrench's aircraft appeal reached the desks of the four British colonial Governors of West Africa, and all of them, to varying degrees, responded positively. The Governor of Sierra Leone even visited Evelyn Wrench at the London headquarters of the Overseas Club in August 1915.[10] His name headed the list of subscribers for the reconnaissance aeroplane *Sierra Leone*, with a donation of £100.[11] Gambia's gift was made in mid-1917, and consisted of £10,000 voted by the Colony's legislature for aeroplanes simply entitled *Gambia Nos. 1-4*. It was shared equally between the RNAS (two Sopwith Camels) and the RFC (two RE8 biplanes, improved replacement for the reconnaissance BE2c also fitted with machine-guns).[12] This was a handsome sum from such a small territory, but although initially disrupted by war, Gambia's groundnut exports had recovered and were fetching good prices that year from Britain, and its budget was in healthy surplus.

In Nigeria, the decidedly autocratic Sir Frederick Lugard—the very theorist of indirect rule—was in touch with Wrench.[13] He even permitted fundraising among his staff: A benefit match at the Lagos Tennis Club in September 1915 saw the Governor's Deputy and the Administrator paired against the Director of Marine and First Assistant Secretary of the Central Secretariat, the proceeds from entrance fees (2s 6d a head) being maximised by a Mrs. Lambert 'who sat at the gate … stoutly refusing to give change.'[14] By the close of 1915 the Nigeria Aeroplane Fund had sent £3,000 to London for two presentation BE2cs.

Subscriptions for *Nigeria No.2* included £800 from the Alake (traditional ruler) of Abeokuta and his Chiefs—a town that until 1914 and forcible integration had been virtually an autonomous, mission-dominated, Yoruba state.¹⁵ (One of the Chiefs—the Olota of Ota—was fined £50 for misappropriating £11 from the collection.)¹⁶ It also included a contribution of £79 'from the Kroo boys'—that is, the seafaring Kru of Liberian origin who had been working European trading ships all along the coast of West Africa since the eighteenth century, who numbered an estimated more than 2,500 at Lagos. (There were plans to raise 10,000 Kru labourers from West Africa for munitions work in Britain during 1916 that had to be dropped in the face of trade union opposition.)¹⁷ One year on, and the Fund presented its final reconnaissance aeroplane, *Nigeria No. 3*.

There was one other aircraft gifted from Nigeria, in 1917. It was allocated the rather ungainly name *Presented by the Native Administration of Benin in Southern Provinces of Nigeria*. For shortly before the outbreak of the Great War, Benin was given its Oba (king) back. In 1897 the former Oba—Ovonramwen—had been deposed, and the royal palace sacked and stripped of its treasures following massacre of a British expeditionary column. (A London auction of artworks from the Benin palace paid for the punitive expedition that ensued.)

When Ovonramwen died in exile the ban on kingship was revoked in favour of his son, who was crowned Oba Eweka II in July 1914. Eweka II's accession fell squarely within Lugard's indirect rule strategy, but some of the administrative details for the Benin Native Authority remained uncertain for a time. Even by the first quarter of 1916, the new Oba's stipend and that of his chief adviser (the Iyasheri) was still not finally settled, although Lugard advised the Colonial Office that they should not be less, when funds permitted, than £1,500 and £750 respectively.¹⁸ On 24 July 1917 (incidentally, the third anniversary of Oba Eweka II's accession) Lugard informed London that he had received, and gratefully accepted, an offer from the Oba to contribute £1,000 from the Benin Native Treasury for expenditure on such war purpose as the Governor should think fit.

It seems that Benin's final accounts for 1916 had revealed a much larger surplus balance for the Benin Native Treasury than previously estimated. He explained that the Oba fully appreciated the significance of his action, and in discussing the matter with him made the observation: 'If a man cannot fight he can still give nine-pence out of every shilling that he owns.'¹⁹ Despite misgivings about the state of Benin's finances, the Colonial Office thus agreed that since it was not a recurrent charge it could be accepted in two instalments, to go towards the purchase of an aeroplane for use by the Imperial Government, as Lugard suggested.[20] In September 1917 the Press Office in London was therefore pleased to disseminate news of an aeroplane gift from the son of Oba Ovonramwen of 1897 Benin massacre fame.

However, the truly surprising engagement with Wrench's aircraft campaign was that of the Gold Coast, which provided no less than twenty-seven presentation aeroplanes in all, eleven by public subscription from a wide social and geographical spread, and sixteen by vote of a Legislative Council which was newly reconstituted in 1916 to include a larger and more representative African voice than hitherto. It was the most striking aspect of the Colony's financial involvement, but there were others, since Gold Coast was broadly supportive of Britain in many ways during the war, the educated coastal elite through war funds of their own establishment. They also addressed meetings in 1917 to encourage military recruitment for the East Africa campaign (to which the Gold Coast Regiment was sent after Togoland and Cameroon), for they hoped thereby for a wider role in post-conflict decision-making.[21]

Nor did any of the inland kingdoms or polities brought into the British sphere in recent decades view the Great War and the military preoccupation with Europe as an opportunity to rebel—even Ashanti, which had not been finally subjugated until 1901. Indeed the Governor, Sir Hugh Clifford, noted that the chiefs and people of Ashanti displayed as keen a desire to assist and support the Government as anything shown by their neighbours on the coast.[22] Although, as the Governor openly admitted, it would be too much to assume that British colonial rule was popular, he assessed that it was certainly regarded as preferable to the German alternative.[23] Coastal intelligentsia and rural Chiefs alike collected for presentation aeroplanes. Evelyn Wrench, surprised at this wave of support for the Overseas Club Aircraft Fund from a totally unexpected direction (darkest Africa!), recorded in early 1916:

> We have just received the money for two more aeroplanes from the Gold Coast [making seven in all], £1,500 from the Chiefs and people of Eastern Krobo and £1,500 from the Head Chief, Chiefs and people of the new Juaben Settlement. It is wonderful thinking of all these natives, who a hundred years ago were practically savages, sending us all this help.[24]

These gifts attested to the attractiveness of Wrench's scheme, as well as the availability of surplus cash in the cocoa-farming areas of Gold

Coast. They had much to do with the personality of a popular Governor, Sir Hugh Clifford, and his personal enthusiasms.

When Clifford arrived as Governor at the end of 1912, the Gold Coast in its current shape was little more than ten years old. However, the British had been trading with the various small Fante states at the coast since the late fifteenth century (until 1807, mainly in slaves, many of them war captives exported by the inland Ashanti kingdom). The British had also been skirmishing on and off with Ashanti for much of the nineteenth century. In 1874, a strong British army expedition equipped with Enfield rifles and seven-pounder guns beat back an Ashanti invasion of the Fante and allied states, and sacked and burnt the Ashanti capital Coomassie (Kumasi), exiling the Asantehene.

The various British forts and settlements on the coast were then converted into a Crown Colony, and the southern states into a Protectorate.[25] After defeating the Ashanti yet again in a nine-month 'war of Ashanti Independence' that broke out in 1900, the British annexed the kingdom. In addition they annexed lands to the north of Ashanti (the Northern Territories). Only the Northern Territories were unsuitable for cocoa production, and untouched during 1914–18 by the consequent economic revolution, and they provided the majority of the recruits for the Gold Coast Regiment that fought in the First World War in Togoland, in Cameroon, and (with distinction) in East Africa.

Sir Hugh Clifford was one of the brightest stars of the British Colonial Service, and regarded as a very able administrator. Son of a once important, but now impoverished, Catholic branch of the English aristocracy, a relative then holding the Governorship of the Straits Settlements (Sir Frederick Weld) secured Clifford's first post with the Malayan Civil Service in the early 1880s. His talents brought him a succession of others of increasing responsibility, in several Malay states; and in 1903, appointment as Colonial Secretary of Trinidad (where his first wife was killed in a cart accident), then later, Ceylon. He received his KCMG in 1909 at the early age of forty-four, and was made Governor of Gold Coast in 1912.[26]

When he arrived, he found a country in rapid economic development. It had become the world's largest cocoa-producer the previous year, and achieved this through independent African peasant production and enterprise, not big European plantation companies. Clifford saw it as his role and duty to further this economic progress; his programme of road construction dramatically improved access to markets for African farmers.[27] More would have been done had it not been for the Great War, and a planned railway project was shelved until afterwards. As it was, 165 miles of hard-surfaced roads were built during his term of office (1912-19), and over 650 miles of secondary roads. Construction of the latter was mainly by rural work-parties organised by Chiefs opening up routes for the lightweight trucks of the cocoa-buying companies.[28]

The ARPS was a body drawn from the educated coastal elite that also claimed to represent the Fante chieftaincy. It had originally been formed to protest proposed British land legislation of 1897, and had successfully achieved its withdrawal. Early in his Governorship, the ARPS tackled Clifford, and challenged him to appoint 'competent and worthy natives' to administrative positions, a request ignored by previous Governors.[29]

One of the Society's leading lights was the Cambridge-educated barrister, journalist, writer, and—for that era at least—political radical, Joseph Ephraim Casely Hayford. He was another strong character, like Clifford, and born in the same year (1866); both also wrote fiction that examined the colonial encounter, each from their own perspective. (Casely Hayford's *Ethiopia Unbound* was published under his pen name of Ekra-Agiman; Clifford's novels and short stories were set in Malaya, where his colonial service career began).[30]

In his somewhat barbed address of welcome, Casely Hayford looked forward in May 1913 to cooperation with the new British Governor, and alluded to the alleged success of Japanese colonialism in Formosa (Taiwan) in seeking to educate the local population to the status of citizenship:

> It precludes the idea of their being forever hewers of wood and drawers of water ... We hope to see revived in the time of the present administration the ideal of citizenship, so that the people of this country may take their true place as citizens of the British Empire.[31]

As with early nationalist politicians elsewhere in the world outside Europe, Japan's success in modernising itself and in challenging the West militarily served as a source of inspiration for Casely Hayford (and apparently even as a coloniser).[32] He was also inspired by Abyssinia and the Emperor Menelik's victory over the Italian army at the Battle of Adowa in 1896.

In fact Clifford, not at all enamoured of the ARPS in general and very unwilling to allow them any ammunition for their claim to speak on behalf of the Fante Chiefs, accepted their grievances on this particular point of discrimination in employment and advancement. Just as he was delivering on the extension of the road network for the rural cocoa-producers, Clifford thus also took action to address the main grievances of the ARPS with respect to access to senior professional posts: He secured the appointment of E. C. Quist as the Gold Coast's first African Crown Counsel, and carried out a long private correspondence with the Colonial Office denouncing the colour bar on appointments to the government medical service across West Africa as a self-serving device maintained by European medical staff.

Behind his back, his views on the West African Medical Service and the need for change were strongly opposed by Sir Frederick Lugard in Nigeria.[33] So although the Aborigines' Protection Society of London welcomed the news in late 1915 that the Secretary of State for the Colonies had agreed the creation of six Gold Coast medical posts for 'qualified West African natives',[34] this was not the general opening across the region that Clifford had been urging. Nonetheless, his efforts were appreciated, and the degree of Clifford's resultant popularity as Governor can be gauged by the fact that when his early transfer was rumoured, press protest ensued, and a call by the ARPS for a popular petition to London to urge his retention.

For his part, Clifford more or less credited the ARPS with popularising aeroplanes in the Gold Coast (though he does not bring himself to refer to the Society by name). He recorded that there was widespread sympathy for the British cause right from the start of the war. Soon, however, the more educated members of society were taking an intelligent interest in the details of the struggle. Stories of the new flying engines being used in warfare began to filter through by this route. (Despite their use in East Africa, aircraft played no part in the Allied military campaigns in either Togoland or Cameroon.) Collections for presentation aircraft came into fashion in Gold Coast from August 1915, and—in Clifford's view—while many contributions were prompted by an instinctive desire to help rather than anything else, most donors had some idea of the military significance of their gift, and took pride in a machine built with their money and carrying the name of their community as taking an active part in the war.[35]

There was a certain amount of rivalry within the ARPS. At the start of the war, J. E. Casely Hayford initiated the Gold Coast Imperial War Fund from his base in the town of Sekondi, in Western Province, without consulting the rest of the leadership. Clifford agreed to act as Patron and made a personal donation. By December 1914 over £3,700 had been forwarded to London; and the Fund closed in August 1916 with a grand total of nearly £30,000—the vast majority of subscribers, according to Clifford, being natives of West Africa.[36]

Joseph Ephraim Casely Hayford, undated photograph
Northwestern University archive (public domain), Wikimedia Commons

The ARPS launched their own separate fund in September 1914 'to demonstrate in a practical form their gratitude and loyalty to His Majesty's Government', and called on the Fante Chiefs to act as its agents. Only £600 had been collected by March 1915. But the arrival of Wrench's popular Imperial Aircraft Flotilla scheme in August 1915 changed all that, and the ARPS' Fund very quickly attracted the £1,500 necessary for their first aeroplane, and two years' later, *Gold Coast Aborigines No. 2.*

It all started with the following circular that issued on 31 July 1915, addressed to British colonial officials in Ashanti and the southern provinces (but not the poorer Northern Territories):

> I am directed by the Acting Governor to forward you a copy of a letter and its enclosure from the Honorary Secretary of the Over-seas Club dealing with the formation of an Over-seas Aircraft Flotilla.
> The presentation to the Imperial Forces in the Field of an aeroplane or aeroplanes by the Colony, or its Dependencies or, possibly, by a particular Native Division or other section of the community and bearing their names is an attractive proposal and one of a nature to commend itself if not to the community at large at any rate to certain sections of

it, who would perhaps feel a sense of gratification and almost of personal service at the direct participation in the European conflict of a Gold Coast unit or units of the Air Service. His Excellency regrets, however, that at the present time it is not possible to make a grant for the purpose from the Public Funds, so that any action in the matter must be of the nature of private effort. It must be remembered also that the generous contributions to the War Fund render it highly undesirable that this fresh appeal should be unduly pressed if it is not likely to meet with a spontaneous response. Moreover, although the cost is not a large sum, representing roughly one day's pay of the Government service, it is rather the number of subscribers than the size of individual subscriptions that enhances the value of the response to an appeal of this kind. I am therefore to ask you to be good enough in the first instance to ascertain local feeling on the subject and to report the result to me by telegram at an early date so that if general sentiment is favourable Subscription List can be opened at various centres without delay.[37]

There was an early and enthusiastic response. On 5th August the Chief Commissioner Ashanti wired that the Coomassie Chiefs would like to guarantee at least one aeroplane called *Ashanti*. The movement was said to be attracting warm approval in Accra itself. The ARPS, based in Central and Western Provinces, forwarded a cheque for £1,500 from their War Fund before the month was out, attracting a comment from the Acting Governor that it was 'gratifying to find that the attractive proposal of the Overseas Club has had the effect of accelerating the practical progress of that fund'.[38] Their gift of *Gold Coast Aborigines No. 1* was the first plane presented, followed by a wave of apparent friendly community rivalry in fundraising, resulting in aircraft from Gold Coast entitled *Ashanti*; *Accra*; *Akim Abuakwa*; and *Ashanti No. 2* (in January 1916); *Manya Krobo*; and *New Juaben Settlement* (March 1916); *Kwahu District* (October 1916); *Western Province* (January 1917); *Accra No. 2* (April 1917); from the ARPS *Gold Coast Aborigines No. 2* (in May 1917); and finally *Ashanti No. 3* in August 1917.[39]

There may have been a certain amount of local politicking involved in the fad for aeroplanes bearing community names. For example, Ofori Atta, Omanhene of Akim (or Akyem) Abuakwa in Eastern Province, was the most influential traditional ruler in the Gold Coast from his accession in 1912; the British thought highly of his abilities and character.

Ofori Atta with entourage, after unknown photographer
© The National Portrait Gallery, London

He was in dispute during the First World War years with Mate Kole—the Konor, or ruler—of the Manya Krobo, another significant figure whom Ofori Atta replaced on the Gold Coast Legislative Council in 1916. They were contesting legal jurisdiction over cocoa-farming lands leased within Akim Abuakwa territory and known as the 'Krobo Plantations'.[40] Each ruler, therefore, had good reason to chalk up their loyalty with the British (though the British eventually declared themselves baffled by the issue and unable to make a ruling). Both were also distinguished by their efforts in 1917 to stimulate their subjects to volunteer for the Gold Coast Regiment by offering bounties—with limited success, for cocoa-farming normally paid better than soldiering.[41]

There was, on the other hand, co-operation as well as competition, and donors may simply have been motivated by a desire to be helpful in the war effort. Following an Ashanti civil war in the nineteenth century, Ashanti refugees from the dissident chiefdom of Juaben (Dwaben) had established the settlement of New Juaben on land purchased from Akim Abuakwa. They made up part of the shortfall for *Ashanti No. 3* in 1917, following an initial contribution of £1,000 by the Omanhene of Adansi (one of the most powerful Ashanti Chiefs); this was quite apart from already having presented their own BE2c in 1916 entitled *New Juaben Settlement*. The Overseas Club in London also covered a deficit of £600 for the aeroplane subscribed by Western Province; and in December 1917, the people of Quittah (Kwitta) District, near Togoland, forwarded £374 14s for the purchase of an aeroplane to be named *Awuna* (which may possibly never have seen the light of day under that name—but the amount was forwarded to the Overseas Club and probably put to the Overseas Aircraft Fund in general).[42]

At the start of Clifford's Governorship in 1912 the structure of the Legislative Council had remained unchanged for more than half a century. It comprised four officials and four 'unofficials' (six out of the total Europeans, with just two African nominees). In 1916 Clifford increased the African representation on the Gold Coast Legislative Council from two to six, all nominated, and halved the European membership. Three of the African representatives were Paramount Chiefs, chosen to represent the people of their region, and three were educated men representing the people of the coast.[43] The Paramount Chiefs were Ofori Atta, representing the Twi peoples; the Omanhene of Anamabu, Amonoo V, a Fante Paramount Chief of good education and strong character according to Clifford; and Sri II, the Fia of Awuna-Ga, the literate Chief of the Ewe-speaking peoples who, while not particularly well-educated, was described by Clifford as having been helpful to the Military Authorities during the invasion of Togoland.

The 'educated men' from the coast comprised three barristers: Thomas Hutton-Mills (one of the two African representatives on the previous council); Emmanuel Joseph Peter Brown, the Secretary of the ARPS; and Joseph Ephraim Casely Hayford. Clifford remarked of Casely Hayford that since there was no Paramount Chief who was both literate and otherwise suitable, so he had to select an educated native permanently resident to represent Western Province. (A statement to be taken at face value: for in his previous post as Colonial Secretary in Ceylon, Clifford persuaded the Colonial Office to reject modest reform proposals from Ceylon's educated elite as the unrepresentative opinion of denationalised politicians, when the true voice of the people was that of their traditional leaders.)[44] Moreover, 'though somewhat given to fomenting agitations against the Cape Coast Government' Casely Hayford strongly professed his loyalty. It was better, Clifford argued, for him to raise issues openly on the Legislative Council than 'relegated to the more or less hole-and-corner methods to which his energies are at present restricted.'[45]

At its opening meeting on 25 September 1916, the Legislative Council expressed gratitude for the increased representation, declared loyalty to His Majesty for victory in the war, and passed a resolution to increase the Gold Coast war contribution from the £80,000 voted in December 1914, to £200,000. This extra sum was to be paid by annual instalments of £20,000, arrears on account of 1915 and 1916 being charged to the revenue of the current year. The Legislative Council also expressed the hope that eight more aeroplanes should be presented to the Army Council as soon as possible.[46] And so it was that eight fighter planes were presented to the RFC, all of them FE2bs (*Gold Coast Nos. 1-8*), and then a further eight (*Gold Coast Nos. 9-16*) a year later. Photographs of these aircraft were hung in the Council Chamber.[47]

J. E. Casely Hayford served as a nominated member of the Gold Coast legislature from 1916 until 1926, and following the introduction of elective representation, as an elected member until he died. However, his path increasingly diverged from the rest of the ARPS leadership. Already influenced by newer and more radical strands of black political thought and the Pan-Africanist and Garveyist ('back to Africa') movements in America and the West Indies, he came in touch with such leading black political figures as W. B. Du Bois, Edward Blyden and Booker T. Washington; and he came into contact with Marcus Garvey through John E. Bruce, who acted as his literary agent in the US for *Ethiopia Unbound*.[48] After the war ended he organised a new movement, the Congress of British West Africa, which aimed to draw support from the coastal intelligentsia in all four British West African Colonies.

The first Congress was held in March 1920 in Accra, bringing together fifty-two delegates—six from Nigeria, three from Sierra Leone, one from Gambia, and forty-two from Gold Coast. It called for reform of the system of Crown Colony Government to include elective representation and appointments on merit to the civil service, and welcomed the principle of self-determination adopted by the Paris Peace Conference. But delegates also expressed concern over the arbitrary partition of former German Togoland and Cameroon between France and Britain, especially the division of the Ewe-speaking peoples, also living in Gold Coast, between the British and the French Togoland Mandates.

Renamed the National Congress of British West Africa it met another three times between 1923 and 1930: in Freetown, in Bathurst, and in Lagos (with attendances less skewed towards Gold Coast delegates). There was domestic opposition from ARPS' leaders, however, who stressed a national and not a pan-West African agenda; from Ofori Atta, who repudiated the claim by the western educated to speak on behalf of everyone else; and from colonial governments, including from Clifford, then Governor of Nigeria. It was a declining influence and collapsed after Casely Hayford's death in 1930.[49]

The Gold Coast's engagement with the Imperial Aircraft Flotilla scheme during the First World War was very striking. Its contributors covered a wide range of the social, cultural, and political spectrum of the Colony. It is all the more striking since there was a price slump of 50 per cent in cocoa prices in the early months of the war over those of 1913, and wartime shipping shortages created severe export problems;[50] at one point Ofori Atta tried unsuccessfully to charter a ship to carry produce out.[51] An export tax of 1s 3d per 60 lb. load first levied in 1916 had to be reduced to 1s per load in 1917, and by 1918 transport costs exceeded prices to farmers in some areas, so that they declined to harvest the crop.[52] Thus, despite the rapid growth of the pre-war years, the cocoa farmers of Gold Coast did not experience an era of smooth expansion during the Great War itself. Unlike many other areas that contributed significantly to the Imperial Aircraft Flotilla, Gold Coast did not do so out of swelling pockets from sustained good prices for strategic exports.

The original circular that went out from the Governor's Office in 1915 effectively instructed British officials to float the scheme widely, and invited them to open subscription lists if the response was positive. Possibly Clifford saw in Wrench's scheme a chance to involve both established Coast society, and inland Chiefs and communities in the common war effort. This, however, might be reading too much into it. For Sir Hugh Clifford was also himself an aviation enthusiast, and it eventually became his consuming hobby.

A tall, powerful, man, who enjoyed speed, first at the controls of motorcycles and automobiles, then aeroplanes, it is not certain when his interest first started; although there is one reference to a first flight made with Grahame-White at Hendon in 1912, the year he came out to Gold Coast.[53] Yet his activities as a pilot only came to the fore after he left in 1919. Clifford took up flying as a hobby in the early 1920s, and bought his own aeroplane in 1929 when it had become an obsession.

He filled successive British Governorships: in Nigeria; then in Ceylon 1925–27; finally he was appointed Governor of the Straits Settlements and High Commissioner to Malaya (where his colonial service career began, and where his heart lay). His flying exploits in his later career coincided with increasingly eccentric patterns of behaviour and an accelerating mental disintegration. Clifford had shown signs of strain and of depression during his Gold Coast days, but this was quite understandable. On top of his public duties (which included administrative responsibilities for Togoland after its conquest) he had the personal anguish of losing his only son on 1 July 1916, the first day of the Battle of the Somme, and then that September his younger and only brother, to whom he was close, also at the Somme.

Sir Hugh Clifford with family June 1915, including only son, who was to die at the Somme, Bassano Ltd.
© The National Portrait Gallery, London

Sir Hugh Clifford with his brother, Col. Henry Clifford, also to fall at the Somme, Bassano Ltd.
© The National Portrait Gallery, London

Some of the stunts in which he was involved made him a rather newsworthy British Governor. In October 1926, while Governor of Ceylon, he was catapulted from the deck of HMS *Hermes* in a seaplane.[54] He was by now also beginning to exhibit episodes of manic behaviour. In Singapore he took an interest in the development of commercial airlinks in the Far East and was a member of the Flying Club. His exploits included an attempt on his sixty-second birthday to take a seaplane up to 15,000 feet (he managed to ascend to 11,000 feet).[55] In 1927 onlookers were astonished to see him balancing on the wings of a French seaplane (in which he was to have been a passenger) in the waters of Singapore harbour for some two hours; but it could be explained as an attempt to prevent the craft capsizing in a squall.[56] He was catapulted on a demonstration flight in a seaplane from the deck of HMS *Vindictive* in March 1928; a week later he presided over Singapore Flying Club's AGM and it was announced that he was to fly one of the club's two new planes.[57]

Soon thereafter he underwent a complete mental collapse. Following his enforced retirement from the Colonial Service, he progressively declined into insanity. (Perhaps, it has been speculated, the long-term outcome of syphilis contracted in his youth.)[58] Victor Purcell, sinologist and former colonial official in Malaya, wrote of him landing his light plane on friends' lawns in England, and recounts an occasion on which Sir Hugh entertained the staff of the Athenaeum Club at a teashop in London 'turning up in what he called his "flying uniform", designed by Clifford himself, with a scarlet turban and adorned with medals and orders and the sash of the GCMG'.[59] For the final years of his life, until his death at the end of 1941, Sir Hugh Clifford was confined to a private nursing home in England.

Country	Approx. population	Number of planes
Gambia	Less than 200,000	4
Gold Coast	Less than 2 million	27
Nigeria	More than 18 million	4
Sierra Leone	Less than 2 million	1

Chapter 10:
The Rhodesias—friends in high places, a Grey area?

The course of the Aeroplane Fund in Southern Rhodesia could not have been in greater contrast. In October 1913 Evelyn Wrench had visited as part of his Overseas Club tour, with introductions doubtless courtesy of Albert Earl Grey, who was on the original board of directors of the BSAC, and BSAC Administrator of Southern Rhodesia 1896–97. Wrench's sister, Winifrede, wrote of their reception at Bulawayo Public Library as well attended, considering that no branch of the Overseas Club was then in existence there, 'but the people are much too aristocratic for us, officials of the Chartered company, land owners, mining magnates, and prosperous shop-keepers, some of them quite recently out from Home.'[1]

The country was still run by the BSAC, but its Royal Charter, granted in 1889, was due for renewal in 1914 and there was a strong chance at the time that the white settler community would press for self-government instead. In the event the Great War intervened, and the whole issue of self-government was shelved until October 1922 (when a referendum indeed opted for self-government rather than union with South Africa).[2]

Many of the older white residents of Rhodesia had already fought in wars. Rhodes established a privately paid paramilitary force, the British South Africa Police (BSAP) in 1890. That year, a Pioneer Column comprising some 500 BSAP and 180 settlers pushed into Mashonaland, establishing an administrative headquarters at a town they named Salisbury (now Harare). The expedition included eighty-four ox-wagons 'trained to maneuver with military precision', and was equipped with automatic weapons and seven-pounder guns.[3] The adventurer and big-game hunter, Frederick Selous, acted as scout. In 1893 the BSAC's first Administrator, Dr. Leander Starr Jameson, provoked the first Matabeleland War. He advanced into Matabeleland with a settler force armed with machine-guns and artillery and quickly defeated Lobengula's army, which suffered heavy losses.

These unprecedented deployments of white power in East and Central Africa were in stark illustration of what chartered company rule and a settler economy portended. The conquest was marked by settler participation and speedy South African economic expansion, so that the new settlement of Bulawayo in Matabeleland soon overtook Salisbury. There was no attempt to accommodate, and indeed little attempt to administer, the conquered: in the aftermath of the first Matabeleland War they were under what has been described as a frank military despotism by Jameson's white police.[4] The Ndebele monarchy was destroyed, and most of the kingdom's cattle looted—what was left was decimated by an epidemic of rinderpest.

In late 1895 Jameson mounted his abortive Raid into Transvaal in an ill-fated attempt to remove the Kruger Government. With most of Rhodesia's white police held captive in the Afrikaner Republic, the conquered Matabele secretly planned an uprising at home. It launched in March 1896 as Albert Earl Grey was on his way from South Africa to take over the position of BSAC Administrator from the disgraced and imprisoned L. S. Jameson. None of the settlers had any inkling what was brewing. By mid-April, Bulawayo was almost surrounded by rebel forces, and 145 whites including women had already been murdered in outlying areas.[5] Earl Grey eventually had to call for intervention by an imperial military force, sent up from South Africa; Cecil Rhodes, assisted by Earl Grey, negotiated Ndebele surrender in late 1896. The rising was primarily a reaction against forced labour and other abuses, and taxation, rather than the widespread alienation of land (the effects of which were not yet felt in matters of actual tenure).[6]

In the meantime, the majority Shona population rose up in June 1896, with dreadful consequences. While many white men—settlers and miners—were away fighting in Matabeleland, their families were vulnerable; many in outlying parts of Mashonaland were wiped out. There was an acute sense of treachery and betrayal. In Matabeleland, a large proportion of the Native Police (recruited by the BSAC from Lobengula's former crack regiments) had joined the revolt with their arms. But white vengeance was directed with most concentration against the Shona, whom they had previously considered to be victims of Ndebele raiding, and had not expected to rebel. Events were violent and desperate in nature. European casualties were higher than in any comparable revolt against colonial rule in Africa—about 10 per cent of the entire white population was killed.[7] It took many months to stamp out all resistance in Shona areas, and this was achieved by such extreme measures as dynamiting the caves in which the rebels were sheltering.

The Risings left a legacy of mutual suspicion and bitterness between black and white and exacerbated tensions between white settlers and the BSAC, held responsible for withdrawing BSAP personnel for the Jameson Raid. The BSAC for its part had to meet expenses of about £2.5 million for military operations, and also paid compensation of some £350,000.[8] (The Company paid no dividends to shareholders until 1924.) Following suppression of the revolts the BSAC reorganised, and extended a more systematic form of administration over the whole country; and in 1898 European settlers gained a measure of representation in Government through the establishment of the Legislative Council.

Another legacy of the 1896 Risings was new constraints on BSAC freedom of action consequent upon the Jameson Raid: it could no longer raise armed forces without the permission of the Colonial Office in London. By the time of the First World War, defence and security matters fell to the Commandant-General—a professional British soldier seconded to the BSAC, who worked with administrators on the ground but reported directly to the South Africa-based British High Commissioner, Lord Buxton.[9]

With the British declaration of war on Germany in 1914 there was a wave of 'patriotic' pressure from white public opinion to commit a Rhodesian force to the fighting in Europe, but this did not happen. As a commercial enterprise there was the problem for the BSAC of expenditure; a small force of volunteers (some three hundred strong) was eventually sent but absorbed into existing British units. Rhodesian military action from August 1914 therefore took place in Africa itself. Elements of the 1,150-strong BSAP were quickly sent to guard the bridge over the Victoria Falls from possible attack from German South West Africa (now Namibia). Subsequently the First Rhodesian Regiment was formed in late 1914, initially to help put down an Afrikaner rebellion inside South Africa against that country's military involvement in the war, but it was then diverted to the German South West Africa theatre until the surrender of Windhoek in early 1915, and later disbanded; the Second Rhodesian Regiment went straight to East Africa.[10]

Memories of the Risings of 1896–97 still fresh in the minds of the white settler community (and with black labour required on farm and mine) Africans were not recruited for military service until mid-1916, when the Rhodesian Native Regiment (RNR) was formed to reinforce the East African Front. The RNR also operated in areas of South West Africa nearest to Rhodesia, and in pursuit of von Lettow-Vorbeck's forces when they raided into Portuguese East Africa (Mozambique) and, in the closing phase of the war, into Northern Rhodesia (Zambia). In all 2,700 Africans served with the Rhodesian forces, initially Ndebele, but later recruited from labour migrants from north of the Zambezi.[11]

Most Rhodesians who fought in the Great War, however, were white and most of them fought on the Western Front and in British units. Most of them also made their own way to Europe to enlist independently as volunteers: by as early as October 1914, three hundred had already done so. Some 40 per cent of white adult males from Southern Rhodesia had seen military service, in Europe and in Africa, by mid-1916. Of the 5,716 white Rhodesians who served during the Great War there were more than 700 fatalities, or a 12 per cent death rate.[12] The number involved, and the cost in casualties for so small a community (about 28,000 strong), was significant: the reason for disbanding the Second Rhodesian Regiment in 1917 was simply that casualties had outstripped any capacity to replace them.[13]

While there was no Rhodesian Regiment as such serving in Europe, many gravitated towards the same British army units to enlist:

> Rhodesians had two superimposed images of their identity. They saw themselves as a British people, a part of the Empire and therefore obliged to fight for, and under, the Union Jack. But they also saw themselves as Rhodesians, a separate breed of Britisher. Even though at the start of the war few people could have been in the country for more than the twenty-four years it had existed as a nation since 1890, and though most had arrived more recently, a remarkably strong 'Rhodesian' identity had already formed. Men wanted to fight in purely Rhodesian units if they could and in their letters and diaries always identified themselves as Rhodesians first and Britons second ... There was a consciousness among the colonists that they were on show as Rhodesians and they wanted to do their infant nation proud.[14]

The biggest concentration was in the Second and Third Battalions of the King's Royal Rifle Corps (KRRC), and they had their own distinctive 'Rhodesian' war cry.

Hazelton Nicholl's identification with Rhodesia was then quite recent and still incomplete, but his personal memoirs show that he regarded himself as one of the British Empire's southern Africa pioneers. He was certainly a product of that empire. Born in Calcutta in 1882, his Scottish grandfather had built railways and bridges in British India, but the family moved to England when he was still an infant. At age fifteen he went to work as a clerk and bookkeeper in a City of London shipping firm with extensive India interests, until the sudden death of his father propelled him, aged twenty, to seek improved earning prospects abroad, the better to help his family.[15]

Securing a variety of employments in the Southern Rhodesian goldfields and mining camps, he eventually became part of a four-man Syndicate that leased two goldmines. Later, he participated in a traction engine transport business that carried supplies and copper ore to and from mines located in a tsetse fly-infested area of Northern Rhodesia and adjacent Katanga in the Belgian Congo—an area where draught animals could not survive and railways had not yet penetrated; however when his New Zealand partner in the enterprise died of black water fever he sold up and returned to gold mining.[16]

In Southern Rhodesia, the First World War placed great pressure on manpower, but at the same time brought a measure of economic prosperity. Britain's munitions factories devoured Southern Rhodesia's base metals: chrome, copper, tungsten, antimony; also asbestos. And gold production reached an all-time high in 1916.[17] However, Hazelton Nicholl had already disappeared, to start a new career in the British flying services. His interest began back in 1911, while on six months' home leave for George V's coronation and to see his family, when he witnessed the Round Britain air race start and finish at Hendon.[18]

Early 1914 found him in Bechuanaland (Botswana) as manager of a gold mine, in which he acquired interests. The outbreak of war, however, decided him on return to Britain to join up. He was precipitated into sudden action by the Afrikaner revolt in next door South Africa against military involvement in the war, which threatened rail-links, ('I couldn't leave my job until my relief arrived, but I actually climbed on board the train in my shirt sleeves about ten at night, thinking it might be the last train to get through before the raiders cut the line.')[19] At Cape Town he took a ship to England, determined to join the RFC. After a number of rebuffs he finally succeeded. He was then thirty-three years old, ten years older than the norm, and it is said that he owed his enlistment to the influence of his relative, Sir David Henderson, Director of Aeronautics at the War Office.[20]

As in other parts of the empire, local 'patriotic' funds sprang up. Colonel Raleigh Grey's Overseas Contingent Fund initially aimed to support the formation of a distinctively Rhodesian force for service in Europe, but switched to assisting volunteers for service in Northern Rhodesia, after what was hinted to have been pressure from the BSAC and Government.[21] When Wrench launched the Overseas Club Tobacco Fund in September 1914, Rhodesia responded with its own move to send raw tobacco directly through the BSAC; bought by the Rhodesian public, it was shipped in bags supplied by the tobacco industry. This turned additionally into a project to send cigarettes and pipe-tobacco in tins and packets advertising the attractions of Rhodesia as a destination for further white emigration. Tins of Navy Cut tobacco carried a map of Africa with the sun shining on Rhodesia and the slogan 'The World's Great Sunspot'; 'Sunspot' was also the name on Rhodesian cigarette labels.[22]

The Rhodesian Aeroplane Fund was established in response to a message from the British Foreign Secretary, Sir Edward Grey. It was outside his remit as Minister in the Asquith Government—Southern Rhodesia was the concern of the Colonial Office, not his Foreign Office, which was already lending its services to propagate Lord Selborne's Patriotic League of Britons Overseas (see chapter one). However, the Secretary of State for Foreign Affairs, driven by a sense of public duty rather than personal political ambition and progressively losing his sight, was depressed by the terrible conflict that had overwhelmed Europe and the world; he believed that there was little that he himself, or the Foreign Office and the British diplomatic service, could usefully do, apart from subordinating themselves to the task of serving the interests of the service chiefs.[23]

In the same way that he lent the services of the British Consular network to help raise money for a battle cruiser for the Admiralty (with little success), utilising his own connections to further the Imperial Aircraft Flotilla appeal in Southern Rhodesia could be interpreted as a displacement activity—an expression of diplomatic impotence to affect wider events. However, his intervention is also open to other interpretations. Quite apart from his third cousin and friend, Albert Earl Grey, Sir Edward Grey had other family links with Southern Rhodesia. Two of his cousins had been wounded while taking part in the Jameson Raid (of whom Colonel Raleigh Grey, injured in the foot, was one).[24] His younger brother, George Grey took part in the First Matabeleland War in 1893, and during the second, in 1896, raised a troop known as 'Grey's Scouts'; as brothers, George and Edward had been particularly close.

George Grey had mining interests in Africa. In 1908, Tanganyika Concessions was formed in London to explore and develop copper mines in Northern Rhodesia and neighbouring Katanga in conjunction with the Belgians, and George Grey led a small prospecting expedition based at Tete on the Zambezi in Portuguese East Africa. It became clear, however, that an essential prior condition for sustainable profitability was the establishment of a rail network. In 1910 George Grey returned to his previous haunts on the Copperbelt, with as his travelling companion none other than Hazelton Nicholl. (The latter, however, declined an invitation to accompany him further to the coast at Mombasa—fortunately for him, for George Grey was mauled by a lion, and died of his injuries in January 1911.)[25]

Sir Edward Grey had other more distant relations in Southern Rhodesia too.[26] Perhaps his family network gave the British Foreign Secretary an inside track on internal white Rhodesian politics. By going public in a local newspaper, the British Foreign Secretary could have been deflecting Colonel Raleigh Grey from ill-advised conspiracies. Whether then in a quasi-official capacity, or purely unofficially, in mid-1915 Sir Edward Grey was in cable communication with unnamed parties in Bulawayo about funds collected from the children of the country for a motor ambulance gift. According to the Bulawayo press, he proposed that Southern Rhodesia should cooperate with other parts of the empire in a scheme already approved by the British Government for the creation of an Imperial Aircraft Flotilla, adding that by increasing the sum to £1,500, they could purchase an aeroplane called 'Rhodesia'. Already one had been promised to the Overseas Club: theirs would be No. 2, *but the first locally named*.[27]

To this the reply went out that although it was not possible to alter the object of the Children's Ambulance Fund at that point, having contributed to this mission of mercy, it would be well to contribute to the offensive output of the empire. Indeed, the newspaper revealed, steps were already in hand for a private collection, and they were now issuing an additional appeal to the general public, and proposed that the Mayor of Bulawayo open a fund for this purpose.[28]

The private collection to which they alluded was in the hands of Sir Edward Grey's cousin, Colonel Raleigh Grey CVO, CMG, 'Rhodesia's self-appointed military expert and adviser',[29] who had led a British Army unit in the First Matabeleland War of 1893 and later commanded the Mafeking column that joined up with Dr. Jameson's forces. As an officer of the 6th Inniskilling Dragoons seconded to the Bechuanaland Border Police, he had been handed over to the British Government for trial—and sentenced to five months' imprisonment for his part in the Raid.[30] However, his CMG had been announced in the *London Gazette* on 1 January 1896 (that is, on the very eve of the Raid's ignominious end). After his spell in jail, he went on to command a unit of the Rhodesian Field Force in the Boer War.

Over time, respectability restored, Raleigh Grey had become an elected member of the Legislative Council for Salisbury; a director of several mining companies; and General Manager of the United Gold Fields Rhodesia Co., a subsidiary of Cecil Rhodes' Consolidated Goldfields of South Africa.[31] He was awarded the CVO in 1910 in his capacity as commanding officer of the Southern Rhodesia Volunteers. (In 1919, he was to be awarded the KBE. He was not alone in this return to social prominence: L. S. Jameson himself was sentenced to 15 months imprisonment but pardoned, served as Prime Minister of Cape Colony 1904–1908, and was, incidentally, also an Overseas Club Vice-President by his death in 1917. Another leader of the Jameson Raid, Colonel Harold Maxwell Grenfell, career British Army officer and nephew of Lord Desborough—see chapter eighteen—was later invested with the MVO and CMG.)

Officers of the Jameson Raid, 1895/6, with L. S. Jameson 4th from left standing, and Lieut. Colonel Raleigh Grey centre in belted jacket and light-coloured trousers
© The National Portrait Gallery, London

Colonel Sir Raleigh Grey in 1914, then a member of the Southern Rhodesia Legislative Council, courtesy of www.rhodesia.me.uk

Colonel Raleigh Grey advised the newspaper that about £1,200 had already been privately subscribed by a number of wealthy donors, but since a desire had been expressed to open the list to public subscriptions, these could be sent to the manager of the Standard Chartered Bank at Salisbury, or to Colonel Grey himself. It seems, however, that he had ruffled feathers through this initiative of his, and the Mayor of Bulawayo called a public meeting to discuss his action.[32] The restricted subscription list, on which the local press spotlight had been turned, was controversial, although the private donors in question remained anonymous. Even the Overseas Club in London was not fully in the picture, for Evelyn Wrench wrote to the Colonial Office to enquire:

> We understand some weeks ago from Lord Grey's cousin, Mr. Raleigh Grey, of Salisbury, Rhodesia, that he was collecting money for a Rhodesian Aeroplane, and I noticed a paragraph in the papers yesterday, saying that the sum of £1,500 has been cabled by the Administrator. Have you received this so far?

He explained that he only wished to keep a complete and accurate record.[33]

The Bulawayo press hinted at significance in the future choice of name for this Rhodesian presentation aircraft. For that which had come to head the Imperial Aircraft Flotilla list in London following its launch at Farnborough by Queen Alexandra, had become *No. 1 South Africa—presented by Residents in the Union of South Africa and Rhodesia*.[34] It replaced *Overseas No. 1*, as previously. Now, Colonel Raleigh Grey was known at the time to support the merger of Northern with Southern Rhodesia,[35] which was also a policy of the BSAC under its Administrator since late 1914, Sir Drummond Chaplin. Chaplin, former general manager of Consolidated Goldfields in Johannesburg, enjoyed the confidence and support of BSAC Directors and was expected to lead the merger of the two Chartered Company administrations.

Colonel Grey further supported the eventual union of 'Rhodesia', the new entity, with South Africa, a future aim also of the BSAC and presumably of Consolidated Goldfields. Many settlers in Southern Rhodesia on the contrary wanted self-government, no union with either Northern Rhodesia or South Africa, and good riddance to the BSAC. The suspicion may well have been that hidden away from public scrutiny, the name chosen by Raleigh Grey's anonymous donors would have contained a similar subliminal puff for political amalgamation. (However, the immediate project of union with Northern Rhodesia was to be finally blocked by the Colonial Office and members of the Rhodesian Legislative Council at the end of 1917.)[36]

The net result was the establishment of a Matabeleland Fund, throwing the collection open to public involvement (and the settlers in Mashonaland later joined in). The Fund made up the balance for *Rhodesia No. 1* and contributed £1,500 for a second aeroplane in August 1915, the Rhodesian press noting pointedly that residents of Mashonaland and Matabeleland had provided the money for *Rhodesia Nos. 1 and 2* that now occupied eleventh and twelfth place respectively on the Imperial Aircraft Flotilla listing. A *Rhodesia No. 3* was presented subsequently, in January 1916.[37] In addition, the gold-mining town of Gatooma (Kadoma), where Hazelton Nicholl had recently lived and worked, created their own Gatooma and District Aeroplane Fund, closing in October 1915 with a total of £1,554 9s 7d from three hundred donors.[38] (The very collection to which 2nd Lieutenant Hazelton Nicholl, RFC, referred in his letter that month to Charles Alma Baker in the FMS—see inset on page 44).

In early 1916, a report on the activities of *Rhodesia No. 2* appeared in the press. While on reconnaissance duty, the War Office wrote, its Lewis gun had fought off attacks by two German planes, one of them a Fokker firing through its propeller. The communication also sent thanks for *Rhodesia No. 3* and promised to forward a photograph to the donors via the BSAC Administrator's Office, and in due course notification through this same route of any 'good work' done by the machine.[39] A photograph of *Gatooma* (subscribed out of white gold miners' wages) was later sent and exhibited first in the window of the Rhodesia News Agency before being enlarged to adorn the boardroom of Gatooma Town Hall.[40]

Apart from the attraction of trying to spike Raleigh Grey's guns, there were other reasons for popular Rhodesian engagement with fundraising for aircraft. There were a number of airmen from Southern Rhodesia in RFC ranks from the early days of the war who wrote home, and whose letters were published. A large number of white 'colonials' were taken on by the RFC in 1917 to make good heavy losses of British pilots and observers. But in fact there had been Canadians, Australians, New Zealanders, South Africans and Rhodesians, not to mention first and second generation Britons resident in other countries throughout the empire and beyond, who enlisted in England after pilot training there from long before this. 'Colonials' who led an outdoor life were believed to be good shots, with sharp eyesight; but above all, the RFC maintained that good horsemen had the relevant natural skills to make good aviators, and it was known that the authorities were predisposed for this reason towards southern African applicants.[41]

From early in the war there were long waiting lists of British Army officers seeking to transfer into the RFC, but they could be ill spared by their units. 'Colonials' were usually civilians when they arrived in England, who then enlisted into the Special Reserve. Of the other trainees alongside him trying for their Aero Club certificates at Brooklands at the start of 1915, Nicholl recalled, there was another from Rhodesia, two from Canada and Australia respectively, and one each from the West Indies, Calcutta, Ceylon, Hong Kong, America, and Argentina. Only one of them was already in England when war was declared.[42]

Hazelton Nicholl graduated as a military pilot at the RFC's Central Flying School in April 1915. Crossing the Channel his plane developed engine trouble and nearly ditched in the sea, and for the first six months with No. 8 Squadron in France the biggest risk was engine failure and forced landings.[43] Seven of the twelve pilots in his squadron were killed in combat, in accidents resulting from shattered nerves or incompetence, or captured.[44] He remained with 8 Squadron until just after the Battle of Loos, before being sent back to England for a rest, and to become a flying instructor. At the beginning of 1916, Rhodesians learnt that he had been made a member of the French Legion of Honour.[45]

Rhodesian flying cadets occasionally mentioned presentation planes in their letters home. In August 1915, 2nd Lieutenant W. Gordon Pender wrote that he was one of about forty pupils at the Central Flying School in England, most of them from South Africa, Australia, and Canada. He planned, when fully qualified, to apply for one of the Rhodesian aeroplanes, but would be in competition with quite a large number of Rhodesians and other colonials in the RFC, and might not succeed.[46] Lieutenant A. R. Howe Browne was killed flying *Gatooma* soon after arriving in France in December 1915.[47] Since he hailed from Umvuma (Mvuma), about 100 miles to Gatooma's southwest, it shows that the RFC did on occasion match presentation aircraft with pilot provenance. But not everyone wanted to pilot a presentation plane. Another Rhodesian wrote of his monoplane training in 1916:

> They are much more difficult to land well with than the biplanes I have been flying. The type of machine being supplied by many of the Colonies and also Rhodesia [the BE2c] is a stable machine; that is, it flies itself without using one's hands to so great an extent as the others ... I prefer one that is not stable; then you know you have got to fly it all the time and it does not get a chance to get out of control.[48]

Most of these Rhodesian pilots, for most of the war, were scattered across different squadrons. The son of Frederick Selous, the big-game hunter and guide to the 1893 Pioneer Column, flew as a pilot with No. 19 Squadron RFC at the time of the autumn 1916 Somme offensive, as did the son of Lieutenant General David Henderson, Ian Henderson.[49] (Selous went missing, presumed dead, in January 1918; Ian Henderson died in a flying accident in Scotland in June the same year.) There was, however, one unit in particular in which Rhodesian pilots were clustered, and that was No. 44 Squadron RFC, formed for Home Defence in reaction to daylight raids on London in May and June 1917. An airman of 44 Squadron who later served as an MP in the Rhodesian Parliament, Captain G. H. Hackwill, was involved in what has been described as the first unqualified night combat in January 1918 when he shot down a German Gotha bomber headed for London.[50]

Arthur Harris, head of RAF Bomber Command in the Second World War and future Air Chief Marshal, had been living in Rhodesia for some six years when the Great War started and continued to identify with the country. He initially served with the First Rhodesian Regiment in German South West Africa, but in 1915 he shipped back to England, where (like Hazleton Nicholl) he was enabled to join the RFC by an influential relative. He flew as a fighter pilot in France and—as something of a night flying specialist—on Home Defence against Zeppelin and aircraft raids in the Midlands and London with 44 and 45 Squadrons.[51] Southern Rhodesian pilots of the RFC (and later the RAF) are thus remembered as playing a significant part in the country's wartime record. Other prominent Rhodesian airmen included Major Robert Hudson MC, who commanded an RFC squadron in France (like his brother, Major Frank Hudson MC) and later returned to become Southern Rhodesia's first Minister of Defence in 1924, and later Chief Justice.[52]

At the time of the First World War, however, there were two Rhodesias, both of them under BSAC Administration. The other was

Northern Rhodesia, today's Zambia, and before an adequate transport infrastructure made the mining of copper profitable in the early 1920s, an impoverished backwater that acted mainly as a labour reserve for the more prosperous Southern Rhodesia. Its role in the Imperial Aircraft Flotilla scheme was minuscule, a mere footnote, but revealing in its own way of another facet of wartime donor motivation. For in April 1915 a subscription list to the Overseas Aircraft Fund was circulating among European residents of Fort Jameson (christened in honour of L. S. Jameson, but known before and since colonial days as Chipata). It was then a small trading and service centre for European tobacco planters and BSAC officials just five miles from the Nyasaland border. Some of the local Angoni (or Ngoni) Chiefs of East Luangwa District expressed a desire to contribute, and were advised by their BSAC Native Commissioner to establish their own list, which he undertook to transmit to London along with any monies collected on their behalf.[53]

Like the Matabele of Southern Rhodesia, the Angoni had been cattle-keepers and cattle-raiders, with a stratified society and an army based on age-grade regiments. Like the Matabele also, the Angoni of Northern Rhodesia had been crushed (in 1898) by superior British firepower and suffered the loss of large herds of cattle. There were two other closely related Angoni groups living within neighbouring Nyasaland, from whom the Fort Jameson Angoni had been administratively separated by British colonial boundaries. All three Angoni communities were cultural cousins not only of the Matabele but also of the Swazi, the Nguni, and the Zulu peoples to the south—like them forged of the violence and great population upheavals set in train during the 1820s and 1830s by the rise in Natal of that unbalanced military genius, Shaka Zulu. Other Angoni lived over the borders in Portuguese East Africa.

Chiefs and sub-Chiefs of the Angoni settlements in Northern Rhodesia and in Nyasaland had been co-opted by British stipends as the cheapest agents of administration on the ground. During the First World War years the Paramount Chief of the Fort Jameson Angoni was Mpeseni Jele (or Jere), known as Mpeseni II. His grandfather, Mpeseni I, had been exiled by the British in 1898, allowed to return one year later, and died in 1901. (The British shot Mpeseni I's eldest son, the father of Mpeseni II, for rebellion.)[54] The defeated Angoni of Fort Jameson had been recruited into the ranks of the Northern Rhodesia Police (NRP), and during the Great War the NRP worked closely with the RNR in East Africa (which, like the KAR, had many Angoni recruits from Nyasaland in its ranks). Indeed, during 1914–18 the majority of Fort Jameson's Angoni youths were enrolled as soldiers and carriers on the Allied side.[55] For the Angoni fell squarely within that recognised warlike category of the day, and the British counted them amongst the so-called 'martial races' of this world that made the best soldiers.

There were widespread impressments of carriers for the East Africa campaign throughout the East and Central African region through the agency of Chiefs, involving many different ethnic groups, and leading in southern Nyasaland to a rebellion that broke out at the beginning of 1915. It was an armed protest with millenarian overtones known as the Chilembwe Revolt, and was put down after two months. It centred on Chiradzulu District, about 200 miles from Fort Jameson: a Nyasa, not an Angoni, area. John Chilembwe, a mission-educated African of mixed Nyasaland tribal origin, was enraged at the area's engulfment in a war of white colonial powers, which saw German forces attacking Nyasaland by lake and by land from the north. He protested especially at forced recruitment of carriers for the East Africa Front from people dying in British service yet still required to pay hut tax.[56]

It was the most significant protest mounted against the war in British Africa, though there were later and far more serious risings in French and in Portuguese African territories. In French West Africa the Volta-Bani War of 1915–16 was sparked by military conscription, and was viciously put down by French colonial troops with heavy civilian casualties.[57] The Portuguese raised all of 39,000 troops to serve in their East African colony during 1914–18, almost half of them black, and around 100,000 carriers.[58] The resultant Barue Rebellion of 1917 was lit by conscription and forced labour, and it spread along both banks of the Zambezi River.[59] It was incidentally suppressed with the assistance of local Angoni auxiliaries of the Portuguese military, who were paid 10s a month and allowed to keep all the booty that they could carry, including women and children.[60]

At the end of May 1915 the BSAC Administrator of Northern Rhodesia sent a dispatch to the British High Commissioner in South Africa enclosing the sum of £32 0s 11½d collected by a number of Angoni Chiefs and sub-Chiefs of East Luangwa District. They included Mpeseni II himself. Forwarded with his dispatch was a translation of the letter that they wished transmitted to HM King George V, along with a subscribers' list detailing their individual subscriptions. It read:

> King George, Our Chief.
> We have heard that you are fighting with the Germans there. We are sending you our help to do what is necessary to make a military airship. We are all sorrowful to find that this year there is not the good peace there was before: war is in all the country: we do not understand how God allows it. We shall rejoice if the little gift, which we, our people, and our friends, are sending, has been accepted.[61]

That same month, the East Luangwa District Native Administration bombarded BSAC headquarters with reports received from Angoni Chiefs of the Fort Jameson area alleging subversion of their moral and political authority by African mission teachers in the area. Against the recent background of the Chilembwe Revolt in neighbouring Nyasaland, BSAC officials were alarmed at the threat to the position of Chiefs entrusted with the task of recruitment for the imperial war effort.[62] Chiefs Maguya, Sayiri, and Madzimawe had jointly composed the letter covering the remittance.[63] The correspondence was laid before King George V, who asked for the Chiefs to be informed of his appreciation of this 'proof of their loyalty and goodwill.'[64]

The following month, the Fort Jameson Native Commissioner duly received a list compiled by Chief Madzimawe of six teachers whom he accused of adulterous relations with wives of husbands absent on military service, thereby undermining further recruitment of—presumably now wary—spouses. More seriously, Chief Sayiri alleged to a British official on a recruitment tour for the NRP in September that teachers were inciting young Angoni to refuse carrier service on the grounds that 'this is the white man's war. Let the white men fight it themselves.'

Despite the confiscation of weapons after the 1898 conquest, and consequent breakdown of the age-set regiments, there was most likely sufficient residual warrior ethos amongst the Angoni of Fort Jameson to give soldiering a definite appeal. Nonetheless, there was no glory at all in being an African carrier in the Great War, just the prospect of exhaustion and disease; and many African porters engaged in the East Africa campaign were literally worked to death and never returned home. So, while the Angoni Chiefs were probably taking the opportunity to diminish the domestic threat to their authority from Christian missions,[65] there is also a strong possibility that they may have been running into increasing problems in providing the necessary numbers of recruits, particularly for carrier service. Seen in this light, the aircraft contributions were probably calculated to impress the East Luangwa Native Administration with the donors' loyalty and willing support in the war effort: a 'charm offensive' of sorts. They may well have wished to cover their backs against British suspicions of a lack of zeal.

As suggested in the Administrator's dispatch to London, the War Office did supply photographs of an aeroplane (a BE2c) to the donors; in fact, the War Office sent out twenty copies for distribution. Yet the suspicion must be that the recipients were even more enchanted with the British official witch-hunt against African mission-teacher 'subversives' that ensued from their complaints. It was sharpened by the fact that the dominant mission in the Fort Jameson area was that of the Dutch Reformed Church, which was held suspect by the British of involvement in the Afrikaner revolt of late 1914 against South Africa's military invasion of German South West Africa and conscription.

Country	Approx. population	Number of planes
Southern Rhodesia	Less than 900,000, of which fewer than 30,000 whites	4
Northern Rhodesia	Less than 900,000	-

BE2c 2119 *Gatooma*—probably the plane in which Rhodesian pilot A. R. Howe Browne died in a dogfight soon after arriving in France, courtesy of Cross & Cockade International Archive

BE2c 2578 *Rhodesia No. 3*; Overseas Club symbol of a circumscribed S within a circle showing clear on the rudder,
courtesy of Cross & Cockade International Archive

Chapter 11:
The Basuto nation, the British sovereign, and 25 Sopwith Camels

When the Union of South Africa came into being on 31 May 1910 it was as a self-governing Dominion of the British Empire and a political union of British and Boer Provinces. Two precepts of British colonial doctrine had long been in conflict with regard to South Africa. The first was devolution of authority and the eventual self-government of (white) settler colonies, and the second, the responsibility on the part of the metropolitan power to protect the interests of the natives ('trusteeship'). The inability to square a circle *vis-à-vis* South Africa when the natives were in a majority in the land, but the white settler minority was large and powerful, and more than half of it Afrikaans-speaking, made British policy shifts contradictory, and confusing.

The dominant concern in Whitehall after the end of the Boer War was to conciliate the two former belligerent white populations, and coloured and African interests were subordinated to this end. Consequently, in 1910 the existing 'colour-blind' franchise was frozen to the Cape, and only white representatives were to be present in the new parliament. Jan Christiaan Smuts, Cambridge-educated lawyer, former Boer General, and recent State Attorney of Transvaal, had been instrumental in framing and negotiating the Constitution, on which English-speaking and Afrikaans-speaking politicians from all four provinces, Transvaal, the Orange Free State (OFS), the Cape, and Natal, agreed to unite.

The new 1910 Constitution also provided for the incorporation of Bechuanaland, Swaziland, and Basutoland (today's Lesotho) into the Union of South Africa—but with certain safeguards regarding notably native land, and without a fixed timescale. The safeguards were introduced in the form of a Schedule to Section 151 of the Constitution, for which Lord Selborne was largely responsible (in relation to Basutoland, it specified that in the case of transfer it would be unlawful to alienate *any* land).[1] Pledges were also given in the British Parliament that the wishes of the inhabitants would be taken into account before any transfer took place. Basutoland was not reassured however, and there were rumours that the country would be seized and divided up into Boer farms.

In March 1914 Lord Selborne addressed the African Society in London on the question of Basutoland: he began by outlining some of its distinctive features. Its highest peak stood at 12,000 feet, but although its flocks and herds were sent to the high valleys in summer, human settlement was at the level of 4-6,000 feet. Perhaps 70,000 out of a population of 350,000 were Christians. The British authorities, Lord Selborne said, supported the Paramount Chief in retaining tribal customs and administering civil law, and they always tried to work through the Chiefs:

> Intellectually, the Basuto are head and shoulders above any other native tribe and they have always shown that they have an excellent fighting capacity, although they were never aggressive in the sense that the Zulus certainly were... the Basuto will never give any trouble, unless they are misgoverned.

His concern in introducing safeguards into the draft South African constitution for such future time as Basutoland should pass from under the immediate responsibility of the Imperial Government, he declared, had been that it should not be subject to the Parliamentary system of South Africa, since the Basuto, who would be unrepresented in that Parliament, would have no control over the use that would be made of their taxes.[2] (The truth probably being that Lord Selborne, from his time in South Africa in the aftermath of the Boer War, had developed a soft spot for Basutoland and the Basuto.)

An exceptionally able and subtle leader, Moshoeshoe—Moshesh to the British—had laid the first foundations for a Basuto (or Basotho) nation in the early nineteenth century. It was a time of great turbulence and danger stemming from the subjugation and violent displacement of clans by the Zulu expansion in Natal, which pushed desperate armed bands over the Drakensberg range of mountains. His Sesuto-speaking people exploited good agricultural land between the Caledon and Orange Rivers, but in the 1820s Moshesh, a sub-Chief, established a new centre of settlement on a defensible mountain plateau: Thaba Bosiu ('mountain of the night') was protected by steep passes that could be sealed by boulders, and he incorporated refugees willing to man defences, and established alliances with potential attackers, and his community grew. Then, in the middle decades of the nineteenth century, the evolving Basuto nation came into danger from another quarter—pioneering Boer farmers equipped with effective firearms moving into the fertile lowlands.

Thus began Moshesh's alliance with the British at Cape Colony in search of support and protection. In 1868, after a Boer blockade of

Thaba Bosiu lasting several years had brought the Basuto to the verge of starvation, Britain annexed Basutoland (in part for their own geopolitical reasons). The settlement arrived at formalised the Basuto loss of arable land to the Boers, and the shallow Caledon River became Basutoland's western border with Boer territory. By the time of the First World War, Basuto Chiefs were still referring to the events of 1868 as pivotal to their survival as a nation, in consequence of the alliance between 'Moshesh the Wise' and Queen Victoria, despite nonetheless continuing to claim lands lost to the Free Staters. Thereafter, the country's boundaries were essentially set, so that after 1910 it existed not only entirely surrounded by a unified South Africa, but bordered in the west by its most aggressively 'Boer' province, the OFS.

With the loss of much of their arable land, the Basuto became increasingly dependent on wage labour on Free State farms and in the mines of the Transvaal. They also moved further up into the highlands in pursuit of pasturage; overstocking and soil erosion gradually resulted over time. They adapted to a more difficult environment and harsher winters, and their hardy mountain ponies became not only the principal mode of transport, but also a standby for war service. The nation did go to war again, in 1880–81, this time against the British Cape Colony authorities under which care they had been placed, and won. That administration had unwisely attempted to confiscate the guns obtained by individual Basuto from the proceeds of their labour on farm and in mine. At the request of Cape Colony, Great Britain resumed direct control of Basutoland in 1884.

There was a great deal of ambiguity in the manner that Basutoland was administered thereafter. After 1884 the country was perhaps a British ruled Crown Colony in legal terms, but was treated (more or less) as a Protectorate.[3] Even the Colonial Office, as well as its officials in South Africa and Basutoland, was confused about its status.[4] Under Moshesh (who died in his eighties in 1870) and his descendants, all adult male Basuto had had the right to speak freely at a gathering of the whole nation called a *pitso*. This eminently democratic institution would no doubt have been rendered impractical over time by population growth and expansion into more remote upland areas. But in 1903 the *pitso* was marginalised by the creation of a new institution, the Basutoland National Council (BNC), established to facilitate dialogue between British colonial officials and the Basuto Chiefs—a sort of indirect rule;[5] the *pitso* becoming a largely ceremonial assembly at which proclamations were read, and the visiting British High Commissioner from South Africa (Lord Buxton during 1914–20) addressed large public gatherings.

In its final form the BNC was the creation of Sir Herbert Slolely, Resident Commissioner to Basutoland for thirteen years from 1903, of whom the *Bloemfontein Post* once commented dismissively that he had never served any part of his working life outside southern Africa, and his little office in Maseru crowned with a Union Jack constituted 'the only visible symbol of sovereignty in all that broad land.' Born in Calcutta in 1855, his southern Africa career began with the Cape Rifles but then settled into long service in Basutoland, first with the Basutoland Mounted Police, then with the administration.[6]

The BNC comprised all the most senior Chiefs. It had been given statutory force as an advisory body in 1910, with ninety-four members nominated by the Paramount Chief (who presided over it) and no more than five members nominated by the British Resident Commissioner.[7] Probably no other representative body in a British Crown Colony could equal this size of local presence.[8] Although unelected, the BNC was more than just a sounding board. While Basutoland also lacked the usual Crown Colony institutions of Executive and Legislative Councils, the BNC drafted or re-stated customary law, and also amended it, effectively legislating, though there was no statutory basis for such 'laws'.[9]

The upshot of all this is that the British more or less left the Basuto Chiefs alone to run internal matters for much of the time, especially so since the books balanced and the budget did not go into deficit—indeed, there was usually a healthy surplus, much of it generated by labour contracts to South Africa. The Chiefs were accordingly comfortable with their Resident Commissioner, to the extent of having even liked and respected him; though to one Johannesburg lawyer who crossed his path in later years, he was overly biased in favour of the native authorities, and inured from his long years in Basutoland to some very tough methods of tribal justice.[10] (Such, indeed, was the position achieved by the Basuto Chiefs in Slolely's time that popular protest later led to reforms to reduce both their number and their powers.)[11]

The BNC's debates were recorded, giving the Colonial Office in London a much greater insight into Basuto concerns than was the norm in those parts of the British Empire lacking the mechanism of an elected parliament. Such records show that at the time of the Great War the Chiefs still clung to the alliance with Great Britain begun by

Moshesh as a vital matter of national survival. They seem to have regarded the relationship as somewhere between an alliance of equals and a duty of loyalty towards the British Crown of the kind required by a liege lord of a (willing) vassal state. But this was a time when their protector, Great Britain, was locked in a most grave world conflict, and counted amongst its close allies the Union of South Africa led by Louis Botha and Jan Smuts (both admired by the British as war leaders)— that is, the enemy from which the Basuto themselves wished above all to be protected, and into whose folds Basutoland was threatened with envelopment at some unknown, but possibly imminent, future date.

There was an unusual degree of heed paid to Basuto opinion in official circles in London. Firstly, as an unconquered people the Basuto benefitted from contemporary British regard for 'martial races', combined with apprehension that if pushed, they just might go to war again. This was no small threat, given the difficulties of the terrain, and the reputation that Basuto horsemen enjoyed for daring and cunning. A 1910 estimate hazarded that in the case of a call to war, the nation would be able to field at least 60,000 armed men, most of them mounted, and mobilise them very quickly; though they would be individually equipped with guns of widely varying degrees of effectiveness and antiquity.[12]

Finally, because of Moshesh's strategy of wooing missionary support (in large part, because he believed this would aid the search for modern weapons) the Protestant Paris Evangelical Mission Society (PEMS) was a long established institution in the land, to which it had brought western education and a printing press. Literacy was not uncommon, and there were about 22,500 children enrolled in mission schools in 1914–15.[13] Labour migration had also brought the Basuto into contact with modern ways; and there was already a tradition of free speech and debate. In other words the Basuto were regarded as both 'traditional' and 'progressive', and the British Establishment liked this. Moreover, they were vocal in their loyalty to the British Crown and this was pleasing.

African Congresses led by western-educated Africans had come together in South Africa in protest against the Act of Union. In January 1912, at Bloemfontein in the OFS, they agreed to form the South African Native National Congress (SANNC)—a forerunner of the African National Congress (ANC) and a pan-South African movement. Delegates from Basutoland were believed present at that Convention, representing the BNC and the then Paramount Chief, Letsie II (who died just one year later).[14] The period 1912–14 was one of African protest in the OFS bordering Basutoland that included a women's anti-pass campaign at Bloemfontein and Winberg; and the SANNC was actually in session at Bloemfontein in August 1914 when news came in of the outbreak of war in Europe. They terminated the work of their delegation to Britain, dispatched just the previous month in order to protest the Union's Land Act of 1913, and suspended further political agitation in South Africa until the end of hostilities.[15]

Basutoland was also seriously affected by several major developments in the OFS. In late 1913, there had been a large-scale strike at the Jagersfontein diamond mine, and serious rioting by many of the 8,000 Basuto workers in protest at the kicking to death of one of their number by a white miner; a number of strikers were shot dead by troops sent in from Bloemfontein to contain the revolt.[16] The country was itself already suffering the influx of Basuto sharecroppers displaced in great numbers from white farms in the OFS by the effects of the South African Land Act. (This was a second Basuto displacement from land originally lost to the Boers in the wars of the mid-nineteenth century.) 1913 was also the year that a new Paramount Chief came to power in Basutoland: This was Griffith Lerotholi, a recent Catholic convert, who turned out to be quite a devout Christian. (A large expansion of the Church followed, and Catholic converts rose from 6,000 in 1896 to about 50,000 in 1930.)[17]

The response of the new Paramount and the Basuto Chiefs to the outbreak of war in Europe was to vehemently reaffirm loyalty to the British Crown (and only the British Crown—there was largely silence about the British Empire as such, which of course now included a unified South Africa as a self-governing Dominion). The Colonial Office was well aware of feelings on this issue. In August 1914, a Governor General's Fund was established in the Union of South Africa by the wife of Prime Minister Louis Botha as a national fund for the relief of distress of all kinds caused by the war; the separate Prince of Wales' Fund was to be devoted solely to the relief of distress in the British Isles. In Basutoland, Paramount Chief Griffith Lerotholi launched a war fund, which on the advice of Resident Commissioner Sloley was limited to a shilling a head—taking into account the difficult economic conditions in the country, due to poor weather, the influx of displaced Basuto sharecroppers, and war disruption to the trade of Basuto wool; in addition, suspension of operations in the South African diamond mines had laid off migrant Basuto miners (gold production was not interrupted).[18]

The Press Bureau in London, always glad to publicise such gestures, carried Griffith's preliminary message transmitted via Lord Buxton:

> With regard to this war which I hear exists between His Majesty the King George V and the Germans, I ask whether as my King is engaged in fighting his enemies I his servant will be doing well to keep aloof watching him being attacked by enemies.
> As I am unable to be with my King in person, I beg to know whether I may show my loyalty and the loyalty of the Basutos to His Majesty the King by giving monetary assistance, to be raised by calling on each Mosuto to pay a sum of one shilling as a contribution to the funds now being raised for relief of sufferers by the war.
> The Basuto and myself are grieved at seeing our King attacked by enemies when we his servants cannot assist him.[19]

The Press Bureau added that the Government had gratefully accepted the offer.

The message was submitted to the King and also printed for Parliament. At the insistence of the Secretary of State for the Colonies, Lewis Harcourt, the money eventually raised (£2,861) went to the Prince of Wales' Fund in 1915, and not the Governor General's Fund:

> I think Griffith wants to make this gift to *the King* & not to the *Union*. We should therefore suggest to Lord Buxton that the money should come *here*—not on account of its *amount*, but because of its *origin & intention*.[20]

Both sides during the Boer War had advised the Basuto that it was a 'white man's conflict' and did not concern them, and Basutoland had consequently stayed neutral. However this did not prevent them from furnishing the British army with several thousand ponies and valuable military intelligence; during the siege of Wepener on the OFS side of the Caledon River, several hundred mounted and armed Basuto prevented Boer troops from crossing the border in order to enfilade the British garrison.[21] Similarly, they were informed again in 1914 that this was a 'white man's war' in which they would not be required to fight. However, the neighbouring OFS was the epicentre of the Afrikaner 'Maritz Revolt' against military intervention in neighbouring German South West Africa, and there was at least one attempt by a rebel leader to canvass support from Basuto Chiefs, but with nil success.

In April 1915, Paramount Chief Griffith Lerotholi led a deputation of thirty Basuto Chiefs to Cape Town, where he delivered an address to Lord Buxton containing fulsome expressions of loyalty, to be met with British assurances of the preservation of Basuto land and commendation for their conduct during the rebellion in the Union—a probable indication that the Basuto were on the alert and passing on information.[22] In London, King George V read Griffith's address in Cape Town 'with interest and satisfaction.'[23]

More expressions of Basutoland's loyalty were to be brought to the King's attention, like those contained in Lord Buxton's despatch on his first visit in August 1916. A crowd of 15–20,000 greeted him at a *pitso*, about 12,000 of them mounted. This was fewer than expected because drought had reduced the stamina of their ponies and made it difficult for those coming from a distance to secure enough water for the journey; only a third of the usual crop was reaped in some districts in 1915–16, and still less in others.[24] The Colonial Office reported that the King 'was pleased to receive very graciously the message of loyalty and devotion to which the Paramount Chief gave expression ... His Majesty was also pleased to direct that his thanks should be conveyed to the Paramount Chief for his message of condolence and sympathy in the loss which the Empire has sustained in the death of Lord Kitchener.'[25] However, the loyal Basuto were soon to be presented with a dilemma.

At the beginning of 1916, Basutoland lost their Resident Commissioner, Herbert Sloley, to retirement. A farewell address by Basuto government employees regretted his departure at that crucial juncture:

> While there is still before us the dreaded question of the incorporation of our territory within the Union ... regarded by us, the Basuto, as the fording of a swollen stream, whose drifts are unfamiliar, which, were our wishes to be done, we would be glad to be with you, when we crossed it.[26]

In his place they got Robert T. Coryndon instead, whom they did not take to at all. He arrived from his previous position as Resident Commissioner to Swaziland disappointed at not getting a higher posting, but keen from the outset to let the Basuto know who was in charge. Educated Basuto elite and Chiefs alike regarded him as unbending and dictatorial, and he reciprocated their lack of warmth.[27] Coryndon was South Africa-born (from the Cape) and a protégé of Cecil Rhodes and one of his twelve original so-called 'Apostles'; he was a muscular expansionist imperialist who saw Basutoland's future as part of the Union of South Africa. (Luckily for all concerned he stayed less than two years, receiving news of his promotion to Governor of Uganda in October 1917.)

In Coryndon's first address to the BNC, he appealed to the memory of his direct predecessors and other members of the British administration (all better regarded by the Basuto than he, as he was no doubt aware):

> The High Commissioner [Buxton] spoke of the war. We feel this Great War very little in Basutoland. The people pay a little more for their blankets [worn as wraps or cloaks against the cold], but still you would hardly know there was a great war in which the whole English people were fighting unless you were told so. But it is very serious. There are few Englishmen here who have not lost a friend either wounded or killed in this war, and many have lost relations. There are twenty-two officials of this Administration, including Dr. Long, now serving in the war in Europe. One of Sir Marshal Clarke's sons was killed whilst fighting in an aeroplane, also one of Sir Godfrey Langdon's sons has been killed in France and another son has been wounded. The son of Sir Herbert Slolely, the boy whom you all remember in Maseru, is now nearly old enough to go to fight for his country. It is probable that he also will join in the war next year. And as regard money, the cost is very heavy indeed. Almost every white man in the country is paying some part of his pay every month to the war. Every person who is loyal to the King should do all he can to assist him. If one cannot help by fighting for the King one can help by paying money to the King for the war. But I wish to make it quite clear that any contribution of this nature must be entirely voluntary.[28]

The Chiefs reminded him that they had been told that this was a white man's conflict, in which they were not asked to fight, but that they all sincerely wished for a British victory:

> We sympathise with Lady Clarke and Sir Godfrey who have lost their sons, but we praise these young men because they have died for their country. We have a saying that every man should die by the spear. We still hope that our King shall come out victorious in this war.

Nonetheless, the message Coryndon's words had most probably conveyed to his audience was that the proceeds of the shilling war fund did not suffice, and they had to do better than that.

Paramount Chief Griffith Lerotholi responded by imposing a *sethabathaba* throughout the country—a traditional mechanism invoked by Chiefs when local or national projects needed to be financed. Individuals were customarily expected to pay according to their means. However, in this case each adult male was required to contribute an animal, or £3 in cash.[29] His intention was apparently to prove Basuto loyalty directly to King George V. In February 1917, £40,000 was forwarded to Lord Buxton as the Basuto national contribution to Imperial War Funds. The British press release (with no sense of irony) described the gift as 'entirely voluntary and unconditional, and its collection owed nothing to any kind of control by the Government.' The total was made up of 4,400 cattle, 5,754 small stock, and £21,565 in cash.[30] It included a personal contribution of £100 from Griffith himself. A further Basutoland contribution of £10,000 was sent in September 1917, the long delay possibly due to the exceptionally severe southern African winter that year, which in late July had left passage blocked by snowdrifts fifteen feet deep in parts of the country.[31]

Hardly was collection of the national levy underway when the Chiefs were required to supply Basuto recruits for the South African Native Labour Contingent (SANLC), established to remedy the severe shortage of manpower at the Front and in French ports in the wake of the Somme offensive. (A proposal to ship Basuto to England to work in the munitions factories was dropped in the face of trade union objections at the very beginning of 1917.)[32] Recruitment began in South Africa, Bechuanaland, Swaziland and Basutoland in September 1916, and over 20,000 men from those countries were to go to France in SANLC units by 1918. However, the *sethabathaba* had been imposed *in lieu* of war service, since the Basuto had been told they were not required in the white man's war, and the level of recruitment fell well below expectations. Coryndon also believed that the Chiefs were deliberately dragging their feet, and there may very well have been truth in this too, for the SANLC was organised and trained in South Africa, and placed under the control of South African officers.

By the time the first SANLC contingent shipped out to France in October/November 1916, Basutoland had supplied only a fifth of the number of recruits expected. Then on 21 February 1917 the *Mendi*, a transport ship, was rammed and sank off the Isle of Wight, killing 615 of the second wave of SANLC who had embarked at Cape Town, among them at least twenty-five Basuto. In landlocked Basutoland, where drowning was regarded as a particularly horrible death, this did little to encourage further recruitment. In order to overcome the resistance of those who regarded the SANLC as a South African scheme, the British military authorities also promised that Basutoland companies would be treated as separate entities, under British command, and not under South African control.[33]

Herbert Slolely was approached in his retirement to advise on the selection of British officers and to undertake periodic welfare visits to Basutoland's labour contingent in France.[34] This brought him into close association with the former Aborigines' Protection Society of London. Launched in 1836 and dominated by Nonconformist Christians, especially Quakers, the Society published accounts of injustices against native peoples in the British Empire and lobbied the Colonial Office in defence of their rights, especially over white settler threats to their lands. It had supporters in Government and Parliament, and was close to a number of Governors and Administrators overseas, as well as enjoying strong links with resident missionaries such as those of the PEMS in Basutoland, who alerted them of colonist encroachment on Basuto territory.[35]

Known as the Anti-Slavery and Aborigines' Protection Society after its merger in 1909 with the larger and older British abolitionist body, during 1913 it had staged a London conference on Basutoland addressed by the country's first Resident Commissioner, Sir Godfrey Lagden, and by leading PEMS missionary, Edouard Jacottet. During the Great War itself, the Society lined itself up with the war effort. It published propaganda materials and gave wartime lectures that denounced German administrative practice in its colonies, and atrocities such as the genocide in German South West Africa that followed the Herero Rebellion of 1904; and it claimed credit for the loyalty of Britain's African and Asian colonies.[36] In 1916, it also set up a Committee for the Welfare of Africans in Europe, which organised the provision of warm clothing, recreation materials, and so on to the SANLC.[37] Chaired by Lord Selborne, it included several MPs. Herbert Slolely, who was involved in welfare visits to France on behalf of the War Office aimed particularly at the Basuto component, praised their work.[38]

Griffith and the BNC were uneasy about the relative failure of recruitment, lest the British should count it an exhibition of disloyalty. Two Basuto Chiefs nominated by Griffith Lerotholi finally travelled to France at the end of 1917, and were met by Sloley in London.[39] One Basuto member of the SANLC in France recalled that the Chiefs included in their party forty of their followers who had volunteered as an example to others. Soon after their arrival, all Basuto were extracted from their existing SANLC units and dispatched to Le Havre, where they were grouped together under British command.[40] This was late in the day, however, and less than 1,500 from Basutoland had served in SANLC ranks by the time it was wound up in early 1918.

Griffith and the BNC need not have worried overmuch about the recruitment issue. What had made an impact in Great Britain was the publicity given to the first *sethabathaba* gift of £40,000 sent in early 1917, together with a loyal message to the sovereign from Griffith and the Basuto nation. Lord Buxton had suggested that the King might indicate the purpose to which it was to be devoted: 'It will no doubt give satisfaction if sum could be applied to some specific military object.'[41] Accordingly the Army Council was consulted, and King George V asked to approve their suggestion that the £40,000 'be used for purchasing a number of aeroplanes, this being, in the opinion of the Army Council, the most tangible and popular form of gift at present.' He did indeed 'quite approve' the Army Council's suggestion;[42] and thus the Colonial Office was able to announce that the gift of £40,000 had been warmly acknowledged on behalf of His Majesty, who had approved its use for that very purpose.[43]

The Paramount Chief was therefore invited to submit names for inscription. The list he provided is telling, comprising as it does the main Chiefs in line of descent from Peete the grandfather of Moshesh (Moshoeshoe), and ending with the mountain stronghold of Thaba Bosiu. The list ran as follows: *Peete*; *Mokhachane*; *Moshoeshoe*; *Letsie I*; *Lerotholi*; *Letsie II*; *Griffith*; *Makhaola*; *Bereng*; *Maama*; *Molapo*; *Jonathan*; *Masupha*; *Lepoqo*; *Majara*; *Makhabane*; *Posholi*; *Mohale*; *Basuto*; *Thaba Bosiu*.[44] Twenty Sopwith Camels were inscribed accordingly, half going to the RNAS and half to the RFC.[45] Then in September 1917 it was announced that HM the King had expressed 'high appreciation' of the further gift of £10,000 from the Paramount Chief and Basuto nation, to be used, once again, for the purchase of aircraft. A further five Sopwith Camels were inscribed with the names *Api*; *Masupha II*; *Nkwebe*; *Matheadira*, and *Theko*.[46]

The Basuto were already well aware of the role of aeroplanes. Back in September 1911, pioneering South African aviator John Weston (who owned a farm in the OFS) staged a flying display before a ticket-buying audience at Bloemfontein racecourse. Before a crowd of some four thousand from all over the OFS, Transvaal and Basutoland, Weston carried out four successful circuits in his 50-hp. Bristol biplane, attaining a height of about 120 feet.[47] There will almost certainly have been Basuto observers of this performance—not among the ticket-holders inside the enclosure, but outside it.

'A military correspondent' writing in the *Bloemfontein Post* in mid-1912 even foresaw a role for aeroplanes in regional reconnaissance—

over the mountainous terrain of Basutoland, for example. (And it would be surprising had local Basuto readers of the paper not brought the content of this particular article to wider notice on the other side of the border.) Bloemfontein Town Council granted Weston a site for a flying school at the very beginning of 1913, and he was in discussion with South African Defence Force (SADF) commander General Lukin about military aviation training, but money was lacking. In February, however, a fire at Weston's farm at Brandfort destroyed his workshop and all his premises and plant. In the event, Weston's rival, Compton Paterson, established South Africa's first military flying school at Kimberley instead, on a site provided by De Beers.[48]

In November 1918, four thousand Basuto gathered outside Maseru to hear Resident Commissioner Colonel Garraway (Coryndon's successor) read the terms of the Armistice. Translated into Sesuto, it took 35 minutes. The audience reportedly paid close attention and seemed fully to grasp its import. Referring to the Basuto nation, one Chief reminded the meeting that the Sovereign had saved their nation when they were cornered as the Germans were now, and Basutoland 'would not be in existence if their father Moshesh had not asked Queen Victoria to take them under their wing.'[49]

At their next session in May 1919, the BNC proposed that the Paramount Chief visit England to convey to His Majesty the nation's great joy at his victory, as well as their desire to remain outside the Union of South Africa. One speaker pointed out that despite all its horrors and tremendous bloodshed, it was through the recent Great War that small nations were promised their right of self-determination, and this presented them with the opportunity to lobby against the incorporation of their country into the Union.[50]

This was to be the first ever visit by a Basuto Paramount Chief to England. Colonel Garraway was enthusiastic, and even managed to steer Griffith away from his desire also to visit Rome (lest George V be upstaged by the Pope). Griffith was, however, eventually allowed to include his (French) Catholic priest, Father Valat, in his party, for purposes of confession and sacrament.[51] The party, which included twelve Chiefs and two interpreters, arrived at Southhampton on 18 October 1919.[52]

WITH THE PARAMOUNT CHIEF, GRIFFITH LEROTHOLI, IN THE CENTRE: BASUTO CHIEFS AT SOUTHAMPTON.

Illustrated London News, 25 October 1919, © Mary Evans

A large crowd assembled to greet them at Waterloo Station, where onlookers were surprised to find that all appeared in European suits of the latest cut.[53] One amongst them had served with the SANLC in France, but most had not been on the sea before, and they had found the journey somewhat dreary, though enlivened by a pod of nine whales that suddenly appeared in the Bay of Biscay.[54]

Their programme included excursions to provincial cities where they toured munitions factories. They visited Windsor Castle, and the Royal Farm; and they placed a wreath on Queen Victoria's tomb at Frogmore. On 1 November they were taken to Northolt, where Griffith and another of the party were given a half-hour flight that included a spin around London, while the others made shorter circuits: Griffith was quoted in the press as expressing his pride in being the first of his race to fly.[55] But the main business was the Royal Audience on the 7th November, with presentation of the loyal address from the BNC on the King's victory, and, of course, the petition about the status of Basutoland.

In a personal address, Griffith expressed the hope that the existing bonds between the Basuto nation and the King and his successors, according to the law, would remain 'the silken but enduring fetters of today.'[56] He was echoing imagery employed in a previous address to the Imperial War Conference of 1917 by New Zealand Premier William Massey,[57] but also subverting Massey's message by diverting its object from the future peacetime shape of the relationship between

Great Britain and the Dominions, to bilateral ties between Basutoland and Britain, and the continuance into the future of the Basuto nation's direct relationship with the British Crown.

Part of the petition on incorporation into the Union, as drafted by the BNC, read:

> Since 1910, the settled Native Policy of the Union of South Africa, has appeared ... to be a veritable compromise between the policy of the late Cape Colony and the policies of the late [Boer] Republics. This means that the administration of the Union of South Africa apart from the fact that the Union Jack flies as its symbol, inspires us with even less confidence than that of the late Cape Colony. [Against which they fought the Gun War of 1880–81.]
>
> The day may come when we will wish to be united to the Union. It will come when the sobs of the Natives in the Union have been stilled for a generation. But as yet we hear them crying. We have read the 1913 Land Act of the Union and we have watched that Act in operation. Tens of thousands of Native victims of that Act have crowded into Basutoland in the six years since 1913, and the iron has entered the souls of the Natives of the Free State.[58]

Secretary of State for the Colonies Lord Milner later replied on the King's behalf: His Majesty's Government had received no proposals for the incorporation of Basutoland in the Union, but if and when such a proposal was made the people of Basutoland would have full opportunity to express their views.[59]

After their return, Paramount Chief Griffith Lerotholi and the BNC continued to work diplomatically on the relationship with the British Crown, and enlisted the symbolic support of the Basuto nation in this endeavour. 12th May 1920 saw the celebration of a newly created public holiday in Basutoland—'Moshoeshoe's Day', commemorating the day in 1868 on which Moshesh placed himself under the protection of Queen Victoria. A public feast was held at Matsieng, the Paramount Chief's headquarters, accompanied by a programme of entertainment comprising (bareback) pony racing. At the end of proceedings, King George V's gift to Griffith of a fine silver-mounted and ivory-handled revolver was exhibited to the admiring crowd.[60] Griffith's gift to King George V consisted of three Basuto ponies shipped out to the Royal Mews at Windsor.[61] Colonial Office papers do not reveal whether they had been amongst the prizewinners.

Country	Approx. population	Number of planes
Basutoland	c. 400,000	25

Sopwith Camel B3866 *Basutoland No. 2 Mokhachane*, photographed in France with its 3 Squadron RNAS pilot, courtesy of Cross & Cockade International Archive

Chapter 12:
Swaziland, Major Miller, the Union of South Africa, and Jan Smuts

In 1918 two SE5a fighting scouts—one of the most effective British aeroplanes of the Great War—were presented by Swaziland. British aircraft production had swollen enormously since the beginning of the war, but so had losses, and between the start of the massive German spring offensive on 21st March 1918 and the end of April, the British flying service on the Western Front lost 1,032 aircraft from all causes out of a total of 1,232.[1] Presentation planes were still welcome to Britain, but as much for their symbolic value as anything else, even if the contribution was now a drop in the ocean. A cabled message from King George V acknowledged the first Swazi remittance of £1,000 in March that year, and announced that the aircraft would be inscribed: *Presented by The Chief Regent, Chiefs and People of Swaziland.*[2] During the minority of her grandson, the future Sobhuza II (installed in 1921), the Chief Regent in question was Queen Labotsibeni. The Regent, who was approaching sixty, was a very capable—and even formidable—ruler, who had dominated Swazi politics for decades.

Like Basutoland and Bechuanaland, Swaziland had a British Resident Commissioner who came under the authority of the High Commissioner in South Africa. There was no institution similar to the BNC in Swaziland however, and the British thought it unlikely that such a body could work there, since the Swazi Chiefs were all too intimidated by Labotsibeni to express independent views. Unlike Southern Rhodesia, white settlement in Swaziland had been entirely peaceful. Many of the kingdom's problems derived, however, from the profligate way in which Labotsibeni's late husband, Mbandzeni, had distributed overlapping land and mineral concessions to British and Afrikaner settler alike—often under the influence of European advisers. The British Government, which since the end of the Boer War had maintained a Protectorate over Swaziland, was her best hope for redress.

Lord Selborne, at that time the South Africa-based High Commissioner for Swaziland, later described the situation as a nightmare:

> Every acre of land in Swaziland had been 'conceded' by the Swazi chief to some white man for grazing, for tillage, for forestry purposes, and

for the exploitation of minerals; the concessions never coincided in area or boundaries or time limit, and were usually owned by different persons on the same piece of land according to their nature.[3]

He appointed George Grey (Sir Edward Grey's brother) to divide the land held by concessionaires, giving one-third of it back for Swazi usage. Grey finished early in 1909, and produced a partition that gave a portion of the better agricultural land and pasturage back to the Swazis. The Queen Regent subsequently encouraged them to work in the South African mines and send back money to buy up more.

The first Swazi gift of £1,000 in February 1918 represented part of an ongoing collection made by Labotsibeni and her Chiefs for unspecified British war purpose that she wished transmitted to His Majesty George V. It followed the much larger war gifts from Basutoland in the previous year, which had been devoted to presentation aeroplanes, and Lord Buxton suggested that it be used to the same end.[4] Given the timing, King George V was able to approve the money as a contribution to the new British unified air service that was to come into being on 1 April 1918,[5] and the two Swaziland aeroplanes were probably amongst the first presentation aircraft earmarked for the RAF rather than the RFC or RNAS. The second and final remittance of £2,000 in August 1918 was collected partly from Swaziland citizens working in the South African mines, but also included contributions from ethnic Swazis of Barberton district of South Africa, just across the border, who regarded Labotsibeni as their Chief.[6]

As well as coinciding with the birth of the RAF, the announcement of the gift was timely in other respects too. It preceded an air tour of the country by RAF Major Allister Mackintosh Miller DSO. He arrived in Mbabane in April 1918 after a flight from Johannesburg with his father as passenger.[7] Since the Major's father was the leading white resident of Swaziland, who had once acted as secretary to the late king Mbandzini, it must be presumed that Labotsibeni knew all about it. The father, Allister M. Miller senior, was a journalist born in Scotland who had settled in Swaziland as a young man and launched the *Times of Swaziland* in 1897.[8] Apart from during the period of the Boer War when the British settler population evacuated the country, and Miller's newspaper ceased publication, he had been there ever since.[9] In 1908 he co-operated with George Grey in the process of partitioning the concessions, of which he was a major holder under the umbrella of the Swaziland Corporation Ltd.

During their air tour of Swaziland in 1918, Major Miller and his father covered almost the whole of the country, from the border with Portuguese East Africa to the border of Zululand. An estimated 60,000 Swazis witnessed the flight out of a total population of some 100,000 or so. It was a sensation. At the start, just outside Mbabane, crowds of Swazis had stayed out on the *veldt* around the aeroplane all night, waiting to see it leave in the morning. The air tour covered well over 800 miles and was a truly pioneering one, over country that had never before witnessed an aeroplane in flight. A feature of the return journey to Johannesburg was a non-stop run of over three hours from Mbabane in clear, but bad, weather for flying. Bad, the *Rand Daily Mail* explained, inasmuch as the powers of the sun and rapid evaporation of moisture on the surface of the earth had the effect of causing 'bumps' even at as high as 5–6,000 feet, whereas in Europe aircraft would leave such phenomena behind at a height of 3,000 feet.

The twenty-six year old Major had been born and brought up in Swaziland, reputedly the first white baby to be born in the country. Allister Mackintosh Miller had been educated at Rhodes College in South Africa, and afterwards went to London to study engineering. When the Great War broke out he joined the Scots Greys, transferring to the RFC a year later.[10] But he was much less widely known in Swaziland than his father, confusingly also known as Allister M. (for Mitchell) Miller. The press carried a telling anecdote from the trip: when a broken wire forced a landing some distance to the west of Mbabane, they attracted a number of curious Swazi onlookers from the surrounding area who had never set eyes on a plane before. They eventually concluded after much speculation and debate that A. M. Miller senior, whom they recognised, was paying a visit in a new type of motor vehicle capable of flying, and that Major Miller (whom they did not) must be his driver.[11]

A small group of South Africans had flown with the RFC from early on, and performed so well that the British authorities decided on a recruiting campaign in South Africa—or so the story goes—and charged then RFC Captain Allister Miller with this task in 1916. However, the unique touring role that he was to play may well have owed much to his father's personal connections from Boer War days. For in December 1901 the new head of British military intelligence in South Africa was none other than Lieutenant Colonel David Henderson of the Argyll and Sutherland Highlanders, and it was he that commissioned fellow Scot A. M. Miller (senior) to act as adjutant in a new unit known as the Lebombo Intelligence Scouts (LIS).

The role of the LIS was to guard the border with Portuguese territory in order to prevent Boer commandos infiltrating into the eastern Transvaal through Swaziland, and they established themselves in the Lebombo range above the Ngwavuma River.[12] At that time Henderson held the office of Director of Military Intelligence in South Africa under Lord Kitchener, and was to serve under Kitchener again as Director of Aeronautics during the First World War. In this latter role Henderson facilitated RFC admission for a number of Southern African applicants, at the behest of old contacts from his earlier military career,[13] but no other was to be given such a special role in recruitment as Miller.

For his first recruiting tour of South Africa in 1916, Miller shipped out with him at least one of the reconnaissance aircraft presented by British communities in Latin America, and on an immensely successful second tour in 1917 he employed two: BE2c A3110 inscribed *Rio de Janeiro Britons No. 2* and BE2e A3109 (a later version of the BE2c) inscribed *Presented by the Rio Gallegos Britons Argentine*.[14] They featured again during early 1918. Major Miller's 1916 round had attracted 1,700 applicants for commissions in the RFC, of whom more than 400 were accepted for pilot training in England. Only two of those chosen failed to achieve the required standard. When Miller went out again in mid-1917, accompanied by Major Bagshaw from Port Elizabeth, he was aiming for one thousand South African flying cadets.[15] Their exhibition flights throughout the country included a 'thrilling display' by *Rio Gallegos Britons* at Kenilworth racetrack near Cape Town before a crowd of thousands; and further displays at Turffontein Race Course near Johannesburg and at Kimberley. After the Kimberley performance Miller was inundated with applications to join the RFC.[16]

In between his recruiting trips to South Africa, Major Miller flew with distinction on the Western Front. Indeed, in the curious etiquette of chivalry that then still obtained between enemy flying services he was chosen to drop the RFC's wreath in memory of the great German aviator Max Immelmann, who was brought down in July 1917 by Lieutenant McCubbin DSO:

> Since a South African aviator had brought him down it was fitting that a South African should be chosen to show the RFC's respect to his memory. Captain Miller took the wreath over to a large German drome and, to make sure of dropping it without damage, descended to a level of 200 feet. He met with a shrapnel reception which crippled his engine so badly that he just managed to get back to our lines. Be it recorded, however, to the credit of the German Air Service, that as soon as they perceived the wreath their fire ceased.[17]

It must have been odd, commuting between the Western Front and recruitment tours of South Africa. Quite apart from the itinerant flying displays there were talks and lectures in all the main urban centres. After his Swaziland tour in early 1918, Major Miller embarked on another leg, this time flying from Johannesburg to Natal and Zululand and covering about 1,800 miles in the air with an actual flying time of almost twenty-four hours, all told:

> A feature of the flights was again the extraordinary effect of the machine's appearance on the natives at Eshowe, Umzinto and Richmond. They came in sometimes from as far afield as 40 or 50 miles ... on several occasions Major Miller addressed them, and explained in simple language the possibilities of an aeroplane, supported by instances of what the Air Force had done in France. In all instances his hearers were immensely impressed.[18]

All South African recruits for the RFC had to be white, however, and this was the rule of the British military authorities though there is no doubt whatsoever that the South African ones would also have insisted on this. Candidates had to satisfy the following conditions: a) be between 18 and 30 years old; b) be of pure European descent and the sons of British subjects (in doubtful cases the burden of proof was to rest upon the candidate); and c) be reported fit for active service and medically fit according to the existing standard of entry into the RFC as pilots.[19] More than three thousand South Africans eventually served with the RFC and Major Miller was responsible for recruiting the great majority of them, who were popularly known as 'Miller's Boys'. On his 1917 recruiting round in South Africa he also raised £13,000 for the RFC hospital in England—a scheme under the patronage of Lady Henderson and object of another Overseas Club fundraising campaign.

The Governor General, Lord Buxton, reported that six hundred candidates had been accepted for the RFC on Miller's recruitment round by the end of 1917; and he described it as of the greatest value that the power of the aeroplane should be known as widely as possible in South Africa at that time. Flying, he wrote, appealed particularly to 'the young Dutchman', and the fact that Major Miller had nominated eight Nationalists as flying cadets and had applications from many more was the best evidence of its political value. In addition, 'the natives' were much impressed with the aeroplane, and as there had been 'slight unrest' amongst them, the flights over native territory were 'most useful'.[20]

Major Miller's touring aerobatic displays were exciting, gruelling, and unpredictable. His April 1918 tour of Swaziland was postponed from an extended recruitment round of exhibition flights throughout South Africa planned initially for 6–24 November 1917. That tour had been dogged by mishaps and interrupted by ill health. It began inauspiciously. At noon on 7 November he landed on Port Elizabeth Golf Course after a five-hour flight from Cape Town, the first long-distance flight in South Africa:

> The great crowd assembled to celebrate the unique event sighted him way out over Emerald Hill ... Ten minutes later he volplaned down to the edge of the fairway of the eighteenth hole, dashed toward the green, crashed into the bunker and buried the nose of his machine in the turf. When he alighted he was travelling fast, a little too fast as events proved, and the cheers of the crowd turned to cries of apprehension ...
> 'I saw', he said, 'that if I swerved to right or left I would dash into the crowd and kill somebody so I steered her for the bunker.' As his machine took the ridge he drove her head hard down, and thus at the risk of his own life averted what would have been a disaster. Within two minutes souvenir hunters were scrambling and fighting for the splinters of the propeller which were showered around over a wide radius.[21]

Repairs were initially estimated to take a week, but waiting for spares to arrive delayed matters. On 22 November he was able to depart for Grahamstown and East London, but only after several hours' delay caused by weather conditions and the demands of photographers:

> At last he was seen climbing into his seat, and the drone of the engine started. Half a dozen preliminary turns of the propeller followed, and then it stopped. Once more the engine droned, the wings were tilted,

the propeller swung round swiftly ... and a second later the aeroplane itself came bounding down the fairway ...
Major Miller is evidently fond of giving his spectators thrills. Again he raced down the course until it appeared that nothing could save him from further disaster at the bunker, but at the moment when the crowd held its breath the aeroplane rose gracefully over the mound and over the heads of the people.[22]

He gave an exhibition flight over East London at 9.30 on 24 November, and at 12.40 started for King Williamstown. He arrived at 1.15 and was entertained to lunch by the Mayor. He departed for Queenstown at 3.50 but was turned back by heavy rains, and tried again next day, arriving at 1.10 pm after a rough passage over the Amatolas Mountains due to strong head winds—the journey had taken two hours. His onward journey to Bloemfontein was delayed initially by problems faced by his transport officers, then by strong winds, and then by Major Miller's ill-health—due to a recurrent bout of malaria. (The Air Board in London issued a tongue-in-cheek advisory to airmen recommending golf as a means of keeping fit off-duty.)

On 3 December he was in the air again, and resumed his tour, flying to Bloemfontein. But there were further incidents. He arrived in Kimberley on 7 December and put on his flying exhibition; he was flying with a damaged propeller, so as not to disappoint his audience. On 17 December it was announced that all further long flights were postponed on doctor's orders, and that he had been ordered to rest for some weeks.

The tour resumed in March/April 1918. At the end of his Swaziland trip, Major Miller arrived in Maritzburg from Dundee. After leaving Dundee the left wheel of his aeroplane came off in the air, but it was picked up and forwarded to Maritzburg by train. The authorities sent an ambulance to the landing field, as a precaution, and 'Left Wheel Missing' was painted in large letters on the ground:

> In landing, Major Miller coasted the machine on to the only wheel and ran up the ground until the speed was reduced and then the machine toppled over on to the axle and skidded slightly. The Mayor welcomed the airman.[23]

Cartoon of Major Miller DSO 'the flying man'
Rand Daily Mail, 11 December 1917

After the war ended, Major Miller attempted to establish an air transport business in Rhodesia, but it failed in the early 1920s and he returned to South Africa.²⁴ He subsequently founded a mail and passenger service that was to form part of the state-owned South African Airways in the 1930s, where he worked as chief publicity officer after the Second World War; during the war itself he served in the South African Air Force (SAAF). His two presentation planes *Rio de Janeiro Britons No. 2* and *Rio Gallegos Britons Argentine* stayed in South Africa in 1919 and were later used for flying displays, carrying mail, and even for carrying Governor Buxton on a ceremonial occasion.²⁵

Support for the Imperial Aircraft Flotilla scheme came largely from South African cities where English-speakers predominated. Its appeal to British Empire solidarity did not grate on their ears, as on those of many Afrikaners, especially in the OFS where support for the Nationalists was strong (even if piloting a plane did appeal). Johannesburg alone had some 4,000 members enrolled in the Overseas Club at the very beginning of 1915, and British Governor General Lord Buxton presided over the Club's activities in the Union of South Africa as a whole.²⁶

As in other parts of the empire, 'patriotic' funds were established, and £75,000 was collected throughout the country in 1915 to equip South African troops. Some of it was deflected to the Overseas Club

Aircraft Fund after Lord Kitchener issued a statement turning down the contribution for machine-guns. The War Office in London explained that the existing limitation on machine-gun availability was not that of money, but of productive capacity, since every available factory, practically throughout the world, was working flat-out to satisfy demand by the Imperial Government. A message went from Evelyn Wrench at the Overseas Club to the Ladies' Committee of the Machine Gun Fund encouraging a switch to aircraft: 'A gift of aeroplanes would ... be timely, and we have Lord Kitchener's authority for saying that it would be very welcome.'[27]

Defence Minister Jan Smuts initially encouraged donors to contribute to the Governor General's Fund. But in recognition that contributions had been intended to support the war effort directly, Defence Headquarters in South Africa followed up with a press statement that offered four alternative destinations for existing donations: supplementary equipment for the South African Expeditionary Force; equipment for a South African General Hospital; sheepskin coats for the troops; or aeroplanes:

> It is impossible to have an aeroplane made to your order and delivered within a few weeks or so to a particular flying unit or a flying man. The War Office will, however, gratefully accept the gift of an aeroplane, value £1,500, from any South African or group of South Africans, and assign to a new aeroplane, when brought into use, the name of any South African place (not person) which the donor wishes to have associated with his gift. Thus, for example, should the people of Springbokfontein subscribe £1,500 for an aeroplane, and so desire, an aeroplane called 'Springbokfontein', will within a month or so be in the sky searching the enemy's lines, perhaps with bombs, perhaps for information.[28]

This reflected a new steer from Smuts, approving presentation aeroplanes that bore South African place names.[29] It also proved to be the most popular donor option: of the slightly more than £6,000 re-allocated from the city of Cape Town's Machine Gun Fund, £4,500 went to three reconnaissance planes named *Cape Town Nos. 1-3*, the rest to other purposes.[30] BE2cs presented by locations elsewhere in South Africa in late 1915 included *Pretoria*; *Kaffraria* (from East London); and *Johannesburg Nos. 1 and 2* (these from the women of the city).

Given the exposure of the South African public to air displays, both by Major Miller from 1916, and by own home grown aviation pioneer John Weston and also Compton Paterson before the Great War even began,[31] the Overseas Club appeal for an Imperial Aircraft Flotilla might have been expected to find a ready audience. But black and coloured South Africa was not a target of the appeal and white South Africa had its divisions during the First World War; hence Lord Buxton's comments on the beneficial political dimensions of Miller's tours.

The first Prime Minister of the Union of South Africa, Louis Botha, and his Defence Minister, Jan Christiaan Smuts, both former Boer Generals, had wished to bring English-speaker and Afrikaner together within a politically unified South Africa that, as a Dominion, would play its full part in shaping the future of the British Empire. They saw military engagement in the Great War as a means towards this end; and, in addition, they had their territorial ambitions in Africa. They committed the SADF to the conquest of German South West Africa (and, indeed, completed its conquest by July 1915).

However many Afrikaners had not forgiven or forgotten the Boer War, and still yearned for a Boer Republic, not a place in the British Empire. A rebellion broke out in September/October 1914 against South Africa's military intervention in the German colony, but was suppressed by Union forces, including very many Afrikaans-speakers who remained loyal to Smuts and Botha. A small Afrikaner civil war, the 'Maritz Revolt' was all over by the beginning of February 1915, but cracks remained. While the British press lionised Louis Botha, both for his domestic policy of reconciling Afrikaans- and English-speakers, and for his conquest of German South West Africa—a clear and welcome victory to lift spirits downcast by continuing stalemate on the Western Front—many of those at home in South Africa, perhaps half of the Afrikaner population, did not agree. The 1915 General Election saw the opposition Nationalists take 16 out of the 17 seats in the OFS, and attract a total of 77,000 votes against 95,000 for the ruling South Africa Party in the country as a whole.[32]

Both Smuts and Botha influenced opinion in Britain. For British public and politicians alike, Smuts had conducted a daring campaign in East Africa that captured large swathes of territory from the enemy, in marked contrast with the grinding immobility of the Western Front, where heavy artillery caused more deaths than disease, and movement was limited by far more than the length of supply-lines. The positive public image of Smuts' military leadership was nurtured by his own communiqués that emphasised his successes in East Africa—reflected in turn by British journalists trawling for good news to report.[33]

The two South African leaders also influenced British government decisions. The strong opposition expressed by Prime Minister Louis Botha to raising and arming black combat troops for service in Europe was decisive in ensuring that only labour auxiliaries were recruited from southern Africa, with the Union taking the preemptive initiative to raise the force. It was also at the insistence of the South African authorities that the SANLC was housed apart from others in France, under the closed compound system used in the South African diamond mines, and brought under the command of ex-personnel of the Union's Native Labour Department or former mining officials.[34]

Jan Smuts became an even greater hero of wartime British public opinion than Louis Botha. Indeed, he was beloved of senior British politicians too, as military leader, high-minded statesman, and scholar-philosopher. Prime Minister Lloyd George's war memoirs heaped praise on him:[35]

> Smuts is one of the most remarkable personalities of his time. He is that fine blend of intellect and human sympathy which constitutes the understanding man. Although he had proved his courage in many enterprises which demanded personal valour, and although he had shown his powers in many a fight which had called for combative qualities, his sympathies were too broad to make of him a mere fighting man. His rare gifts of mind and heart strengthened those finer elements which are apt to be overwhelmed in an hour of savage temper and pitiless carnage. Of his practical contribution to our counsels during those trying years, it is difficult to speak too highly.

His closest friends in England were radical females—feminists and pacifists who had campaigned to draw public attention to the treatment of women and children in the British-run concentration camps during the Boer War, and worked to improve their dire conditions. The foremost figure was Emily Hobhouse, but Smuts also corresponded regularly with the Quaker sisters Margaret Clark Gillett and Alice Clark throughout his life.[36] Margaret Gillett's son recalled wartime visits to the family home in Oxford by General Smuts when he was a member of Lloyd George's War Cabinet; on occasion he accompanied the Gilletts to the Oxford Friends' Meeting wearing his military uniform.[37]

Yet Jan Christiaan Smuts was at the same time flawed by what has been termed an almost visceral fear of Africans.[38] After taking part in the capture of German South West Africa, Smuts was called on by the British to lead the imperial forces in the East Africa campaign. His address to South African troops at Johannesburg bound for the East African theatre illustrates his deep-seated phobia that sat so uneasily alongside his intellectualism:

> You are going to fight in East Africa not a civilised foe, but hordes of barbarians who have been scientifically trained by German officers, and they are said to be good fighting material ... but we are versed in this kind of work. For two hundred years now we have been engaged in struggling and wrestling this land from barbarism.[39]

The only non-white South Africans allowed to bear arms in the First World War were the 'coloureds' of the Cape Corps, a unit of which served in East Africa during 1916 as part of Smuts' command.[40]

Jan Smuts was responsible, as South African Minister of Defence, for the formation of the SADF, and a flying arm was envisaged from the very beginning. Pre-war exhibition flying by civilian aviators had half an eye to military use. A display at Kimberley as far back as April 1912 involved Compton Paterson's partner, 'Bok' Driver, demonstrating a bombing run by means of 'melons ... dropped with remarkable accuracy from a considerable height upon a tarpaulin.'[41] A handful of South African officers had already been sent to England for pilot training before the war, back in early 1914. At the beginning of 1915 a South African Aviation Corps was officially established, initially for service in South West Africa. After further training in England it became a part of the imperial forces in East Africa under Smuts' generalship as No. 26 (South African) Squadron of the RFC, before disbanding.[42]

Smuts, however, had a wartime career split between Africa and Britain, and also contributed to the formation of the RAF. The outstanding intellectual figure of the Imperial War Cabinet—that gathering of senior Dominion politicians and British Ministers that met in session in London during March–May 1917—he was the only one of their number to join Prime Minister Lloyd George's five-man British War Cabinet, as Minister without Portfolio.[43] During 1917-18 Jan Smuts occupied an office in London adjoining that of Lord Milner, the War Cabinet's most senior member save for Lloyd George himself.[44]

Spurred by daylight bombing raids on London, the British War Cabinet agreed in June 1917 to a large-scale increase in aircraft production, followed by a decision to virtually double the number of RFC squadrons, with a matching increase in the size of the RNAS. Smuts was charged with a radical reappraisal of British air policy, public and parliamentary opinion having been inflamed especially by the raid of 13 June by Gotha bombers that resulted in 162 dead and 432 injured within a one-mile radius of London's Liverpool Street Station.[45]

Smuts' first Report, in July, made recommendations for the improvement of London's air defences. The second was delivered to the War Cabinet on 17 August and proposed the establishment of an Air Ministry and the amalgamation of the RFC and RNAS into a single force (Smuts following the advice of Henderson in this matter). Hence the RAF duly came into being on 1 April 1918.

The Union of South Africa provided over a dozen presentation planes to Britain, half of them following the closure of the Machine-Gun Fund in late 1915. Four more were presented to the RFC during 1916–17, mainly by local branches of the Overseas Club. The last two were gifted to the RAF in 1918; one provided by the Overseas Club branch at Benoni on the Reef, another, *South African Aviators*, by Walter Greenacre MP of Durban. By this time handover ceremonies between the Dominions and Britain had become quite elaborate, and replete with speeches underlining wartime solidarity. Henry Burton, South African Minister of Railways and Harbours, ceremoniously handed over the two aeroplanes at Brooklands in July 1918 with verbal tributes to the three thousand South African pilots of the RFC and RAF. Receiving them on behalf of the Air Ministry, Major J. E. Baird lauded the activities of South African airmen in South West Africa and in East Africa, where malaria had increased their hardships. He described the machines in question as symbols of empire unity—built in Britain, presented by the Union of South Africa through a South African Minister, to be flown out to France by two pilots from Canada and Australia respectively, and greatly appreciated as gifts by the RAF.[46]

The symbolism turned out to be misleading. The sacrifice by the South African Expeditionary Force at Delville Wood in July 1916 certainly ranked in the annals of the First World War alongside that of the Canadians at Vimy Ridge, or ANZAC soldiers at Gallipoli, but most of the troops concerned had been English-speakers. Most of the troops in South West Africa and subsequently East Africa were Afrikaners, and regarded by many as traitors to the republican cause, so that the role of those fighting in these campaigns was later elided from South African memorial.[47]

After the Armistice, Jan Smuts helped draft Britain's peace terms and (together with Botha) represented South Africa at the Paris Peace Conference of 1919. Regarded internationally as a leading world statesman by contemporaries, his ideas contributed materially to the shaping of the League of Nations and the system of Mandates for the administration of Germany's ex-colonies, as well as the evolution of Dominion status to fully sovereign, independent, statehood. For many white South Africans, however, he was tarnished by a too willing engagement with the 'British' world.

When Louis Botha died in August 1919, Smuts became Prime Minister of the Union of South Africa, but the Nationalists won the 1920, and then 1924, General Elections on a republican platform, and Smuts (who had managed to form a coalition government in 1920) was finally ousted. He returned as Deputy Prime Minister in 1933, and was South African Prime Minister during the Second World War (and appointed an Honorary Field Marshal in the British Army in 1941), but he lost the General Election of 1948 to the National Party. For the last two years of his life he was Chancellor of Cambridge University.

As for incorporating Bechuanaland, Swaziland, and Basutoland into the Union, South African leaders raised the issue again and again, to be fobbed off by British delaying tactics on each occasion. The whole saga was set out in an official British Command Paper: 'Basutoland, the Bechuanaland Protectorate and Swaziland: History of Discussions with the Union of South Africa 1909–1939'.[48] Generally it was Swaziland that topped Union claims, for it had once been a British-Boer condominium, and once also a Protectorate of the Transvaal Republic. (Although for anyone gazing at the map today, it is the continued separate existence of Basutoland entirely surrounded by South Africa, and its independence in 1966 as the sovereign Kingdom of Lesotho, that causes the main wonderment). The foot-dragging by the Colonial Office (and later the Dominions Office) and reluctance to countenance changes to the *status quo*, as promised in 1910, was due to insistence on 'trusteeship' doctrines,[49] perhaps reflecting counsel from Whitehall's legal experts—but in any case, transfer of *any* of these territories became unthinkable after 1948 and the National Party's electoral victory that inaugurated full-blown *apartheid* in South Africa.

Country	Approx. population	Number of planes
Swaziland	c. 100,000	2
South Africa	More than 5 million, of which about 1 million whites	13

Chapter 13:
The Indian Empire:
The sub-continent and Burma

Just as in the Great War the Indian sub-continent was the largest source of military manpower for the imperial war effort, it was also the largest single source of presentation aeroplanes for the RFC: at least 175. (Had Calcutta's Aeroplane Fund not diverted its subscriptions to motor ambulances in 1915, India's tally would have fallen not far short of two hundred.) Probably the greatest number represented gifts of the princes who still held sway over a third of the land area and about a fifth of the population, some of them very large gifts indeed. The Maharajah of Bikanir (Bikaner) provided the funds— £17,000—for twelve presentation aeroplanes; the Nizam of Hyderabad, eighteen; and the Gaekwar of Baroda nineteen.[1]

This was just part of an extravagant flow of funds and materiel from the rulers of the Indian princely states that supplemented the military expenditure of the Government of India. Over the course of the Great War, their gifts were estimated to exceed £4 million in value.[2] They loaned and gifted money, aeroplanes, motor ambulances, armoured vehicles, machine guns, hospital ships, horses; and of course, men, for all those who maintained soldiers for imperial service offered contingents for the war, sometimes even accompanying them abroad.

Historically furnishing a large troop reserve for imperial use and supported by the Indian taxpayer, the Indian Army itself already numbered nearly 242,000 in 1914.[3] By the end of the war, almost one and a half million Indians had served, including 400,000 non-combatants. In addition to gifting £100 million to the British Treasury, the Government of India met the cost of supporting these troops, some £20–£30 million a year.[4] They were the only non-white British Empire troops used in a purely combat capacity on the Western Front. Two Indian infantry divisions were diverted to France following initial heavy losses by the BEF in the first months of the war. They fought at Neuve Chapelle in March 1915, Festubert (late May) and Loos in the autumn.[5] Before the onset of a second European winter, surviving Indian infantry corps went on to join others in Mesopotamia (Iraq), although some cavalry units remained in France throughout the war.

Indians also fought at Gallipoli and in Egypt, Palestine, and East Africa (as well as half a Sikh battalion that took part with the Japanese in the capture of Tsingtao in November 1914), but Mesopotamia was the main theatre of operations for most of the war. The Indian involvement began as an action to safeguard the Anglo-Persian Oil Company's installations on the Persian Gulf, which supplied fuel for the Royal Navy's new oil-driven battle cruisers, and widened into a campaign against the Turks in Mesopotamia. Nearly 589,000 Indian soldiers and some 293,000 labour corps and other non-combatants served there.[6]

An Indian Flying School had been established at Sitapur in early 1914. It was staffed by British officers of the Indian Army who had learnt to fly at their own expense while in England on leave, and then completed an RFC course at Farnborough. The School's own first course of instruction was due to begin in September when the Great War intervened, and staff and equipment were packed off to Egypt following the Turkish attack on the Suez Canal. There they flew reconnaissance for the Indian Expeditionary Force, while a squadron of the RFC was only later dispatched to India to replace them.[7]

The Mesopotamia campaign was initially under the direction of the Government of India, and Viceroy Lord Hardinge protested the lack of air support.[8] Australia answered the Viceroy's appeal by loaning pilots and ground crew for a 'Mesopotamian half-flight', as it was called, that arrived in late May 1915. The Maharajah Scindia of Gwalior (a friend of the Viceroy) had stepped in with an offer to fund four aeroplanes. Ordered via the War Office in London they began to arrive in Bombay in April, and thence onwards, to be flown by the half-flight's four Australian aviators.

The first of the Maharajah's reconnaissance aircraft to arrive were two Maurice Farmans, to be joined in mid-July by two new Caudron biplanes.[9] Reports of their activities were submitted via the Viceregal Lodge:

> My Dear Maharaja, July 28, 1915
>
> I think you would like to know that our recent success on the 24th on the Euphrates was largely due to the employment of the aeroplanes which Your Highness so generously presented to the Government. We were informed that the troops could not advance, as it was found impossible to locate the position of the enemy and their guns; but as soon as the two aeroplanes arrived, they were able to make a successful reconnaissance, showing up the whole of the Turkish position, with the result that the attack was completely successful. Without aeroplanes our losses would probably have been very heavy. I assure Your Highness I am very grateful for that gift of yours.
>
> Yours etc.,
> Hardinge of Penshurst.[10]

A further four gift aircraft from the Maharajah Scindia (making eight in all, at a total cost of £14,400) were evidently treated as part of the Imperial Aircraft Flotilla scheme. *Gwalior No. 3* was issued to the RFC in France, but at least two others of the series (BE2cs all), did find service in Mesopotamia.[11] The Australians were later joined by airmen of the Indian Army released from Egypt, along with further trained men from India, but this composite force was to suffer severe losses at Kut-el-Amara in early 1916; and the Indian flying corps as a separate body had in any case already ceased to exist in late 1915.[12]

Many other presentation aircraft were funded through newspaper campaigns and private subscription in India, but they went to the RFC. In response to an appeal on behalf of the Overseas Club by the Governor of Bombay, the cotton-mill magnates Sir David Sassoon (of the wealthy Baghdadi Jewish dynasty) and Sir Shapurji Broacha (a leading member of Bombay's Parsee merchant community) financed two of that city's presentation aeroplanes, and the Bombay Cotton Trades Association a third.[13] Madras also provided a couple bearing the name of the city.

Subscribers to a collection in Calcutta included the Japanese firm Mitsui Bussan Kaisha, along with many British enterprises and a sprinkling of Indian contributors. However, on the advice of its Chairman, Sir John Hewett, the large sum of £35,000 raised by the Calcutta Aeroplane Fund was devoted to motor ambulances instead. This was after Sir John, who also chaired the Indian Soldiers' Fund Committee in London, was advised that aircraft manufacturers were already working to full capacity on British government orders and could not supply—suggesting that he tried unsuccessfully to place orders in Britain for the direct benefit of the Government of India and the Indian Army.[14]

The Punjab Armoured Aeroplane Fleet Fund, to give it its full title, had as its original aim to raise an air fleet that would be employed primarily in those areas where Indian troops were engaged. This was not to be, but may explain its enormous success in northern India, for Punjab made by far the largest contribution in manpower to the Indian Army during the Great War, alone supplying 360,000 recruits.[15] It started off naming its gifts after rivers in the province, but ran out of rivers for its eventual tally of fifty-one presentation fighter planes and had to replace them with less evocative place-names. Rulers of the princely states subscribing one or more aircraft through the Fund included the Maharajahs of Nabha and Jind; the Rajah of Faridkot; the Nawabs of Bahawalpur and of Ala Bagh; as well as the Commander-in-Chief of the Kashmir Army, Rajkumar Hari Singh (who paid £10,000 for the names *Punjab Nos. 12-15, Kashmir*). By the time it closed, in March 1916, it had taken all of £96,000.[16] And more was to come: in addition to two aircraft already provided through the Fund, the Maharajah of Nabha subsequently provided another six outside it.

Only a handful of the very many presentation aeroplanes from India were destined for Egypt, East Africa, or the Mesopotamian theatre where the largest part of the Indian Army was fighting. This handful included all three of those presented by the Maharajah of Rewa, but he was probably a special case, as the donor of an aircraft to the Flying School at Sitapur who had taken an active interest in aeronautics prior to the First World War.[17] A few were used close to home, on the North-West Frontier and elsewhere, including two of the three reconnaissance aeroplanes presented by the Khan of Kalat, the ruler of Baluchistan,[18] source of one of the first Indian infantry regiments to fight on the Western Front. However, the majority, like presentation aircraft from other parts of the empire, ended up being flown by the RFC in France, or used in Home Defence against German Zeppelin or aeroplane raids on English towns.

Most of India's westernised elite supported the British war effort, including the country's moderate nationalist movements, the Indian National Congress and the Muslim League, who cooperated with each other and looked to the wartime British discourse about democracy to deliver evolutionary change. Mohandas ('Mahatma') Gandhi returned to India in 1915 after almost two decades in South Africa, where he had begun to develop his philosophy and method of non-violent political agitation; however both there and in India he encouraged support for Britain in the war. There was a revolutionary political movement at work at home and abroad at the time, but *Ghadr* met with a very limited response. Mainly externally based (with its beginnings in 1913 amongst Sikhs on the western seaboard of America) it disseminated propaganda urging Indian troops to mutiny and targeted its message at Muslim soldiers, playing on a reluctance to fight against the forces of Ottoman Turkey, and it received monetary and logistical support from Germany.

The British authorities regarded *Ghadr* for these reasons as a serious potential threat, especially following the mutiny in Singapore of the Rajput wing of the Fifth Light Infantry in February 1915: a mutiny in part sparked by rumours that they were to be sent to fight fellow Muslims.[19] The British fear was clearly one of contagion. Yet when in addition to propaganda activities the *Ghadr* leadership became involved in far flung arms smuggling plots they over-extended themselves, and were compromised by a German double agent working for the British, and by British interception of their messages sent via German embassies. Thus a conspiracy to foment an armed uprising among Indian troops of the Calcutta garrison was decisively quashed in December 1915.[20]

In 1917, two prominent Indians (the Maharajah of Bikanir and Sir S. P. Sinha) were included for the first time as their country's representatives at an Imperial Conference in London (and the first Imperial *War* Conference), in recognition of the weight and importance of India's contribution. In the same year, Edwin Montagu, Secretary of State for India, promised the progressive realisation of responsible government in India as an integral part of the British Empire. While his undertaking raised nationalist expectations of progress to Dominion status, the political reforms actually introduced by the Government of India Act of 1919 fell far, far, short. The same year saw the massacre in Amritsar of four hundred unarmed demonstrators by General Dyer; and in 1920–22, the serious growth of Gandhi's mass non-cooperation campaign for immediate self-rule. The rest, as they say, is history, though for the Indian princes, that history eventually rather left them behind.

The Nizam of Hyderabad's gift of presentation aeroplanes was made in the last year of the war. Mir Osman Ali Khan—the seventh Nizam, last representative of the Mughal Empire and ruler of some 15 million people in central-southern India—donated money that uniquely furnished a single squadron—No. 110 Squadron RAF. It formed part of the Independent Force established under Major General Sir Hugh Trenchard. A strategic bombing unit with the remit to attack industrial targets inside Germany, the Independent Force was in action from August 1918.

Major Hazelton Nicholl RAF (a flying instructor in England since late 1915) was given command of 110 Squadron. They were equipped with the new DH9A bomber powered by the 400-hp. American 'Liberty' engine, capable of carrying a bomb load of up to 460 lb. with a flying range of four and a half hours. The squadron was based in southeast France near the Vosges Mountains and just within range of the nearest Rhine towns. Since the average flying height on a bombing raid was 17,500 feet the cold was intense, and at the start they flew without oxygen though this was later remedied.[21] In complete contrast to other large contributions on the part of the Indian princes, or for that matter from the Malay Sultan Ibrahim II whose gifts had been dispersed around different RFC units, they formed the squadron's entire complement of eighteen bomber aircraft (one of them incidentally numbered *No. 12A* so as to avoid 'unlucky' 13).[22] Each one inscribed as a gift of the Nizam, to Hazelton Nicholl these presentation planes demonstrated 'just what the loyalty of the Indian Princes meant to Britain.'[23]

During the Great War the Nizam had ruled Hyderabad directly, as his own Chief Minister. One estimate put his contribution towards the imperial war effort in men, materiel, and money as worth up to £2 million.[24] Welcome as this was, probably even more valuable to the British authorities had been the appeal he was persuaded to issue back in November 1914, calling on the Muslims of India to support Britain's cause despite Turkey's entry into the war on the side of Germany.[25] His reward was to be made an Honorary Lieutenant General of the British Army, and in the 1918 New Year's Honours List to be elevated by King George V from 'His Highness' to 'His Exalted Highness'. The King also conferred on him the title of 'Faithful Ally' of the British Government, and he became the only Indian ruler entitled to a 21-gun salute (giving rise to jealousy among others, none of whom rated more than 19-guns).[26]

Although No. 110 squadron disbanded in 1919, the Nizam went on to contribute towards the cost of no less than three RAF squadrons in the Second World War, and thus a resurrected 110 Squadron RAF received the name 'Hyderabad'.[27] The British, however, had come to regret plying the Nizam with titles that only increased his own delusions of grandeur. His aspirations for an independent Hyderabad later ended in tragedy in the aftermath of Partition, when in September 1948 troops of an Independent India rolled into his state. A Hyderabadi volunteer force had perpetrated atrocities on the populace, and the Indian intervention was followed by violent Hindu retaliatory action against Muslims. Of the total Muslim community of the State, between one in ten and one in five adult males were believed killed.[28] But even after Hyderabad's surrender, the Nizam remained one of the richest men in the world, or perhaps even the very richest, one estimate of his personal wealth putting it at around £100 million.[29] The Nizam died in early 1967.

A nation of a little over twelve million at the 1911 census, Burma was ruled as an adjunct of British India following the Third (and final) Burma War of 1885 and abolition of the Burmese monarchy. The last king, Thibaw died in exile in India at the end of 1916. The annexation of Burma had been the personal policy of Lord Randolph Churchill, Secretary of State for India, completely bypassing Parliament.[30] Although swiftly accomplished by a British military force, prolonged and widespread resistance had followed Thibaw's surrender. In the process of British 'pacification' all existing structures of power were swept away and replaced by an unusually centralised colonial administration (at least for the British Empire). Instead of a Governor, Burma was given a Lieutenant Governor, answerable to the Viceroy of India.

The country's external trade was good in the First World War years: oil for British ships exported by the Burmah Oil Co.; timber of all kinds for Mesopotamia; and teak especially for the Indian Military Department. The war also stimulated a strong British demand for wolfram, used in steel manufacture, of which Tavoy in Burma became an important supplier.[31] A Burman company of Military Police was recruited for the first time in 1916–17, and Burma supplied a force of Sappers and Miners for Mesopotamia comprising some 500 officers and almost 12,000 men, many from the Kachin hills.[32] The country also sent a 2,000-strong labour contingent to France in 1917, half drawn from the majority Burman population and half Northern

Chin.[33] It was not without repercussions—serious riots ensued that year in the Chin Hills of Burma and neighbouring Assam in India against further recruitment for overseas service.

Burma was the source of six presentation aeroplanes, three of them subscribed in 1915. British officials of the Hong Kong and Shanghai Bank and Bank of Rangoon set up a memorial fund shortly after the death in June that year of Flight Sub-Lieutenant Reginald Warneford RNAS, who was awarded the VC for downing a Zeppelin over Belgium but died shortly afterwards in an air accident. Warneford had been born in Darjeeling, and before enlisting worked for the British India Steamship Co., from whence—presumably—stemmed his connection with Rangoon. Subscribers to the *Warneford* aeroplane were mainly Britons, but donors' lists always contained a good sprinkling of Burmese, Chinese, and Indian names.[34] Buddhist contributors could opt to subscribe towards motor ambulances, and the fund consequently presented a number to the War Office, as well as the aircraft.

The British community was imprinted with a strong Scots character. There were long-established Scottish firms in Burma: the Bombay Burmah Trading Corporation involved in the logging business; the Irrawaddy Flotilla Co, dominating inland transport; and Steel Bros. rice traders; last but not least, there was the Burmah Oil Co. headquartered in Glasgow, the parent company of the Anglo-Persian Oil Co. (forerunner of British Petroleum).[35] Whether or not attributable to famed Scottish financial prudence, evidently there had been some local expatriate resistance to collections for presentation aircraft along the lines (as in Singapore) that provision of aeroplanes should properly fall to the British Government, not private subscription. Rangoon's English-language newspaper—unsympathetic to this reasoning—called it a form of 'passive resistance' by those required to pay no taxes to the British Government yet who nonetheless proved reluctant to contribute voluntarily to the war effort.[36]

Two other aircraft were presented through separate funds established locally in 1915. *The Akyab* was provided by residents of the northwestern coastal port of that name in Arakan district (now Sittwe), which handled Burma's rice exports across the Bay of Bengal; and the name *Toungoo District Burma* came from the centre of the teak industry in Lower Burma. Subscribers to the latter (some of whom took the 'Buddhist option' and earmarked their monies for motor ambulances instead) counted very many Burmese names, as well as those of (probably) Indian and Chinese traders.

All three (*Warneford*, *Akyab*, and *Toungoo District*) were initially presentation RE7s—precursor of the RE8 and one of the most unsatisfactory types of the Great War, beset by problems—their later replacements were FE2s of various models. In Pegu district, north of Rangoon, British, Burmese and Indian court officials, lawyers, and honorary magistrates opened a similar fund;[37] but although it presented motor ambulances, there is no evidence for a 'Pegu' aeroplane, so the amount collected for that particular purpose probably fell short of the minimum sum required.

Long after the various local aeroplane funds had closed, a Burma War Fund was established in late August 1916 with the encouragement of a new Lieutenant Governor of Burma, Sir Harcourt Butler. Following an inaugural mass meeting, a Rangoon-based Central Committee was established to include community representatives willing to organise collections. In addition, War Fund organisers wrote to the Commissioners of Burma's administrative divisions, as well as to the Superintendents of the Thai-speaking Northern and Southern Shan States, enclosing a Report of the first meeting and urging their cooperation:

> You will notice that the substantial sum of Rs.2,90,000 has already been secured; that the movement has the approval of His Honour the Lieutenant-Governor; and that a strong and thoroughly representative Committee has been elected to carry out the aim in view, which is that everyone in Burma, of whatever rank, should be afforded an opportunity of expressing by means of a monetary donation his appreciation of the fighting forces of the Empire, which continue to hold the foe at bay and thus ensure the safety of life and property in Burma as if the greatest struggle in history, now proceeding, were not a reality …[and] it is hoped a very large sum will be collected to be presented to the Viceroy [of India] during His Excellency's visit to Burma in December next.[38]

Small contributions were made to the War Fund from all over Burma. Subscriptions were itemised by the *Rangoon Times* administrative division by administrative division and name by name, however tiny the sum. Certainly very many people donated. However, in interpreting the published donors' lists, it is difficult not to be influenced by George

Orwell's portrayal of the prevailing colonial order in his novel *Burmese Days*—seeding the suspicion that anyone in government employ, or seeking to find favour with British officialdom, must have found it politick to add their mite, and get their name recorded amongst the newspaper columns of the virtuous as loyal supporters of the imperial war effort.

More substantial contributions from the Shan States should probably be interpreted as tokens of allegiance, however. Bordering other small Shan polities situated inside the Chinese province of Yunnan to the north, and the kingdom of Siam to the south, the Northern and Southern Shan States of Burma were administered as British Protectorates. Their hereditary Chiefs thus acted as instruments of British indirect rule over Burma's remote frontier lands, while enjoying at the same time a large degree of local power and autonomy—certainly more than any other part of Burma.

Before the imposition of British colonial rule, they had been tributaries of the Burmese kingdom, and actually experienced a reduction in revenue demands with the coming of new, British, overlords in the nineteenth century.[39] They had also begun to benefit of late from the extension of the railway system into their region, though progress had been halted by the advent of the Great War. By 1916, the Shan Chiefs had established a reputation as notably open-handed contributors to British war funds; and Hkun Hsan Gawn, ruler of Tawnpeng, a small but prosperous highland tea-growing area, headed the list of donors to the War Fund with an early substantial contribution.[40]

The Indian *Ghadr* movement established training camps along the Burma-Siam border and smuggled in arms during 1915. Tipped off by the British, the Siamese authorities mounted raids and rounded up several hundred revolutionaries in the frontier areas.[41] Trials of seventeen so-called Indian 'seditionists' were held at Mandalay in Upper Burma between March and August 1916.[42] During his three-week tour of Burma at the end of the year, Lord Chelmsford, Hardinge's replacement as Viceroy of India, was handed a large cheque for 26 lakhs rupees as a first instalment from the War Fund.[43] On that leg of his trip that took him into Shan country, he lauded the rulers' role in the events of the preceding year:

> [Whether] in establishing and maintaining at their own expense patrols on important roads and ferries to prevent the entrance of hostile and seditious emissaries, or in showing their people an example of unswerving loyalty or in subscribing with the greatest generosity to

many objects connected with the war and especially to the Burma War Fund, they have rendered valuable services for which I am glad to have this opportunity of thanking them in person. The *Sawbwa* of Kengtung [occupying a strategically placed salient between Yunnan and Siam], in particular, has shown most commendable energy in causing ill-disposed or seditious persons entering his State to be promptly arrested.[44]

There was to be a further generous gesture of allegiance. At the end of March 1918 three new RE8s inscribed *Burma Nos. 1-3 Presented by the Chiefs of the Northern Shan States* issued from Coventry Aircraft Park.[45] Thus the Northern Shan States became responsible for providing no less than half of Burma's overall contribution to the Imperial Aircraft Flotilla, and in good time for use by the new, unified British flying service, the RAF.

As elsewhere in the empire, British residents enlisted in the forces, and some applied to join the flying services. Lieutenant Short, who transferred to the RFC from the Indian Army and qualified as a pilot/artillery observer, was awarded the MC in September 1916 at age thirty-one;[46] in May 1917 his sister in Burma was informed of his death in action in France. Most unusually, in 1918 a Burmese was gazetted a probationary flying officer. 2nd Lieutenant Lou Htin Wah became the first Burmese to receive a King's Commission in a combatant branch of the British forces.[47] A former pupil of Rangoon College, he had studied at Middlesex Hospital Medical School from June 1915 until November 1917, and was qualified in physics and chemistry, as well as having some knowledge of photography.[48] He relinquished his temporary RAF commission at the end of his employment—then in the RAF's administrative branch—in late 1920.[49]

The RFC/RAF had by the later stages of the war somewhat relaxed its colour bar on recruitment to flying commissions, though fitfully and in response to specific circumstances, rather than as a matter of general policy. In practice, there had always been the odd anomaly despite official insistence on officer recruits of solely European descent. Initially, for example, applicants for the RFC's flying school outside Toronto had been required to be matriculates, and to be of pure European ancestry.[50] However, both educational standards and age requirements were relaxed in October 1917 in order to make good serious RFC pilot losses on the Western Front, and the training facility was also allowed to recruit directly from the Canadian Army.[51]

Evidently, the colour bar on RFC flying commissions was thereby also circumvented, for three Canadian Mohawk Indians of the dissolved 114th Battalion of the CEF—Lieutenants James David Moses, John Randolph Stacey, and Oliver Milton Martin—served as pilots with the RFC/RAF. (Martin survived the war to rise eventually to Brigadier-General—the highest rank ever reached by a native Indian in the Canadian forces.)[52] All appear from their service records to have been seconded for duty with the RFC in late 1917.[53] Apparently a former sailor of Miomac Indian descent, Harry Wambolt trained at Dover and was flying with 1 Wing RNAS even earlier, in 1916,[54] although RNAS recruitment criteria were certainly just as racially restrictive as those of the RFC.

In addition, the Government of New Zealand precipitated an official exemption of sorts when in June 1917 it formally enquired of the War Office in London whether any objection would be raised to candidates of Maori blood from their Canterbury Aviation School applying to the RFC for flying commissions. The War Office eventually informed New Zealand that there was none so long as the applicant was judged acceptable officer material for the New Zealand forces (though this statement was later qualified, see page 300).[55] But in any case, racially exclusionary criteria had not been applied in any official or systematic sense in relation to non-commissioned officers—such as, for instance, Flight Sergeants McIntosh and Clarke from Jamaica—especially where promotion on merit from the rank of Air Mechanic was involved. (There was also a strong class bias in operation, especially early in the war, against white British non-public school pilot officers.)

Even before New Zealand's approach to the War Office, however, the RFC's first Indian officer cadet, Hardit Singh Malik, had already been recruited, and three other Indians were to be admitted as flying officers before the Armistice. A member of a well-to-do Sikh family from Rawalpindi, Malik's motives in seeking to join the British flying service had been complex and his route indirect. According to his autobiography (published posthumously), he was studying history at Oxford when war broke out. In sympathy with nationalist aspirations for India, he was ambivalent about joining a so-called 'war for freedom' when his country was under foreign rule, and he regarded the attitude of the Indian maharajahs as sycophantic. As almost all his British friends at Oxford had joined up, however, he felt the urge to do so too, and resented the attitude of the British military authorities, which, he recalled, seemed to regard all Indian students as potential revolutionaries and terrorists not to be trusted in the fighting services.

Initially, the French Red Cross recruited him as an ambulance driver through contacts of his Oxford tutor, but attracted during his time in France by the romance of flying, he sounded out the French authorities with respect to training as an airman. It was in consequence of these developments that Malik was interviewed by Sir David Henderson at the War Office, and subsequently admitted as an RFC cadet in April 1917—after the same former Oxford tutor who had secured his French Red Cross appointment contacted Henderson and told him that it was scandalous that the British Armed Forces had no place for Malik while the French were willing to enlist him.

Showing real aptitude in training, he was amongst those selected to progress from BE2cs to more advanced fighter pilot instruction on faster but less stable aircraft. (Those less skilled moved on to the heavier multipurpose RE8 scout.) He completed training in June 1917, and from that October flew on the Western Front with 28 Squadron, a new fighter unit equipped with Sopwith Camels, including at Passchendaele. For a while he also flew against the Austrians in Italy, wearing his turban beneath an oversize helmet as part of his RFC uniform. Later, he joined 11 Squadron in France.

The RFC's second Indian pilot recruit was Indra Lal Roy, who joined as an officer cadet in July 1917 straight after leaving school in England. He was killed in action in France in July 1918, his posthumous award of the DFC citing his action in shooting down nine enemy aircraft in thirteen days.[56] Hardit Singh Malik was luckier and survived the war. After it ended he entered the Indian Civil Service, and in 1947 became independent India's first High Commissioner to Canada.[57]

An RFC unit (No. 31 Squadron) was stationed in India from the end of 1915, and as well as training flights carried out occasional operations on the North-West Frontier. There were plans to establish an independent air service for India with a view, specifically, to policing action there (and in June 1917 fourteen machines were indeed deployed in a 'pacification' campaign in Waziristan).[58] During 1918 a second squadron was formed, bringing RAF strength in India to eighty officers and six hundred men.[59] A large expansion in Egypt was additionally envisaged and Brigadier General Geoffrey Salmond, who headed the RAF's Middle Eastern force, proposed training Indian personnel in order to make good service shortages that had followed the German spring offensive, and the consequent diversion of much RAF manpower to the Western Front.

With Air Ministry and India Office sanction, cadet selection was to begin in the autumn, initially for one hundred Indians 'of high physical qualifications and good family' to be enlisted 'on exactly the same terms as British officers' and trained in Egypt, alongside members of British forces in the East and the existing Australian and South African trainees.[60] But the plan fell victim to the general retrenchment of the flying service after the end of the conflict. Besides, as Secretary of State for War with ministerial responsibility for the RAF 1919–21, Winston Churchill, with his notorious mistrust and dislike of India, its religious and communal passions and its politics, lent no support to the scheme, and cheerfully ruled out the possibility of Indians becoming pilots.[61] RAF post-war expenditure on the subcontinent was also slashed by the Government of India in the interests of economy, and though further RAF squadrons were added in 1919–20, they were cut back in 1921; by 1922 they had but few aircraft in a fit state to fly.[62] The subcontinent had to await the 1930s to get its own air force.

During the inter-war years the RAF's official colour bar on officer commissions was also allowed to persist—probably due to institutional inertia as much as racist attitudes within the service itself. Most of the RAF's squadrons (reduced to just twenty-five) were meanwhile deployed in an imperial policing role: in India; in Egypt; in Mesopotamia and in Aden.[63] Otherwise obsolete First World War bombers like the DH9A thus found a role in post-war colonial anti-insurgency operations by the RAF on India's North-West Frontier and elsewhere, especially Mesopotamia and Palestine, becoming the workhorse for RAF bombing raids on rebels and recalcitrant populations.[64]

Country	Approx. population	Number of planes
India	c. 300 million	175 +
Burma	over 12 million	6

Chapter 14:
Birds of Ceylon—a very strange campaign indeed

The directly ruled Crown Colony of Ceylon formed no part of any self-government plan at this period. Educated Ceylonese had been calling for a greater elective voice on the Legislative Council for some years. However, by the time of the 1911 election only one token elected seat had been conceded to them, and fewer than 3,000 Sinhalese, Tamils and Muslims qualified to vote for it.[1] The British presence was well entrenched. The coastal regions of Ceylon had come under East India Company rule (from the Dutch) in the Napoleonic wars, and with the incorporation of the ancient Buddhist kingdom of Kandy in 1815 the whole island became a British Crown Colony. While 75 per cent of the population was Sinhalese, there existed important South Indian (mainly Tamil) minorities, and also a Eurasian population ('Burghers') of Portuguese/Dutch origin. There was in addition a substantial British-born population of more than 6,000, largely comprising planters or administrators in a respective ratio of about two to one.[2]

A new Governor arrived in 1913 with no experience of colonial administration, but with a strong interest in Ceylon's ancient Buddhist civilisation. This was Sir Robert Chalmers, a talented public servant who had risen through the ranks at the Treasury to become the main architect of Lloyd George's redistributive 1909 'People's Budget'. Son of a bookseller and publisher, Chalmers was a Liberal by conviction, but fell out with Lloyd George in 1913 and may himself have requested the move from the Treasury to Governorship of Ceylon.[3] In any case, the post seemed made for him. Under his other, private, hat, Chalmers was a Pali scholar who published in learned journals.[4] He was in communication through the Pali Text Society (PTS) with other linguists and Buddhist scholars in Ceylon and India, as well as members of Siam's royal family.[5] But at the centre of his PTS circle were its founders, Thomas and Caroline Rhys Davids, whose only son, Arthur Rhys Davids—an RFC fighter 'ace'—was to go missing in action in France, aged barely twenty, in October 1917.[6]

Chalmers hoped for the establishment of a university in Ceylon that would become a centre for Sinhalese and Buddhist learning, but in 1914 the world went to war. At the outbreak, existing companies of Volunteers (comprising Europeans and some Burghers) were called out to help man Colombo's defences; and in October 1914, a Colombo Town Guard was formed that included practically every adult male European fit for service who was not the member of an existing volunteer corps. The major and important harbour at Colombo occupied a key position on the sea routes and was initially threatened by the activities of the *Emden*. The commerce raider roamed the Indian Ocean, wreaking havoc with British shipping. On 22 September 1914, its captain, Commander Müller shelled the Burmah Oil Company's coastal oil tank farm in India, immediately to the south of Madras, destroying 346,000 gallons of fuel in a visually sensational attack that was perhaps even more embarrassing to the British authorities than economically damaging.[7] The *Emden* then moved to the west of Ceylon, preying on the busy sea-routes of the western Indian Ocean. After the shelling of Madras, searchlights scoured the entrance to Colombo harbour, the difficulties of tracking down the light cruiser compounded by the immensity of the Indian Ocean itself.

After the cruiser was run aground by HMAS *Sydney* at the Cocos islands in early November 1914 (having in the meantime sunk another five merchant vessels and carried out its spectacular raid on Penang harbour), Colombo was a secure haven again. It served throughout the rest of the war as port of call for ANZAC contingents and British forces from the East *en route* to the Front, and for returning casualties. In monetary terms, the Colony's Government provided £2 million directly towards British war expenses; it met the cost of a Ceylon Planters' Rifle Corps Contingent, and of a Sanitary Company for Mesopotamia; and it contributed to the passages of those volunteering for active service.[8] By 1917, nearly 900 British planters had left Ceylon to join the army: a very heavy percentage of those of military age resident on the island.[9]

British tea and rubber planters contributed generously to relief funds and war charities. Their gifts included four presentation aircraft provided by a Ceylon Aeroplane Fund, while a further two were gifted directly by prominent Sinhalese. However, the press campaign on behalf of the island's aeroplane fund had some peculiar features, which (partially at least) need to be set against the background of events on the island in 1915, and the Governor's response to them. For Robert Chalmers had two sons, Ralph and Robert, one already a professional soldier, and one a barrister who enlisted in the British Army after war was declared. In May 1915 the Governor and his wife were informed that both sons had fallen at Ypres: Ralph killed in action on the 10th and Robert dying of wounds on the 25th.

While the Governor was still in a state of shock, rioting broke out at Gampola, near Kandy, between Sinhalese Buddhists marking Wesak Day (28th May and anniversary of the Buddha's birth) and Moors (a Muslim trading community of South Indian origin). The Moors were trying to bar a Buddhist procession with music and elephants from approaching near to their mosque, initially through legal prohibition. In the event, rioting ensued, and spread throughout the western part of the island over the next few days. As it progressed, it drew in criminal elements, and developed into looting, and attacks on the businesses, homes, and persons of the Moors. The disorder was communal and religious in origin but it entailed commercial rivalries and jealousies. It was, however, entirely unconnected with the war.[10]

On 1st June rioting reached Colombo. Chalmers declared Martial Law the following day, putting restoration of public order into the hands of the GOC, Brigadier General Malcolm. Martial law was not lifted until the end of August although the rioting had largely died down after the first week. Makeshift field courts were set up in late June, and as a result of summary trials under martial law by Commissioners who had been hastily sworn in for the purpose, many Sinhalese peasants experienced lashings as well as being sentenced to long periods of penal servitude (fourteen years and upwards in many cases). Courts martial tried 412 people, of whom 358 were convicted, while civil tribunals, which sat throughout, convicted 4,855 persons and acquitted 3,573.[11] Sentences of execution were swiftly carried out at the prisons—at least six by early July,[12] while summary shootings by the military occurred after the rioting had ended.

Although in his early reporting to the Colonial Office Sir Robert Chalmers judged the riots to have no political undertones, later, vague references to an alleged backstage conspiracy by leaders of the proto-nationalist Buddhist temperance movement creep into his dispatches, based apparently on police intimations and advice.[13] Arrests spread outward to encompass anyone who had questioned the government—not only labour leaders but also the well-heeled and decorous proponents of constitutional reform from Ceylon's landed and professional elite. Many prominent Sinhalese, who almost certainly had no part in, or connection to, the rioting, were thus held without trial on suspicion of conspiracy and subversion. By July, order—of sorts—had been established. However by Chalmers' own account, the riots cost between 106 and 116 dead, possibly more, of which 39 were killed by rioters, 4 by persons unknown, and no less than 63 were killed by military and police.[14]

Martial law was lifted at the end of August. On 26th September leading Sinhalese addressed an overflowing public meeting in Colombo. An estimated 5–6,000 people from all parts of the island were present to hear speakers appeal for a Royal Commission into the handling of the riots.[15] That meeting was restricted to Sinhalese only, but the one elected non-European and non-Burgher member of the legislature, Ponnampalam Ramanathan (a Tamil), made impassioned speeches in the Legislative Council fiercely condemning the way in which the disturbances had been suppressed and refuting the supposition of conspiracy.

Subsequently, the most articulate of the 'constitutionalists', E. W. Perera, made the long and perilous sea journey to England in order to urge the release of those leading Sinhalese still held in detention, complaining that it was impossible to get access to Sir Robert Chalmers.[16] He remained a lobbyist in Britain for four years, joined for three of them by D. B. Jayatillaka.[17] There were questions in the British Parliament. Under pressure of public opinion in England and Ceylon, Sir Robert Chalmers was quietly recalled—officially requested to return to help out at the Treasury—which he did with apparent relief at the end of 1915, being made Joint Permanent Secretary.

Early in 1915 the Governor had established The Chalmers Oriental Text Fund to publish and make available 'scholarly editions of the whole Pali Canon and of the Commentaries thereon in a uniform shape and price'.[18] His successor as Governor, Sir John Anderson, arrived in April 1916 with a different priority. He quickly released eight hundred prisoners sentenced to prison terms of a year or less; and also undertook to review personally all court martial sentences brought up on petition, and all cases where innocent persons had allegedly been convicted of offences connected with the riots. In June 1916 he advised the Colonial Office:

> Petitions are pouring in and I am just managing to keep abreast of them. Some of them are simple, but others are giving me a lot of trouble. The truth is that many of the sentences are vindictive and absurd and if I could get all the compensation money in, I shall release all except ringleaders and those guilty of damaging mosques, of arson, murder, or rape. The promiscuous shooting which took place after the riots were over is very nasty. The fact is that the military got completely out of hand, and let some hot headed young planters shoot almost as they pleased.[19]

An Indemnity Act passed before Chalmers left meant that officials could not be prosecuted for measures taken to suppress the riots. However Anderson appointed a local Commission (comprising the

Chief Justice and a barrister who had held acting judicial posts) to enquire into the most flagrant incident at Kagella district, midway along the Gampola to Colombo road. His coruscating dispatch forwarded an advance copy of their Report to London in May 1917. It censures several men, but pins primary responsibility on F. N. Sudlow, who led an artillery contingent of the Colombo Town Guard in the area. In Anderson's words:

> He received from the Inspector General of Police instructions to deal vigorously with actual disturbances, and seems to have construed them into a commission to administer *lynch law* throughout the area prescribed for his patrol, and to have considered that their effect was to make him the leader of a *posse of vigilantes* sent out to deal with desperadoes in the manner depicted in cinema shows and dime novels of the 'Wild West'.[20]

In the light of all this, it will come as no surprise to the reader that Ceylon provides an example of the failure of a fundraising newspaper campaign to percolate very far beyond the bounds of the resident white planter community, despite vigorous promotion efforts. The timing can hardly have been worse. An appeal by Evelyn Wrench for an aeroplane from Ceylon to join the Imperial Aircraft Flotilla was supported by an editorial in the *Times of Ceylon*, which launched a fund for the purpose at the beginning of August 1915, when martial law was still in full force—although it did provide alternative copy unlikely to incur any problem with the censor. The avian theme that was to dominate the paper's correspondence columns for the rest of the year opened with the proposal that the country's first gift should be called *Paddy Bird*.[21]

And so it was. The European planters of Ceylon adopted the scheme as their own. Much of their involvement no doubt stemmed from a straightforward wish to help the war effort, in response to a further editorial that stressed the effectiveness of aviation in the great struggle on the Western Front:

> Its reconnaissance work has largely removed the 'fog of war' ... [and] proved itself invaluable, as a director of distant artillery fire on land ... their usefulness has been increased by the introduction of wireless telegraphy in a form sufficiently portable to be attached to a plane, and equally important has been the addition of photographic appliances, whereby it is possible to take a telephoto picture of the country below an altitude of 6,000 feet. It is not difficult to appreciate the great assistance this has been to the commanders in this 'war of trenches', where the position has not changed for months at a time. The aeroplane today has in fact become the eyes of the army.[22]

Most contributions were modest, but there were many of them: A large proportion of the resident British community must have subscribed to presentation aircraft during 1915.

The European planters had a trade organisation based in England as well as Ceylon. The President of the Ceylon Association in London, Sir Edward Rosling, called in on Overseas Club headquarters to formally hand over the £1,500 for *Ceylon No. 1 Paddy Bird* in September 1915,[23] and was subsequently included on its Central Committee as Ceylon representative.[24] The self-same month also saw the additional payment of £2,250 from the Ceylon Aeroplane Fund for a 100 hp. Gnome Vickers fighter plane to be called *A Devil-Bird from Ceylon*, and in November, the same again for *Ceylon No. 3 The Nightjar*.[25]

The list for *Ceylon No.4* opened with the sum of Rs. 5,000 donated by a company of the Colombo Town Guard from their riot pay, plus a cheque from a resident of Kandy who wrote: 'I am glad to see that your third egg is nearly hatched, and I'm sending you a cheque to *start a fourth* as I am unable to go to the front myself.' Readers wrote in from their estates all over Ceylon with suggestions of what to call it: Jungle Cock; King Crow; The Harrier; Ceylon Honey-bird; Cingalee Robin; Snipe; Parakeet; Backamoona; Kingfisher; Shrike; and so on. One wrote: 'Sorry this bird is taking longer than the rest to hatch out. Why not call it "Banji" or "Bangey"—I don't know how you spell it—but it's the bane of a tea planter's life.' It even drew suggestions from two Sinhalese readers (for *Lanka*, and for Magpie or *Pol-Kicha*).[26]

Now, bird imagery was quite commonly employed with respect to aviation during the Great War, perhaps even more so in the Colonies than in Britain, for in recent years they had all been required to pass legislation protecting 'birds of plumage' (a move that suggested the influence of Sir Edward Grey, a noted ornithologist, who had become sick of seeing his friends adorning ladies' hats). Nonetheless, enough was enough, even in Ceylon, and the newspaper closed this correspondence by adopting the suggestion from one planter of *The Flying Fox from Ceylon*. The paper even issued a special supplement, a sketch entitled 'The fifth Ceylon Bird will soon be on its way Home', with sari-clad figure waving farewell to a flock of aeroplanes in flight.

A well-known Colombo lawyer had already presented a second Ceylon plane outside of the main aircraft series and independently of the Ceylon Aeroplane Fund (of which more later), and therefore this 'fifth bird' was actually *Ceylon No. 4, The Flying Fox*. It was presented in February 1916,[27] just a few weeks before Ceylon's new Governor, Sir John Anderson, arrived with a mission to undo some of the harm wreaked under martial law.

Supplement to the *Times of Ceylon*, 21 January 1916

It was to be the Aeroplane Fund's third FE2b (at £2,250). Taken together with its first gift of £1,500, that made a grand total of £8,250 collected by the Fund well within six months. Moreover, it was collected very largely within a British community only some 6–7,000 strong, though it was not subscribed by them exclusively. A small handful of Sinhalese planters were listed as contributing to *Ceylon No. 3 The Nightjar*;[28] and in December the *Times of Ceylon* reported that Misses Amy de Saram and D. Jayatilleke played a pianoforte duet that opened an Aeroplane Fund concert, in which a Mr. E. S. D. Oluma sang a topical song about aeroplanes and Zeppelins.[29]

At the time the Ceylon Aeroplane Fund sent its first remittance of £1,500 for *Paddy Bird* there were thirteen men from Ceylon who were members of the RFC or RNAS, and it was requested that one of them be allowed to pilot the plane. The War Office replied that they would do their best, but it might prove very difficult to arrange.[30] The London correspondent of the *Times of Ceylon* subsequently advised that it had proved impossible:

> [However] we can hardly feel disappointed on this account. ... Our chief feeling must be one of pride that the machine is there. [*Paddy Bird* having just arrived in France.] At any moment we may hear that the gun biplane provided by the fund is there also. What about the second gun biplane? We suggested the other day that its gift would be an admirable means of enabling the people of Ceylon to commemorate the 500th anniversary of the Battle of Agincourt.[31]

Later a 'Letter from a Fighting Man in Belgium' was published, so full of bird imagery it could almost have been penned by a journalist on the paper, writing anonymously in support of the Fund. Here is a very short extract:

> Five of the 'super-avian' birds yesterday evening utterly distracted the Hun batteries along our front. The air spaces above were spotted with shrapnel puffs... The hawks, if low down, and in great danger, dodge the shells by continually shifting their angle of flight, darting about here and there ... We have seen flights where it seemed impossible for the hawk to miss a shell, and then, when the hawk had reached safety, we have seen him deliberately turn back and return to the same danger zone ... One hawk did this five times while we watched from the front trench, and when he finally decided to go home to roost, and regained safety, it was a great relief to cheer him, and I hope he heard that bottled-up explosion of relief we gave him.[32]

Obviously genuine letters from the Front were also published, drawing upon the in-house discourse featuring birds. A soldier from Ceylon serving in the Royal Engineers wrote from Belgium remitting money towards *Ceylon No. 3, The Nightjar* (in what might well be a unique example of money for a 'colonial' aeroplane fund flowing in an opposite direction):

> Sir—I enclose my cheque for Rs.500 for my feather in the 'Third Bird'. We are within shelling distance—we spend our evenings occasionally watching the bursts of the German shells as they try and 'strafe' our aeroplanes, six or seven of which are usually up in the evenings, patrolling and scouting.

To which the editor added that the welcome 'our birds' would get when recognised could be imagined, so the sooner 'our third bird joins the flock the better.'[33] Captain Elton Lane of 23 squadron RFC wrote from France in mid-1916 to inform the readership that *The Nightjar from Ceylon* (FE2b serial number 5249) had been transferred to his squadron a few days' previously, and in an exchange for one of his machines was to be posted to his flight. Given the danger from artillery fire he hoped that it would not 'lose too many feathers on the way' in a reconnaissance he was soon to lead.[34]

What was going on? The planters of Ceylon, the Colombo Town Guard, even 'Ceylon men' at the Front in Europe, were communicating through a jocular language created around the Ceylon Aeroplane Fund, reinforcing wartime solidarity between planter society in the Colony and its men on the Western Front. Was there also some element of hope that this 'patriotic' endeavour would absolve them from possible censure for martial law excess? They must have been aware of expressions of disquiet in the British Parliament about events in Ceylon, even while martial law was still in force, including a question about executions directed at the Secretary of State for the Colonies, Andrew Bonar Law. He replied in late July 1915 that sentences of death had been passed in certain cases, but he was not aware whether they had been carried out.[35] (Some certainly had.) Yet less than two months later the truth was out, and Bonar Law stated to Parliament that eighty-three persons had been sentenced to death under martial law, and thirty-four had been executed, of which twenty-six were convicted of murder. Martial law, he said, was withdrawn on the 30th August, and the condition of Ceylon was now 'normal'.[36]

Yet there were other factors also at play within the British community, including an intensely competitive spirit to emulate, and if possible surpass, the Malaya Air Fleet Fund and attract contributions widely from all communities, and a sense of thwarted ambition at the poor response. Witness this outburst of irritation from the paper's letter columns at the general lack of subscriptions from wealthy Sinhalese, from 'the Chetties' (a South Indian community) 'who rule the rice trade' or indeed from others:

> How about the wealthy gem merchant ... What has become of our wealthy Sinhalese gentleman who would think nothing of sending Home the price of an aeroplane for an English horse with a chance of winning the Governor's Cup? ... Do they understand the difference between the mild rule of England and the iron grip of Germany? ... Tea and rubber are again to bear the brunt ... while the wealthy inhabitant of Ceylon who does not own tea or rubber escapes very easily.[37]

In a couple of instances, planters congratulated themselves upon collecting widely amongst the Tamil workforce on their own estates. The following from Trincomalee Estates Ltd., forwarding Rs.52.40, 'being amount I have collected from all the Company's employees, for the most part coolies. They have given me one day's pay most willingly. Trusting the aeroplane will soon be flying.'[38]

Giving to the Fund, the *Times of Ceylon* suggested, presented an opportunity for Ceylon 'the Premier Crown Colony' to make its mark, and hope for favourable treatment in any new dispensation for the countries of the British Empire, after the Great War was all over; it should not be said that only the Dominions contributed to victory. One subscriber invoked the spirit of public school team games:

> Sir—If thirty other East Anglians and (or) Old Marlburians will contribute to the Ceylon Aeroplane they will draw a third subscription from myself. Marlborough is near the top of the Public Schools in numbers at the front, and as for Norfolk, Suffolk, Essex, and Cambridgeshire, see the casualty lists daily. No objections to the other schools cutting out Marlborough in subscriptions.[39]

Ceylon was also viewed as in competition with other British Colonies in adding aircraft numbers to the Imperial Aircraft Flotilla:

> From 'Our London Correspondent' 3 February 1916:
> I presented Ceylon's fourth splendid gift to the Empire's defence last Tuesday to the Overseas Club, and mentioned that, whilst the whole island had taken part in the subscription, the girls and children throughout Ceylon, and even the coolies on the estates, had taken their

part in sending this beautiful weapon of defence into the air. I see Sir Hugh Clifford [a former Colonial Secretary of Ceylon] is not behindhand in this good work. A further sum of £1,526 has been subscribed by the people of Ashanti for the purchase of an aeroplane to the Royal Flying Corps through the Overseas Aircraft Fund. This is the fifth aeroplane to be presented by the people of the Gold Coast and its dependencies. Thus Ceylon and the Gold Coast are running a 'neck and neck' race.[40]

A Tamil benefit concert held in Jaffna in October 1915 raised Rs. 1,000 for the Fund and the small Muslim community of Talawakelle (where the mosque and bazaar had been torched and destroyed in early June) separately subscribed Rs.126.20.[41] Rather too much was made of such scanty involvement, and despite ingenious appeals from European planters the Sinhalese majority largely stood aloof:

> An appeal by a Buddhist to fellow Buddhists:
> Although I am open to be criticised for inviting my co-religionists to break indirectly the foremost of the five vows which we are bound to observe ... I would point out ... that we present the aeroplane as a symbol of our loyalty to our King, and do not ever wish that anyone should get close to the machine to be killed.[42]

But the entire Buddhist Sinhalese press had been suspended since early in June. Its editors remained in detention until martial law was lifted,[43] when a Special Tribunal handed out fines to those deemed guilty of publishing material liable to promote hostility between Sinhalese and Moors.[44] Even when free to do so, it is unlikely that the vernacular press would have been much of a mind to further the campaign.

Two prominent Sinhalese did each donate presentation machines, but not through the Ceylon Aeroplane Fund (and neither requested the presentation name of flying creature, whether bird or mammal). Frederick John de Saram, JP, a barrister and head of a well-known Colombo firm of solicitors, met the costs of a fighter aeroplane for the RFC in September 1915.[45] His letter, informing Governor Chalmers of the War Office's acceptance of his offer, requested that it be given the name *Ceylon*.[46]

Then in June 1917, the landed proprietor and mine-owner, Henry Lawson de Mel, JP, donated £2,500 through the Colonial Office for a seaplane for the RNAS (put toward a naval patrol floatplane).[47] Like de Saram's gift to the RFC, he simply asked that it be inscribed *Ceylon*. However, his somewhat verbose accompanying letter to the Governor also proclaimed his loyalty to the British Empire and his helpful public influence on fellow Sinhalese:

> In public life I have over and over again impressed my fellow countrymen how much we were indebted to His Majesty's Imperial Navy for our safety, our food, and the sale of nearly all our products ... For the past few months I have been lecturing in Sinhalese on the War in several towns and villages ... and at two public meetings at Colombo and Moratuwa when several thousand of Sinhalese were assembled I moved from the Chair two resolutions unanimously passed praying for the early and successful termination of the War and calling upon all Sinhalese to support the war by service or contribution.

In accordance with de Mel's expressed wishes it was announced only that he had made a generous contribution for war purposes, without specifying the amount or its exact object.[48]

Henry de Mel (a lawyer before taking on the family business) had as his prime concern damage limitation, and managing the economic effects of war on the island. He had indeed delivered a recent series of public lectures, and earlier helped avoid a run on the Savings Bank by issuing appeals to depositors through the Sinhalese press.[49] However, he had also been one of those prominent Sinhalese at the mass meeting of September 1915 that called for a Commission of Inquiry into the riots; and his letter to the British authorities offering money for the seaplane, although couched in reassuring terms of his good intentions and support in the war, was probably also exploratory of the official response to his more recent political activities.

Elected as a member of Colombo's Municipal Council to represent the Low Country Products Association, Henry Lawson de Mel was a proponent of local self-government. In addition, he was a prominent member of the newly formed Ceylon Reform League, which listed the campaigners E. W. Perera and D. B. Jayatillaka as its agents in London.[50] A press notice announcing the League's establishment in mid-June 1917 gave as its stated purpose to secure 'such reforms in the administration and government of Ceylon as will give the people an effective share therein'.[51] Soon thereafter, de Mel transmitted a Reform League memorial to the Governor that—very politely—urged change at the local level. In forwarding the document to London, Anderson explained that it was to H. L. de Mel, a man of education and ability and a leading light in the Low Country Products Association, that the Colonial Government turned for help and advice on matters affecting coconut and plumbago interests.[52]

It is not difficult to discern which of the two was foremost in official thinking. H. L. de Mel managed some fifty estates (coconut, cinnamon and tea) owned by his father or himself, and while the virtual collapse of the coconut industry, on which so many relied for their livelihoods, was a cause for concern, plumbago—or true vein graphite—was used in munitions production. Ceylon supplied the Allies, and the US was its principal customer. De Mel, who chaired the Plumbago Merchants Union, owned the large Ragedera mine, a thousand feet deep and producing the highest possible grade of graphite with just one per cent ash when fired at high temperatures. Used in crucibles, it was employed in the production of explosive shells, heavy artillery, and armour plating. In 1913, Ceylon as a whole had exported just 15,000 tons, but this rose to at least 59,607 tons during 1916 and 1917, and de Mel's mine played an important part.[53] He was the first person from the island to be awarded a CBE.[54]

Apart from the Ceylon Aeroplane Fund, there was another War Fund established with the primary aim to present an aircraft to the RFC. It was set up by a representative of the Church Militant who encouraged enlistment in the British forces: This was the Rev. A. G. Fraser, Principal of Trinity College, the Church Missionary Society (CMS) leading private boys school. Subscription lists show that all communities at the school contributed to the fund, but its priorities shifted from aircraft in late 1915 (when the *Times of Ceylon* Passages Fund ran out of money) to providing passages for army volunteers.[55]

As well as teachers and alumni of Trinity College who were drawn from all Ceylon's communities, some Burghers and other Eurasians also sailed from Ceylon for the purpose of volunteering for the British Army, despite initial War Office reluctance to accept them.[56] (They were eventually absorbed into various British units: two half-brothers, K. Visuvalingam and A. W. Viswa, were reported to have been discharged back in 1917, wounded and with shell shock, both the sons of A. S. Brown, estate-owner at Gampola; they had served in different regiments.)[57] Of the 65 volunteers from Trinity College itself, 13 were killed; 18 wounded or gassed, and 2 taken prisoner. The Rev. A. G. Fraser himself served as an army chaplain on the Western Front from autumn 1917 until gassed and invalided out in mid-1918.[58]

By September 1917 the Report of the Kegalla Shootings Commission, as it was known, had been published in Ceylon. The white planter reaction was one of dismay and fury. They were incensed as much by the language used in the Governor's presentation of its findings—

which described the action of those implicated as 'incomprehensible [for] an Englishman in an English Colony'—as by the perceived injustice of its findings.[59] Anderson was unrepentant, telling the Colonial Office that his action had gone far to dispel strong feelings amongst Sinhalese about the 'serious blot [these incidents had created] on the traditions of British administration, which had impaired their confidence in the impartiality and honesty of their rulers [...] the result at which I aimed and if it has been attained its value far outweighs any temporary soreness on the part of a section of the community.'[60]

The Planters' Association of Ceylon therefore resolved with the help of the London Association to counter the 'false version ... given to certain members of parliament [in London]',[61] and they produced a memorial setting out their case. It called for the reinstatement and exoneration of the four men named and dismissed from their positions, which it maintained were blameless because they had acted in good faith. Sir John Anderson suppressed the document on the grounds that it was almost certain to evoke a Sinhalese counterblast.[62] However, he died on 24 March 1918, a week after an operation to remove an abdominal growth; he had been ill, at times gravely, for over a year, though with periods of remission.[63]

The planters thereupon returned to the charge, plying the colonial administration with their memorial endorsed by some 1,600 or so signatories, including that of the Bishop of Colombo.[64] But the Secretary of State for the Colonies was dismissive:

> Mr. [Walter] Long ... cannot admit that the emergency existing at the time in that area was so urgent as to require the immediate execution of men who were arrested without difficulty and could have been held for trial as so many hundreds were held in other districts. As the Commission of Enquiry pointed out, the cases before them were the only cases proved to have occurred in the Colony in which persons had been executed after a summary enquiry and after rioting had ceased.[65]

Blame was apportioned locally in other quarters too. An English-language newspaper close to Ceylon's educated, reformist elite, the *Ceylon Daily News*, began publishing in January 1918. It commented of the choice of a Governor to follow Anderson that people had come to appreciate the importance of the individual occupying the office. The rule of Sir John Anderson had been 'personal' as well as 'independent, and fearless, and just'. Without once mentioning the name of Sir Robert Chalmers, it added that the people of the country now had a lively sense of the difficulties facing a Governor of Ceylon, whereby 'the kindliest intentions may be frustrated and unmerited hardships ensue':

> One pitfall in particular they have reason to dread ... We are aware of the existence of a class of 'imformers' [sic.] in this country—persons whose habit it is to distort facts and invent fears, who make it their business generally to misrepresent the mind and the feeling of the people, for the advancement of their selfish ends. At a crisis, these persons attend with evil counsel. In the absence of a crisis they seek to generate an atmosphere of suspicion which may engender some momentous misunderstanding.

Hopefully, it said, the next Governor might have 'some experience of the winning ways of the habitual informer' and thus will be 'able to estimate these interesting elements in our political situation with accuracy, and eliminate them with discretion.'[66]

The Ceylon Reform League, to which H. L. de Mel belonged, merged in 1919 with the older—and even more resolutely respectable—Ceylon National Association, to form the Ceylon National Congress;[67] contributing to the post-war growth of Ceylonese political nationalism. Memories of Governor Chalmers' role nevertheless remained curiously muted, later writers recalling him as an inexperienced figure, stampeded into extreme measures while afflicted by grief, and Brigadier General Malcolm appears to have carried the main opprobrium for the abuses of 1915.[68]

It is tempting to wonder what divergent path the Imperial Aircraft Flotilla scheme might have taken with no riots, and no martial law. Chalmers might well have passed Wrench's appeal to the Sinhalese Buddhist press, as well as the planters' mouthpiece, the *Times of Ceylon*; the PTS with its connection to the Rhys Davids family might even have had some role. At the very least, the campaign would probably have been associated less closely with a rather closed and blinkered British community. There was no inherent reason why the contrast with the Malaya Air Fleet Fund should have been quite so stark.

Country	Approx. population	Number of planes
Ceylon	More than 4 million	6

FE2b 6338 *Ceylon No. 3*—A Nightjar from Ceylon in German hands, early 1916 (the FE2b of which Captain Elton Lane wrote home in mid-1916 was its replacement), courtesy of Cross & Cockade International Archive

Chapter 15:
Furthest ripples of the Great War reach Abyssinia and Siam

The British Empire sent huge numbers of migrants around the world. In 1913 alone, 389,394 people travelled overseas from Britain, 73 per cent of them to destinations within the empire, especially the white Dominions.[1] It also distributed Indian indentured workers about in large numbers, many originally to fill the labour gap left on colonial sugar-estates by the emancipation of black slaves in the 1830s. In the decades leading up to the Great War, Indian labour migrants also harvested new cash crops, like rubber, or old ones like tea. Despite the ending of indentured labour in 1917, by 1921 there were still 2.5 million Indians living outside the sub-continent in Britain's colonial empire.[2] Chinese 'coolie' labour was also transported about in quantity, especially from southern China to the tin mines and rubber estates of the FMS.

Migration by traders and settlers from India and China (and elsewhere) had of course also gone on independently of the British for centuries, and continued, as opportunity beckoned. By the First World War, there were 'Asiatic' trading communities of persons born in British India or in British Colonies, and therefore British subjects, scattered not only within the empire, but outside it; sometimes in countries that had (somehow) avoided being colonised by the European powers at all. Those British subjects fell under the wing of the British consular service, controlled by the Foreign Office in London, and were not the direct concern of the Colonial Office. Yet although the rulers of the countries in which they resided might have been on the fringes of the conflict, they had their own interests in the outcome of a Great War that was convulsing both Europe and the Ottoman Empire.

As we saw in chapter one, at the end of 1914 the Foreign Office under Sir Edward Grey sent instructions to its Consuls and heads of Legation abroad (then usually called Ministers rather than Ambassadors) to recruit 'patriotic' Britons to a League established in London to raise funds abroad for the Admiralty; failing to collect sufficient for a warship, however, the Patriotic League of Britons Overseas turned to seaplanes for the RNAS instead. In mid-1915, administration of the

League's seaplane fund was taken over by Evelyn Wrench, author of the Imperial Aircraft Flotilla scheme. In addition, during 1915–16 Charles Alma Baker's Malaya Air Fleet Fund was enjoying great success in attracting subscriptions from beyond the bounds of the resident British expatriate community in the FMS and Straits Settlements. This influenced British representatives in foreign countries outside the empire to look to 'their' locally resident British subjects for contributions.

Contemporary British involvement with the ancient Christian kingdom of Abyssinia in the Horn of Africa, source of the Blue Nile, was largely geopolitical and strategic, rather than economic or commercial in nature. Abyssinia owed its continued independence to the resounding victory of the Emperor Menelik II over the Italians at the Battle of Adowa in 1896. Menelik, however, had been realistic enough in the years that followed to mesh the consolidation of his own empire with the interests of Britain, Italy and France in the region. In extending his control from Abyssinia's Christian highland core out over adjacent lowlands (including areas imprinted with an Islamic rather than Coptic Christian character) he was careful to legalise the kingdom's boundaries through frontier agreements with the neighbouring European imperial powers—Britain in Sudan and Somaliland and the East African Protectorate; France and Italy. Among the new or long abandoned areas Menelik incorporated into his empire were the Ogaden, the mediaeval walled trading city of Harar, and the lands of the Oromo.[3] Great Britain, France and Italy had accommodated to the fact of Menelik through the Tripartite Agreement of 1906 that recognised Abyssinia's independence, but they qualified this with an envisaged three-way carve-up in the event of a breakdown of government.

Foreigners in Addis Ababa constituted only about 2–3,000 persons out of a permanent population of a little over 60,000, of which Greeks were the largest community, followed by Arabs, Indians and Armenians. There was a British Legation to the Emperor Menelik's court occupying land they had been granted on the outskirts, as well as French, Italian, Russian and German Legations, and American, Turkish and Greek Consulates.[4] Wilfred Thesiger (brother to Lord Chelmsford, Viceroy of India 1916–21) had arrived to head the British mission in December 1909, and remained for the next ten years. However, just two months before his arrival, a massive stroke had left Menelik paralysed and unable to speak. Menelik's designated heir was his young grandson Lij Iyasu (or Iyassu, or Yasu), supported by an appointed regent. But in early 1911, the regent died, while the Emperor Menelik II lived on, in a completely incapacitated state. Iyasu, then sixteen, self-indulgent, arrogant, headstrong, and devoid of commonsense, became *de facto* ruler, but he was never crowned. On 13 December 1913, Menelik finally died.

The youthful Iyasu spent most of his time outside Addis Ababa, expressing open contempt for the Shoan aristocrats and government officials running the Kingdom. During the Great War he played a disastrous hand. Iyasu's attempt to favour Muslims in his administration (and his taking of Muslim wives) was perhaps an attempt at assimilation of the borderlands, as he claimed, but it nonetheless further alienated the Shoan aristocracy and the Coptic Church Establishment. After Italy entered the war on the side of the Allies in May 1915, his actions attracted the attention of the Central Powers, and Turkey set out to woo Iyasu.[5]

A year on, the British Minister reported to London that Iyasu had presented the Turkish Consul with an Abyssinian flag 'on which was embroidered the Turkish crescent, and the Mohammedan profession of faith', causing consternation amongst Coptic Christians.[6] Turkish propaganda denouncing the Arab Revolt appeared on display in Harar (published on orders from the Turkish Consul, with Iyasu's permission). It charged that the British had 'bought' the Sheriff of Medina and the Bedouin tribes in an attack on Islam, and called for *jihad*.[7] While existing opinion in Abyssinia lacked confidence in an Allied victory, Thesiger believed that the fall of Kut-el-Amara in Mesopotamia (at the end of April 1916) had increased Turkish military prestige, itself already enhanced by the British evacuation of Gallipoli; although Iyasu himself remained personally indifferent to Germany's fate (not necessarily Turkey's) and the ultimate outcome of the war.[8]

Moreover, Lij Iyasu infuriated Great Britain, in particular, by flirting with their opponent in British Somaliland, Seyyid Muhammed Abdullah Hassan (the so-called 'Mad Mullah') to the extent of supplying some rifles and ammunition. Equally, Iyasu's attempt at alliance building appeared treasonous to domestic critics, since the Dervish leader opposed Abyssinian control of the Ogaden, with its Somali population. In any event, in September 1916 the Allies sent a joint formal note to the Foreign Ministry in Addis Ababa protesting Iyasu's actions and announcing an arms embargo.

Some two weeks later, he was deposed by a group of Shoan nobles on the ostensible ground of apostasy, for which, according to one historian, the Allies provided ammunition in the form of forged pictures and documents; the date chosen for the coup was 27 September 1916, an Orthodox Christian holiday commemorating the finding of the True Cross.[9] In a very modern touch, the conspirators were frustrated in their attempts to keep the Allies out of the picture by the Italian Vice-Consul, an electrical engineer by profession, who tapped the wire between the Shoan headquarters and Addis Ababa, which he connected to the Italian Legation.[10]

Iyasu's distant cousin Tafari (or Taffari) Makonnen—subsequently Ras Tafari, and still later the Emperor Haile Selassie—was almost certainly one of the leading players in the conspiracy. In August, Iyasu had removed him as the Christian Governor of the important, and largely Muslim, eastern province of Haraghe, and therefore of the city of Harar itself, where the Turkish propaganda effort was concentrated. Of highborn Shoan pedigree, he was promoted to Ras (Prince) Tafari immediately after Iyasu's deposition, and nominated as regent and heir apparent to a new Monarch, Menelik's daughter, Empress Zewditu. She was little more than a pious figurehead, however, overshadowed by Ras Tafari—twenty-four years old to her forty, but wily, sophisticated in his international dealings, politically astute, and personally courageous. Iyasu fled, initially to Harar, while his father, Negus Mikael of Wollo, raised an army to march on Addis Ababa.

The Thesigers at the British Legation had a son born in Addis Ababa in June 1910, and also named Wilfred Thesiger, who was to become the well-known British explorer and writer.[11] According to his autobiography, *A Life of My Choice*, his father the British envoy had been on leave in England when war was declared, and served in France with the rank of Captain in British Army Intelligence through the retreat from Mons, before returning to Addis Ababa with his family in January 1915 at the end of that leave. (There is nothing to indicate that his military position was temporary, however, and Wilfred Thesiger, senior, is sometimes referred to as Captain Thesiger in contemporary correspondence with London.)

A Life of My Choice also recalls that when the writer was himself six years old, the infant son of Ras Tafari, Asfa Wossen, was brought to his mother for safekeeping after Iyasu's deposition; and of his father making arrangements for the three hundred British subjects in Addis Ababa—Europeans, Indians and Arabs—to take refuge in the Legation grounds if Negus Mikael should emerge victorious. His father feared that restoration of Iyasu would constitute a propaganda success for Ottoman Turkey at the very least, and at the worst might even bring Abyssinia into the war, at a time that the British were fighting the Germans in East Africa, the Turks in Sinai, Mesopotamia and the Aden Protectorate, and the Dervishes in Somaliland.[12]

The short but bloody civil war was resolved by Negus Mikael's defeat by the Shoan army at the Battle of Segelle to the north of Addis Ababa on 27 October 1916, thereby removing any threat of the Central Powers making political inroads in the Horn of Africa.[13] Zewditu's coronation as Empress took place in February 1917—the first ever attended by official European representatives—and was hailed in the British press as the accession of 'The New Pro-Ally Ruler of Abyssinia'.[14]

Events must have provided British subjects with some reassurance that they would not need to seek sanctuary at the British Legation after all—in the short term at least—even though times were still turbulent and Iyasu himself remained at large. He was captured and imprisoned a few years later, and died, or was murdered, in 1935 at around the time of the Italian invasion.

Mrs. Kathleen Thesiger, the British Minister's lively and adventurous wife, was responsible for the wartime collection for Addis Ababa's presentation aeroplane. In May 1918 she remitted a contribution of £2,026 to the recently merged Overseas Club and Patriotic League in London on behalf of its Addis Ababa branch (which had in previous years made modest contributions to the League's Seaplane Fund). She wrote an accompanying letter which pointed out that of the three hundred or so British subjects resident in the Abyssinian capital, few were wealthy, and only a dozen were Europeans. The money was provided by a small, mainly Indian community, a large proportion of whom were low-paid clerks and shop assistants, and trade had been very depressed over the preceding year, so that they had made a real financial sacrifice to do so.[15] Their resulting fighter aeroplane was presented to the RAF in August 1918: SE5a serial number F9029, inscribed *Overseas Club and Patriotic League Addis Ababa Branch* being among the aircraft donated to the Dominions at the end of the war. It went to Canada in 1919.[16]

Ras Tafari formally succeeded Zewditu as the Emperor Haile Selassie at her death in April 1930, but he had been steadily accruing influence for years—not without opposition—and had undergone a coronation of sorts two years previously, with Zewditu's compliance. During his regency he was characterised by the wife of Addis Ababa's

Reuters representative as 'inclined towards aeroplanes, the League of Nations, and the progress of science'. His interest was perhaps reinforced by the British use of air power against the Dervishes in Somaliland at the beginning of 1920. Although not totally successful (their strikes did not succeed in instilling the total demoralisation hoped for, and the 'Mad Mullah' Seyyid Muhammed Abdullah Hassan escaped into the Ogaden, only to die, probably of influenza, some months later): This, however, was one of the first occasions aeroplanes were used in warfare in Africa outside the Great War itself.[17]

As elsewhere in the world at the time, aviation signified modernity and progress, and its defence possibilities were very interesting indeed. After his 'coronation' in 1928 (but before formally becoming Emperor):

> King Taffari was bold enough to purchase one or two French aeroplanes and secure the services of a competent French pilot. Then another plane appeared on the scene, this time German, with two German pilots, both young titled men ... Opposition to Taffari as King had been expected, but he was slowly preparing to meet and quash [this] with the aid of his 'planes, and well drilled and decently equipped little force of soldiers.[18]

On 28 March 1930, the Empress Zewditu's former husband, Ras Gugsa Wule, despite her pleas rose in armed rebellion against him. According to one account, Tafari's three biplanes flew over Gugsa's lines and dropped leaflets that carried the text of an Episcopal anathema signed by the Patriarch and five new bishops threatening excommunication from the Church; when the biplanes reappeared again, after battle had commenced, it was to drop small bombs and hand grenades.[19] (An alternative version held that there were three bombing runs made by the Imperial Air Force in the guise of one biplane with a French pilot.)[20] A couple of days after her ex-husband's defeat, Zewditu died (of natural causes); simultaneously with the news of her death in April 1930, Ras Tafari's succession as Emperor of Abyssinia was announced.[21]

Country	Approx. population	Number of planes
Abyssinia	More than 10 million; c. 300 British subjects	1

Siam was a Buddhist kingdom of 8.8 million at the time of the Great War.[22] It owed its continued independence to Siamese royal statecraft and astute diplomacy, rather than victory in battle. Even the European colonial powers themselves had come to value having a friendly, modernising buffer state interposed between British Malaya and French Indo-China. But the kingdom had lost a good deal of territory to France and Britain, and been forced to accept unequal treaties conceding extra-territorial rights to the western powers. When Vajiravudh came to the throne in 1910, both British and German influence and commercial activity were strong in the kingdom. Until 1917 Siam, with no essential national interests involved, remained a neutral in the Great War.

Although British influence in Siam was not exclusive, it was important. Of the more than two hundred foreign advisers employed by the Siamese Government, over half were British. They were also well dispersed through the bureaucracy, and present in each and every department dealing with natural resources or finance.[23] As at Addis Ababa, a British Envoy Extraordinary and Minister Plenipotentiary to the Royal Court headed the British Legation in Bangkok: this was Sir Herbert G. Dering during 1915–19. (He was one whose long career in the Foreign Service had had its exciting moments—as Second Secretary in Peking he had been present during the Boxer Rebellion and was awarded the China Medal and Clasp for Defence of Legations.)[24] A British Consulate provided the point of reference for resident Britons in northern Siam, many of them involved in the teak business.

Both the British Minister at Bangkok and the Consul in Chiengmai (Chiang Mai) were in receipt of the Consular Circular that issued from the Foreign Office on 17 December 1914, urging them to seek out local Britons willing to establish a branch of the recently launched Patriotic League of Britons Overseas and further its fundraising efforts for a warship. Two branches of the Patriotic League were formed in early 1915. Mr. Hamilton Price, a prominent businessman, agreed to act as president of the Bangkok branch, and the British Consul, W. A. R. Wood, became president of the Northern Siam—or 'Upcountry'—one.

Of the two, it was the Upcountry branch that flourished, despite the scattered nature of its membership (a large proportion failing to attend the first annual general meeting in April 1916, due to 'absence in the forest').[25] Northern Siam was in fact one of the League's rare success stories, along with the notably generous Shanghai branch. As of late May 1915, £458 had been collected for the Seaplane Fund from a membership of only forty-five; by the end of 1916 the branch's contributions totaled £1,666.[26] In consequence, the name *Britons in Siam* could eventually be painted on a Sopwith Triplane,[27] a lethal new fighter plane flown by the RNAS that was introduced in the first half of 1917.[28]

A British Military Aeroplane Fund was additionally established in September 1915. By the following April it had presented two reconnaissance planes to the RFC, one of them—*Chengwa (North Siam) Britons No.1*—subscribed entirely by upcountry residents, and also one fighter plane.[29] Two more fighters were forthcoming later that same year. If the RNAS Triplane is included in the tally, that made five aircraft in all from Siam.

Those final pair of presentation aircraft from Siam were subscribed on an entirely new list however, one that was set up at the instigation of the British Legation specifically to collect from 'British Subjects' in the country. The inspiration probably derived in part from Bonar Law's appreciative official response to the Malaya Air Fleet Fund's first gift of ten aircraft to the RFC, for in his message of January 1916 the Secretary of State for the Colonies had pointedly noted that subscriptions had come from all nationalities including the Chinese of the FMS, and *Reuters* news agency carried his communiqué round the world, including to Bangkok.[30]

During the month that followed that communiqué, Straits Chinese resident at Bangkok formed an Association of British-Chinese Subjects, its purpose to collect funds for the Red Cross. Prominent figures heading the association's twenty-four man Committee included the *comprador* to the Chartered Bank of India, Australia and China in Siam, Chea Chee Seng (from Penang), and the Singapore-born Seow Keng Lin, a major broker who handled the entire rice output of many Bangkok mills.[31]

Many of the better-heeled British subjects resident in Siam at the time were, in fact, Straits Chinese businessmen involved especially in the milling and wholesale distribution (including the bulk shipping) of rice. There was also a substantial Chinese trading community in Siam of non-British subjects (one press estimate of the urban population of Bangkok in this period put the Chinese, or part Chinese, proportion at up to a third). However, those Chinese who *were* British subjects normally had this status by virtue of having been born, and often educated, in the Straits Settlements, many originating from nearby Penang island, an entrepôt serving southern Siam and elsewhere in the immediate region.

On 20th July 1916, Herbert Dering called a meeting of British subjects at the Legation, with the express purpose to attract subscriptions for a fighter aircraft for the RFC. Some three hundred 'European and Asiatic' British subjects attended, with a strong showing reported on the part of Indians 'of all races', Straits Chinese, Burmans, Shans, Malays, and others, all of whom subscribed 'according to their means'. With a little over 13 *ticals* to the pound sterling, close upon 50,000 *ticals* were given or promised, that is, more than enough for the first fighter:

> One prominent and respected member of the British-Chinese Community alone signed for 6,000 *ticals*, while various well-known Sikh residents and other Indians of the different races represented made donations of conspicuous sums individually, ranging from 2,000 *ticals* downwards.[32]

On 4th August, second anniversary of Britain's declaration of war, Dering announced £2,250 for a fighter plane to be inscribed *Presented by British Subjects of All Races in Siam*. Less than two months later a further £2,250 was remitted from the Siam British Subjects Aeroplane Fund for another fighter for the RFC, *Presented by British Subjects in Siam No.2*.[33] Leftover funds of £465 were sent to London for upkeep of the planes.[34]

A final published account broke down contributions by community, though without giving any indication of donor numbers or overall size of the community in question. The list nonetheless indicates that the two contributor groups with the largest financial input were the Europeans and the Straits Chinese, and this probably reflected their overall respective financial clout. It will be seen that the Indian contribution was set out under distinct community sub-categories (and the possible regional security implications of this at that time are examined in the concluding chapter, pp. 325–7).

Table III: Contributions to the Siam British Subjects Aeroplane Fund:

Subscribed by:	Ticals:
Europeans	28,082.50
Chinese	20,456.00
Sikhs	4,629.00
Borah community	3,737.00
Southern Indians	2,986.00
Northern Indians	1,384.75
Suratis	1,336.00
Burmese	1,126.88
Shan	434.83
Malays	164.00
Anonymous	155.00
Sundries	137.00
Bank interest	36.77
Grand total -	Ticals 64,817.68

NB: the sums given do not quite add up to the stated total
(Source: *Bangkok Times*, 22 January 1917)

A vivid account of the destruction of one of Siam's presentation aircraft came from its unnamed RFC observer writing to his brother in Siam. As the paper commented, it was rare for such a small community as theirs to be so nearly and personally connected with the action of one of the aeroplanes that they had contributed to the war. (It is also rare to encounter such eloquence and immediacy of expression in a letter from an RFC airman tasked with what is often assumed to be the mundane task of photographic reconnaissance.) The name of the presentation reconnaissance aircraft from Siam that was destroyed is unstated, but of Siam's gifts to the RFC, a possible candidate is the reconnaissance biplane *British Residents in Siam* first presented in 1915:

From the Bangkok Times, 19 June 1917:

I am alive, actually alive! By all the laws of chance I ought to be dead at the present moment. There was a photographic reconnaissance this morning; I led in the 'Siam' machine. We must have been a fine sight leaving the aerodrome—the camera machine (myself with two long blue streamers followed by the spare camera machine with one streamer) then the escorting battleplanes, and about ten fast scouts skimming a thousand feet above us. Off we went to do the dirty work. Before we started we had seen bunches of Huns wandering about in fives and sixes.

This morning the air was full of them, and Archie had three weeks shells to work off. As we started in the first square shells were bursting all around us, hundreds of them above us and below us. One came through the wing and a strut about two feet from the engine. Fortunately, it did not burst. At the 14th square there was a deadly pause—you could almost feel the stillness. Then suddenly from the clouds above us and from all sides came the rat-tat-tat of the machine guns—Huns appeared from nowhere, dived on our tail, shot at us as they passed underneath. I got the rear gun on the nearest one and emptied a drum into him at close range. I think he was astonished as the back of the machine is supposed to be the blind side and so the one to attack from, but we now have two guns. He came so close I held my breath and waited for the crash, but he just managed to turn, stuck his nose up for a bit, fell over on one wing, dived down thousands of feet and vanished in a cloud. I think I must have shot him.

Meanwhile it was impossible to tell what was going on, —everything seemed to be going round in circles, one minute we were lying on our backs, the next minute pointing downwards at the earth. You could catch a glimpse of a Hun diving past after someone, or perhaps being himself chased—just in time for a few hurried shots at him, then snatch up the rear gun and blaze away at someone swooping down on your tail. Suddenly a big hole appeared in the spare petrol tank, and the petrol spouted out and blew over the engine; two wires suddenly curled up and flamed out in the wind. I signed to go home and we dived down, looking more like a bundle of wires and ribbons than anything else. The engine had stopped, but we were fortunately up about ten thousand feet.

We just managed to glide into the first square, the Huns giving us H... from the trenches. We landed with a bump between the lines and just managed to crawl to a shell hole before we got hit. There wasn't much left of the machine by this time, so we left it there and crept back into our own lines when it grew dark. The photos were excellent and were the only bunch secured 'over' today.

Right from early days, the link between the Patriotic League and the Overseas Club caused controversy among the British community in Siam, not on account of Evelyn Wrench himself, but because of its President, Lord Northcliffe. The objection was ostensibly to the *Daily Mail*'s 'political views of which many men out here disagree'. Since, however, the newspaper's opinions were of a flag-waving imperial variety, it was probably the populist and demagogic nature of Northcliffe's paper that irked, as well as his attacks on members of the wartime leadership. At the 1917 annual general meeting of the Bangkok branch, Hamilton Price, chairing, regretted that the League was becoming increasingly tainted, via the Overseas Club, by its association with Northcliffe—the man 'who tried to down Lord Kitchener'—and his 'blatant journalism'.

Because of this apparent loathing of Lord Northcliffe and all his works, Siam remitted its contributions directly to the War Office via Dering at the Legation, bypassing the Overseas Club Aircraft Fund altogether. When in 1918 news arrived from London that the Overseas Club and Patriotic League were to merge, the Bangkok branch of the League voted a resolution proposed by Hamilton Price and seconded by Dering to dissolve itself, and constitute a new British (Siam) War Aids Association instead; and the Northern Siam branch followed close on its heels.[35]

In parallel with the collections for presentation aeroplanes within the British community and by British subjects, Siam was independently establishing its own embryo air force. King Vajiravudh took a strong interest in defence matters. When he ascended the throne in October 1910 he was already bent upon fostering military modernity and a nationalist spirit in his people. Mastery of the new technology of flying promised to do both, as well as demonstrate to the Western nations Siam's equal capabilities.[36] The beginning of 1911 had seen an Aviation Week at Bangkok at which the Belgian aviator, Charles Van den Born, gave a series of exhibition flights. Among the passengers he carried were two of the King's brothers, Prince Chakrabongse, Chief of the Army General Staff, and Prince Parachatra, Commander of the Army Engineers (as well as Mrs. Hamilton Price).[37] The military interest was patent, and an army passenger dropped a mock bomb in front of the lawn on one circuit.[38]

Three Siamese officers of the Royal Army Engineers were sent for instruction to France in February 1912, and after several months of learning the language they completed their pilot training courses in August 1913. Major Luang Sakd was the first to gain his Aero Club of

France qualification and go on to secure a certificate as a military flyer; he commanded the Siamese air service 1914–1932.[39] The air fleet was initially made up of three Breguet biplanes and four Nieuport II monoplanes purchased from France by the Ministry of War, and a fourth Breguet bought by a wealthy resident of Cambodian extraction (setting a precedent for gift aeroplanes that was followed by others in Siam over the next decade).[40] After witnessing a flying display by all three of the country's military aviators on 13 January 1914, the King recorded in his diary: 'I am delighted that we Thai are not bested by the Westerner; truly we can do whatever they can do.'[41]

Although he led a country initially committed to neutrality, King Vajiravudh's wartime sympathies were barely hidden. He had been educated in England, including at Sandhurst Military College as well as Oxford University, and while in Britain served as a lieutenant with the Royal Durham Light Infantry. In 1915 and in 1916 he made two separate donations of £1,000 to the widows' and orphans' fund of his old regiment; and in mid-1915 Vajiravudh and George V exchanged honorary ranks of General in each other's armies.[42] However, in the matter of state policy, he acted on his considered assessment of the national interest, which for the first two years of the war was to maintain strict neutrality.[43]

The King, however, had already published a long anonymous article in August 1915, deploring the German sinking of the *Lusitania* as a violation of international law. It was the resumption of unrestricted submarine warfare and consequent declaration of war on Germany by American President Woodrow Wilson in April 1917 that precipitated a change of policy.[44] The King argued to his Ministers that US engagement was about to tip the balance of war in the Allies' favour, so that Siam's interests were no longer served by staying neutral. If Siam entered the war now, it could hope for future concessions in the matter of its unequal treaties with the European powers. The loss of Siamese investments in Germany would be balanced by the seizure of German steam-ships anchored at Bangkok.[45]

Siam entered the war on 22 July 1917. The 2–300 Germans resident in Siam, one-third of them in employment as Government Advisors and the rest engaged in commerce, were expelled to British India, and German assets seized. The King followed the advice of his chief diplomatic representative in Paris, Prince Charun, who proposed that the country should 'take some active part or make a bit of a show' by dispatching a contingent of Air Force pilots and ambulance drivers to

France.[46] The Ministry of War therefore issued an announcement inviting applications for a Siamese Expeditionary Force (SEF) to Europe, especially from airmen, motorists able to both drive and repair, and doctors and nurses:

> It is considered that this Expeditionary Corps will serve to display in Europe the Siamese National Flag as an emblem of His Majesty's honour and show the Siamese National dignity, giving concrete proof that we are in alliance with the Great Nations. It is, furthermore, considered that the members of the corps will gain valuable experience by their own participation in the war as well as by learning from the Allies who have been carrying on the war for already over three years. They will thus be able, when they come back, to enhance the quality of the Siamese Army as a whole. The Expeditionary Force will be equipped as a Flying Corps with aviators, motor mechanics, and medical staff, complete.[47]

In June 1918 the 1,200-plus SEF finally set sail after a number of major transportation hitches. It included an aviation corps of 370, of which about a third had undergone some pilot training already at Siam's own Aviation School. On arrival in France at the end of July they were divided into separate medical, automobile, and aviation contingents. The pilots were placed at Istrès, near Marseilles, for further training, and were still there by the time the Armistice was signed in November 1918, awaiting attachment to French air force units.[48] Ninety-four pilot trainees (out of 106) had qualified as military aviators.[49]

There had, of course, also been undercurrents. There had been a half-baked coup attempt against Vajiravudh back in 1912, and in early 1917 Bangkok was awash with rumours about a plot to replace him with his half-brother, backed by the Germans, but when questioned about this the King intimated to Dering that all was well in hand.[50] During 1915 Siam had also been a locus of *Ghadr* conspiracies, highlighted by a British held trial of Indian 'seditionists' at Mandalay in Upper Burma during March–August 1916, with press allegations of German support and hints at involvement in counter-measures on the part of British Consulates in Siam.[51] However *Ghadr* was of much greater concern to the British than the Siamese authorities. In declaring war against Germany in 1917, Siam's chief aim was an uncomplicated one: to assert its right as a member of the family of nations, influenced by the repeated declaration by the Allies that the war was being waged so that every nation, however small, should be free to develop along its own lines. In this matter, tangible gains were indeed made.

Less than a year after their return from France, the aviators began staging provincial air displays in order to promote popular support for aviation and the construction of new landing grounds. The aerobatic displays and passenger circuits were hugely popular, attracting large crowds from the surrounding areas.[52] While there was no public campaign to raise funds, voluntary contributions for the purchase of aeroplanes poured into the Ministry of War, especially from the further provinces, and Siamese aeroplanes were named after the provinces that had subscribed money. By the 1920s, Siam had over one hundred pilots, and was running an airmail service within the country.[53]

Vajiravudh's calculations had paid off (even if government extravagance on aviation, amongst other things, did create large financial problems). The aviation contingent and also the motor mechanics and drivers had received valuable technical training in France; Siam had the opportunity to unfurl its new flag at Victory Parades in Europe (the present tricolour, designed by the King himself); and the kingdom secured a seat at the Paris Peace Conference of 1919 and the formal abrogation of all German treaty rights in Siam. The US surrendered its treaty rights in 1920, and by 1924–25 all ten European states concerned, including importantly France and Britain, had cancelled their respective extraterritorial treaties.[54]

However the Siamese engagement in the war had encountered no obstacles.[55] In contrast, Ras Tafari had been willing to break off relations with the Central Powers under certain conditions in 1917–18, the most immediate of which centred on supply of rifles, and which also included a seat at the Peace Conference. The British and the French were willing to supply, but met with strong resistance from the Italians, who were even more strongly opposed to the suggestion from the French Government that Abyssinia should furnish a contingent for the war in Europe: if they became actual belligerents, they could claim to be represented at the Peace Conference, which was regarded as out of the question. Thus, any move by Abyssinia was blocked, in the way that Siam was not.[56]

Country	Approx. population	Number of planes
Siam	8.8 million; nos. of British subjects not known, at least many hundreds	5

SE5a F9029 gifted by the Addis Ababa branch of the Overseas Club and Patriotic League and flown by nascent 1 Squadron Canadian Air Force at Shoreham, Kent in 1919, maple leaf symbol on its fin, courtesy of Cross & Cockade International Archive

BE2c 2592 *Contributed to by British Residents in Siam*, the country's first presentation: the formulation 'contributed to' instead of the more usual 'presented by' was chosen by the War Office to acknowledge receipt of £500 in October 1915 from a fund that was still open, and actively receiving donations for the aircraft, courtesy of Cross & Cockade International Archive

Chapter 16:
Big and small donors: The Shanghai Race Club and Argentine Britons

On the outbreak of war, German merchants and their families were the largest foreign element in the British Crown Colony of Hong Kong (though the British community was ten times larger). German women and children were obliged to leave, and male nationals of military age were interned and their businesses taken over by Government—by 1916 their firms had all been liquidated and assets sold off.[1] It was a more complex story in the Straits Settlements Colony. On 7 August 1914 a number of German reservists attempted to leave Singapore by ship for the express purpose of joining the garrison at Tsingtao. They were made prisoners of war, but were released on parole. All German nationals in the Straits Settlements were then made subject to certain restrictions. Following the attack by the *Emden* on Penang harbour, however, instructions issued for their internment.

This action was followed by legislation for the compulsory confiscation and liquidation of enemy companies,[2] though the Colonial Secretary at Singapore conceded that most German residents had behaved in an exemplary manner at a very difficult time, and there was no evidence whatsoever that information of the movements of British shipping had reached the *Emden* through any breach of their parole. But German business with neutral states that in turn traded with Germany—a reference to the neighbouring NEI under the neutral Dutch—made it difficult to prevent money and information filtering through from the Colony into enemy countries.[3]

During the Singapore mutiny of February 1915, one group of Indian mutineers made for Tanglin prison camp to release German internees, arm them and invite them to lead the rebellion against the British. This proved to be the last thing the majority of the German civilians wanted, but captured sailors from the *Emden* held alongside them, and the reservists, did collaborate. Soon after, the authorities at Singapore quietly shipped all their German prisoners off to Australia for the remainder of the war.

Such measures were not open to the British in neutral zones, such as the Treaty Ports where German businesses operated freely until

China declared war on Germany in 1917. Shanghai's was something of a special situation. Opened as a Treaty Port in 1843 at the end of the Opium Wars, two foreign enclaves existed administered by their own municipal councils: the International Settlement, and the French Concession. In 1915 the entire British population resident in China outside of Hong Kong numbered 8,641. Of this total, 681 lived in the French Concession and 4,822 in the International Settlement.[4] The Chinese State had ceded neither enclave to any foreign power, and their legal status was opaque. The often freebooting—even some amongst them, criminal—'international' inhabitants were thus able to exploit their considerable leeway to dodge the control of any authority: whether it should be that of their own Government, or of China.

Shanghai Britons had long coexisted and traded with German businessmen in the International Settlement. Although British wartime legislation prohibited trading with the enemy, disentangling Anglo-German commercial ties in Shanghai was far from easy.[5] The British Consul General in Shanghai since 1911 was Sir Everard Fraser KCMG, and Archibald Rose was the British Commercial Attaché. Under the principle of extraterritoriality, Shanghai Britons came under the jurisdiction of their Consul. However, he lacked authority over the body elected each year to administer the International Settlement: the Shanghai Municipal Council (SMC). Elected on a property-based franchise by foreign ratepayers, it was nonetheless dominated by a local British oligarchy that controlled the largest number of seats (six).

In the absence of real executive authority, but expected to further British policies during the Great War, Sir Everard Fraser became an inveterate joiner and patron of 'patriotic associations' that promised to exercise a moral suasion over the British community. Fraser was already president of the Navy League in Shanghai, but on receipt of the Consular Circular from the Foreign Office enjoining British Consuls to support the aims of the Patriotic League of Britons Overseas, he convened a meeting at the Town Hall on 9 February 1915 to discuss the formation of a local branch. It would not be superfluous, he promised—the Navy League was more home-orientated and existed to help support sailors in port, while the Patriotic League was overseas-orientated, and had as its main purpose to buy a warship for the Royal Navy.[6]

Speakers at what was reported to have been a large and enthusiastic gathering included the presidents of the various British national societies in Shanghai: St. George's, St. Andrew's, St. Patrick's and St.

David's. An Australian speaker outlined his country's contribution in the war, while Edward Isaac Ezra, whose family business in Shanghai dealt—in descending order of importance—in yarn, opium, real estate and finance,[7] spoke of India and its support, and vouched that the Jews of the Empire were willing to do their share, and sometimes more. A first meeting of the Committee of the Patriotic League, held at the British Consulate under Sir Everard Fraser's presidency, decided that it would be open to all British registered subjects regardless of age, sex, or race. Donations to the warship (to cover the first year's subscription to the League) were to be paid into the Hong Kong and Shanghai Bank.[8]

They were tapping a rich seam: there was wealth in Shanghai. Most donations for the warship came from the British business community in the International Settlement, but employees of the Shanghai-Nanking and Shanghai-Hangchow-Ningpo Railways also made contributions, and their lists included both British and Sikh names.[9] The Patriotic League's Report for the first half of 1915 shows that of the total £37,000 received from branches worldwide, £15,000 came from China, and £10,219 of that from Shanghai.[10] By the end of 1916, Shanghai had provided the League with over £13,000 more.[11]

A Shanghai branch of the Overseas Club also formed in early 1915, and Sir Everard Fraser was elected president of that too;[12] by June it had over 900 members. Soon the respective members of both organisations were writing to the press to condemn trading with the enemy. For instance:

> Sir—The Shanghai Branch of the Patriotic League of Britons Overseas is now a pretty formidable institution, and it is to be hoped that in addition to collecting funds towards presenting a battleship to the Government at home, active interest will be taken by the committee in promoting wherever and whenever possible British interests in China ... it is a matter of common knowledge that certain Banking Institutions in this port have since the outbreak of war rendered financial assistance in one way or another to German firms, but if the reports which have reached me are correct, I think the majority of Englishmen in Shanghai would be astounded to know to what extent this 'financial assistance' has grown. It is alleged that a large number of German firms are enabled to carry on a regular import and export business solely by the facilities granted them by the Banks here, and I would suggest that a representative and influential committee of the League be formed to investigate this matter thoroughly.[13]

A British Chamber of Commerce was formed in Shanghai in May 1915 with Fraser as honorary president and Archibald Rose, vice-president, but lacked powers, so British firms were urged to take independent action in the matter.[14] Other clubs and associations swung into action, ostensibly galvanised by the German sinking of the *Lusitania*. The British-dominated Shanghai Club requested German nationals to refrain from using club premises, and the forty German members of the Shanghai Race Club received a letter asking them 'not to make use of the Grand Stand, premises or compound of the Club until further notice.' For its part, the Shanghai Marine Insurance Association (nine out of ten of whose members were British or Allied nationals) 'most strongly deprecated' members insuring risks on cargo owned by persons or firms of enemy nationality, either directly or indirectly, by way of reinsurance.[15]

As we already know, the Patriotic League's proposed gift of a warship to the Royal Navy never materialised. In September 1915, the Shanghai branch received a letter from Lord Aldenham to inform them that the League had purchased ten seaplanes instead, and that subscription lists for the Seaplane Fund would be kept open until further notice. He explained that the Seaplane Fund was quite independent of the Aeroplane fund, which was being organised *within* the empire by the Overseas Club, an association with which the League was working in close and friendly cooperation.[16] By the end of 1917 Sir Everard Fraser was able to report that the League in Shanghai had subscribed three seaplanes to date, each costing £3,500, named *Shanghai Britons Nos. 1, 2, and 3* and in addition one aeroplane, *Shanghai Britons No. 4*. The total amount forwarded to London came to £19,585.[17]

However, Shanghai was by then also a contributor to the separate Overseas Club Aircraft Fund through H. H. Read, who started collecting in April 1915.[18] He was well placed to do so, as Treasurer of the Shanghai Race Club, one of the Society hubs of the International Settlement. Its famous racecourse (sister to Hong Kong's Happy Valley) was the largest in China, occupying a prominent position in the centre of the city, in what is now People's Square.

Reid's collection was not an instant hit. A subscriber wrote to the paper in June 1915 to ask what had become of it. Reid explained in reply that since the total sum in hand had only amounted to about $400, it had been put towards the general collection (for *Overseas No.*

1). Apart from a few 'sportsmen' the public response had been indifferent. Recalling that Hong Kong had already sent £4,500 to London, Reid urged Shanghai to make its own worthy contribution. Though not of the empire, he wrote, Shanghai had 'sprung up from a mudflat' chiefly through British energy and initiative, and so he was now addressing his appeal to 'sportsmen' in the knowledge that there were hundreds unable to serve their country militarily, but who were eager in some way 'to play the game'.[19]

In its early formative years, aviation itself had been seen as something of a sporting pursuit for gentlemen, and the original 1912 RFC had recruited from fox-hunting ex-cavalry officers; an image and ethos of cavalier daring had carried over, with those who could afford the cost of pilot training in England in the initial years of the Great War attracted by its 'sporting' and 'gallant' image.[20] This time round Reid had much greater success in attracting contributions, perhaps the result of networking at the racetrack.

In July he was able to acknowledge 'a most generous' contribution from a member of the Shanghai Stock Exchange, which resulted from an appeal from its Chairman for members to show their appreciation for the windfall many dealers had reaped from the wartime demand for raw rubber. Many fortunes had been made by men who had purchased at low rates, while others who had 'got stuck' during 1910 (with the collapse of an artificial rubber boom in a rigged market) had been relieved of heavy burdens: Read hoped that other recent beneficiaries of the rubber boom would follow the stockbroker's example.[21]

In late 1915 subscribers to the fund learnt that 2nd Lieutenant Colquhoun-Symington was flying the city's first aeroplane presented through the Overseas Club, *Shanghai Britons*, (a BE2c) in France. He had been awarded the MC for 'conspicuous gallantry and skill' in demolishing part of a moving train with bombs dropped from a height of 500 ft (but his flying career was to end some months later in serious injury in an air accident).[22] That Christmas of 1915, an exhibition of 'Pictures, Arts and Crafts' held at the Town Hall raised sufficient for a Vickers Gunbus called *Shanghai Exhibition*.[23] The greater part of Shanghai's contribution to the Overseas Club Aircraft Fund derived from the racecourse however. Five presentation planes were subscribed there starting with £1,500 for *Shanghai Race Club No. 1* at the Autumn 1915 Race Meeting.

Subscribers were not generally named in the press, so that much about their identities must be surmised. However, there are some clues, and some circumstantial evidence. Britons dominated the Shanghai Race Club membership anyway. But the racing fraternity also included amongst them their commercial allies and business collaborators drawn from a Jewish merchant elite, originating historically in a Sephardic flight from persecution at Baghdad. They were British subjects who had been attracted to settle in Shanghai initially (via Bombay and Hong Kong) by the lucrative opium trade from British India to China.

Over time, opium was overtaken by trade yarn, cotton and Indian produce; and David Sassoon and Company Ltd., the most important such business, additionally developed extensive interests in shipping and real estate. By 1914, the firm had branches at Manchester, Bombay, Calcutta, Karachi, Baghdad, Hong Kong and Hankow, as well as Shanghai. But its directors lived in England and its head office was located in London, from whence its worldwide commercial and financial operations were run.[24] Sir Philip Sassoon (military secretary to Field Marshal Sir Douglas Haig 1915–18) was a British MP and the Company Chairman. For the City of London was at the same time both a cosmopolitan and a British institution:

> The great Jewish families [like the Sassoons] epitomised this duality, combining country houses, sons at Eton and Harrow, and outspoken loyalty to the crown and the empire with a global spread of personal and economic connections which stretched well beyond the limits of formal British influence. (Cain and Hopkins, p.127)

The flamboyant and undoubtedly gay Sir Philip was also a prominent Society host and aviation enthusiast, who was later to hold two periods of office as British Under Secretary of State for Air.

The most prominent Baghdadi Jewish name at Shanghai was indeed that of the Sassoons, followed closely by the Ezras. Despite possible latent anti-Semitism, Shanghai's British community maintained less rigid social barriers at the upper levels than in the usual run of British colonies. The Baghdadi Jews, for their part, had adopted an Anglicised way of life, belonged to a club, and acquired a taste for whisky. Between 1869 and 1921, the Baghdadi Jewish mercantile elite elected a councillor virtually each year as part of the British quota of six on the SMC:[25] in 1913, Shanghai-born Edward Isaac Ezra held the seat.[26]

Although never taking to cricket, or other English team sports, they developed a passion for riding and breeding racehorses, activities in which the Sassoons and the Ezras were both prominently engaged.

The Ezras owned one of the largest and most successful stables in China and were counted amongst the best riders.[27] The Sassoon family competed across several generations in the China Race. Inter-city racing had been established in the early 1900s to allow the Hong Kong Jockey Club and racehorse owners of the Shanghai Race Club to compete against each other, and in 1914 a certain M. S. Sassoon had been appointed Time-keeper for the Hong Kong Jockey Club, with which members of the family had been associated as owners and riders since at least 1867.[28]

The Sassoon family had one leading member and racehorse owner in the British flying services during the Great War, although he was not Shanghai-resident until later. (Ellice) Victor Sassoon served as an RNAS observer in France from the end of 1915 until an air accident in 1916 left him, then an acting Flight Lieutenant in his mid-thirties, walking with two sticks for the rest of his life. Fluent in French, he was then given administrative responsibilities in France, with the eventual RAF rank of Captain.[29]

He had been raised and educated in England and was an older (by seven years) second cousin of Sir Philip. Victor Sassoon was also amongst the earliest of England's pre-war pioneers to gain his aviator's certificate. A prominent figure at Brooklands, he qualified in January 1911 (as 'E. Smith'), a few weeks ahead of Gustav Hamel and several months before David Henderson. He then put up the money for *Aeroplane* magazine, which he co-founded with Charles G. Grey, its editor;[30] and even contributed a couple of articles personally (E. V. Sassoon, 'The Royal Flying Corps and the Civilian' and a debonair 'Experiences in the "Circuit d'Anjou"' accompanied by his own photographs).[31]

London-based Chairman of the family's private banking arm before the war, Sir Victor moved to Bombay in 1924 on the death of his father (Edward Elias Sassoon), where he managed the family textile mills and served on the Indian Legislative Council. But he shifted his wealth and residence to Shanghai in the late 1920s for tax reasons, establishing himself as a major real estate tycoon and property developer, and the most prominent Sassoon to be linked with the city. Widely known as a *bon vivant*, he owned racing stables in Hong Kong (the Roman Stable), and in England (the Eve Stud outside Newmarket, which bred the winners of many famous races).[32]

A fellow Shanghai resident was to be closely associated with Sir Victor Sassoon's Shanghai property ventures during the twenties and thirties—becoming known as 'his' man on the SMC.[33] This was H. E. Arnhold, whose position had been an uncomfortable one in the early days of the Great War. Not of Shanghai's Baghdadi Jewish community, but of German Jewish origin, Harry E. Arnhold was a Hong Kong-born British subject who had been educated in Britain. However, he had inherited a German-registered company. In early 1915, the British Commercial Attaché, Archibald Rose, complained to London that a British subject, H. E. Arnhold, was carrying on business as a British firm, but continued to utilise the organisation and resources of the German firm of Arnhold Karberg & Co. He expressed regrets that he was powerless to do anything about it.[34]

By the autumn of 1917 (after China had entered the war) it seems that a way had been found to regularise this awkward situation, for on 1st October Arnhold Bros. & Co. was incorporated under British law in Hong Kong, with its head office in Shanghai. The successor to Messrs. H. E. Arnhold, China, it advertised its Agents and Home Offices as Arnhold, Karberg & Co., London and New York.[35] Therefore it was most probably no coincidence that amongst the contributions to war funds collected by the Shanghai Race Club at its Autumn 1917 Race Meeting was the sum of $10,500 for a fighter plane, to be called *Shanghai Race Club No.5 The 'Oriole'*. Far from indicating that Shanghai was emulating Ceylon with presentation aircraft named after birds, the full title— *'The Oriole' Presented by Mr. H. E. Arnhold of Shanghai*—holds the key.[36] His presentation scout (a Sopwith Pup) was named and inscribed after Harry Arnhold's very own leading racehorse.[37]

This suggests that it was 'high rollers' and racehorse owners like Arnhold who fed the Aircraft Fund. Meeting the cost of an entire aeroplane may have been Harry Arnhold's gesture of loyalty (and thanks?) towards Shanghai's British consular authorities with respect to his newly legitimised company. The fact that the earlier aircraft in the series—*Shanghai Race Club Nos. 1-4*—had all carried no such individual attribution implies that several owners might have contributed. Moreover, only $20,000 of the $60,000 collected at the Autumn race meeting of 1917 was identified as having derived from voluntary contributions, and Arnhold had provided a good half of it for his presentation plane. This leads to the conclusion that the remainder ($40,000) probably derived either from the proceeds of a direct levy on ticket sales, or a betting tax. The Stewards distributed that sum to numerous causes, which included The Sikh Wounded, as well as French, Italian, Belgian, Portuguese, and Russian war funds.[38]

Country	Approx. population	Number of planes
China (excluding Hong Kong)	c. 452 million; 8,641 British residents	20 in all
Subscribed by:		
Shanghai	British subjects c. 5,500	12
Peking		3
Tientsin		2
Hankow		1
Yangsee Valley		1
North China		1

Unlike certain other Latin American nations that followed the US in declaring war on Germany in 1917, Argentina declared for 'benevolent neutrality' while 'recognising the justice' of the American action.[39] Continued neutrality was a close-run thing after German torpedoes sank Argentine merchant ships in September 1917 and the Argentine Chamber of Deputies voted by a majority for a break in relations;[40] but President Hipólito Yrigoyen stalled for time, and never signed the necessary decree. It is not difficult to see why the country remained neutral throughout. 1914 found Argentina in the midst of a profound domestic commercial and industrial crisis, with steep falls in the value of property and widespread bankruptcies due to over-speculation in real estate and reckless borrowing.[41] The Great War initially disrupted shipping and freight charges but the Argentine economy subsequently recovered ground to the extent that the banks started lending again.

Argentina sought to export to all sides. Although wheat prices remained low, demand for canned bully beef for the troops lifted the profits of meat-producers and allied industries; Argentine horses were shipped to the British army in France despite German protests; even Argentine wool started fetching unprecedented prices and was sold to whomsoever paid—the largest buyer was Germany in 1916, America in 1917.[42] In early 1918 Argentina did recall its military attachés from Berlin and Vienna after an Argentine steamer was torpedoed in the Mediterranean, and notified Brazil that it considered its declaration of war on Germany to have been just and proper,[43] but that was as far as it went.

Argentina had carried out a census in mid-1914. It found the total population to number 7,885,237; of whom 2,357,952 were foreign nationals, born outside the country. They included 26,995 Germans, 38,123 Austro-Hungarians, and 27,692 British.[44] In each case, the enumeration underestimated the overall size of the community in question, for all children born in Argentina were recorded in the census returns simply as Argentines. The English-language press in Buenos Aires hazarded that in 1915 the British community in Argentina stood somewhere short of 35,000.[45] It was the biggest British community in any foreign country outside the British Empire and its self-governing Dominions, apart from the US. The social span was also quite wide, encompassing British ranchers and engineers; as well as middle-level and clerical employees—many of them on fixed term contracts tied to British companies such as railways, banks and importers; but also shepherds of Irish and Scottish descent long settled in the far windswept south of Argentina; not to mention a Welsh-speaking agricultural colony established in Patagonia's Chabut Valley for close to half a century.[46]

The British community therefore included temporary male migrants out on contract (most of them probably of military age) who would expect to return to Britain in due course, as well as established, rooted, communities. A Buenos Aires-based British Patriotic Committee was formed at the start of the war to lead the Argentine British war effort, comprising British consular officials and leading members of the community, and chaired by the British Minister, Reginald Tower. It provided passages to England for those volunteers unable to meet their own transport costs, and organised contributions to war charities, such as shipping donated livestock to help support Belgian refugees in England.

In March 1916 the British consulate in Buenos Aires started circulating a 'black list' of firms trading with Germany, bringing official Argentine objections that many of those listed were in fact Argentine-registered. Nonetheless neutral Argentina, with one-third of its population citizens of countries at war, did offer a prime opportunity for propaganda and counter-propaganda efforts. The British Society printed and distributed 5,000 pamphlets in Spanish in late 1914, setting out Great Britain's case for its participation in the conflict.[47]

Established in Buenos Aires in 1912 (and not to be confused with the Patriotic Committee), the British Society had begun as one of several Anglo-Argentine cultural associations in Buenos Aires, its UK parent body being the League of the Empire, formed in 1901.[48] The League's main role was to link London with educational bodies abroad for the purpose of such as teacher-exchange programmes, and it was strongly associated with Lord Meath's Empire Day movement for schools.[49] Rather to its surprise, the League was to act as the conduit for subscriptions to presentation aircraft from the River Plate region.

The British Society launched its campaign for a fighter plane on 2 August 1915. The press appeal expressed the hope that every section of the community would contribute:

> We realise, of course, that here the commercial conditions make it impossible to raise large sums, but £2,250 for a biplane, complete with machine gun, ought not to be beyond our resources if a united effort is made, and we trust that for our credit as British subjects that the flotilla of airships now being formed will contain at least one unit provided by the River Plate.[50]

Within one month the fund was oversubscribed. The Society's chairman sounded both excited and overwhelmed:

> During the 'last lap' ... contributions in large and small amounts were being received in the British Society's offices from early in the morning until six o'clock at night, with scarcely a moment's pause ... The result is very gratifying: all the more gratifying by reason of the fact that there has been no delay in raising the amount required ... When so many take part the burden is lightened and it is calculated that 1,500 to 2,000 British residents in Argentina have contributed something.[51]

All the subscriptions derived from private individuals, and none from big firms, banks, or large business houses. The honorary treasurer expressed his belief that the spontaneous popular response was due to the nature of the appeal, which gave every subscriber a personal sense of involvement in the war and the feeling that they were striking a direct blow against the enemy.[52] It was therefore decided to keep the fund open, and at the christening ceremony at Farnborough for *River Plate No. 1* in November 1915, Lord Meath read a cable confirming that the money for a second plane entitled *River Plate No. 2* (a less costly BE2c reconnaissance aircraft) had been collected. A toast was drunk at the British Society office in Buenos Aires to coincide in real time with this event.[53]

Possibly half of Anglo-Argentine males of military age volunteered for the British forces, their presence on French battlefields supplying a strong sense of community engagement. At that time almost two-thirds of Argentina's over 22,000 miles of railway were owned and worked by British capital under British management, and a Railway Contingent of more than a thousand from Argentina was recruited to serve with the British Army on the Western Front, with the promise that the volunteers would be reinstated in their jobs when the war ended. Eight thousand railway employees subscribed a BE2c on their own list raised in parallel with that of the British Society in late 1915. It was named the *Central Argentine Railway Aeroplane* and it joined *River Plate Nos. 1 and 2* in France,[54] to make three in all from the central region and the capital.

4,852 volunteers from Argentina are believed to have fought in British ranks on the Western Front, distributed across various units (of whom 528 were killed).[55] The RCI ran a scheme to supply them with the local preferred smoke (*cigarillos*), and to judge from letters to the press, recipients appreciated this particular comfort from home above all else.[56] Many of those Anglo-Argentine recruits, especially from the rural areas, initially served in the 2nd King Edward's Horse. This regiment, drawn entirely from overseas, was raised by private subscription at the beginning of the war and was later adopted by the War Office as a British regular cavalry unit.[57] Disbanded in August 1917, many of its members transferred to the Tank Corps after a desolate combat experience as cavalry.

One sight that haunted many from the battle of Festubert was a parapet one hundred yards long part composed of German corpses.[58] Captain Edward McCorry had been amongst the first volunteers to leave Argentina. At the time of writing to his brother Enrique in Patagones he had been eight months at the Front in France:

Extracts from a letter published in the Buenos Aires Herald, 28 January 1916:

Dear Old—   2nd King Edward's Horse, France

It is not often I get a chance of writing, sometimes when I do get a moment to myself I don't feel up to it. We have been out of the trenches now for three weeks. They call it a rest, but at night we have to go up to the firing line and dig trenches or put up barbed wire, etc. This is what they call a rest. We hear that on Wednesday we return to our old place at--------------.

Our Brigade hold the record as cavalry for being the longest time under shellfire. ... I don't think we have one hundred of the old lot left. It was at Festubert, our first engagement where we lost most of them. Great God! It was an awful four days that we held a captured German trench—and a damned rotten one at that... They rained shells on us night and day. The fourth day they attempted an attack but we gave them hell. It was then that poor old Wyn Fisher was killed; shot through the eye. The Germans held a portion of the trench on our right and the word was passed for the bombers to precede us and bomb them out. We took over about 200 yards of trench. The German dead were piled on top of one another. In places where the parapet had been blown in they had built it up with their own dead, with sandbags placed on top of them. They must have been there for weeks, all one could see were heads, arms and legs projecting from the sandbags— and the stench! It was awful ...

At Festubert a sergeant of our division was taken prisoner. A few days afterwards, when we advanced, he was found by his own men crucified with bayonets to an old door. Of course he was dead when they found him [...]

Something tells me that perhaps in six months time the enemy will ask for peace on any terms. You should see some of our guns, 'some' guns they are—not to be too explicit—plenty of shells to feed them with now. You will be surprised to hear that I have been offered a commission in the Welsh Guards, which means that I shall be in London when you receive this, learning infantry drill. They are picking experienced men from the ranks for officers, a thing they ought to have done long ago.

When you write address letters to Argentine Club, Hamilton Place, London.

Your affectionate brother,
NED

Argentine Britons also served as airmen in France. Bristol Fighter 'ace' Capt. Thomas Colvill-Jones initially joined the Artists' Rifles and later transferred to the RFC. In mid-1918 he died of wounds a prisoner-of-war in Germany; while his brother Robert, MC, an observer, was killed only shortly before the Armistice, also shot down. Lieut. W. Beresford Melville left in April 1916 for pilot training in England, later joining 56 Squadron, and he survived the war.[59] But it was not just that the RFC favoured 'colonials' like Melville for officer commissions. Argentina was the first South American country to incorporate aeroplanes with its army,[60] and had its own pilot training facilities. The following news item appeared at the beginning of 1916:

> Mr. Hubert F. Fisher and wife will leave by tonight's boat for Montevideo, there to take passage for England by the *Remuera*. Mr. Fisher goes to volunteer for service in the Royal Flying Corps, having recently taken out his 'brevet' as pilot in the San Fernando Aviation Schools. He bears letters from influential members of the British community to authorities at home recommending that he be allowed to pilot one of the River Plate aeroplanes. [Result unknown, but such requests were usually unsuccessful.] The best wishes of the whole community will accompany him.[61]

Born in Gloucestershire in 1884, Hubert Fisher had been ten years as an engineer in South America, boasted experience in aircraft construction, and had flown a wide array of aircraft models as an amateur. After entering the RFC in England he piloted fighters with 11 Squadron in France, before being appointed an instructor at the Army's Oxford Aviation Training School. Promoted from Captain to Major in September 1917, he was briefly attached to the Canadian Military Flying School outside Toronto as Chief Instructor. However, he was one of those unfortunates who survived the war only to fall prey to the Spanish 'flu epidemic, dying at the RAF hospital in London in March 1919.[62]

As elsewhere in the world with combatants on the Western Front, many Argentine subscribers for presentation aircraft were probably motivated by the urge to extend protection to their own—so often how the role of aeroplanes was perceived at the time. Rural communities in Patagonia as well as those from the greater River Plate area had sons in the war and were involved in fundraising, but there is scant information on their campaigns at that distance from Buenos Aires. Rio Gallegos in southern Patagonia was a region of vast scattered sheep *estancias* developed in part by settlers of Scottish origin from the Falkland Islands.[63] The area was reportedly subscribing an aeroplane for the RFC in mid-1916, but nothing further appeared in the English-language press of the capital, which had no wireless link with the region and no thought of one until mid-1918.[64] Little trace would have remained had Major Miller, RFC, not started using *Rio Gallegos Britons* on his aerobatic tours of South Africa. (A reconnaissance aeroplane simply named *Argentine* has also been recorded—but its exact provenance and all else about it remain a mystery.)

From Argentina's neighbour came *Britons in Chile*.[65] There was almost another, subscribed by the thinly scattered English-speaking communities of the Patagonian far south of both Chile and Argentina that were served by the *Magellan Times*. Founded in 1914, this weekly was published from Punta Arenas on the Strait of Magellan. It launched an Aeroplane Fund in May 1916, citing the feat of Lieutenant Warneford RNAS in downing a Zeppelin over Belgium—'one thrills at [the] exploit'. Within a month the paper had collected a little over £810. It comprised two donations of £100 and two of £50, but also very many small sums, showing that all economic levels contributed.[66]

In July 1916, however, Sir Ernest Shackleton arrived at Punta Arenas in a continuing effort to organise a rescue of the twenty-two men of his Antarctic expedition. They had been stranded for many weeks on Elephant Island in the South Shetlands (so named on account of its population of elephant seals), after their ship became trapped in ice. Most subscribers to the Aeroplane Fund agreed the diversion of monies towards an urgent rescue attempt. Together with further donations, £1500 was raised and devoted to chartering a ship. That perilous effort also failed,[67] but eventually the stranded men, many suffering from frostbite, were saved in August 1916 by a tugboat of the Chilean navy.

Country	Approx. population	Number of planes
Argentina	7.9 million, including a British community up to 35,000 strong	5
Chile	c. 3.6 million	1
Falkland Islands	c. 2,220	1

FE2b *River Plate* written off after crashing into a telegraph pole, 1916, courtesy of Cross & Cockade International Archive

Chapter 17:
Charles Alma Baker and the
Australian Air Squadrons Fund

The Australian Air Squadrons Fund was established in mid-1916 and became a mass campaign, and a channel of popular support for Australian troops on the Western Front and in the Middle East. However Australia had already presented at least two aeroplanes to the RFC before Charles Alma Baker arrived on the scene to further awaken public opinion to the cause. For in 1915 the Tasmanian Government provided a BE2c named after the territory, and the State public subscribed *South Australia* at the start of 1916.[1] By the Armistice there were some fifty-four Australian presentation aircraft all told, forty-one of them donated through the Australian Air Squadrons Fund, or the renamed 'Victory' Fund also organised by Charles Alma Baker; Overseas Club branches had separately gifted several others, amongst them *The ANZAC*, which was presented jointly with New Zealand.

The First World War is often cited as a major turning point in Australian national consciousness: from 'South Briton' at the outset to a distinctively Australian identity. Out of a population of just 4.9 million, nearly 417,000 Australians enlisted during 1914–18, and almost 65 per cent fell casualty—26,000 in the ill-fated Gallipoli campaign alone;[2] and dispatches from Australian newsmen helped create the heroic ANZAC legend.[3] However, Australian national identity also coalesced on the Western Front, in the skies over France, and in the Ottoman territories of the Middle East, where the Australian Light Horse were engaged so effectively on the ground. About a third of Australian pilots (179 airmen) were killed, wounded, or captured in the war.[4]

Australian airmen, some drawn from the ranks of the Light Horse and trained by the RFC in Egypt, flew as part of the Egyptian Expeditionary Force (EEF), and eventually also in Palestine, Syria, and the Jordan valley. Their key role as part of the Palestine Brigade of the RFC was the photographic reconnaissance of vast stretches of country for new military maps that were compiled by the Royal Engineers,[5] and this involved a central role in pioneering entirely new aerial survey methods over virgin terrain.⁶ They provided air support for T. E. Lawrence and the Arab force with which he was associated alongside the RFC's Arabian Detachment, or C-Flight of 14 Squadron RFC, and its successor, X-Flight,⁷ and they bombed Turkish work parties trying to restore railway lines cut by Arab attack. Their often merciless bombing and ground strafing of Turkish lines and troop columns played a significant part in the culminating stages of the Palestine campaign. As part of the final battle of Megiddo (biblical Armageddon) in September 1918, it included obliteration of fleeing Turkish columns by machine-gunning and bombardment from the air.⁸

Given its vast distances, it was natural for Australia to evince an early interest in the possibilities of aviation, but apprehensions about Japan's rise as a Pacific power also factored aircraft into Australia's coastal defence planning.⁹ By the time of the Great War, a Central Flying School was in operation at Point Cook in Victoria, and Australia became the only one of all the Dominions to establish a flying arm that served from early days through to the Armistice.¹⁰ Some thirty-odd Australian airmen (four pilots, and ground crew) were sent to Mesopotamia in early 1915 to support the Anglo-Indian force, but taken captive by the Turks at Kut-el-Amara, few survived. There were also other Australian airmen serving with British squadrons in France, who had enlisted as individuals prior to the formation of the Australian Flying Corps (AFC) in 1916.

Although they formed part of the Australian Imperial Force (AIF), the various squadrons of the AFC usually fell under RFC command. 1ˢᵗ Squadron AFC initially flew outdated BE2cs and similar machines in the Middle East. In October 1917, they were joined by 111 Squadron RFC in a new 40ᵗʰ Wing under the command of Lieutenant Colonel A. E. Borton. Australian airmen in the Middle East were reputed to be naturals as fighter pilots. During early 1918, 111 Squadron were equipped with SE5as, and 1ˢᵗ Squadron AFC transferred from their older aircraft to all eighteen of the recently introduced and very effective F2b Bristol Fighters, together bringing air ascendency to the imperial forces in the Palestine campaign led by General Allenby.¹¹ Each of the new fighter-bombers that the Australians flew bore a presentation name that identified it as Australia's gift.¹² AFC officer L. W. Sutherland recalled that B1229 *NSW No. 11, The Macintyre Kayuga Estate* was often out on loan to T. E. Lawrence.¹³

From the latter part of 1917 Australian airmen also served on the Western Front as the 2nd, 3rd, and 4th Squadrons AFC (though under different RFC designations).[14] Additionally, four AFC training squadrons were established in England. They too, were all to fly aircraft bearing Australian presentation names, because in one respect Australian fundraising for the Imperial Aircraft Flotilla had a unique outcome. Unlike other donor nations, from summer 1917 until the end of the war Australian pilots became the ones flying the aeroplanes they provided. For in addition to the Australian service side of the air war, there were domestic political aspects pertinent to the unfolding of the Australian fundraising campaign. They provide the main subject of our story.

Charles Alma Baker arrived in Australia accompanied by his family in March 1916, intending to stay no more than two or three months, and leaving his mining manager, Frederick Shepherd, in charge of the Malaya Air Fleet Fund. However Sidney Kidman, the so-called 'Cattle King' and self-made millionaire, persuaded Alma Baker to join him as an investment partner in a number of cattle stations in western New South Wales (NSW); Alma Baker therefore decided to stay and set up a new aeroplane fund.[15] In addition to a claimed go-ahead from the War Office in London, by early July he had secured permission for the launch from Australia's Minister of Defence, Senator G. F. Pearce.[16]

Apparently the Overseas Club felt rather put out when they got wind of it, but Lieutenant General Sir David Henderson in London was reluctant to intervene. As he advised Sir Ernest Birch, Overseas Club Central Committee member but also personal friend of Alma Baker:

> It is a little difficult for me to interfere between the Over-seas Club and Mr. Alma Baker, but I certainly think that any funds which come from Australia for the purchase of aeroplanes should come through the Over-seas Club. We owe a great deal to Mr. Baker for his efforts on our behalf in the Malay Peninsula, and I am anxious that he should not be discouraged from further efforts, but I can quite see that the Over-seas Club may look upon Australia as being within their particular province. I do not know anything of a particular War Office approval for Mr. Baker to raise money in Australia, and if such approval has been given, I am sure that there was no intention to interfere with the privileges of the Over-seas Club.
>
> I have already written to Mr. Steel-Maitland [Parliamentary Under Secretary at the Colonial Office] on this subject to the same effect, but

I hope very much that the matter may be settled privately without calling on the War Office to interfere.[17]

In the event, Evelyn Wrench let matters ride, and the controversy over Alma Baker's fundraising, when it came, was initially concentrated at the Australian end.

By the Armistice, the total amount paid over to the War Office by the Australian Air Squadrons Fund amounted to £109,500.[18] The first aeroplane, *Australia No.1, South Australia No. 1, The Sidney Kidman*, was the gift of Alma Baker's new Australian business partner, costing £2,700 (another, *Mrs Sidney Kidman*, became *South Australia No. 2*). The second in the national series, *Australia No. 2, New South Wales No. 1, The White Belltrees*, bore the name of the State and the donor's homestead, farm or ranch, as so many others were to do. After that, however, the inscriptions became increasingly baffling, as serial numbers running by the nation as a whole (the Commonwealth of Australia) diverged more and more from those of the State, so that *Australia No. 40* was also *New South Wales No. 30*. (It certainly baffled those responsible for inscribing them at the depots in England, for there were several complaints of mistakes.)[19]

In the campaign's initial stages, Alma Baker had the support of several Australian politicians. Mac Abbott, a Nationalist MP in the NSW Legislative Assembly, accompanied him on a tour of his own constituency of Upper Hunter, with the result that almost £6,500 was forthcoming in one day. Abbott wrote that the appeal of the scheme to the 'hard-headed businessmen' who donated lay in the fact that Alma Baker paid for all expenses out of his own pocket, and the Union Bank of Australia handled all subscriptions. It delivered swift results, for it was only a matter of a couple of months between the donation being made and the machine flying to the Front bearing an inscription of the donor's State, his name and locality. It thus constituted 'a splendid message of support to the lads at the front, associated with or hailing from the town of such donor or locality, as the case may be.' But it was also a people's movement, as the MP for Upper Hunter explained, since the poorest person giving his shilling or less was directly contributing to the actual fighting.[20]

Front cover of the *Austral-Briton* special war edition, 16 September 1916
© The British Library Board

While Mac Abbott stressed the modest cost involved, 'namely £2700 per aeroplane, as against the cost of say, the Queen Elizabeth, which approximated £3,500,000', an Australian motoring magazine made this appeal to British Empire solidarity:

> Obviously, the possession of swarms and swarms of aerocraft [sic.] must help the British armies considerably. It must expedite the accomplishment of victory; it must save hundreds of thousand of valuable lives and millions of treasure in the course of a year. Therefore, our British Imperial forces SHOULD have those clouds and clouds of aeroplanes.[21]

In addition, Alma Baker brought his very own inimitable style to the campaigning, succinctly described by a periodical for returned Australian soldiers and sailors:

> There is a man named C. Alma Baker. He is reported to be very wealthy. If the tenacity he is displaying in connection with the Battleplane Movement prevailed in business we do not wonder at it. Baker wants funds to keep going an Australian Battleplane Squadron serving on the Western Front and he keeps inundating us with literature to that effect. Space is valuable, but we wish the man success for the cause is good. If you are interested, as you should be, write to him c/o Union Bank, Sydney.[22]

Although Mac Abbott's constituency lay in a coal-mining area, press coverage suggests that Alma Baker directed his message at a mainly rural audience elsewhere. There was a distinctly bucolic feel about much of the fundraising. In October 1916, for instance, it included a 'Queen of the Day' carnival and a cattle sale for the Tweed No. 1 Battleplane Fund.[23] Half the £2,700 that went to *Australia No. 10, NSW No. 9 'The Tweed'* (an FE2d—a later and improved version of the FE2b) was thanks to 150 local farmers who put their best milch cows up for auction, while others gave various forms of farm produce: 'Mr. E. Haydon, of Bloomfield, Blandford, has given to the Battleplane Fund a fat bullock and a bale of wool; Mr. Reynolds, of Somerton, Port Macquarie, two fat sheep.'[24]

An address to the Farmers' and Settlers' Conference of July 1917 illustrates the particularly emotive tone Alma Baker used in Australia. Every contribution, be it £2,700 for a complete 'battleplane' (as he now always called them in his appeals), or only a few pounds or a few shillings toward one, was 'worth the life of one of our boys, was helping to stop the big shells of the enemy, and preventing countless casualties.' At times the tone of the speech verged on emotional blackmail:

> Imagine for one moment how you would feel after long days and nights of intense fighting in the trenches if you saw in the aerodrome behind your lines when you came back for short relief a battleplane bearing the name of your own district: perhaps the name of a relation or friend in the dear land you came from. Would this not generate kind and grateful thoughts for those who, although remaining behind in safety and comfort, beyond the sound of shot and shell, beyond the cries of the distressed, had thought of you, and had sacrificed a few hard-earned pounds to help send for your protection one of these highly specialised and valuable engines of war? Is not a battleplane that will carry your name, or the name of your district over the heads of our boys into the battles for victory, worth any sacrifices you can make?

He continued with some very dubious accounting:

> Lord Kitchener had stated that a squadron of battleplanes (16) was equal to an army corps. On this basis each battleplane in a squadron is equal to two thousand men, and every pound subscribed towards that battleplane stood for a man's life. Every British battleplane was equal to at least two German machines. Every battleplane Australians could send and did not send was thus tantamount to making a present of four battleplanes to the enemy.
> Remember, the boys fighting for you want your help now. Remember that every pound you can spare for a battleplane is worth one of our boys' lives. Remember that every battleplane you send, or help to send, will help to save thousands of brave lives and countless casualties. Remember that your help will enable many of your kith and kin to come back to their homes who would otherwise never return.[25]

In contrast to other Dominions, there was a dearth of presentation aeroplanes named after Australian cities;[26] and the rare exception to this rule appears to have been gifted independently of Alma Baker's campaign, like the *City of Adelaide*, presented by Mrs. Harry Bickford through the Overseas Club at the end of 1916. The relevant background during later 1916 and throughout 1917 was one of party political schisms over conscription in Australia, and two referenda that defeated the Government's attempts to introduce it. August to October 1917 also saw serious labour unrest in Sydney and the formation of a farmers' army of strike-breakers 7,300 strong.[27] There was a move from within their ranks to present a plane called 'The Volunteer Loyalist of New South Wales',[28] and this may be a pointer to the conservative 'loyalist' outlook of many of the supporters of the Australian Air Squadrons Fund at that time.

That gift materialised in 1918 under the ponderous title *Australia No. 40, NSW No. 30, 'The Victory' presented by Loyalist Volunteers, Farmers and Settlers, Residents of Collarenebri and Wahroonga*. It was after Alma Baker had re-launched his appeal in the middle of the year, this time for so-called 'Victory' Battleplanes. The renamed 'Victory' Fund came under the patronage of the Governor General of the Commonwealth of Australia, and of the Governors of NSW, of Queensland, of South Australia, of West Australia, and of Tasmania.[29] This new level of official support was, in fact, a new level of official scrutiny of the aeroplane fund on the part of Australia's imperial representatives, though if Alma Baker realised this, he did not admit it publicly. It was in no way due to any question of financial impropriety or lack of administrative competence on his part, but almost certainly because of constitutional issues that had developed during 1916–18 into a clash between NSW, the most populous and important State in the country, and the Federal (Commonwealth) Government of Australia. The second (and last) of the new series, and the country's final presentation aeroplane before the end of the war was *Australia No. 41 'Victory Scout'*, which was presented by the Residents of the Northern Territory and other parts of Australia shortly before the Armistice.

Just one year before the outbreak of the Great War, the writer Sir Rider Haggard reported on a visit to Australia as a member of a Royal Commission on the Dominions. He labelled the country a 'Heptarchy'. For including the Federal Parliament there were fourteen Houses of Assembly, seven of them Upper, and seven Lower, each with its paraphernalia of Ministers and officials, and its separate Imperial Governor. It was not too much to say, said Rider Haggard, that every one of these States was jealous of the other, and that all of them viewed the central Federal Government with dislike and apprehension:

> To such an extent is this true that the surest way not to get one of the State Governments to do anything, is to prefer the request through an

officer of the Federal Government. What the Federal Government says ought to be done the State Government will say ought not to be done.[30]

That was precisely what came to bedevil the question of pilot training in Australia and, by extension, the Australian Air Squadrons Fund: even despite (or perhaps because of) the War Precautions Act of 1914, through which the Commonwealth Government gave itself sweeping powers to issue wartime regulations without parliamentary scrutiny, potentially overriding State rights by arguing the exigencies of national defence—a Federal preserve.[31] Matters evolved into a constitutional issue for the Colonial Office in London, and rather turned its officials against the innocent Charles Alma Baker, whatever good work he had done for the imperial war effort.

On 28th August 1916, little more than a month after the Australian Air Squadrons Fund launched, Gerald Strickland, NSW Governor 1913–17, officially opened a new aviation school. Special trains took visitors out from Sydney to Clarendon, the station nearest the aerodrome. Alma Baker was a special guest at the ceremony. The Chief Instructor, Mr. Stutt, entertained the crowd with some spectacular stunt flying—including aerobatics with the Governor's fearless daughter aboard.[32] He thrilled spectators with a number of sudden sensational vertical dives and turns. Returning from one trip:

> Mr. Stutt suddenly dived and pretended to go straight for a party of press photographers, who hastily separated, but … after flying about 15 ft. over the heads of the crowd, [he] suddenly swept upwards again. He also skimmed just over a passing railway engine, showing fine control of his machine.

Relating all this with verve, the *Sydney Mail* nonetheless sounded a note of caution:

> This State effort has come in for some censure on the ground that it is an interference with Federal duties. The government's answer to this is that it has had the endorsement and assistance of the Commonwealth Government, the Defence authorities, and of the Imperial Government. Nevertheless, as all Defence matters are supposed to be controlled by the Commonwealth, the Clarendon school will no doubt eventually be taken over by the Federal Government, which already has established a similar institution in Victoria.[33]

It was only a partial misreading.

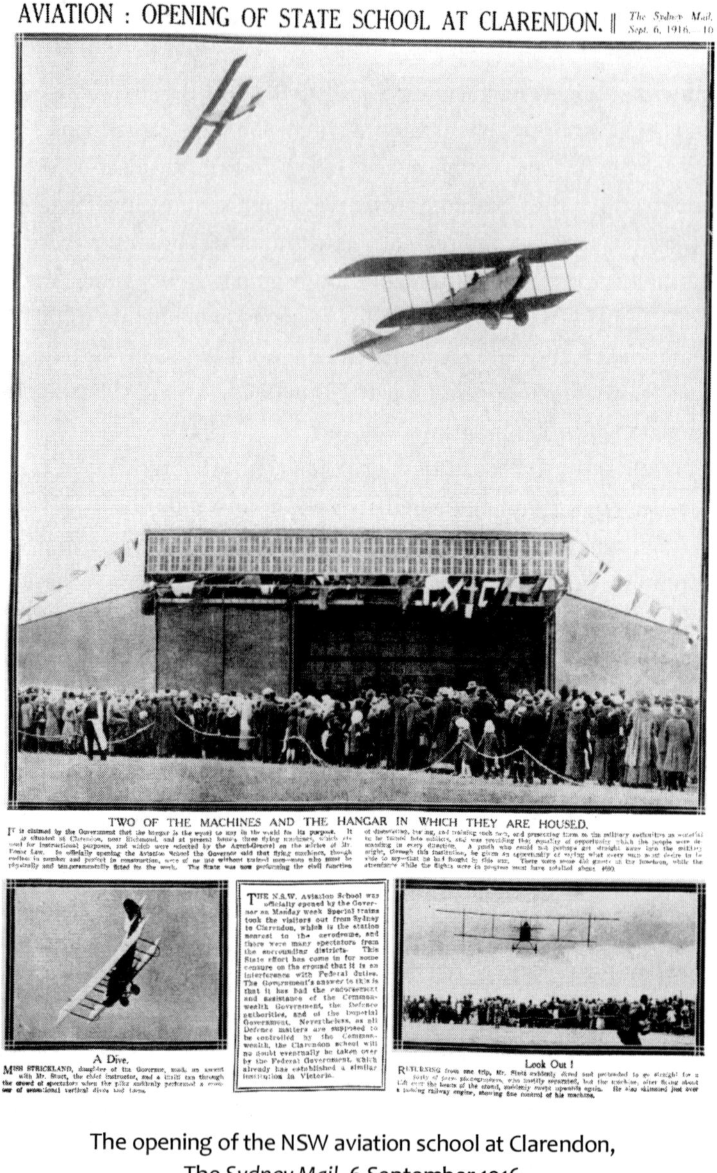

The opening of the NSW aviation school at Clarendon,
The *Sydney Mail*, 6 September 1916

THE FIRST FLIGHT AND SOME OF THE AVIATION STUDENTS. *The Sydney Mail, Sept. 6, 1916.*

MISS STRICKLAND ABOUT TO ASCEND IN CHARGE OF CHIEF INSTRUCTOR STUTT.

THE STUDENTS AND THEIR PILOT-INSTRUCTORS.

The first flight with the Governor's daughter, and staff and students,
The Sydney Mail, 6 September 1916

Establishment of the flying school had been with the consent of Australia's Defence Minister, Senator Pearce, but he had also insisted that defence was a Federal prerogative and could not fall to the State authorities. Therefore the NSW School came under the wing of the NSW Minister of Education (for education *was* a State concern) and pilots were only to be trained to a standard sufficient for an Australian Aero Club certificate, not given *military* aviation instruction, unlike those at the Central Flying School in Victoria, which prepared pilots for the AFC.[34]

The Premier of NSW, William Holman, one of Australia's foremost politicians, was nonetheless an enthusiast for the School and clearly had ambitions for it that went beyond civilian matters, and for Alma Baker's campaign equally. Holman committed to match every plane subscribed by the public within the State with the gift of another from NSW Government funds. In addition, Holman announced before the assembled gathering at the School's opening that the State would soon have twelve presentation aeroplanes for Britain, six from the public and another six from his State government; he promised that the first twelve pilots trained at the aviation school would go to Europe to take charge of those machines.[35]

It was not to be. A lengthy constitutional tussle ensued, whereby the Federal Government jealously retained control over recruitment and disposition of Australian pilots in the war, and this included applicants for both the AFC and the RFC from the NSW Aviation School. It was despite vigorous attempts by Holman to circumvent the approved channels of communication and deal directly with the War Office through the NSW resident Agent-General in London. The Colonial Office supported the Commonwealth of Australia and insisted on the correct procedures being followed: All correspondence on defence matters to go through the Federal authorities, and all selection in Australia of candidates for the RFC in England to be their final responsibility too. It all became tetchy and tediously bureaucratic.[36] The main sufferers were the NSW pilot trainees stuck in limbo.

A solution of sorts was arrived at during NSW Premier Holman's visit to London in July 1917. He complained, nevertheless, that the Colonial Office was obsessed with the idea that all matters of the slightest military bearing could only be negotiated with the Commonwealth of Australia, even though education was entirely a State concern and

NSW students did not become military trainees until they entered RFC ranks. After several interviews with the Secretary of State for the Colonies, and with Henderson at the Military Aeronautics Directorate, Holman recorded that it was General Smuts who finally put the issue directly before the War Cabinet.[37] Thereafter, it appears that pilots with Aero Club certificates from the NSW School went through the prescribed Federal channels before applying to the RFC, and any NSW cadets enlisting in the RFC as civilians had to go through the entire British military flying course when they arrived in England.[38]

The chill from all this extended to Whitehall. In March 1917 the Colonial Office icily requested the War Office to inform the Army Council that in future *all* acknowledgments of sums received from NSW for aeroplanes through the Australian Air Squadrons Fund should be sent via the Colonial Office, for communication *through* the Governor General of the Commonwealth of Australia to Charles Alma Baker, and not sent direct.[39] A final statement of accounts for the Australian Air Squadrons Fund showed £21,600 collected from the NSW Agent-General by the Union Bank of Australia's London branch for the cost of eight 'battleplanes' in all, in duplication of the first eight machines subscribed for privately in the State (thus adding a third set of serial numbers to confuse the Australian series: such as *Australia No.11, NSW No.10 'Duplicate Tweed No.9'*).[40]

As for Holman's desire to see the NSW's planes flown by NSW pilots in the war, this is quite likely what stimulated the official request for *Australian* pilots to fly *Australian* presentation planes in the first place. In April 1917 Colonel Thomas Griffiths, Commandant, had written to the War Office from the AIF's London headquarters:

> It is understood at these headquarters that a number of Aeroplanes have been donated by the various State Governments of Australia and also by private individuals resident therein.
> I am to say that it would be a great compliment to the Australian Flying Corps and also to the donors if these machines could be allocated to the Australian Squadrons.
> I am to ask whether this wish could be gratified please as it would give great pleasure to the Australian Imperial Forces.

It could not have been more nicely put, and drew the response that steps would be taken in future to allocate such machines to the Australian Squadrons, as requested.⁴¹ It all sounded so guileless. The timing, however, had quite conceivably been dictated by Holman's planned visit to London that summer; either to forestall him, or smooth a solution to the quarrel, or both. Consequently the RFC received instructions to transfer Australian presentation names onto planes being flown by Australian squadrons on the Western Front, in the Middle East, and by training squadrons in England.⁴²

At a time of such titanic world conflict and massive bloodletting as the First World War, it seems extraordinary that so much energy should have been spent on bureaucratic battles, but such is human nature. Considerations of Australian national prestige added a further dimension. During 1917–18 the Australian authorities were raising additional AFC Squadrons for service abroad, and they highlighted the unique nature of the country's military contribution. This all fed into efforts to promote Australia's image among the Dominions. Whilst in Britain during 1918, Australian Prime Minister Billy Hughes stressed the AFC's autonomous role in the imperial war effort, emphasising that it preceded the recently announced Canadian air service by some three years.⁴³

Alma Baker thus unwittingly blundered in with both feet into disputed domestic political terrain that eventually entailed respective Federal and State constitutional rights and responsibilities, as well as wider issues of military pride and national identity. He muddied the waters in a more minor matter too, although in contrast to the Colonial Office, the British air authorities seem not to have taken umbrage. His campaign leaflet for the Australian Air Squadrons Fund stated in early 1917 that there existed an urgent need for many more aeroplanes than were provided for by the War Office official programme. The campaign leaflet also contained the following passage, which was headed in capitals BUILDING CONTRACTS:

> Contracts for building the Aeroplanes presented are let by the War Office from time to time when funds for each complete Aeroplane are available. The building of presented Aeroplanes will not interfere with the progress of the large Army Official Programme, but is carried out by smaller outside firms, and so provides a valuable addition to our Aerial Forces.⁴⁴

The degree of truth embedded in this claim is unclear: Monies from the Union Bank of Australia on behalf of the Australian Air Squadrons Fund were paid into an Aeroplane Gift Suspense Account at the Bank of England, an arrangement similar to that for payments by the Malaya Air Fleet Fund established by Alma Baker in 1915. However, while Alma Baker was not above bending facts if he thought it would add to donor appeal, it is feasible that contracts for presentation aircraft subscribed from abroad were handled differently from others, especially in the early days, when the RFC was in great need of aircraft and in competition with the Royal Navy for scarce aero-engines.

Until 1917, design and production for both RNAS and RFC had been under the separate departmental control of the Admiralty and War Office, but in January that year the Air Board took over design, and in March 1917 the supply of aeronautical material to both became the responsibility of the Ministry of Munitions.[45] In April 1917 Alma Baker sent his Australian Air Squadrons Fund leaflet to Lord Cowdray of Midhurst, an industrialist and leading public works contractor who had been brought in by the new government of Lloyd George to head the Air Board.[46] Lord Cowdray sought clarification of Alma Baker's claims. A brief was produced that appeared to refute them, but without directly addressing the point about the selective allocation of building contracts:

> With regard to Mr Baker's statement that 'everyone of these Presentation Battleplanes is an *extra* fighting machine which otherwise would not be here', this is not correct, and all enquirers have always been told that gifts of money cannot strictly be said to enable us to add to the number of aeroplanes at the disposal of the Army, but can only be utilised to pay for aeroplanes already ordered, since orders have already been placed for aeroplanes to the utmost extent of the capabilities of manufacture. They were also told, however, that such gifts were accepted by the Army Council with very great pleasure as an indication of the desire of a patriotic organisation Overseas to assist the common cause.[47]

Right from the beginning of the war, most of the aircraft ordered by the Army were built by private manufacturers, though back in the days when the BE2c dominated production, they mainly worked to Royal Aircraft Factory designs.[48] In his letter of October 1915 to Charles Alma Baker about the satisfactory performance of the BE2c that he was flying, RFC 2nd Lieutenant Hazelton Nicoll (Henderson's relation) thought fit to mention that *Malaya No. 3—presented by C. Alma Baker* had been manufactured by a small independent company (Ruston Proctor & Co. of Lincoln).⁴⁹ Perhaps the RFC in the early days quietly maximised the funds available to them for production by allocating presentation names to machines already coming off the production line, but allocated the money received from abroad to *new* aircraft contracts through small independent manufacturers who could be trusted not to advertise the fact to their Navy rivals? Remember what happened when the Admiralty came to hear of Dominica's £4,000 gift voted for the RFC in October 1914—they claimed half of it for themselves.

Be that as it may, by the end of the war, Charles Alma Baker was still regarded favourably by the War Office and by the Air Ministry and RAF, but he was certainly not in good odour with the Colonial Office, precisely because of the Australian constitutional wrangle. In November 1917 the Straits Settlements Governor, Sir Arthur Young, recommended him for a CBE, but Alma Baker requested a deferral until victory in the war was won, lest it adversely affect his fundraising in Australia.⁵⁰ (Needless to say, there was a States versus Federal Government spat at the time over whether the relevant State Governor or the Governor General of the Commonwealth of Australia should hold responsibility for putting names forward to London for the award of honours.)⁵¹ At the beginning of 1919 the Governor at Singapore renewed his recommendation for Alma Baker but suggested a higher honour, the KBE. However, notwithstanding lobbying by Sir Ernest Birch in London, he was awarded the lesser CBE.⁵²

In May 1919 Brigadier General A. E. Borton—later, Air Vice Marshal Borton, RAF—former Commander of 40th Wing in Palestine, addressed the following letter to Sir Arthur Young in his capacity as Governor and Commander-in-Chief Straits Settlements. His letter was clearly expected to find its way into the newspapers, and may have represented the RAF's tribute to Alma Baker and his wartime fundraising. ('Biffy' Borton, incidentally, was known for having set a long-distance record the previous year, by flying a Handley Page bomber from England to Egypt.)⁵³

Penang Gazette and Straits Chronicle, 30 May 1919:

YOUR EXCELLENCY, -
I have the honour to bring to the notice of Your Excellency certain data in connection with the Malayan Air Squadrons Fund which I am in a position to give from personal experience, and which it is suggested might prove of interest to the subscribers whose patriotic effort had such a direct influence on the War, especially General Allenby's magnificent victory in Palestine.

2. At the time of the successful operations in that Theatre, No. 1 Squadron of the Australian Flying Corps under my command was entirely equipped with Aeroplanes provided by the Fund, and it was largely the possession of this type of machine that enabled our pilots to obtain that complete mastery over enemy aircraft, which General Allenby in his despatches referred to as having such a marked influence on the success of his operations.

3. During the period prior to the operations, in addition to carrying out daily reconnaissances and bombing attacks far behind the enemy's lines, and engaging in frequent successful combats with enemy aircraft, these machines enabled our pilots to take photographs of an area of 1,500 square miles from which were prepared maps of the greatest value to our troops during their advance.

4. I will not attempt to give details of all the enterprises which the pilots of these machines successfully carried out: it will be sufficient to quote, as an instance of the variety of the nature of these duties, the fact that by carrying supplies of horse-shoes etc., to our advanced Cavalry at a time when no other means of communication was available, they were enabled to continue the advance which otherwise would have been seriously delayed.

5. I am unable to speak from personal experience of the activities of Aeroplanes of the Fund in other theatres, but in Palestine their value cannot be overstated.

I have, etc.

(Sgd.) A. E. Borton, Brigadier-General, Royal Air Force.

Though describing them as gifts of the 'Malayan Air Squadrons Fund', he was in fact writing of the Bristol Fighters flown by the 1st Squadron AFC in the Middle East that had been presented under the *Australian Air Squadrons Fund*, and his attribution was no doubt a deliberate mistake rather than a slip (one alone of the Malaya Air Fleet Fund's presentation aircraft is known to have ended up in that theatre).[54] As intended, his letter appeared in the press not of Australia, but of the FMS and Straits Settlements. This was all of a piece with the War Office's practice after the Australian constitutional row blew up, at least when entering into correspondence with the Colonial Office about Alma Baker. They avoided incensing their Whitehall counterparts by omitting any mention of his Australian fundraising, even citing his old address at Batu Gajah, Perak, FMS, rather than his then current address in Sydney.

After the war Alma Baker privately published a souvenir volume about the Malaya Air Fleet Fund and Australian Air Squadrons Fund. It occasioned some disobliging internal Colonial Office comments on his Australian fundraising, showing that he not been forgiven his perceived spoiling role in the NSW flying school imbroglio.[55] Bound in vellum and illustrated by the Australian artist Fred Leinst, the book was given a restricted (but rather grand) circulation that included members of the Royal Family. *94 Gift Battle Planes which Fought in the Great War 1914–1918*, as titled, paid tribute to donors in both Malaya and Australia, but this lavish publication also cast Charles Alma Baker's own role in a prominent light.

The rest of his life was spent in travelling, deep-sea fishing, and in experimental biodynamic farming activities in New Zealand that indulged his interest in the operation of what he termed 'cosmic forces' in the soil, and which eventually began to accumulate debts.[56] *En route* from Sydney to London in 1919 to oversee the final publication details of his book and receive his CBE from the King, he spent time at the Tuna Fishing Club on Catalina Island off California, where his passion for game fishing began, and he struck up sporting friendships with Western movie star Tom Mix, and Zane Grey, writer of Western novels.[57]

He returned to Malaya during the early part of the Second World War in declining health, and donated £30,000 for the purchase of six Hurricanes for the RAF (all of it borrowed). Four of the presentation planes were to be called *The Alma Baker*; *The Alma Baker Malaya*; *The Alma Baker Australia*, and *The Alma Baker New Zealand*. He died in Penang in his mid-eighties during April 1941 (eight months before the Japanese invasion).[58]

Country	Approx. population	Number of planes
Australia	4.9 million	c. 54
		+ 1 from Australia and New Zealand

Charles Alma Baker CBE, in a press photograph,
Sonoma California, 28 October 1919
Author's own collection

Part III—How it ended, and epilogue

Chapter 18:
New Zealand and Britain's aeroplane gifts to the Dominions

New Zealand sent almost one in five of its adult male population overseas during the First World War, 40 per cent of those eligible.[1] At the outset a New Zealand force seized German Samoa, while the Australians took New Guinea, both key stations on the German wireless network. Like the Australians, the New Zealanders were on the Western Front, and at Gallipoli, and the New Zealand Mounted Rifles played an important role in desert warfare alongside the Australian Light Horse in the Middle East. Although (like Australia again) Gallipoli overshadowed other theatres of war in popular perception, the Western Front took the greatest toll in casualties and fewer New Zealand troops died at Gallipoli than later at Passchendaele.[2] Indeed, 50,000 out of New Zealand's total of 58,000 casualties were incurred in France and Belgium.[3]

Most unlike Australia (and indeed all the other Dominions), however, New Zealand's native inhabitants were full citizens under the law, and were in 1914 represented by four Maori MPs. In cooperation with the Maori Committee, the New Zealand defence authorities raised a Maori force for service abroad. Although at first destined for garrison duties in Egypt, in 1915 it was decided to employ them as pioneers: that is, infantry units performing frontline combat engineering assignments, and in September 1917 the New Zealand (Maori) Pioneer Battalion was officially formed.[4] (This was the army corps in which Charles Alma Baker's illegitimate son, Pita Heretaunga Baker, served.) The Maori Contingent (and later Pioneer Battalion) served at Gallipoli in 1915 then on the Western Front, suffering over a thousand casualties, or some 40 per cent of the total sent overseas.[5]

New Zealand was surprisingly ahead of its time in certain respects. In the 1890s the Government in Wellington introduced an array of measures that put it in the reformist vanguard, well ahead of similar provisions in Britain. They included a graduated land tax, progressive labour legislation, and old age pensions. The House of Representatives voted to extend the franchise to women back in 1893—the first country in the world to do so (although women did not become eligible to stand for parliament until 1919).[6] In early 1913, George V inspected New Zealand's Dreadnought gift to the empire. Interested in the workings of the 13.5 inch guns and the new gyroscope compass, it being the first vessel to be fitted with this innovation, he was also much tickled to find the midshipmen quarters of HMS *New Zealand* decorated in the suffragette colours of green, white and purple; so absorbed was he in the inspection that he was late for lunch.[7]

Perhaps partly in symbolic recognition of the large gift of HMS *New Zealand*, the Dominion was the first recipient (in 1913) of a presentation aeroplane from Great Britain. The gift to New Zealand was organised by the Imperial Air Fleet Committee (IAFC) and financed by various British businessmen and companies (including Shell Motor Spirit, which donated £1,000).[8] It was the Blériot monoplane in which the British aviator, Gustav Hamel, had made his non-stop flight from Dover to Cologne in a time of 4 hours 18 minutes under IAFC sponsorship. Former New Zealand Prime Minister, Sir Joseph Ward was a Vice President and founder member of the Committee, newly established that February. Ward, defeated in the 1912 elections, had taken his wife and daughter to England at the beginning of 1913, returning to New Zealand as Leader of the Opposition towards the end of the year. Doubtless he was the other main reason for the choice of New Zealand.

William Grenfell, Lord Desborough, was IAFC President. Athlete, sportsman, and public servant, he was known for twice swimming across Niagara just below the falls; climbing the Matterhorn by several routes and forming the British Olympic Committee to organise the 1908 Olympics in London after Rome pulled out. The Grenfells were old friends of Lord Kitchener, who often stayed with them at Taplow Court, near Maidenhead, when he was in England. Indeed, during a return stay as Kitchener's guest in Egypt, Lord Desborough was out hunting hippopotami and giraffes at Fashoda (Kodok) in Sudan when he cabled home to accept the IAFC presidency.[9] Kitchener was close to the whole family, especially sons Julian and Billy who were both to die at Ypres, in May and July 1915 respectively. On hearing of Julian Grenfell's death, he broke down—the only occasion during the Great War when he was known to have left his desk to recover composure.

Lord Kitchener also acted as godfather to the Grenfells' youngest daughter, Imogen.[10]

Taplow Court on the Thames had acted as the pre-war hub for gatherings of the 'Souls'—writers; wits; and politicians of both Tory and Liberal, established and up-and-coming varieties (with the young Winston Churchill in this last category):

> The Souls, hugely influential in the world of politics and the country-house weekends that characterized the last flowering of the British aristocracy, included among their more prominent members [Lord] Curzon [of India]; ... his fellow Tory grandee, Arthur Balfour, prime minister before he was ousted in the 1906 Liberal landslide; and the great hostesses, Lady Elcho, Ettie Grenfell [Lady Desborough] and the duchess of Rutland.
> Although discreet, corridor-creeping adultery in country-houses was part and parcel of the Souls' way of life ... confiding their secrets only to those with a need to know—and often not even to them.[11]

Lady Ettie Desborough, described as probably the leading British aristocratic hostess of the late Victorian and early Edwardian eras, fascinated as well as attracted male followers, who became habitués at Taplow. Arthur Balfour had romantic attachments (and possibly more, despite his bloodlessness) with the two leading female Souls, Lady Desborough and Mary Elcho.[12]

However Ettie Desborough was nothing if not discreet. (In the words of her biographer, 'padlock was her word for secret confidence, and "dentist" was her word for a searching, intimate tête-à-tête.')[13] Albert Earl Grey had once been among Lady Desborough's more ambiguous affairs—perhaps platonic flirtations—that later extended to his younger cousins John (the banker) and Maurice Baring.[14] The latter was the man of letters who during the Great War was to serve both Henderson and Trenchard in turn as *aide-de-camp* and interpreter in France, acting as the RFC's main liaison with French manufacturers and suppliers of aero-engines.[15] The mother of Haig's private secretary, Philip Sassoon, had been one of the 'Souls' and he had grown up alongside Julian and Billy at numerous house parties at Taplow; Lady Desborough was to remain Philip's lifelong friend.[16]

Inspired by Hamel's pre-war achievements, Lord Desborough aimed to ensure the absolute superiority of the British Empire as much in the skies as on the high seas. The IAFC's aeroplane gifts were intended to encourage the Dominions to take up flying, and thus lay the foundations for an 'Imperial Air Fleet' as a 'new link' of Empire Union.[17] The entire Grenfell family was smitten by flying: the eldest daughter Monica had her first flight with Claude Grahame-White at Hendon, and in 1924 was to marry Air Marshal Sir John Salmond, RAF. They were also smitten with the dashing young Gustav Hamel, who was closely associated with the IAFC—like Grahame-White and other leading aviators.[18] Hamel was a frequent guest of Lord and Lady Desborough until his untimely loss over the Channel in May 1914, only a few days after he had 'looped the loop' at Maidenhead with one of Taplow Court's society ladies the passenger.[19]

In an 'interesting and unusual' ceremony at Hendon in May 1913, Lady Desborough christened the 80-h.p Blériot monoplane in which Gustav Hamel had undertaken his Dover-Calais flight. She named it *'Britannia'*, and New Zealand's High Commissioner in London, W. T. Mackenzie, officially received it for his Government. His people, he declared, would regard it as a forerunner of extensive developments in inter-Imperial communication, 'as they in New Zealand had more to do with peace than war'. Gustav Hamel 'pointed out to Lord and Lady Desborough the various features of the monoplane, which looked very smart decorated with the Union Jack and the New Zealand flag'.[20] And the portly Sir Joseph Ward, unable to fasten the belt to strap himself in, described his flight that day as Hamel's passenger (his first ever) as one in which he had 'to hang on like grim death in a thunderstorm'.[21] (In return, Hamel was the recipient of a 'wonderfully perfect' silver model of *Britannia* 'made to scale by Mappin & Webb, Ltd., for the proprietors of Shell Spirit.')[22]

New Zealand's only military trainee pilot was still under instruction in England when the plane, promptly dismantled and shipped out in a crate, arrived by sea that September, and anyway it was found that it had been forgotten to pack the propeller, which followed on later. The IAFC's song 'Britannia must Rule the Air' was sung publicly for the first time in June 1913 by a New Zealand tenor at a banquet in London.[23] However *Britannia* only flew a few times in New Zealand, and then piloted by civilians and all in January 1914. With the outbreak of war it was returned to England for the use of the RFC, who employed it in training.[24]

At Hendon, May 1913, IAFC booklet, 1920
© The British Library Board

Sir Joseph Ward climbs aboard *Britannia*, IAFC booklet, 1920
© The British Library Board

The IAFC launched a public subscription for further machines for the Dominions in June 1913, but it met with little success. In the first half of 1914 the IAFC aimed another appeal at Oxford graduates, for an aeroplane called 'The Oxford' to be presented to Australia, but that flopped too.[25] In the opening month of the Great War, however, the Liverpool businessman, William E. Cain, additionally presented a machine to Australia through the IAFC, named after his home city, and there matters stood. It was not until 1916 that a move to raise money from British cities began to pick up a head of public steam, and local centres of industry and commerce in Britain responded to the appeal to fund aeroplanes for the use of overseas forces, whose heroic role in the war was now an established fact for the British newspaper reading public. This meant the Dominions and India.

Unless higher Dominion dignitaries were present in Britain for an Imperial Conference, the aircraft subscribed and presented by British cities were handed over in formal ceremony to the relevant High Commissioner (or representative of the Government of India), along with emblems and badges of IAFC design; Pathé made film recordings of the event, staged before large provincial audiences with Lord Mayor and local dignitaries in attendance. Like overseas presentation aircraft, the names were transferred onto any replacements. The original *Liverpool I* was the first Renault BE2c to fly under service conditions, before being struck off charge in August 1915 having logged 139 hours flying: after transfer to a second BE2c, the name was carried in turn by a large Martinsyde Elephant fighter bomber; a BE2e; and an RE8.[26]

In June 1916, the *Leicester* was formally presented to the Canadian High Commissioner, to be flown by Canadian pilots of the RFC. It was followed by the gift of *Leeds* to India in the presence of Lord Islington, Under Secretary of State at the India Office and a former Governor of New Zealand (as well as brother-in-law to Sir David Henderson). Then, in May 1917, the London Chamber of Commerce presented the DH4, *South Africa*: at the handover ceremony General Smuts represented the South African Government.[27] There followed during 1917–19 these additions to the Imperial Air Fleet: *Sheffield* to Newfoundland; *Nottingham* to New Zealand; *Huddersfield* to Canada; *Manchester* to India; *Liverpool No. 2* to Newfoundland; *City of Hull* to Australia; *City of Glasgow* to Canada; *City of Edinburgh* to New Zealand; and *City of Birmingham* to South Africa.[28] Crowds of 40–60,000 were normal. Over 80,000 people attended the presentation of *Sheffield* to Newfoundland.[29]

Vast crowds attended these ceremonies: At the presentation of
City of Hull to Australia in 1918, IAFC booklet, 1920
© The British Library Board

General Jan Smuts at the presentation of DH4 *South Africa* by the
London Chamber of Commerce in 1917, his expression evocative of
his Afrikaans nickname of *slim* (sly or crafty) *Jannie*, IAFC booklet, 1920
© The British Library Board

Hardit Singh Malik with *Manchester-India*, March 1918
Courtesy of Cross & Cockade International Archive

At the beginning of March 1918, a Sopwith Camel gifted by the Manchester Chamber of Commerce was handed over, Sahibzada Aftab Ahmed Khan representing the Government of India. Lieutenant Hardit Singh Malik (the pilot only accepted by the RFC as a candidate for a flying commission after Henderson's intervention) took part in the ceremony.[30] A telegram from Lord Islington referred to the distinction Malik had earned in the service of the RFC, and to the demonstrable effectiveness of airmen in the special conditions of frontier warfare, citing operations in Waziristan. The plane's bronze mascot (a tiger) duly affixed, Lord Desborough promised that the name *Manchester* would be transferred to any replacement machine, and thus be perpetuated the length of the war itself.[31]

The IAFC-donated aeroplanes were to have been flown on the Western Front until the end of the war, and were then to be returned to the respective Dominion (or India as the case may be) to which they already 'belonged'. This did not always happen. The *Nottingham*—an RE8 donated to New Zealand by that city's Chamber of Commerce, was launched at on official function before a crowd of 40,000. New Zealand flags were presented to dignitaries, and a bronze mascot with a representation of a kiwi together with the New Zealand motto of 'Onward' and the IAFC's motto of 'Heaven's light our guide' was attached to the fuselage. Despite the promises, *Nottingham* did not come to New Zealand after the end of the war,[32] but post-war vacillations in New Zealand air policy may have been at least partly to blame.

In late 1915, the campaigner of New Zealand origin, Charles Alma Baker, had appealed to fellow residents of the FMS to furnish:

> Aeroplanes and such an Air Force as will adequately represent the Loyalty and Patriotism of the 'Entire Population of Malaya', and be such a record that this, the 'Golden Link' in the Imperial Chain, can look back upon with justifiable pride.[33]

At the Imperial War Conference that opened in London in March 1917, New Zealand's Prime Minister, William Massey, employed a similar metaphor when he called for the forging of bonds between the countries represented there that would need to be 'while stronger than steel yet as light as silk' if the unity between the empire's disparate parts was to endure.[34] Such shared imperial imagery drawn on by Premier Massey, of a flexible cord or chain, became common currency in discourse about the future peacetime shape that an otherwise disjointed and dispersed British Empire might take.

With regard to that particular gathering in London of senior empire politicians, it also reflected Dominion ambitions for greater equality, and a future say in the imperial order after all the sacrifices of the war. For while from a long-term historical perspective British imperial policy towards the settler colonies had tended to be loose and devolved, the Great War had paradoxically both fostered further Dominion autonomy, and briefly, and under practical pressures, saw a major concentration of power in London through an Imperial War Cabinet with selective Dominion input.[35] Although Jan Smuts accepted Lloyd George's invitation to stay on as a member of the British War Cabinet and a continuing Dominion presence between Conferences (Premier Billy Hughes of Australia declined a similar invitation),[36] the problem still remained of how the post-war future was to be shaped.

Some believed that by overcoming geographical separation, air connections might help point the way ahead toward greater economic and political cohesion. Likewise, the IAFC wooed financial support from British provincial Chambers of Commerce with the prospect of improved trade links with the Dominions and India, and a stopover or station on future air routes to be established in peacetime. They published a 'Red Route' map of Britain showing cities that had contributed to the Imperial Air Fleet, with the implicit possibility of privileged inclusion in a 'New Red Route of Aeroplanes round the British Empire' that would establish a 'New Link of Empire Union'.[37] At the handover of *Manchester-India* the IAFC also ceremonially presented the Director of the Great Central Railway Company with a trophy of flags of those British towns on his rail system that had contributed aeroplanes to the scheme.[38]

Clearly the IAFC's imperial propaganda was not without its more pragmatic appeal to the municipalities. At the ceremonial presentation of *Liverpool* to Newfoundland, the Lord Mayor declared hardheadedly:

> The idea underlying the presentation of the craft is to establish a practically All-Red route in the air throughout the planet. That is the business aspect of the movement, and it is an aspect that must appeal strongly to all concerned in British trade and commerce. The quick perception of the potentialities of the aeroplane as a means of transit for goods as well as for passengers shows an intellectual alertness worthy of the best traditions of British captains of industry.[39]

As well as the IAFC's dreams for civil aviation when peace should finally arrive, ambitions for a role in imperial defence plans crept into Dominion thinking. They evidently included setting up air bases. In early 1917, Charles Alma Baker wrote from Australia to the Under Secretary of State for the Colonies in London:

> With reference to the battleplanes presented by the various parts of the Empire, may I be permitted to ask if it would be possible, when the war is over, for the presented machines to be returned to the different localities that present them? I ask this, as I think in the near future air power will be even more important than sea power, and that Imperial federation of the air forces of the Empire must come soon; also that aerial bases for the protection of the Pacific will be established in Australia, New Guinea, New Zealand, Fiji, Borneo, Hong Kong, Penang, Singapore, and the Federated Malay States, and if the machines are sent back after the war a large number of the most improved types of aeroplanes, and pilots who have learnt the latest tactics in war, will be at the disposal of Governments of the different parts of the Empire.[40]

He was advised through the Governor General of Australia that it was somewhat premature to consider the matter, but no doubt some thought would be given to the areas providing the aircraft in due course.

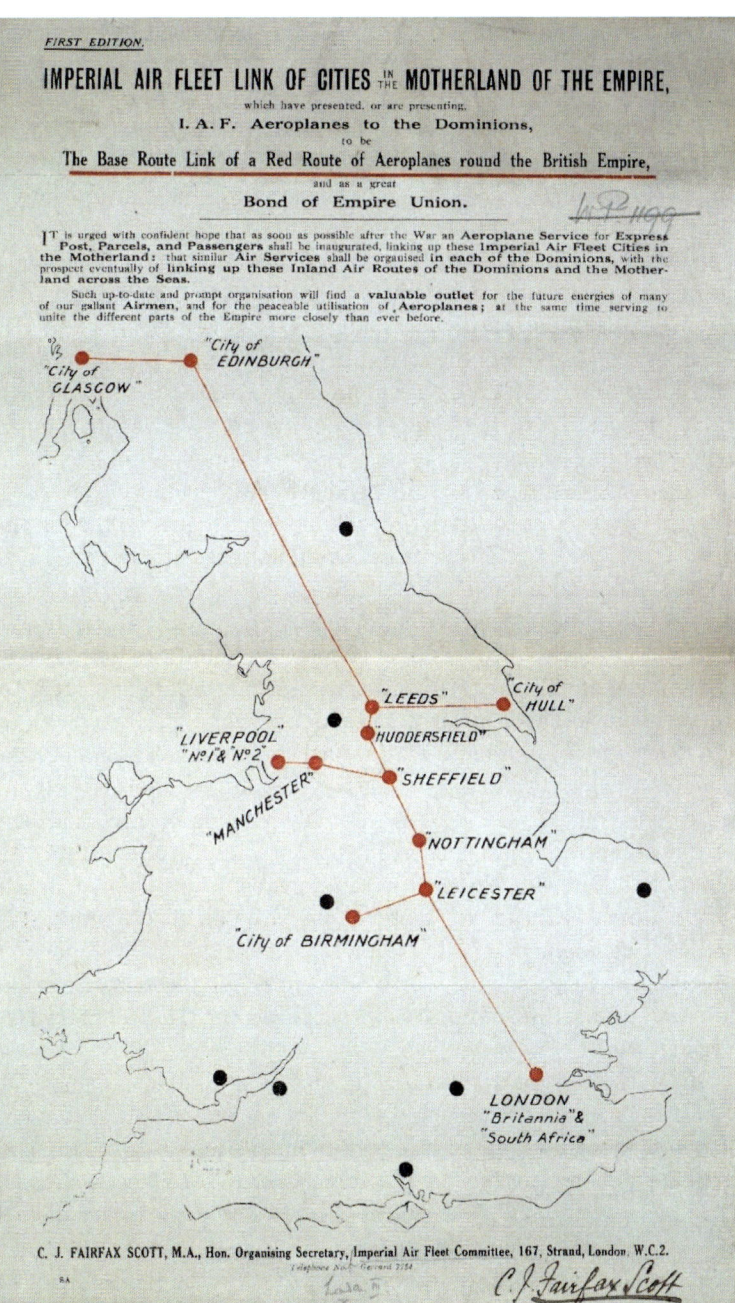

The IAFC's 'red route' map, IAFC booklet, 1920
© The British Library Board

After the Armistice, Alma Baker returned to the charge, passing copies of his letter and the reply from the Colonial Office to the Australian Minister of Defence, Senator Pearce, who sent it on to the Australian High Commissioner in London for follow up.[41] The British Chief of the Air Staff at the time, Sir Frederick Sykes, supported the creation of an 'Imperial' Air Force whose role would be to defend the entire empire, but his plan submitted to the War Cabinet in June 1918 had been rejected as too costly, and he was replaced the following February.[42] (In his new appointment as Controller-General of Aviation he pursued his vision of air-links as a unifying factor for a Commonwealth of English-speaking peoples, but in the civil sphere.)[43]

Then in May 1919 it was announced by way of an arranged parliamentary question in the House of Commons that the Air Ministry would be offering some of its now surplus planes to the Dominions and Colonies as a free gift (though there is no evidence that planes were, in fact, offered to any of the Colonies). Subsequently the Air Ministry wrote offering to each of the Dominions up to a hundred war-surplus aircraft to help them establish their own air force, and 'thereby develop defence of the Empire by air'.

Not everyone took advantage—while Newfoundland was too poor to dream of an air force, Canada was an important beneficiary. The country had supplied the largest number of 'colonials' flying with the RFC/RAF, and an estimated 13–14,000 Canadians were connected in some way with the British flying services during the Great War.[44] More than four thousand of the Canadian flying officers had been trained at the aviation school established outside Toronto in late 1916 in cooperation with the British authorities. They trained on the Curtiss-designed large two-seater biplane of Canadian manufacture, the JN-4, nicknamed the 'Jenny' or the 'Canuck'.[45] Many Americans also trained at the school, which was under the direction of British Colonel Cuthbert Gurney Hoare, especially after the US entered the war in April 1917.

In the twenty-one months the RFC/RAF recruited in Canada, 9,200 Canadian airmen were accepted;[46] and by the end of 1918, Canadians made up at least 15 per cent of RAF flying officers in France.[47] They included a nephew of the late Lord Kitchener, whose fees at Canada's McGill University had been met by his uncle after his father died. In the last year of the war Henry Horatio ('Hal') Kitchener, then aged eighteen, and qualified as a pilot/observer, entered the ranks of the RFC/RAF but was forbidden by doctors to fly above 10,000 feet (he suffered from the family's hereditary deafness that had bypassed his uncle).[48] Arrangements had just been made for two independent Canadian squadrons to work alongside the RAF in France and Belgium when the Armistice intervened; and there were plans for them to return to form the nucleus of a Canadian Air Force, which in fact came into being in 1920.

At the beginning of 1919 the High Commissioner for Canada took formal possession of the three Imperial Air Fleet planes *Leicester*, *Huddersfield*, and *City of Glasgow* at Hendon. Each of them was adorned with the IAFC-designed light bronze badge with beaver and maple leaf design. (Newfoundland's IAFC bronze mascot design was in the form of a caribou's head.) The High Commissioner declared that Canada had started an airmail service already, and the country envisaged using planes for fire-fighting in outlying districts and on scattered farms, maybe using lakes and employing seaplanes to travel over forests to keep down fires.[49] By something of a sleight-of-hand trick, one of those ceremoniously handed over from the RAF had actually been presented by Zanzibar: a Bristol Fighter originally inscribed *Zanzibar No. 17*, but with its name altered to *Huddersfield-Canada*,[50] presumably in hurried replacement of a machine found unfit for purpose.

After the end of the war all aeroplanes bearing Australian presentation names (which had had Australian pilots at the controls for well over a year) were duly dispatched to Australia. Soon after the Armistice, the Canadian military authorities also requested the return of the fifteen aircraft presented by its citizens in order to form the first squadron of a Canadian Air Force.[51] Only seven of them could be found in a fit state to send, but numbers were made up of other aeroplanes presented from elsewhere through the Overseas Club and Patriotic League. Lord Londonderry, as Under Secretary for Air handed over all fifteen aircraft on behalf of his Ministry at a ceremony at Hendon aerodrome in February 1919.[52] A sixteenth aircraft, given by Captain A. M. Simpson in the name of the City of Liverpool, was added at the last moment.[53] (This was not an IAFC gift, and may have been provided through the Liverpool branch of the Overseas Club.) In receiving them officially, Sir Edward Kemp, Minister of the Overseas Military Forces of Canada, added a steely note to the bondage metaphor:

> The ties which bound the Colonies to the Mother Country had been referred to as a silken cord, but war had proved it to be of much stronger material, and he hoped and believed that nothing would happen in the future to weaken it.[54]

Unaccompanied by public ceremony, German planes and parts left Fienvilliers in France on 21 July 1919, additionally destined for the Canadian Government.[55]

The Royal Australian Air Force was formed in 1921 from men who had flown in the war, and what is described as an 'enormous quantity' of aviation materiel sent by the British Air Ministry to Australia after the Armistice, along with one hundred planes.[56] The third major beneficiary was South Africa. The key here, besides the large number of South Africans flying with the RFC during the war, was the keen interest shown by General Jan Smuts, whose report had led to the establishment of the RAF, and who set great store by the future possibilities of aviation.

The London Chamber of Commerce had funded the gift of DH4 *South Africa* in 1917 (with over £1,000 towards it provided by 'British Petroleum'—actually a former German marketing company whose assets in UK had been seized and sold to the Anglo-Persian Oil Co.)[57] In his acceptance speech, Smuts claimed that ultimate victory lay in keeping air supremacy. But when this was achieved the aeroplane would open up vistas of progress for the human race: If the existing obstacles of time and space to a closer union between the scattered members of this 'Commonwealth of Nations' (he did not like the word 'empire' he said) could be overcome by means of an Air Fleet, then the aeroplane would play a most useful part in the new era of peace that would dawn.[58]

The decision to establish a South African Air Force (SAAF) was made in 1919, and one was gradually built up in the early 1920s from aircraft provided by the British Air Ministry. From September 1919 a hundred aircraft arrived in batches together with spares, tools and hangars.[59] The SAAF was formed under the command of Lieutenant Colonel Pierre van Ryneveld, who with Flight Lieutenant Brand had made the pioneer flight from London via Cairo to the Cape from 4 February to 20 March 1920. Described as having opened up the last important empire air route (after flights made by others to Canada, Australia, and India), they had crashed twice *en route*, forcing them to change engines, and finally arrived on the last leg of the journey from Bulawayo to Cape Town in a donated British war-surplus De Havilland replacement, named by Smuts the *Voortrekker*.[60] Four civilian and one RAF aircraft and crew had set off to fly Cairo to Cape that February under the sponsorship of various parties and with the encouragement of Sykes.[61] The South African team were the only ones to make it.

A matter of national pride to Jan Smuts, he lobbied hard to get parity of recognition with the Australian airmen responsible for the earlier Australian flight (who had flown uninterrupted in the same plane from London and became national heroes), eventually obtaining the award of two KBEs for Van Ryneveld and Brand, civil division.[62] The IAFC honoured the South African airmen with a luncheon in May 1920, at which the speaker was Flight Lieutenant Prince Albert, RAF (later, King George VI), the IAFC noting that the Cairo to Cape Town Air Route would pass over Fashoda, within forty miles of which an aerodrome would be established.[63] The ghost of Lord Kitchener, who had faced down the French in the famous clash of imperialisms at Fashoda on the Nile in 1898, Hero of Sudan, was clearly present. He had gone down off Orkney when his ship hit a mine in June 1916, never to enjoy his retirement to his estate in the Kenyan Highlands.

Quite apart from the Imperial Air Fleet planes, British towns and cities, army units (especially reserve units) and factories had been raising money for presentation aircraft for the RFC and RAF in emulation of the Imperial Aircraft Flotilla scheme. The earliest were presented in 1916, but most date from the latter part of the war. At least fifty-two aeroplanes were subscribed in this way. In April 1918, for example, the workers at the munitions factory in Georgetown, Paisley, Scotland, raised £2,500 for a fighter aeroplane as their contribution to War Weapons Week. They achieved this by organising at the factory a 'fancy fair', cinema entertainments, concerts, and a fancy dress ball.[64] Sometimes a single individual would come up with the money: in May, Lieutenant Colonel Sir A. E. Bingham of the West Riding Division of the Royal Engineers, manufacturer and Senior Warden of the Cutlers' Company, Sheffield, presented an RE8, *The Ranby*, to the RAF.[65]

For sign writers and photographers at RAF depots this all spelt an eventual massive accumulation of work. Sir David Henderson's original undertaking that donors of presentation aeroplanes to the RFC would be kept informed of any 'good work' done by their machine had been dropped much earlier. However, the undertaking to transfer presentation names onto replacement aircraft and supply photographs to donors was maintained. By 1919, surviving RFC documentation recorded over 600 separate donations of presentation aeroplanes.

Taking the original named machine and each replacement onto which that name had been transferred, it has been calculated that the number of aircraft carrying those names had amounted to at least 1,400.[66] In August 1918, RAF Headquarters heeded pleas and agreed to allow separate fabric strips inscribed with the relevant presentation name to be sent to a central depot, where they could simply be pasted on to waiting aircraft and photographed when a photographer was available. However, this was to be done *only* for aircraft donated by British towns or army units: all presentation aeroplanes donated from overseas were to be treated in exactly the same way as previously.[67]

New Zealand did not form its own air corps during the Great War. The several hundred pilots from New Zealand mainly flew with the RFC or the RNAS after either initial training at one of New Zealand's two civilian aviation schools or in England. Some also flew with the AFC in the Middle East. The first Maori to qualify as an aviator did so at New Zealand's Canterbury Aviation School in 1917. Ernest Taniwha Sutherland went on to serve as an air observer with the RAF in the final months of the war. Correspondence between New Zealand and the British authorities during 1917 regarding men of Maori blood serving in the RFC as officers resulted in British agreement provided they were considered suitable for commissions in the New Zealand forces. In October 1918 the British Government however stipulated that Maori applicants should have attained a higher educational standard than Europeans, but this new hurdle came too late to have any practical effect on candidates for service in the war. The second Maori to qualify as a pilot in New Zealand was Charles Barton, who did so in 1918, but after the Armistice.[68]

Nor did New Zealand take full advantage of the Air Ministry's offer of war-surplus aircraft in 1919. Despite the recommendations of a British expert air advisor seconded to it, the New Zealand Government decided that it was 'impracticable to involve the country in the large expenditure that would be required for any air scheme which would be of value for defence or postal purposes.' But at the beginning of 1920, second thoughts led to acceptance of whatsoever might still be available. Some months later, thirty-three machines were shipped out, of which the New Zealand Government reserved six for defence use, and lent the remainder to private flying enterprises in the country. New Zealand finally established its own air force in 1923.[69]

Subscribers in New Zealand presented eight aircraft to Great Britain during the war, through both the Overseas Club and the Patriotic League. The first, *Hawkes Bay New Zealand*, a reconnaissance aeroplane, went to the RFC in September 1915. Two Sopwith 1½ Strutters (suitable for long range reconnaissance) called *New Zealand Nos. 1 and 2 'Poverty Bay'* were presented to the RNAS, the first of them in

January 1916. To the RFC again went FE2bs *Maori* and *Auckland* in June and September 1916 respectively. The Auckland Provincial Aeroplane Committee provided the latter, while the Union Steamship Company gifted *Maori* with the special request that a New Zealander pilot it.[70] (Result unknown, but such requests usually failed.) A reconnaissance aircraft named *Otago New Zealand* was presented in December 1916, and *Christchurch Overseas Club* (a DH5) and *Wanganui New Zealand* (an SE5a) followed in August 1917 and May 1918 respectively.[71]

Sir Joseph Ward remained IAFC Vice-President into the early 1920s (he died in 1930), when the organisation's rationale ended with the formation of Imperial Airways in 1924 and it ceased activities. Despite his Irish Catholic origins and public support for Irish Home Rule, Ward was also a supporter of British Empire unity, and had been responsible for the Government's gift of the Dreadnought to the Royal Navy. During most of the Great War he was shackled to his great political rival, William F. Massey, leader of the Reform Party and an Orangeman and Ulster Protestant. On 4 August 1915, first anniversary of the declaration of war, Massey formed a coalition government with himself as Prime Minister and Ward, the Liberal leader, as Deputy Prime Minister and Minister of Finance. Cabinet decisions were to be unanimous.

Not trusting Ward to act as Prime Minister in his absence, Massey had him accompany him wherever he went, and the odd couple travelled to Imperial Conferences in London, on visits to the Front, and ultimately to the Peace Conference in Paris, spending months at a time together outside the country. Ward had been the first Dominion Statesman to 'fly Imperially'—in the IAFC's phrase—in *Britannia*. On a visit to New Zealanders fighting on the Western Front in early November 1916, Massey bested Ward—or at least drew even with him— by flying passenger with the RFC from one of their airfields in France, perhaps the first serving head of government to have done so.[72]

As in other areas settled principally from the British Isles, events in Ireland loomed large in domestic politics, especially following the Easter Rising of 1916. Unlike Australia, New Zealand's coalition government was able to introduce conscription. Yet some of the underlying social tensions between empire 'loyalists' of English, Scots, and Ulster Protestant descent, and those of Irish Catholic background critical of British policies in Ireland, were probably common to both. In the continuing absence from the country of its two senior politicians at the Paris Peace Conference of 1919, the Governor General, Lord Liverpool, commented on the air of unease and discontent prevailing in the country at large. While the prime issue under discussion in Paris was the fate of the former German colony of Western Samoa (for which, in the event, New Zealand was awarded the Mandate) at home the situation in Ireland was considered a far more vital matter, and the Protestants were organising against the Catholics, whom they regarded as untrustworthy.[73]

In March 1917, the indefatigable Evelyn Wrench spent the two weeks awaiting his RFC joining instructions engaged on a mission of conciliation between Dublin and Belfast. He hoped to increase contact between Ireland and the Dominions, and nursed a scheme for the establishment of two provincial parliaments to deal with all internal matters—one in Dublin for Leinster, Munster and Connaught, and the other in Belfast for Ulster. A 'Council of Twenty-Four' consisting of twelve representatives from each, with sessions alternating between the two cities, should deal with matters of common concern, such as customs, railways, postal services and fisheries. However his proposed Irish Unity League to work towards such ends, with its slogan of a 'United Ireland within a United Empire', met with a frosty reception from fellow Ulstermen and he was forced to drop the idea.[74] In mid-1918 he founded the English-Speaking Union instead, to promote Anglo-American amity, and co-operation between the US and the British Dominions (later, the Commonwealth)—a much easier nut to crack.

Country	Approx. population	Number of planes
New Zealand	1.15 million	8 + 1 subscribed from Australia and New Zealand
Great Britain	46 million, including over 4m. Ireland and c. 4.5m. Scotland	c. 52 + 13 IAFC

Chapter 19:
Cast list: minorities, colonials, 'subject peoples' and native rulers

If the play's the thing, then the curtain came down on the Imperial Aircraft Flotilla at the end of the war. Yet even if there were no encores, there were later echoes of the British presentation aircraft scheme that had run from the beginning of 1915 until the Armistice. It may have provided a source of inspiration for the 'Aeroplane Purchasing Campaign' for the Nationalist Chinese air force, launched in a belated Chinese aerial arms race with Japan. It began in August 1936, in both China itself and amongst the overseas Chinese of Southeast Asia. A ceremony at Shanghai that October (a city subject to indiscriminate Japanese bombing in 1932) unveiled ten named aircraft that had been gifted by citizens as a 'birthday present' for Chiang Kai-shek; and it was announced that they were to be joined by two additional aeroplanes as Red Cross vehicles, provided by China's Catholics.[1] The fundraising appeal ran through Chinese communities worldwide during the undeclared Sino-Japanese war that broke out the following year.

During the Japanese military occupation of Malaya and Singapore that began some five years later, resident Chinese communities were grouped locally into a new association, and compelled to provide money for warplanes for the Japanese imperial forces. A direct connection had apparently been perceived between local collections for the air force of Nationalist China and the earlier British fundraising effort—for Dr. Lim Boon Keng of Singapore, who had been heavily involved during the Great War in support of Charles Alma Baker's Malaya Air Fleet Fund, was forced to take on the figurehead role under duress (to end maltreatment of his wife).[2] Previously, in 1938, the Sultans and people of the FMS had quite separately also gifted four Sunderland flying boats for use of the RAF based in Singapore.

A British presentation scheme known as the Spitfire Fund (though it presented other aircraft models too) was established in the Second World War. Superficially similar in conception to that of the First, donors to the Spitfire Fund received photographs of 'their' plane, and attempts were initially made to supply progress reports. However there were important differences. The sum specified for a Spitfire—

£5,000—was nominal, and represented a contribution towards general production costs, but was below the actual cost. The presentation name attached only to the original, and was not transferred to any replacement. No appeal was issued to create a notional 'Imperial' flotilla of aircraft; and there was a much greater proportionate input from subscribers in Great Britain itself.

However, a colonial government providing sufficient funds could have an RAF squadron named after the territory in question, and the name of that squadron was supposed to be perpetuated (though sometimes may have failed to survive post-war RAF reorganisation).[3] An enquiry from the Nizam of Hyderabad at the start of the conflict about what part 'his' squadron would play, along with payment of £100,000, followed six months later by a further £50,000, precipitated this concession on the part of the RAF: No. 110 Squadron, which had disbanded in August 1919 and reformed in May 1937, thus became known as *Hyderabad* squadron, whose pilots wore badges supplied by the Nizam himself.[4]

Charles Alma Baker was personally responsible for several presentation Hurricanes, on borrowed money that created a future headache for the administrators of his estate. There were several other echoes of the past. A gift of £100,000 from the BNC provided a number of aircraft that henceforth flew with the RAF's No. 72 *Basutoland* Squadron, while some 22,000 Basuto served in the British Army's African Pioneer Corps (APC), among them skilled muleteers to carry ammunition and supplies in the Italian mountains and evacuate casualties.[5] And Sultan Seyyid Khalifa and the Government of Zanzibar presented the money for four Spitfires.

Nevertheless, the Imperial Aircraft Flotilla campaign was not replicated in any deep sense, though some of its outward forms were adopted; and could not be, for it had developed and spread organically, under an earlier and much more self-confident British imperial order, convinced of the British Empire's future longevity if not of the precise direction it was heading and shape it was taking. While a titanic European conflict had raged during 1914–18, the Imperial Aircraft Flotilla campaign ran through countries located on the periphery of the Great War and communities living in its shadow.

A combination of publicity by home and overseas newspapers, and active involvement by many British officials worldwide, turned a voluntary scheme, launched by a hyperactive pressman with an empire mission, into a movement that spanned the globe. Although it ran primarily through populations of British blood descent, there were plenty of other subscribers, with motivations of their own that were both many and various. By the Second World War, and even more through the events of that war, and in particular the fall of Singapore, the old certainties on which the appeal to imperial unity was based had largely evaporated.

Many of the subscriptions for presentation aircraft in the Great War had been modest and the motivation for them probably straightforward. Smaller traders and service providers might simply have wanted to keep officialdom sweet with a show of goodwill, while British subjects resident outside the empire may have acted—at least in part—out of an awareness of their reliance on the resident British mission for consular assistance, or even personal security. (At Addis Ababa, for instance, where the threat was serious, the British Legation grounds the designated place of sanctuary, and where the British Minister's wife handled subscriptions.)

The source of larger donations nevertheless provides a pointer to contemporary economic and commercial interests that willingly supported the imperial cause during an era still dominated by the ideal and practice of international free trade, though interrupted by the exigencies of war and soon to be progressively undermined by the growth of protectionism throughout the world. It was also dominated by mainly untaxed entrepreneurial activity and investment. Commercially active minorities and trading *diasporas* were often prominent subscribers, alone, or in combination with others.

The subscription lists for the Malaya Air Fleet Fund in Perak's Kinta Valley notably bore witness to the interdependence (at that date at least) of British and Chinese business enterprise and investment in the tin mining industry. In a broader sense, British colonial penetration of Southeast Asia during the nineteenth century had created challenges for resident ethnic Chinese business communities on this western-most edge of China's maritime trading area. But it also brought access to the British Empire's commercial sea-routes across the globe, especially after the opportunities for expansion created by the opening of the Suez Canal in 1869. If anything, the effect of the Great War appears to have been to enhance those opportunities, in shipping, in banking, and in insurance.

It was a double-edged traffic, however, and the historic trade in opium from British India to China had attracted, amongst others, Sephardic Jewish dynasties of Baghdadi origin that settled and set up businesses in the port cities of South and East Asia, there to become commercial allies of the British in opium and other profitable enterprises. Quite possibly numbering amongst the anonymous subscribers of the Shanghai Race Club, they were represented among larger donors elsewhere by cotton mill magnate Sir David Sassoon in Bombay, and merchant and hotelier Manasseh Meyer in Singapore.

Besides those of British blood descent, there were therefore others that identified their interests with investing in, and upholding, the British Empire, at least as an economic enterprise. Of those occupying a rewarding niche in commerce and the empire's trading networks, there were indeed some with good reason to feel passionately about the events of the Great War, and its outcome. The very small, but relatively well-off, Armenian community of the Straits Settlements Colony was involved in the larger effort by the Armenian *diaspora* to provide relief for refugees and survivors from the large-scale and systematic Turkish massacres and death marches of 1915. Their donations to the Malaya Air Fleet Fund have been touched on already.

There were also others of more slender means. The 'Syrian Christians' of West Africa as they were then known (mainly Lebanese Maronites), were subscribers, although technically enemy subjects. Enterprising migrants from the Syrian provinces of the Ottoman Empire, they were small and medium traders. Their contributions were modest and often went unrecorded, but as a community included some £71 17s 0d to the Nigeria Aeroplane Fund.[6] In Gold Coast they made an initial contribution of £52 10s 0d to the Imperial War Fund established by Joseph Ephraim Casely Hayford, a donation attributed by Clifford to hostility towards the Ottoman Turks.[7] Back in their homeland some 500,000 people—almost half the population—died of famine during 1915-18;[8] and as with the Armenians, Syrian Christian 'colonies' worldwide involved themselves in relief efforts.[9] (However, although the Turks carried the blame, the food crisis was complex in origin: precipitated by the French and British blockade off the Syrian coast, it was exacerbated by diversion of grain to Turkish and German troop detachments in Syria; by effects of the Arab revolt in the Hejaz; and by both bureaucratic bungling and profiteering.)[10]

Did British attitudes to the citizens of their empire change as a result of all this practical support from unexpected directions? Perhaps a little bit. There was some initial surprise at the financial assistance forthcoming from beyond the white Dominions and scattered British expatriate communities at large in the world. The response from Chinese donors in Hong Kong and Southeast Asia was certainly unexpected, and gave rise to comment in London. It also gave rise to some questioning in local newspapers with a British expatriate readership as to whether generous local contributions to the Imperial Aircraft Flotilla, or other funds like the Red Cross, could be described as 'patriotic'—in the sense of upholding the British imperial cause—concluding that Chinese support for war funds had proved so open-handed that it would be churlish to question motivations.

The publicity surrounding gifts from Hong Kong and the FMS and Straits Settlements, and the positive response from the top of the Colonial Office (Lewis Harcourt in the case of Hong Kong, and then Bonar Law with respect to the Malaya Air Fleet Fund) probably also encouraged further collections directed specifically at 'British subjects', such as that initiated by the Bangkok Legation during 1916. In fact, Chinese involvement even extended beyond such established communities in Asia, for instance to members of the Chinese Commercial Society of Kingston (which represented resident shopkeepers and traders in Jamaica of mainly recent Hong Kong provenance) who collectively subscribed to the Alexandra Aeroplane Fund.[11]

At the end of the day, however, it was the Dominions with their great sacrifices in blood by 'kith and kin' that were really remembered in Britain, and it was to the Dominions that war-surplus aircraft, including those bearing presentation names of Crown Colonies and Protectorates, were sent. Since, however, the Dominions (and Southern Rhodesia) had provided the main source of the empire's pilot recruits to the RFC/RNAS/RAF (all of them operating a 'whites-only' recruitment policy, albeit fitfully and with exceptions), they were most probably the only areas with sufficient trained aviators able to use those aircraft. (The independent kingdom of Siam stood as an example of what could be done, but it was a foreign country outside the empire and little known or appreciated in Great Britain.) But in any case, Crown Colonies, which were not self-governing, were not then envisaged by the British authorities as ever raising or running their own air forces, still less Protectorates.

So often subsumed within the broader category of Britons abroad, the Scots were central players in the empire-building project,[12] and prominent as traders and investors, in banking, insurance and mutual societies, as settlers, engineers, doctors, lawyers, missionaries, and other professionals.[13] They were also prominent in the British military where they had had a disproportionate presence at every level including senior officer ranks since the eighteenth century.[14] Scotland sent more volunteers to the Great War in proportion to population than anywhere else in the United Kingdom, and they suffered the highest death rate (26.4% compared with 11.8% for the rest of the British Army). These high casualty rates reflected the fact that the Scottish regiments were regarded as excellent shock troops that could be relied on to lead the line in the opening stages of battle. Consequently, only Serbia and Turkey exceeded Scotland's mortality rate among combatant nations.[15] (West African soldiers employed as shock troops by the French Army also suffered high casualties and a comparable death rate.)[16]

Scotland's leading representative in this story was Lieutenant General Sir David Henderson, Director of Aeronautics at the War Office 1915–17, and after the Armistice, military councillor during the Paris Peace Conference, then Director-General of the League of Red Cross Societies in Geneva until his death in 1921. Like so many other senior British officers of the period, he was a veteran of the Boer war, in which he had been Director of Intelligence. (The GOC Straits Settlements at Singapore, Brigadier General Dudley Ridout, who was not a Scot, had incidentally served as an intelligence officer under Henderson in South Africa.)[17] Henderson's personal contacts most probably informed the choice of Major Allister Miller for his southern Africa mission in 1916. Miller's use of presentation planes for aerobatic displays on his South African recruitment tours raises the further possibility that Henderson and the RFC might have regarded them as a recruiting attraction for 'colonials'.

Higher pay and the excitements of flying were probably the more persuasive factors, however, as the following two letter writers suggest. RFC trainee L. J. Riordan, twenty-three years old and in civil life an office typist in Johannesburg earning £15 per month, wrote home in June 1916:

> By all the rules of modern warfare I ought to be dead long ago, but it's now eight months since I left ... and I'm still alive and kicking. As you know, I was in the Gunners, and then they asked me to transfer to the Royal Flying Corps; more pay if you live long enough and draw it and a bonus. Well, I signed in the RFC for 4 years ... After I get my ticket I get about 3 more months flying all kinds of machines ... Then I have

another exam and get my wings, and am then a fully fledged military aviator. I am getting £26 a month at present, and when I get my wings get ... roughly £37 10s [per] month and bonus of £150 for every year's service in the RFC. Not bad, eh? ... I intend returning to S. Africa after this affair, and am endeavouring to get in the South African Flying Corps.[18]

Victor B. Pare, from Cape Town, now with his RAF wings, wrote in 1918:

> After a few more hours on 'Pups' I'll be put on 'Sopwith Camels'—the service machines that are doing the most damage in France and are most dreaded; they have 2 machineguns in front. Do you remember how curious I used to be to have a look at Patterson [sic.—Compton Paterson] and his old hydroplane? How wonderful I thought it was to see a machine flying alone in the air; and now performing feats that Patterson [sic.] would not think of doing: 'hoops', 'spins', 'rolls', 'Immelman turns', 'vertical banks' and 'falling leaf'.[19]

His elder brother, also in the RAF, wrote home that 'little Vic' was making quite a name for himself as a stunt flyer.

Nonetheless, published letters bear witness that some 'colonials' sought to fly aeroplanes associated with their home country. Others serving abroad wrote back about presentation aeroplanes from home, such as Alfred Horne of Trinidad, Captain Elton Lane of Ceylon and the anonymous observer in the Siam aeroplane (inset on p. 241). The following came from the pen of trooper Roach serving with the 1st Canadian cavalry brigade of the 2nd King Edward's Horse in France:

> ... on Saturday we were relieved by the 7th and 8th Canadians, and took over their billets, a few miles in the rear of the trenches.
> This morning, I went out for a quiet walk, and ... struck upon one of our latest aircraft stations of biplanes. I had a look round, and to my surprise discovered one of 'Good old Shanghai's' overseas subscription biplanes ... It was riddled with bullet holes from German anti-aircraft guns, patched up in a hundred and one places ... On the rudder at the rear of the plane, was the mark of the Overseas Club, and on the side ... in big letters, *Shanghai Britons*.
> I was quite proud to see the old name, and had quite a chat over it with the Major in command. It appears he has written ... acknowledging the receipt of it. [...] I am sure members of the Overseas Club would be pleased to hear of their gift. (*New China Herald*, 29 January 1916)

2nd Lieutenant Hazelton Nicholl's missive of October 1915 to Charles Alma Baker (inset on p. 44) may well have deliberately exaggerated the significance of presentation aeroplanes to airmen in France—perhaps at the behest of Sir David Henderson, who was probably aware of contemporary opposition to the Malaya Air Fleet Fund in Singapore's legislature, and may have wished to provide Charles Alma Baker with ammunition for his cause. But as an individual Hazelton Nicholl also identified with the colonies through personal experience.

Clearly presentation aircraft *did* hold a certain appeal for some at least of the RFC's overseas recruits, and perhaps held real meaning for those like Nicholl with a strong faith in the value of the British Empire. (Which is not to say that the 'colonials' necessarily treated the scheme with solemnity: there were hoaxes—witness the appeal to Trinidad and Dominica for presentation kite balloons, and fake presentation names, such as *'Jack Canuck'* found painted on a fighter plane in France, presumably by its Canadian pilot.)[20]

Yet it is also important to avoid overstating the attraction of presentation aircraft to aviators during the war: If they were of significant importance to very many of the Great War's airmen, even to many of its 'colonials', their published letters and memoirs would mention them more often than they actually do. In fact such references occur infrequently, and have been cited almost wherever found and whenever possible in this book. There is therefore slender evidence of a deep or widespread significance attaching to national units of a notional Imperial Aircraft Flotilla for those actually flying them.

Where entire squadrons were equipped with effective aircraft models that bore names signifying presentation from a single source, it was a different matter; but such examples are rare because for most of the war presentation aeroplanes were distributed randomly across squadrons. However, examples do include the eighteen Bristol Fighters flown by 1st Squadron AFC in Palestine during late 1917–18 which were provided through the Australian Air Squadrons Fund, and which feature (thinly disguised) in Brigadier General A. E. Borton's letter (inset on p. 279); and also the eighteen *Hyderabad* presentation DH9As that equipped 110 Squadron RAF for their strategic bombing role in the war's closing months.

It has been argued that Australia's successful request in 1917 for Australian airmen to pilot Australia's own presentation planes, represented a move in a long running domestic constitutional tussle between Federal and State Governments; but Australian military pride and developing national self-awareness and self-assertion, consciously promoted by Australian Prime Minister Billy Hughes, were also important factors. Doubtless, if it had been possible for the RFC/RNAS/RAF to match overseas pilots with aircraft named after their home areas in this way more often, presentation aircraft would have left a deeper impression on aircrew, but it was rarely practical to accede to such requests. There were nevertheless numerous examples of subscribers requesting just this, that one of their compatriots should pilot their presentation aircraft, usually unsuccessfully. The designated presentation name in itself already provided some sense of local ownership, but many subscribers would have liked to take this further, had circumstances but permitted.

The conclusion must be that the Imperial Aircraft Flotilla struck its main chord with those in the empire and outside it that did not personally fight in the war, but wished to lend their support, and thereby even take a vicarious part in the action. The fundraising scheme gave contributors a sense of direct engagement in otherwise distant hostilities, and, through their chosen presentation name, publicly identified the individual or community concerned with those engaged in the fighting. Thanks to Henderson's undertakings, their presentation name was retained the length of the war itself, no matter how many of the aircraft bearing it crashed or were destroyed.

In addition, an aura of romance and 'gallantry' attached to military aviation in general. For many civilians, at home and abroad, stories of individual air combat harked back to a more chivalrous age, echoed in the codes and rituals observed by air forces on both sides in the skies above France. Pilots were popular press heroes. It was almost as if duels between 'knights of the air' were conceived as staged in some imaginary airy realm, situated both physically and morally above battlefields where massive artillery bombardments and poison gas had eliminated all such redeeming possibilities:

> For airmen, immortalized through their exploits, became *the* heroes of World War I. In Europe, public fascination with these new warriors converged on a single image of individual combat, deadly but chivalrous. In the trenches, mass slaughter on an unprecedented scale rendered individuals insignificant. Aerial heroes provided a much-needed affirmation of the importance of the individual and of youth—despite (or because of) the slaughter of both.[21]

By the closing stages of the war, however, some eight hundred aircraft from all sides were flying on the Western Front, and air fighting had itself become a matter of mass attrition. Less than half of aircrew trained in Britain during the course of the Great War ended up avoiding serious injury or death.[22] The nightmare for many was that of burning alive.

While public glamour attached to fighter pilots regardless, in the early stages of the war especially, when the BE2c reconnaissance aircraft dominated British production, the emphasis of many fundraising appeals was upon financing a protective arm of warfare, the 'eyes' of the army—one that would help safeguard the infantry from enemy attack, especially heavy artillery attack. This was notably so in the Dominions that had troop contingents in the trenches. It was the dominant note in Alma Baker's Australian campaigning, even during 1917–18 when the offensive role of aircraft in bombing and ground-strafing was coming to the fore, and he himself now always referred to them as 'battleplanes'.

Yet in many areas of the world without ground troops on the Western Front, and especially in places where mediaeval European tales of individual knightly contest carried no resonance, aviation was associated much more with science in warfare, with mastery of new technologies, and with notions of modernity and progress. This included amongst those within the empire who felt personally disparaged by contemporary British arrogance towards (and on the part of some, ingrained attitudes of outright contempt for) 'subject races'. It was quite possibly a factor in the popular enthusiasm for presentation aeroplanes in Gold Coast, and for the active involvement of J. E. Casely Hayford—he who wished to see Africans play their full part as citizens of the empire, and not be discounted as little more than 'hewers of wood and drawers of water'. The Jaffna Tamils resident in the Malay States felt slighted by being regarded as a mere 'subject race ... a community of clerks' and 'an indifferent community only' in the eyes of their British colonial bosses. The press evidence suggests that their aim as a community in subscribing for their own fighter plane was primarily to gain greater respect and recognition from that quarter.

Chiefs played a key role in leading collections for aeroplanes in those rural African societies that took part, occasionally perhaps with more than a nod towards influencing the colonial administration in their favour. While normally able to order work parties in the immediate area, they were often placed in an invidious position over supplying human porterage for the long drawn out allied campaign in East Africa. For while Chiefs were on the British payroll, they lacked autocratic powers over their subjects, whose interests they were traditionally expected to represent. Where pressures were acute, African Chiefs risked being caught between British demands to meet fixed manpower targets for military operations, and a growing resistance to especially carrier service from potential recruits. Contributions towards a presentation aeroplane from Angoni Chiefs and sub-Chiefs in Northern Rhodesia may well have been a manipulative response to just such a dilemma, calculated to put them on the right side of the colonial administration while shifting blame for recruitment shortcomings onto others.

In Gold Coast, the involvement of whole communities subscribing their respectively named aircraft set up its own competitive dynamic. But the initial positive response to the Imperial Aircraft Flotilla appeal owed a lot to the personality and policies of the Governor. Those policies combined with the cautionary example of the harsh German colonial order previously in force over the border in Togoland, as highlighted by wartime Aborigines' Protection Society propaganda emanating from London. Much indeed depended on the British Governor or Administrator of the day. In contrast to Frederick Lugard in Nigeria, for example, who directed in late 1914 that carriers be impressed if the situation called for it,[23] Hugh Clifford resisted demands for military carriers for East Africa, arguing that recruitment would undercut the effort to enroll soldiers for the Gold Coast Regiment.[24]

The Basutoland war levy saw serious political concerns writ large at the national level, with the perceived relationship with the British Crown as guarantor of survival in the balance, and a Resident Commissioner more sympathetic to the Union of South Africa than the Basuto holding office during 1916–17. For unlike so many other African countries whose boundaries were arbitrarily carved out by rival European powers at the end of the nineteenth century, Basutoland was a rare example of a political, cultural, and geographical unit, whose national identity had been forged over many decades of resistance to hostile external forces.[25] Since 1868, however, Basutoland had also paradoxically depended upon the British imperial power for its continued separate existence. Yet it was on the advice of the Army Council in London, and with George V's ready agreement that the proceeds from the country's war levy were devoted to presentation aircraft. That is, the levy was not originally raised with the *intent* of contributing to a notional Imperial Aircraft Flotilla. Rather it was a war gift to a British sovereign who in his person offered a more acceptable focus of allegiance than an Empire (albeit British) of which the Union of South Africa was so prominent—and uncomfortably close—a member.

The cast list of larger subscribers to the Imperial Aircraft Flotilla worldwide also included quite a selection of 'native rulers' from different corners of the British Empire. They included some who enjoyed great personal wealth and extensive powers over their subjects, even while independence from ultimate British control remained no more than illusory. In India, the feudal princes (who controlled their own treasuries) were important and seemed to compete with each other in their general munificence during the course of the conflict; in addition, that is, to supplying their own corps of combatants to the war. In the case of Zanzibar, the war in East Africa and past Anglo-German political interference and involvement in dynastic rivalries drew Sultan Seyyid Khalifa right into the thick of things. Moreover, all strands of evidence point to an acute personal concern on his part to cultivate the goodwill of British naval and military personnel on the spot. (Perhaps the Sultan had half an eye to naval evacuation from the island, should the war in East Africa have gone the way of the Germans.)

The rulers of the Northern Shan States, who subscribed all of three aeroplanes, also policed Burma's wild borderlands on behalf of British overlords that otherwise left their small principalities largely in peace, besides bringing certain economic benefits. On the Malay Peninsula the Sultans of Kedah and of Johore were benefactors. In the case of the latter, the substantial gifts made on his account and that of the Johore government followed his role in suppressing the 1915 Singapore mutiny, with the consequent sudden transformation of his previously thorny relationship with the British. (While incidentally providing a vivid example of the contradictions and ironies inherent in indirect rule.) His self-image was already that of the military man of action, and for Sultan Ibrahim II as much as for many of the Indian maharajahs, an existing motoring hobby (and extravagant collections of expensive automobiles) also led naturally to an interest in aeroplanes.

Besides, the Imperial Aircraft Flotilla scheme fulfilled a prestige function for those able to subscribe one or more entire aircraft named after themselves, their businesses, fiefdoms, or principalities. As monies for batches of aircraft were received, letters of thanks went out to the administrators of the various overseas funds on behalf of the British Government and Army Council, listing the presentation aircraft concerned. Those letters were frequently published in the local English-language press. And although donors were not permitted to publish the photographs of 'their' aeroplane supplied to them by the War Office, that did not prevent them from displaying them framed in palace, home, or office. The possibility of recognition in the form of British honours was an extra allure for some:[26] certainly Robert Ho Tung—the richest man in Hong Kong—was in this respect highly susceptible. The Indian princes, in particular, appear to have been especially partial to the outward trappings of imperial pomp and circumstance, though presentation aeroplanes were but one of the many gifts and services they rendered in the war.

The British Crown also maintained an interest and involvement in the scheme and this enhanced popular appeal. Queen Alexandra, the Queen Mother, was very much publicly associated with the campaign through her ceremonial launch of planes from the empire at Farnborough in July 1915 ('as friendly as she could be... took such an interest in everything', according to Wrench in his journal).[27] She subsequently encouraged the Jamaican aircraft fund established in her name with appreciative remarks, prominently reported by the *Gleaner* newspaper, and this was an important endorsement on an island where the British Crown held a central place in popular sentiment.

In receipt of monies gifted for the war George V, Patron of the Overseas Club and of the Patriotic League, welcomed such funds being devoted to aircraft, as was certainly the case for the £50,000 raised by Basutoland's war levy. Genuinely interested in military and naval aviation, the King was also concerned lest the air advantage go to the enemy: a concern expressed through his assistant private secretary, Clive Wigram, who wrote to Henderson in October 1916:[28]

> My dear General,
> The King read in one of the summaries of operations that the Germans had produced some new aeroplanes on our front in the west, and I think His Majesty read in the account from some correspondent that the Germans had a useful new three-seater.
> Would you be so kind as to let me know for His Majesty's information whether you think that these new aeroplanes are in any way the equal of ours, and whether they are likely to cause us much trouble. [...]
> Yours sincerely,
> [Sgd.] Clive Wigram

To which Henderson replied that little had been heard of the three-seater, but the one or two small, fast, new German monoplane models that had been introduced, though still few in number and requiring very good piloting, were likely to prove much more dangerous:

> We are, of course, doing all we can to keep up, and to augment our present superiority. The provision of new machines, in sufficient number, still presents many difficulties, but we have reason to hope for a large increase during the winter, and also for considerable improvement in type.
> I hope you will let me know if His Majesty desires any more information on these points.
> Yours sincerely,
> [Sgd.] David Henderson

Publicised in Britain through the agency of the Press Bureau, regular bulletins on new aeroplane gifts from the empire found their way into the national press, especially the columns of Northcliffe's newspapers. At the outset, when British aircraft were scarce, the Imperial Aircraft Flotilla scheme was a welcome source of practical support for the flying services, yet it was probably the symbolic demonstration of wartime solidarity from across the empire that the British Establishment came to value most. The litany of new presentation aeroplane names constantly joining the Flotilla provided reassurance that all parts of the British Empire really cared, and stood in solidarity in the war.

Chapter 20:
The orchestration of support—the British Empire's last curtain call?

By 21 August 1917, overseas contributors had defrayed the costs of 437 aeroplanes and seaplanes for the RFC or RNAS,[1] and over five hundred and fifty by the Armistice. If gift planes from Great Britain itself are counted, well in excess of six hundred were presented from all sources during the conflict. Their designated names included those of countries, cities, districts, businesses, communities, ranches, homesteads, and individuals, even, in the case of Harry Arnhold of Shanghai, his racing pony *Oriole*. Yet to whatever degree the presentations may have expressed a national, local, corporate, individual (or equine) identity, it was as part of a notional Imperial Aircraft Flotilla that placed them all under the British imperial roof (even Ceylon's birds and flying fruit-bat).

The identity expressed was nonetheless layered—identification with the British Empire at war through the presentation itself, yes, but usually with the subscribers' own named locality or community of reference inscribed on the aircraft, alongside their country. The unit with which they publicly identified themselves through that presentation name could be as encompassing or as specific—even quirky—as desired: country, State and locality in Australia; community of people for Gold Coast subscribers, although with the administrative and political unit *Gold Coast* alone emblazoned on those numbered aircraft voted from public funds.

Scattered Britons and British subjects worldwide had been responsible for many of the presentations, only certain of them covered in case studies here. British residents of Aden provided one aeroplane, and in Egypt, three; Gibraltar and the Falkland Islands gave one each, both named after the dependency in question. In addition, there were presentation aircraft from overseas Britons and British subjects in allied and neutral countries (and their dependencies). Apart from Abyssinia and Siam, China, Argentina, and Chile, Brazil provided five; France, one; Italy, one; Japan, two; Mexico, one; Nicaragua, one; the NEI, two; Philippines, three; and Spain, two—one of them from Britons resident in the Canary Islands. Of the six from the US, the New

York branch of the Overseas Club presented two, the Imperial Order of Daughters of the British Empire another, Mr. and Mrs. H. P. Stromberg of New York City a further two, and there was a sixth named *Chicago*.²

After the end of the war, the British Air Ministry actually approved a scheme to commission silver model aeroplanes as 'thank you' tokens for contributors. But at their 1ˢᵗ May 1919 meeting the Air Council thought better of it and abandoned the idea, which would have cost £13,000 to implement and needed Treasury sanction.³ The shelves were now truly bare, Great Britain having spent going on for £10 billion on the imperial war effort, more than any other single combatant power.⁴ Yet although financially much weakened, and having lost more than 700,000 dead, Great Britain had emerged from the First World War with the greatest fleet in the world still, and had ended up constructing the largest air force.

To echo the words of writer Jan Morris, bigger areas of the world map were shaded (or hatched) in red than ever, and they included for the first time mandated ex-German territories: Tanganyika (former German East Africa), parts of Togoland and Cameroon (divided with France), and suzerainty over former Ottoman lands of the Middle East. But despite appearances, things had changed.⁵ The transformation has been aptly described as leaving 'individuals and societies ... exhausted and introspective compared to the exuberant outbursts that had once characterized the Imperial generation of 1914.'⁶ The very extent of the British Empire was also to create its own overstretch—in the face of early nationalist upheavals in Ireland, in Egypt and the Middle East, and in India.

Profound long-term changes in political aspirations were initiated, or further stimulated, by the war and the peace settlement. Even before the end of the conflict there were stirrings. All the discourse on the Allied side about democracy and the rights of small nations encouraged hopes and ambitions. Dr. Lim Boon Keng in Singapore had already pressed for reforms even before the war began. In October 1917 he appealed in the Legislative Council for greater representation for Asians, arguing that if Britain was fighting to free the people of Europe from German domination, then 'surely the sons of the Empire, men brought up under the flag and trained in the great ideals and aspirations of Englishmen, have the right to expect that under the flag they will have liberty'; and they should not therefore be denied 'the rights and privileges of free men.'⁷ Post-war, Ceylon's educated elite renewed efforts begun in earlier years to gain an effective elective presence on the legislature.

Vajiravudh of Siam, saw—and took—his kingdom's opportunity to enter the war on America's heels and secure a seat at the Peace Conference as a combatant nation, with all that implied. On the pretext of congratulating King George V on his great victory, Griffith Lerotholi and the Basuto Chiefs saw their chance after the Armistice to lobby the British Crown and Government directly against the nation's threatened incorporation into the Union of South Africa. And while the post-war Congress of British West Africa organised by Joseph Ephraim Casely Hayford urged reform of Britain's directly ruled Crown Colony system of government, it at the same time welcomed the principle of self-determination that the Paris Peace Conference had adopted.

Great Britain, of course, already accepted the right of self-determination in the sense of internal self-government of its white settler colonies. Towards the end of the First World War it had, in addition, embraced the notion of equal and independent status—in Jan Smuts' adopted phrase, a 'Commonwealth of Nations' rather than a British-run empire, though it was 1931 before this was formalised in a Statute of Westminster that removed Great Britain's right to legislate for the Dominions. But American President Woodrow Wilson's 'Fourteen Principles' adopted by the Paris Peace Conference of 1919 inaugurated the right of national self-determination as something more—as a guiding international precept. (Though the longstanding British doctrine of 'trusteeship' of indigenous peoples already held the seeds of that notion.)

It was in this sense that the concept of self-determination began to subvert acceptance of a directing metropolitan power as part of the inevitable way of things. Initially selectively applied by the League of Nations (which, ironically, the US did not join), the right of self-determination eventually produced a sea change in the political aspirations of 'subject peoples' throughout the world, although the era of nationalist politics was yet to come. It proved inimical over time to the maintenance of an empire with Britain at the helm, especially as its free trade underpinnings fell away with the rise of protectionism over succeeding decades, though admittedly it took another world war before the imperial edifice was sufficiently weakened to start crumbling away.

At home, all British 'Tommies' over the age of twenty-one were enabled to exercise the vote, for the Representation of the People Act of 1918 removed all property qualifications for adult males. Exclusion of so many who had sacrificed so much was no longer acceptable. Women over thirty with property qualifications were enfranchised for the first time, and in the General Election of December 1918 nearly 10.8 million voted—more than twice the number at the previous election in December 1910. In Britain the great conciliator, Evelyn Wrench, devoted the inter-war years first to the cause of radical constitutional reform in India (admiring, then turning against the doings of Mahatma Gandhi), and later to an ill-advised engagement with the policy of appeasement (his last visit to Germany took place in July 1939, when he attempted to broker a compromise over the status of Danzig).[8] After the Second World War was over he applied himself more fully to the affairs of the Royal Over-Seas League (ROSL), as the Overseas Club and Patriotic League became.

Wrench's Imperial Aircraft Flotilla campaign during the Great War had been an episode, a channel for his energies, signifying neither a beginning nor an ending of anything in particular. But the story of the campaign in its worldwide ramifications casts a light on all parts of the British Empire in that period, when the world was at war and all attention was otherwise fixed on the titanic struggle centred on Europe. What conclusions can be drawn from the story?

The press was important to the fundraising campaign as never before. Many British expatriates throughout the world subscribed to the overseas edition of the *Daily Mail*. It gave Evelyn Wrench channels of communication to many newspaper editors in the Dominions and Colonies, and he was aided by a number of British Colonial Governors and Administrators in receipt of his campaigning literature, who put it out to 'their' local press, and in some instances also brought it to the attention of their district officials or influential contacts. Their willingness to spread the word was encouraged by the large number of Establishment figures associated with the Overseas Club, including former and serving Secretaries of State for the Colonies, Governors, and senior Dominion politicians; and by the King's patronage, as well as by endorsement of the scheme by Kitchener and the Army Council.

Colonial newspapers were often already engaged in their own efforts to whip up 'patriotic' fervour in the imperial cause. But there were other considerations that made the Imperial Aircraft Flotilla concept attractive. Editorials sometimes stressed the chance it offered to lodge the name of the Colony concerned in the consciousness of the powers that be in London, invoking the opportunity of being regarded favourably in whatever new imperial order should be fashioned at war's end; looking forward even, to possible constitutional revisions. Directly ruled Crown Colonies were anxious not to be overlooked in any future dispensation involving a greater degree of autonomy and consultation—perhaps more elected seats on the local legislature, or even a voice that would be heeded by Whitehall. The perceived danger was that of being sidelined in a future new federal arrangement between Britain and the Dominions, which had sent large armies to help the Mother Country in her hour of need.

Yet in reality talk of Imperial Federation belonged to the past and not the future, and federation discourse gave way to the more nebulous language of Commonwealth of Nations post Great War. Not only was the idea of Imperial Federation increasingly irrelevant (if not positively unwelcome) to Dominion Governments, whose desire for autonomy from London, along with national self-consciousness and pride, had grown out of their experiences in the Great War itself; the whole concept also contained inherent problems for non-white elites ambitious for greater power and responsibility. What, for example, would be the relationship between a central imperial 'parliament', comprised of a federation of Britain and the Dominions, and the existing Crown Colony legislatures, on which 'subject peoples' were seeking a much larger voice? For a start it completely ignored the question of India's future constitutional status and whether it would be a member of that parliament or not. In addition, as an editorial in the *Ceylon Daily News* put it, the danger was that such a selective federal deliberative body would 'impose on the weaker races of the Empire the domination of an imperial clique made up of British colonists and Boers.'[9]

In certain Protectorates, as opposed to Colonies, there had been no local English-language press to propagate the Imperial Aircraft Flotilla scheme, so all depended on the keenness (or otherwise) of the British Resident to enlist the support of the local ruler and involve businessmen and traders. Much depended on personalities, and relations with native administrations under indirect rule. Circumstances also differed between countries whose economies suffered during the war, and those whose exports were strategically important, or otherwise flourished; between those directly affected by the conflict and those far removed from it; those with combatants in the war and those without. Certain of the Dominions, Australia and Newfoundland especially, experienced fundraising at a mass, popular, level, and in a smaller way it reached to the grassroots in the Caribbean too. (Basutoland's war levy formed a category all its very own.) Of those British communities living outside the empire, the ready response forthcoming from Argentine Britons, who had significant numbers of their young men fighting on the Western Front, more closely resembled that of the Dominion of Newfoundland than anywhere else.

Of course, any insights into the British Empire and its ways that might be afforded by the story of the Imperial Aircraft Flotilla are, by their very nature, partial. They spotlight 'voluntary' financial support for the imperial air war, and not those indifferent or hostile to the appeal. The other side of the coin reveals itself, however, in seeking to explain the Ceylon Aeroplane Fund's outright failure to reach much beyond European planter society. (Despite two leading Sinhalese presenting aircraft *outside* the Fund, one of them when a new British Governor was in place, determined to address previous human rights abuses.) Conversely, some British officials pushed the boat out in support more than others, and paucity or absence of presentation aeroplanes from any particular unit of the British Empire cannot necessarily be interpreted as a case of donor resistance.

Gold Coast is particularly interesting for the widespread community involvement, as well as the 'official' involvement of the reconstituted Legislative Council, and the part played by a political radical (for that era) and critic of many aspects of British colonial administration, Joseph Ephraim Casely Hayford. But it is impossible to isolate these agencies from the effect of the personality and policies of the British Governor at the time, Hugh Clifford, or, indeed, the influence of the situation in neighbouring Togoland. A really dynamic and dedicated campaigner such as Charles Alma Baker also made a big difference, as the progress of both the Malaya Air Fleet Fund and the Australian Air Squadrons Fund amply demonstrates.

HMS *Malaya* had created a pre-war precedent for defence contributions from the further corners of the British Empire. During the conflict, colonial legislatures that were wholly or largely unelected voted funds for presentation aircraft without wider popular consultation, but also without popular protest. In the case of Mauritius, its Council of Government had a relatively large elected element, but based on a property franchise so narrow as to make it almost completely unrepresentative of the population at large; and the Franco-

Mauritian 'Oligarchs' on that Council voted money from public funds for no less than fifteen aircraft, doubling the sum given by, and on behalf of, the big Franco-Mauritian sugar growers whose interests they represented (and with whom they were often identical). NSW in Australia, with a democratically elected State government, did the same, matching the smaller number of aircraft that were presented by its public, while the unelected Gold Coast legislature actually outdid the already respectable score for presentation planes privately subscribed.

Nevertheless, there is no evidence of British colonial administrations imposing such expenditure, as opposed to instances of collusion between individual officials and local elites. This was perhaps the case in Dominica's original Legislative Council vote of funds in 1914 and, it might be suspected, Mauritius later, and certainly so in the Zanzibar Protectorate where the Sultan and Major Pearce formed a single partnership in the war. Money voted officially frequently sat alongside private fundraising, usually organised through local branches of banks and publicised through local English-language newspapers

Propaganda and counter-subversion also played a part in certain areas. Germany set up a *jihad* bureau in Berlin to stir up revolt among Muslims under Allied colonial rule, with the eighty million or so of British India the prime target. Great Britain, for its part, specifically courted Islamic opinion across the empire after Turkey entered the war on 2 November 1914 and, less than two weeks later, issued a call for international holy war on behalf of the Ottoman sultan. An obliging letter to coastal Muslim rulers on the African mainland from Sultan Seyyid Khalifa of Zanzibar anticipated the call for *jihad*, and was quickly disseminated and widely publicised (see inset on p. 73: in this particular instance the text was published in Rangoon's English-language newspaper).

India's large Army with its many Muslim troops was a particular concern, and the Nizam of Hyderabad, Mir Osman Ali Khan was reluctantly persuaded by the British Resident to issue a supportive statement for mainly domestic consumption, in the form of a letter calling on the Muslims of India to remain staunch in their fidelity to British rule, despite Ottoman Turkey's alliance with Germany. In return he was rewarded with yet more imperial pomp and circumstance than he had already.

After the mutiny of Muslim Indian troops at Singapore in February 1915, the GOC Straits Settlements, Brigadier General Dudley Ridout devoted his energies to combating the influence of *Ghadr* in his capacity as commander of military and political intelligence, and Singapore became something of a clearing-house for secret reports on *Ghadr* activities throughout Asia (he later established Singapore's Special Branch after retiring from the army).[10] Efforts to counter subversion and rally support in which Ridout may be suspected to have had a hidden hand were at several levels, and at the most overt included a mass meeting of Muslims in Singapore that pledged loyalty to King George V. The *Malaya Tribune* reported in glowing terms that:

> The Malays were perhaps strongest numerically, ... clad in their native sarongs and silk caps of multitudinous shades of colour ... Arabian merchants and teachers, picturesquely clad in flowing white robes, turbans and slippers, numerous natives of South Indian origin, a host of men clad in the comely costume of Java and the Southern Isles were there. Egyptian merchants were also present in fez and European dress, as also Parsee business magnates, Tamils and Malabaris.[11]

The four Muslim leaders of that 'loyalty' meeting were subsequently all appointed JPs.[12]

Following a call at their newspaper offices by Alma Baker in person, the *Malaya Tribune* dropped a hint that Dudley Ridout regarded support for the Malaya Air Fleet Fund as a useful indicator of political loyalties:

> [Charles Alma Baker] also drew attention to a letter appearing in the *Malay Mail* of Tuesday last setting out the respective claims and objects of the Malay States War Relief Fund and the Malayan Aircraft Fund. Mr. Baker expressed his thanks for the writer's appeal on behalf of the Fund, but was at a loss to know who were referred to by General Ridout as being 'agin the Government', and as such were accorded an excellent opportunity to show that by this time they are determined to do what they could to further the interests of their country.[13]

Although Ridout was a nominated member of the Straits Settlements Legislative Council at Singapore from April 1915 onwards, it is nonetheless not known how actively he encouraged the fundraising campaign; there is no evidence that he instigated it.

Ghadr was in the end so effectively suppressed wherever it had a presence, its one-time platform so comprehensively overshadowed by later, home-grown, directions in Indian political nationalism (not least, Mahatma Gandhi's passive resistance movement, and the Congress Party's rift with the Muslim League under Muhammad Ali Jinnah), that it is difficult to regard it seriously as a one-time threat. But it was not so for the British authorities at the time of the Great War, when the largest single component of the imperial forces was provided by Indian troops, many of them Muslims at whom the exhortations to mutiny were addressed.

Ridout in Singapore directed counter-subversion operations. He was aided by intelligence reports on the activities of *Ghadr* supporters and networks throughout Southeast Asia and the East; by interception on the part of British Naval Intelligence in London of *Ghadr* messages sent through German embassies; and by German double agent Vincent Kraft, recruited in mid-1915 and ably handled by his Singapore-based personal case officer, former Deputy Superintendent of the Bombay police, Hector Kothavala (a Parsee).[14] With regard to the US, the British had also enjoyed the assistance of a Canadian Immigration Service official subsidised by the Department of Criminal Intelligence (DCI) in India, who generally kept tabs on *Ghadr* in North America until his death in October 1914, when some of this work was taken over by the British Consul-General in San Francisco.[15]

Consequently many mishaps began to afflict *Ghadr* operations, especially after Kraft, completely unsuspected to the German authorities, started working for British Intelligence. On 29 June 1915, the US authorities seized the vessel the *Annie Larsen* and its cargo of arms destined for India. In July, a motor-schooner carrying arms and ammunition was forced to put into the Celebes for repair where it was boarded and searched by Dutch customs officers (tipped off by the British) who impounded the weapons. One of the German-American weapons instructors aboard fled, but was later apprehended by the British *en route* to warn conspirators about the arms seizure. He revealed the location of secret training camps on the Siam-Burma border, and the Siamese authorities duly rounded up several hundred people. A series of lightning raids in both Calcutta and Burma on December 15th 1915 resulted in more than three hundred being taken into police custody.[16]

There was also a *Ghadr* sub-plot centred on the NEI, featuring Kraft (a former resident) that involved propaganda and the smuggling of passports as well as arms shipments. A Dutch journalist and democracy activist from Batavia (Java) banished from the NEI for contravening colonial press laws, was arrested by the British at Hong Kong in late 1915. Brought to Singapore for questioning, he admitted to Dudley Ridout that he was paid to disseminate *Ghadr* propaganda materials, and had been detailed to set up a base for this purpose at Bangkok.

The journalist in question (E. F. E. Douwes Dekker) had friendly links with the early Javanese nationalist organisation, *sarekat islam*. Ridout was therefore confident of the continued cooperation of the Dutch colonial authorities over *Ghadr* activities, since they touched on the internal stability of Dutch rule in the NEI itself, even though the Dutch remained neutrals in the wider matter of the Great War.[17]

In late 1915, Commander D. C. McIntyre, harbour master and port intelligence officer at Penang where the *Emden* had staged its spectacular raid just over a year earlier (and whose lax security had contributed to its success),[18] reported to military headquarters in Singapore. He informed them that a steamer captain at his regular ports of call had noticed an unusual degree of activity amongst German residents at Asahan on the Dutch island of Sumatra. Consequently Ridout sent an agent to investigate. British Consuls in the region formed part of Ridout's networks, and he also instructed the British Vice-Consul at Medan (commercial centre of the main tobacco-growing region inland from Asahan) to carry out enquiries.[19]

In 1916, the same Commander Duncan McIntyre who first reported the matter to Ridout's headquarters became one of three local collectors at Penang island for the Malaya Air Fleet Fund, perhaps fortuitously, perhaps not: Since canvassing for subscriptions around and about the harbour would certainly have given him the opportunity to meet and talk with sympathetic traders, and other businessmen of the various communities linked in some way to the sea-traffic with Sumatra, and other parts of the NEI and the wider region.

There were other shadowy goings-on linked to security measures against *Ghadr* elsewhere in evidence from the latter half of 1915 onwards. A long running conspiracy trial of thirteen Sikhs took place in Mandalay, Upper Burma, during March–July 1916. The proceedings were extensively covered in the columns of the *Bangkok Times*.[20] Sikh Temples in northern Siam and in Bangkok were implicated. The trial touched on an extensive arms smuggling plot involving locations as distant as the US, Hong Kong and Shanghai. It was aimed at an uprising in Burma near the border with Siam. Such developments doubtless also rendered the security cooperation of the strategically located Northern Shan States doubly valuable to both the British administration of Burma, and the Government of British India.

With one exception (found guilty on a lesser count) the accused in the trial were eventually found guilty of both conspiracy and abetment. On 21st July 1916 they were variously sentenced to death, or to transportation for life. An editorial in the *Bangkok Times* carried more than a hint of menace:

> The sentences passed by the Special Tribunal sitting at Mandalay should serve a good purpose. It is true that the *Ghadr* campaign was a futile business. It is also true that in a time of tremendous stress India has been splendidly loyal, but on that account there is all the more reason that the bad spirit existent in certain groups of the population should not be ignored or belittled. There is only one way of dealing with seditious plots in war time ... The outcome may make some foolish people think, and will confirm the ordinary Indian subject in his loyalty. [...]
> [While acknowledging the assistance of the Government of Siam in foiling the plot] one may add that India has reason for also acknowledging the services of the British Consulates in this country. The trial certainly proved how closely and effectively the official hand is kept on the pulse of any movement affecting British interests here.[21]

Some, at least, of those British subjects who attended the fundraising meeting for a fighter plane convened by the British Legation at Bangkok on 20th July 1916, must have been aware of the ongoing trial in Burma. (The meeting, incidentally, was held in the 'Old British Court House' in the Siamese capital the very evening before sentences were handed out at Mandalay.) It is a matter for conjecture to what extent events over the border might have encouraged a readiness on the part of British subjects in Siam to empty their pockets; even whether a wish to gauge loyalties in the war had any influence on Dering's decision to call the meeting in the first place.

Since the beginning of 1915, however, Dering had been called on to act as *de facto* intelligence officer monitoring the movements of Indians in Siam. In August 1915 he was given the support at Bangkok of David Petrie, a Scot responsible for setting up Indian intelligence in the Far East 1915–19 (and who was to end his career as Director-General of MI5 1940–46).[22] Noticeably, the final published account of the Siam British Subjects Aeroplane Fund broke down Indian contributions into five distinct community sub-divisions—Sikhs, the Borah community, Northern Indians, Southern Indians, and Suratis—suggesting a possibly detailed British interest in the response to the appeal.[23]

The nature of the Imperial Aircraft Flotilla campaign lent itself to such usage, although it was not originally conceived as a hard propaganda or policing tool. It is important to realise that of the many large fundraising appeals launched throughout the 'British' world during

1914–18, Evelyn Wrench's Imperial Aircraft Flotilla was perhaps the most overtly political in concept, having been explicitly designed to provide all constituent parts of the British Empire and British communities abroad with a sense of direct participation in the imperial war effort. In supporting a new and apparently effective arm of warfare, donors thereby identified themselves and their community (through their designated presentation name) with the imperial forces engaged in the fighting.

Quite apart, though, from any additional attraction this might have had for those with an involvement in Ridout's counter-subversion efforts (or wishing by a display of loyalty in the war to avoid being regarded as suspect), it appealed to many British colonial officials who believed that by disseminating the scheme locally they were simultaneously helping the common military cause and chalking up the willing support of their own particular corner of the empire, both with the Colonial Office, and the wider powers that be in London. An additional consideration being that unlike the astronomical costs of a battleship, collections for aircraft could be launched in most parts of the empire with the reasonable expectation of reaching their target amount (but also with the *caveat* that the Colonial Office discouraged, or even vetoed, subscriptions from public funds that it deemed unaffordable or unjustified).

Another influential factor was simply sentiment. The fate of those directly engaged in the war loomed large over many of those in a position to support the scheme, or who otherwise played a part in this story. The possibility that those close to them would die or suffer injury on the battlefield was felt in a direct and personal, as well as national, sense, and a large proportion did die: Between September 1914 and May 1915, Lord Desborough, President of the IAFC, lost two nephews (polo-playing twins, one of them, Captain Francis Grenfell, the first officer to be awarded the VC in the war) as well as two out of his own three sons on the Western Front—Julian, the war poet, and Billy, Grenfell. Lady Ettie Desborough not only lost two sons, but also lost Patrick Shaw-Stewart, a Barings banker better known as a war poet and rumoured to be her young lover, to a shell in France on the very last day of 1917.[24]

All the slaughter and the bereavement are aspects of the Great War with which we are already familiar, but it is perhaps still worth pointing out that many of the public figures, and proconsuls and former proconsuls of Britain's colonial empire, shared the anxieties, strains and grief of all those ordinary citizens back home: Sir Robert Chalmers was informed in May 1915 that both of his sons had been killed at Ypres, with serious repercussions for the handling of the Ceylon riots. Lord Selborne lost his second son in Mesopotamia in 1916 and later privately published that son's (rather high-minded) letters home, which looked forward to the ending of the conflict and India's constitutional advance.[25] Sir Hugh Clifford lost his only son, also named Hugh, and his only brother, Henry, an Army Colonel, at the Somme. The only remaining son and heir of Lord Buxton, Governor General of South Africa, died at Passchendaele.

A final observation: Although essentially bounded in time by the Great War of 1914–18, the progress of the various aircraft appeals reveals more about the quiet operation of personal ties and influence across the British Empire than official papers alone. The Imperial Aircraft Flotilla campaign ran through, alongside, and independently of, the imperial bureaucracy and colonial administrative structures. Some of Britain's administrators and senior officials played a much larger part than others. Weaving through the more visible imperial bureaucratic framework ran less tangible threads of kinship and marriage, or common background and shared interests (including the frequently cited ex-public school affiliations). Such influences often operated silently in the background, unmentioned in administrative correspondence and therefore the official record. Wartime voluntary association in this 'patriotic' fundraising endeavour, however, brought some of those normally hidden connections to the fore, if only temporarily, in a swansong performance of imperial unity.

Naturally such networks ran especially densely between Britain (including importantly Scotland) and areas of white settlement—mainly the Dominions along with Southern Rhodesia (where Sir Edward Grey's intervention in the collection for a Rhodesian aeroplane may reveal kinship ties at play at senior British Cabinet level). Albert Earl Grey indeed provides an extreme example of just how far across the imperial world the web of personal contact and influence could extend. Of course professional soldiers had friends and relatives too (and so Lieutenant General Sir David Henderson helped get Hazelton Nicholl into the RFC), but military contacts and favours also dated back to service experience and comradeship from previous wars—the Boer War in Henderson's case. In the Great War they now extended to former enemies such as Jan Smuts, military man and also politician and statesman.

The administration of the empire ostensibly ran on impersonal lines, through its ranked officials, but in truth 'indirect rule', especially, often entailed affective ties, as well as mutual antagonisms (sometimes both simultaneously) and these were highly charged times. An individual's role could also turn out to be quite ironic and contradictory. Sir Herbert Slolely, Resident Commissioner of Basutoland 1903–1916, had counselled a Basuto war contribution of no more than a shilling a head per adult male. The effective catalyst for the Basuto war levy of £50,000, devoted by King George V on the advice of the Army Council to the presentation of 25 Sopwith Camels to the RFC and RNAS, was the threat of incorporation into South Africa and the advent as Basutoland's Resident Commissioner of detested arch imperialist and Cecil Rhodes protégé, Robert Coryndon, who personified that threat.

Rather poignantly, when Slolely's post-retirement engagement with the Basuto component of the SANLC in France was just about beginning, his son, RFC 'ace' Robert Sloley, was reported missing in action on the Western Front shortly after giving an exhibition flight before Queen Mary. Shot down on 1st October 1917, he had flown SE5as with 56 Squadron (so none of Basutoland's Sopwith Camels, though they were already in service in France). Robert Slolely was a friend and colleague of Arthur Rhys Davids, who went missing in action less than a month after his own disappearance both of them aged just twenty.[26] In both cases, a German plane dropped a note over the British lines to inform the RFC of the death.[27]

Annexes

Annex I: The Overseas Club

(*Source*: *Overseas*, November 1916)

Patron: HIS MAJESTY THE KING
Vice-Patron: H.R.H. The Duke of Connaught, K.G.
President: Lord Northcliffe.

Vice-Presidents:
Earl Grey, G.C.B., G.C.M.G.
Earl of Liverpool, K.C.M.G., Governor of New Zealand.
Earl of Meath, K.P.
Earl Selborne, K.G., G.C.M.G.
Viscount Gladstone, G.C.M.G.
Lord Hardinge of Penshurst, G.C.B., G.C.M.
Viscount Bryce, O.M.
Lord Denman, K.C.M.G.
Sir R. Munro Ferguson, G.C.M.G., Governor-General of Australia.
Viscount Buxton, G.C.M.G., Governor-General of the Union of South Africa.
Lord Islington, G.C.M.G., D.S.O.
Rt. Hon. A. Bonar Law, M.P., Secretary of State for the Colonies.
Rt. Hon. Rt. Hon. Sir Robert R. L. Borden, K.C.M.G., Prime Minister of Canada.
Rt. Hon. Andrew Fisher, High Commissioner for Australia.
Rt. Hon. W. F. Massey, Prime Minister of New Zealand.
Rt. Hon. Sir George Reid, M.P.
Rt. Hon. Lewis Harcourt, M.P.
Rt. Hon. Will Crooks, P.C., M.P.
Rt. Hon. William Hughes, Prime Minister of Australia.
Sir Starr Jameson.
Sir John Kirk.
Sir Owen Philipps, K.C.M.G.
Lt.-General Sir Bevan Edwards.
Lt.-General Sir Robert Baden-Powell, K.C.B., Chief Scout.
Sir T. Vansittart Bowater.
General Booth.
Rev. & Hon. Edward Lyttelton.
George R. Parkin, Esq., C.M.G., Secretary, Rhodes Trustee.
Kennedy Jones, Esq.

Central Committee:
W. A. Bulkeley-Evans, Esq. (*chairman*), G. B. Dodwell, Esq.
Algernon Aspinall, Esq., Capt. A. H. Horsfall, D.S.O.
Sir Ernest Birch, K.C.M.G., The Rev. R. L. Gwynne.
Ralph S. Bond, Esq., Gordon Inglis, Esq.
Harry E. Brittain, Esq., Richard Jebb, Esq.
G. McL. Brown, Esq., W. Maxwell Lyte, R.N.V.R.
Percy C. Burton, Esq., Fred W. Hayne, Esq.
Colonel Frank Butler, E. R. Peacock, Esq.
Howard d'Egville, Esq., Sir Edward Rosling.
Sir Frederick des Voeux, Bart, Earl Stanhope.
Francis Deverell, Esq. Murray Stewart, Esq.
C. F. Truefitt, Esq., *Hon. Treasurer*
J. Evelyn Wrench, Esq., *Hon. Organiser*

Annex II: The Patriotic League of Britons Overseas

(*Source: Overseas*, November 1916)

Patron:
HIS MAJESTY THE KING.

Chairman:
*Rt. Hon. Earl Selborne, P.C., K.G., G.C.M.G.

Vice-Chairman and Hon. Treasurer:
*Lord Aldenham.

Central Committee:
Sir Charles Addis.
F. Anderson, Esq.
Sir R. Balfour, Bart., M.P.
J.Beaton, Esq.
F. Faithful Begg, Esq.
Admiral Lord Beresford of Metemmah and Curraghmore, G.C.B
A. A. Booth, Esq.
Charles Bright, Esq., F.R.S.E., M.Inst.C.E.
Sir Arthur Chapman.
Rt. Hon. Earl Curzon of Kedleston, P. C.
*G. B. Dodwell, Esq.
*Rt. Hon. Sir H. M. Durand, G.C.M.G.
*Alexander Finn, Esq.
Admiral the Hon. Sir E. R. Fremantle, G.C.B., C.M.G.
Sir W. H. Haggard, K.C.M.G., C.B.
Sir Robert Harvey, M.Inst.C.E.
*F. W. Hayne, Esq.
Sir R. J. Kennedy, K.C.M.G., D.L.
R. de B. M. Layard, Esq., C.M.G.
Rt. Hon. Sir Gerard E. Lowther, Bart., G.C.M.G.
Rt. Hon. Viscount Milner, G.C.B., G.C.M.G.
J. G. Petitt, Esq.
*Charles V. Sale Esq.
*Sir C. J. Tarring.
Lt.-Col. Sir Henry E. Trotter, R.E., K.C.M.G.
Sir Pelham L. Warren, K.C.M.G.
Sir Hiram S. Wilkinson.
* Signifies Member of Executive

Joint Hon. Secretaries:
*W. Maxwell Lyte, R.N.V.R., A.A.C.   *Evelyn Wrench, Esq.

Annex III: The Imperial Air Fleet Committee

(*Source*: IAFC booklet, *The New Link and Spirit of the Empire: 'Plane Pioneers of an Imperial Air Fleet*, London: 1920)

President:
The Rt. Hon. LORD DESBOROUGH, K.C.V.O.

Vice-Presidents:
The Duke of Portland, K.G., P.C., G.C.V.O., D.L., J.P.
The Rt. Hon. Sir Joseph Ward, Bart., P.C., K.C.M.G.*
The Rt. Hon. Lord Hugh Cecil, P.C., M.P., Lieut. R.A.F.

Council:
The Rt. Hon. Lord Morris, P.C., K.C.M.G., K.C. (Newfoundland).
The Rt. Hon. Sir George Perley, K.C.M.G., M.P. (Canada).
The Rt. Hon. W. P. Schreiner, P.C., C.M.G., K.C. (South Africa).
The Hon. Sir Thomas Mackenzie, K.C.M.G. (New Zealand).*
The Rt. Hon. Sir T. Vezey Strong, P.C., K.C.V.O., K.B.E., J.P.
Lieut.-Col. W. A. Bishop, V.C., D.S.O., M.C., D.F.C.
Lord Carbery.*
Alfred Docker, Esq. (Chairman of Executive).*
Sir Algernon F. Firth, Bart., J.P.
The Hon. Sir John Cockburn, K.C.M.G.
Colonel H. E. Rawson, C.B., R.E.
Major B. F. S. Baden-Powell, F.R.A.S.*
W. H. Butlin, Esq., B.A., K.I.C.*
John Cates, Esq.*
William Coward, Esq.*
E. Marshall Fox, Esq.*
W. P. Gibbons, Esq.*
H. Hirst, Esq.*
P. F. Holmes, Esq.*
A. Montefiore, Esq.*
F. J. West, Esq.*
J. F. Wright, Esq.*
H. James Yates, Esq., F.C.S., M.I.Mech.E.*

Hon. Organising Secretary and Director of Propaganda:
C. J. FAIRFAX SCOTT, M.A.
* The Founder Members

Annex IV: Procedural correspondence and instructions

(*Sources*: TNA AIR 1/903/204/5/799; AIR 1/755/204/4/84)

11th October 1915, C.R.F.C 2024(Q) Major, D.A.Q.M.G, RFC in the Field to Officer Commanding II Wing RFC:
>Could you inform me whether there are any aeroplanes presented by subscription in the Colonies or Dependencies in the Squadrons under your Command? Such aeroplanes have the name of the place presenting them printed on them so that they are easily recognised.
>If there are any of these machines please let me have their RFC numbers and types, with the names of the donors.
>It would also be convenient if when one of these machines is engaged in a Combat in the Air the circumstances could be noted in the usual formal report of the combat.
>It is anticipated that the donors will like to know what has happened to their gifts, and will be vexed if no answer can be given to their enquiries.

13th October 1915, 87/6291 (M.A.1) War Office to GOC 1st Brigade RFC:
>I am directed to request that you will forward a report of any interesting actions in which a part was taken by any of the aeroplanes which have been presented through the Overseas Club and labeled with the name of the donor.
>This information is required to be given to the donors who have generously come forward. I am further to request that any such future action be notified.

14th October 1915, B.M. 4899 (M.A.2.A.), Assistant Director of Military Aeronautics (A.D.M.A) War Office to GOC 1st Brigade RFC:
>I am directed to inform you that it has been decided that in the event of an aeroplane which has been presented to the Royal Flying Corps as the result of a private subscription or a special grant by a Colonial Government, being struck off charge on account of loss or other cause, another machine of the same type shall be labeled with the name of the lost machine. I am, therefore, to request that in all cases where

such a machine has had to be struck off charge you will report the same, giving the number of the new machine which has been given the name of the one lost.

I enclose herewith a complete statement of aeroplanes so far presented, in order that in any case where the machine has been lost a new machine may be given its name in accordance with the above.

16th October 1915, Lieut. Colonel Brooke-Popham to 1st, 2nd & 3rd Wings, Nos. 12 and 13 Squadrons:
>The donors of aeroplanes to the Royal Flying Corps are asking for a record to be kept of the work done by the aeroplanes they have given. These bear special names such as 'SHANGHAI' LIVERPOOL, etc.
>
>Please direct all concerned that when reporting a combat in the air or bomb dropping, in which one of those machines has taken part, that a note is made on the report stating the name borne by the machine.

16th October 1915, Major RFC in the Field to Deputy Director of Military Aeronautics (D.D.M.A) War Office:
>In answer to your memorandum 87/6291 (M.A.1) dated 13th October, there are enclosed some notes as to machines presented through the Overseas Club. It is hoped to see further notes in the future.

17th October 1915, C.R.F.C 2024(Q) Major, D.A.Q.M.G for Commanding RFC, British Army in the Field, to A.D.M.A, War Office:
>In answer to your memorandum B.M. 4899 (M.A.2.A) dated the 14th October 1915, I note that it has been decided that when a machine presented by private subscription, or by a special grant from a Colonial Government, is struck off charge, another machine is to be labeled with the name which had been attached to the one struck off. But it will be better, to save confusion, that when one of the machines in question has been struck off, the naming and labeling of a new one shall be done in England, and that the task of combining the records of the two machines as though they belonged to one shall also be undertaken at home. If this be done, the only duty cast upon the Royal Flying Corps in the Field will be to furnish the War Office with records of the

achievements of all labeled machines. Some of these records have already been sent, and every endeavour will be made to procure full information in regard to such of the machines mentioned in your list as have come to the Royal Flying Corps in the Field, and of any others of the same class that may hereafter be sent out to it in the field.

21st October 1915, B.M. 4899 (M.A.2.A.) War Office to GOC, 1st Brigade RFC:

With reference to your C.R.F.C 2024(Q), dated 17th October, 1915, the procedure proposed by you is concurred in. It will facilitate matters if the striking off of one of the gift machines can be reported at once, and the information not kept for the usual fortnightly return of aeroplanes.

26th October 1915, Brigadier General Commanding to 1st, 2nd and 3rd Wings RFC:

Your attention is drawn to my No. C.R.F.C. 2024(Q) dated 11th October.

Several instances have occurred in which the names of presentation machines have been omitted when rendering reports of combats in the air.

Not infrequently the number of the machines engaged in the combat has been omitted from the report.

Instances of these omissions occurring in your Wing are appended.

Wing Commanders will take such steps as is necessary to ensure that reports of combats in the air are correctly rendered and the orders referred to in the above mentioned letter strictly complied with.

9th January 1916, C.R.F.C 2024/1(Q), Lieut. Colonel, RFC to Officer Commanding, Aeroplane Repair Section:

Whenever an Aeroplane is received from England bearing an inscription plate indicating that it has been presented to the British Government by one of the Colonies you will make a note on your Daily State reporting the arrival of the aeroplane.

This note is to be made on the Daily State and not on the pink card.

Endnotes

Chapter 1: Introduction—gifts for the Royal Navy, and the Patriotic League

1. Quoted in Massie, *Dreadnought: Britain, Germany and the Coming of the Great War*, p. 837
2. Hough, *Dreadnought: A History of the Modern Battleship*, p. 78
3. Massie, *Dreadnought*, p. 832
4. See Mackenzie, 'Canada, the North Atlantic Triangle, and the Empire', p. 579
5. The *Hong Kong Telegraph (HKT)*, 21 May 1913
6. There were other Malay sultanates outside the federation at the time, and the population of the Malay states as a whole may have been up to 2.5 million
7. Officer and Williamson 'Purchasing Power of British Pounds from 1245 to Present'—based on the RPI for 1912 and 2012
8. *Singapore Free Press (SFP)*, 15 November 1912
9. Giving rise to a hoax report in the Madras press that the Indian princes planned to present a number of battleships: news relayed around the world by *Reuters* before being dismissed as false—*SFP*, 11 December 1912
10. *Straits Echo* (mail edition) *(SE)*, 27 December 1912
11. Jagjit Singh Sadhu, 'British Administration in the Federated Malay States, 1896-1920' (PhD thesis, University of London: January 1975)
12. *HKT*, 31 January 1913
13. Lugard, *The Dual Mandate in British Tropical Africa*
14. Williams, *Running the Show*, has a profile: Chapter 11 'Sweet talk and secrets—the rise and rise of Frank Athelstane Swettenham'
15. Swettenham, *British Malaya*, p. 343
16. Swettenham, *Footprints in Malaya*, p. 67
17. *Ibid.* p. 97
18. The *Times of Malaya and Planters' and Miners' Gazette* (weekly mail edition) *(ToM)*, 2 June 1916
19. With the exception of the Boer War of 1899-1902, which had proved a very unpleasant shock
20. Wrench, *Struggle*, Appendices
21. Booth, 'Lord Selborne and the British Protectorates, 1908-1910'
22. *Daily Mail Overseas Edition* or *Overseas Daily Mail (ODM)*, 16 January 1915
23. Mackenzie, *Propaganda and Empire*, p. 148
24. The National Archive (TNA), FO 369/799 'Consular Miscellaneous (General)', Consular Circular No.75275
25. TNA, FO 369/854, 'Consular Miscellaneous (General) 114-359'
26. *Reuters*, 25 May 1914
27. TNA, FO 369/854
28. *Pall Mall Gazette (PMG)*, 6 May 1912
29. *PMG*, 29 January 1914
30. *PMG*, 11 November 1913; 2 December 1913
31. *Overseas*, December 1915, p. 18
32. The *Aeroplane*, 4 August 1915, p. 124

33 Gratton, *The Origins of Air War*, p. 11
34 Mottram, 'The Early Days of the RNAS'
35 Baughen, *Blueprint for Victory*, pp. 51–2
36 Officer and Williamson 'Purchasing Power'
37 TNA, FO 369/854
38 TNA, CO 616/55, Escott/CO, 13 July 1916; Admiralty/CO, 3 September 1916
39 *The Times*, Empire Day Supplement, 24 May 1916
40 *Overseas*, April 1916
41 *Flight*, 26 October 1916
42 Patriotic League of Britons Overseas, *Second Annual Report*
43 Wrench, *Struggle*, Appendices

Chapter 2: And for the Army, Vickers Gunbus Dominica, and a kite balloon ...
1 See Paris, *Winged Warfare*, pp. 89–97
2 *Ibid*. p. 105
3 *PMG*, 27 March 1913
4 With oversight of aeronautics while in command of the RFC in France from August 1914, he returned to head the Aeronautics Directorate at the War Office one year later—H. A. Jones, 'Sir David Henderson, father of the Royal Air Force'
5 Paris, *Winged Warfare*, pp. 80–1; pp. 100–1; Edgerton, *England and the Aeroplane*, p. 21
6 *PMG*, 12 March 1913
7 *PMG*, 29 April 1913
8 Paris, *Winged Warfare*, p. 99
9 *PMG*, 5 May 1913; 7 May 1913
10 *PMG*, 20 August 1914
11 *Flight*, 1 January 1915
12 TNA, AIR 1/903/204/5/779
13 Dominica was later (1937) transferred from the Leeward Islands to the Windward Islands group
14 *Oxford Dictionary of National Biography*
15 *Ibid*; Williams, *Running the Show*, pp. 308–32
16 Bell, *Glimpses of a Governor's Life*, p. 84
17 Honychurch, *The Dominica Story*, pp. 149–152
18 Hulme, 'Islands and Roads'; for Chamberlain's tropical development policies see Porter, *The Lion's Share*, pp. 160–3
19 Bell, *Glimpses*, p. 27
20 *Ibid*. p. 45
21 Hulme, 'Islands and Roads'
22 Honychurch, *The Dominica Story*, p. 152
23 Imperial War Museum (IWM), IWM Cat.no.23153, Robin Hughes Chamberlain taped interviews (1971)—www.iwm.org.uk/collections/item/object/80021 540
24 The *Dominica Chronicle (DC)*, 25 July 1917; 16 June 1917; 20 June 1917; 20 October 1917

25 Nor does Hughes Chamberlain in his series of IWM taped interviews mention Dominica's gift
26 *DC*, 30 September 1914
27 TNA, CO 152/342, Dispatches, 7 October 1914; 10 October 1914
28 *West India Committee Circular (WICC)*, 29 December 1914
29 TNA, CO 152/343, Admiralty/CO, 29 October 1914
30 TNA, AIR 1/366/15/231/6, Military Aeronautics WO/CO, 1 November 1914
31 Honychurch, *The Dominica Story*, p. 177
32 The Virgin Islands, previously under Danish sovereignty and sold to the US in 1916, remained part of the Catholic diocese of Roseau
33 *DC*, 9 September 1914; Hamelius, *The Siege of Liège*, relates a similar Zeppelin legend created by a mistaken 'eyewitness' in the beleaguered city, pp. 45–6
34 West, *MI5 in the Great War*, pp. 170–3
35 Gollin, *The Impact of Air Power*, pp. 313–4
36 Lewis, *Sagittarius Rising*, p. 64: 'If there was ever an aeroplane unsuited for active service, it was the BE2c'
37 Morrow Jnr., 'The War in the Air', p.166
38 Baughen, *Blueprint for Victory*, pp. 122–3
39 *Ibid*. pp. 122–3
40 As per its service history summarised in Vann and Waugh, 'Presentation Aircraft 1914–1918'
41 *DC*, 30 October 1915
42 Grattan, *The Origins of Air War*, p. 35
43 IWM Cat.no.23153
44 Honychurch, *The Dominica Story*, p. 152
45 Bell, *Glimpses*, p. 95
46 *DC*, 3 November 1915
47 *DC*, 30 September 1914; 20 May 1916; 28 July 1917
48 *DC*, 14 November 1914
49 Wrench, *Struggle*, pp. 100–2
50 *Ibid.*
51 British Library (BL), Northcliffe papers, Add/MSS 62223, Empire Day 1918 Overseas Club leaflet
52 Wrench, *Struggle*, pp. 102–3
53 *DC*, 5 May 1917
54 Jefford, *Observers and Navigators and other non-pilot aircrew*, p. 76
55 *PoSG*, 11 April 1916: letter from his brother informed by War Office telegram
56 TNA, AIR 76/455/60, his service record
57 *Dominica Guardian*, 7 January 1915
58 *DC*, 5 May 1917
59 *DC*, 9 May 1917
60 *WICC*, 12 January 1918
61 Colvill-Jones, *Your Ever Loving Son*, p. 69; p. 74; p. 173; pp. 184–6; p. 251

Chapter 3: The Imperial Aircraft Flotilla Takes Off, 1915-1916

1. Lee Thompson, *Politicians, the Press and Propaganda*, p. 14
2. Taylor, *The Great Outsiders*, p. 121; Paris, *Winged Warfare*, pp. 67-71
3. Wrench, *Uphill*, pp. 218-9; Wrench, *Struggle*, pp. 119-20
4. Finnegan, *Shooting the Front*, p. 43
5. Lloyd George, *War Memoirs*, Vol. 2, p. 1095
6. Wrench, *Struggle*, Appendices
7. *Ibid.* p. 140
8. *Ibid.* p. 97
9. Wrench, *Uphill*, p. 304
10. *Ibid.* p. 140
11. *ODM*, 12 June 1915; 5 June 1915
12. Wrench, *Struggle*, p. 142
13. *ODM*, 17 July 1915
14. *ODM*, 21 August 1915
15. TNA CO 323/692/26; CO 323/692/43, correspondence Wrench/CO, August-September 1915
16. *Overseas*, March 1916
17. Tyler, *Labour's Lost Leader*, pp. 197-208—in June 1917 he became the shocked witness to the aftermath of a direct hit by German Gotha bombers on a school in Poplar only yards from his home, killing eighteen children.
18. Sweetman, *Cavalry of the Clouds*, p. 44
19. Royal Air Force Museum (RAFM) Archive, the Henderson papers, AC 71/4/1, no. 18, Letter Henderson/Steel-Maitland, 23 June 1916
20. See Annex IV
21. Vann and Waugh, 'Presentation Aircraft 1914-1918', pp. 51-2
22. Overseas Club booklet, 'The Imperial Aircraft Flotilla', May 1916
23. TNA, AIR 1/113/15/39/33
24. Cooper, *The Birth of Independent Air Power*, p. 34
25. Finnegan, *Shooting the Front*, p. 286
26. TNA, AIR 1/142/15/40/314, cites Army Council letters of 9 December 1916 and 13 January 1917
27. TNA, AIR 1/903/204/5/779, Capt. General Staff for DDMA/GOC 1st Brigade RFC, 13 October 1915, followed by memo. B.M 4899, on procedures—see Annex IV
28. RAFM, X005-0949, AVM Hazleton Nicholl's typescript 'Journeys and Recollections' (1950), p. 7, refers to a cruise in his youth aboard the 75-ton steam yacht of a wealthy Clydeside shipbuilder uncle (as Henderson's father David, of D. & W. Henderson Ltd., indeed was)
29. www.rafweb.org/Biographies/Nicholl.htm
30. See chapter 3, pp. 43-5, and chapter 8, pp. 120-1; 125-6
31. TNA AIR 1/755/204/4/84, 'Performances of Gift Aeroplanes (Overseas Club) 16 October-8 January 1916'
32. TNA CO 323/693, Overseas Club, 14 September 1915
33. Wrench, *Struggle*, p. 158

34 BL, Northcliffe papers, correspondence with Wrench, Add/MSS 62223, Overseas Club Empire Day 1918 leaflet

Chapter 4: Press and personal networks: Canada and Newfoundland
1   Alfred Harmsworth became Lord Northcliffe in December 1905
2   May, 'Founding Father'
3   Lee Thompson, *Northcliffe: Press Baron in Politics*, p. 118; Wrench, *Uphill*, p. 137
4   Wrench, *Struggle*, pp. 93–8
5   Taylor, *The Great Outsiders*, pp. 93–4; p. 101
6   Wills, *The Anglo-African who's who*, p. 156
7   BL, Wrench papers, Add/MSS 59,563-59,566, letter, 14 August 1906
8   Begbie, *Albert fourth Earl Grey*
9   Magee and Thompson, *Empire and Globalisation*, pp. 206–7
10 See Martin, 'The idea of "Imperial Federation"'
11 Judd, *Radical Joe*, p. 180; for the larger implications of his tariff policy see Cain and Hopkins, *British Imperialism: Innovation and Expansion*, pp. 202–25.
12 *Oxford Dictionary of National Biography*
13 BL, Add/MSS 59,563-59,566, letter to his parents, 19 August 1906
14 BL, Northcliffe papers, Add/MSS 62222, Wrench/Northcliffe, 25 June 1912
15 Wrench, *Struggle*, pp. 248–9
16 Wrench, *Uphill*, p. 158
17 Wrench, *Struggle*, p. 249
18 May, 'Founding Father'; Wrench, *Uphill*, pp. 159–62
19 Lee Thompson, *Northcliffe: Press Baron in Politics*, p. 168
20 Lee Thompson, 'Selling the Mother Country to the Empire'
21 Wrench, *Uphill*, p. 225
22 As mentioned in Dafoe, *The Imperial Press Conference*
23 Potter, *News and the British World*, p. 132
24 *Straits Echo (SE)*, 27 December 1912
25 Lee Thompson, *Northcliffe: Press Baron in Politics*, p. 172
26 Wrench, *Uphill*, p. 250
27 Epstein, 'Imperial Airs: Leo Amery, Air Power and Empire'
28 Potter, *News and the British World*, p. 164
29 BL, Wrench papers, Add/MSS 59,570
30 BL, Wrench papers, Add/MSS 59,572
31 May, 'Founding Father'; Wrench, *Uphill*, p. 295
32 Wrench, *Struggle*, p. 94
33 Wrench, *Uphill*, p. 295
34 BL, Northcliffe papers, correspondence with Wrench, Add/MSS 62222
35 Wrench, *Struggle*, p. 132; *Uphill*, pp. 305–6
36 *Ibid.* p. 266
37 Taylor, *The Great Outsiders*, p. 147
38 Wrench, *Struggle*, p. 61
39 They married in 1937 after her husband, Sir Frederick des Voeux, died

40 Wrench, *Struggle*, mentions two information sources—Brigadier General Guy Brooke, former *aide-de-camp* to General French, GOC BEF, and Claude Johnson, Managing Director of Rolls-Royce: p. 147; p. 151; p. 154; p. 166
41 Quoted in Overseas Club booklet 'The Imperial Aircraft Flotilla', May 1916
42 Hart, *Aces Falling*, p. 21
43 O'Brien, 'Out of a Clear Sky: The Mobilization of the Newfoundland Regiment'
44 *Ibid.*
45 *Ibid.*
46 Overseas Club booklet, 'The Imperial Air Flotilla', May 1916
47 Deal, 'Newfoundland's First Air War'
48 *Daily News (DN)*, 14 October 1915
49 Mackenzie, 'Eastern Approaches: Maritime Canada and Newfoundland'
50 Lloyd George, *War Memoirs*, Vol.2, p. 2009
51 O'Brien, 'Out of a Clear Sky'
52 See Mackenzie, 'Canada, the North Atlantic Triangle, and the Empire'
53 *DN*, 31 August 1915

Chapter 5: Sultan Seyyid Khalifa of Zanzibar and the Royal Naval Air Service
1 Zanzibar *Blue Book*, 1913
2 Pakenham, *The Scramble for Africa*, pp. 282–96: the eventual arrangement exchanged a British Protectorate over Zanzibar for Heligoland going to Germany
3 TNA, FO 84/1746
4 Ruete, *Memoirs of an Arabian Princess of Oman and Zanzibar*, p. 228
5 Hernon, *Britain's Forgotten Wars*, pp. 397–404
6 Pearce, *Zanzibar: The Island Metropolis*, pp. 273–4
7 *Ibid.*
8 TNA, CO 618/15; CO 618/20: He died of tuberculosis in Paris on 17 December 1918, still dogged by scandals, in July 1916 a Paris Magistrate had ordered him to pay monies owing to a local brothel-keeper for services rendered
9 Pearce, *Zanzibar: The Island Metropolis*, pp. 281–4; p. 286
10 Ingrams (a former Assistant Secretary of the island), *Zanzibar*, p. 177
11 TNA, CO 618/8, Telegram Pearce/CO, 6 November 1914
12 TNA, CO 323/736, Dispatch, 11 January 1917
13 Paice, *Tip and Run*, p. 26
14 TNA, CO 618/8, Dispatch, 31 December 1914
15 TNA, CO 618/14, Dispatch, 19 July 1916
16 Lonsdale, 'East Africa', p. 535; see also Paice, *Tip and Run*
17 Hodges, 'Military Labour in East Africa and its Impact on Kenya', p. 143
18 Ingrams, *Zanzibar*, pp. 177–8
19 In 1916, the administration of Mafia Island was placed in the hands of the Zanzibar Government, but it transferred to Tanganyika in 1922
20 Dye, 'Royal Naval Air Service Operations in German East Africa: Part I'
21 Ricardo Marques, *Os Fantasmas do Rovuma*, p. 153
22 Layman, *Naval Aviation in the First World War*, pp. 132–7
23 Paice, *Tip and Run*, p. 118
24 TNA, CAB 45/218, 'RNAS operations off Zanzibar 1914–17: a narrative by Wing Cdr. J. T. Cull, DSO, RAF'

25 Cooksley, *Royal Flying Corps Handbook 1914–1918*, p. 103
26 Paice, *Tip and Run*, pp. 178–9; Dye, 'RNAS Operations: Part I'
27 Quoted in Dye, 'RNAS Operations in German East Africa: Part II'
28 *Ibid.*
29 TNA, CAB 45/218, 'RNAS operations off Zanzibar'
30 Layman, *Naval Aviation*, p. 135
31 Dye, 'RNAS Operations: Part II'
32 Vann and Waugh, 'Presentation Aircraft 1914–1918'
33 Marques, *Os Fantasmas do Rovuma*, p. 155; p. 165; Carvalho, *A Guerra que Portugal quis esquecer*, pp. 143–4
34 Urban, *Ned's Navy: The Private Letters of Edward Charlton*, p. 143
35 Layman, *Naval Aviation*, p. 135
36 Pearce, *Zanzibar: The Island Metropolis*, p. 272
37 TNA, CO 618/11, Pearce/Read, private letter 18 May 1915
38 TNA CO 618/15, Dispatch, 12 October 1916
39 Crofton, *Zanzibar Affairs 1914–1933*, p. 3
40 TNA, CO 618/11, Telegram, 30 June 1915
41 TNA, CO 688/21, Zanzibar Protectorate Council Minutes, 24 June 1915
42 *The Times*, 27 October 1915
43 TNA, CO 618/19, CO minute, 10 April 1918; Read/Air Ministry, 13 April 1918
44 Ingrams, *Zanzibar*, p. 178
45 TNA, CO 618/20, Robinson Air Ministry/CO, 18 April 1918
46 Vann and Waugh, 'Presentation Aircraft 1914–1918'
47 CO 448/14, recommendation list April 1918
48 Cannadine, *Ornamentalism*, pp. 96–7
49 Urban, *Ned's Navy*, p. 159

Chapter 6: Tropical Sugarcane Producers: Pacific, Indian Ocean, and Caribbean
1 www.25squadron.org.uk/History.htm, accessed 2013
2 Vann and Waugh, 'Presentation Aircraft 1914–1918': a couple of them were of the later FE2d model
3 TNA, War Cabinet GT series 202, 'Memorandum on the Assistance of Colonies and Protectorates in the War', 13 March 1917
4 Macdonald, *Cinderellas of the Empire*, pp. 115–16
5 TNA, CO 616/28, CO manuscript minute, 30 September 1915
6 TNA CO 752/6, reference to telegram Escott/CO, 20 July 1916
7 McIntyre, 'Australia, New Zealand, and the Pacific Islands', p. 668
8 Scarr, *Ratu Sukuna*, pp. 32–9; p. 53
9 Leclezio, 'People and Politics'
10 The *Planters and Commercial Gazette (PCG)*, 23 May 1916
11 Bell, *Glimpses*, pp. 210–11
12 *PCG*, 19 May 1916
13 From April 1916 onwards, the *PCG* carried almost daily feature articles on the Battle of Verdun drawn from both the French and English press
14 *PCG*, 5 August 1916
15 Darwin, *The Empire Project*, pp. 336–7
16 Jackson, *War and Empire in Mauritius and the Indian Ocean*, p. 23

17 See Morrow Jnr., 'The War in the Air'
18 *PCG*, 22–23 October 1916
19 *PCG*, 1–3 November 1916; *The Times*, 4 November 1916
20 Bell, *Witches and Fishes*, pp. 87–8
21 Williams, *Running the Show*, p. 332
22 De Lisser, *Jamaica and the Great War*, p. 33, pp. 59–60
23 Smith, *Jamaican Volunteers in the First World War*, p. 140
24 Smith, 'Heaven grant you strength to fight the battle for your race'
25 See chapter 13, pp. 211–2
26 *DG*, 8 May 1916
27 De Lisser, *Jamaica and the Great War*, pp. 101–3
28 The *Daily Gleaner (DG)*, 25 November 1915
29 *DG*, 18 September 1915
30 *DG*, 1 November 1915
31 *DG*, 5 November 1915
32 *DG*, 10 November 1915
33 De Lisser, *Jamaica and the Great War*, p. 106
34 *DG*, 15 September 1915; 28 September 1915; 8 January 1916; 13 January 1916
35 *DG*, 1 March 1916
36 *DG*, 14 October 1915
37 *DG*, 18 October 1915
38 TNA, CO 448/14, Dispatch, 4 April 1918
39 *DG*, 22 October 1915: a *quattie* was a small coin worth a penny ha'penny
40 The *Port of Spain Gazette (PoSG)*, 20 September 1914; 7 February 1915; 16 June 1915; 17 June 1915; 2 October 1915
41 *PoSG*, 18 August 1916; 17 December 1916
42 *PoSG*, 5 September 1915; 16 March 1916; 29 March 1916
43 The *West India Committee Circular (WICC)*, 19 October 1916; *PoSG*, 31 October 1916
44 *WICC*, 11 January 1917; 22 February 1917
45 *PoSG*, 5 December 1916
46 TNA, CO 448/15
47 *Daily Argosy (DA)*, 20 May 1915; 23 May 1915; 6 June 1915; 20 July 1915; 1 October 1915; 9 October 1915; 17 October 1915
48 *ODM*, 26 May 1917; *WICC*, 22 February 1917
49 *ODM*, 25 May 1918
50 Cooper, *The Birth of Independent Air Power*, p. 93
51 Penrose, *British Aviation*, p. 606

Chapter 7: Eastern outposts—bankers and philanthropists of Hong Kong
1 *HKT*, 26 March 1915
2 TNA, CO 129/42, Dispatch, 14 January 1915; Cmd. 7875, April 1915
3 Carroll, *Edge of Empires*, p. 73
4 *Ibid.* p. 11; p. 78
5 *Ibid.* p. 66; Miners, *Hong Kong under Imperial Rule*, p. 59
6 *Ibid.* p. 45

7 Sayer, *Hong Kong 1862–1919*, pp. 111–23
8 TNA, CO 129/422, Telegram, 24 May 1915: its name was also rendered in English as Tai Yau Bank or Tai Yuen Bank
9 TNA, CO 129/422, Telegram, 25 May 1915; *ODM*, 5 June 1915
10 *South China Morning Post (SCMP)*, 26 May 1915; 11 August 1915
11 *SCMP*, 30 December 1915, citing a letter from Wrench to the Governor
12 See Annex IV
13 TNA, AIR 1/755/204/4/84
14 *Overseas*, no. 1, December 1915
15 TNA, CO 129/422, Dispatch No. 201, 27 May 1915
16 Lee, *Being Eurasian*, p. 115
17 Carroll, *Edge of Empires*, p. 74; pp. 79–80
18 Zheng, *Chinese Family Business and the Equal Inheritance System*, p. 41
19 *Ibid.* pp. 114–5
20 *Ibid.* p. 112
21 Carroll, *Edge of Empires*, pp. 79–83; Feldwick (ed.), *Present Day Impressions of the Far East*, p. 520; p. 573; pp. 581–3
22 Zheng, *Chinese Family Business*, p. 107; p. 112
23 Tsang, *A Modern History of Hong Kong*, p. 87
24 Feldwick, *Present Day Impressions of the Far East*, pp. 530–1
25 Zheng, *Chinese Family Business*, p. 112
26 Lee, *Being Eurasian*, p. 16
27 And, in 1909, *Notes on Pony and Horse Racing in Hong Kong 1845–1887*
28 http://racingmemories.hk, accessed 2015
29 Carroll, *Edge of Empires*, pp. 100–1; Kwarteng, *Ghosts of Empire*, pp. 340–2
30 Feldwick, *Present Day Impressions of the Far East*, pp. 530–1
31 TNA, CO 129/422, Dispatch No. 216, 5 June 1915; CO 129/423, Loke Yew/May, 1 June 1915
32 Fisher, *Who's Who in Malaya 1925*, pp. 69–70
33 See Mishra, *From the Ruins of Empire*
34 TNA, CO 129/421, Dispatch, 8 April 1915; Manuscript minute on Telegram transmitting representations on the Japanese demands, 6 April 1915
35 Dickinson, 'The Japanese Empire', p. 205
36 *Pinang Gazette and Straits Chronicle* (weekly edition) (*PGSC*), 16 October 1914
37 Dickinson, 'The Japanese Empire', p. 205
38 The Washington Conference on disarmament and the future of the Pacific. See Tooze, *The Deluge*, pp. 396–403
39 TNA, CO 129/423, Dispatch, 3 December 1915
40 *SCMP*, 13 April 1917
41 Photographs published in Jarrett, 'Ho Fook'
42 Tsang, *A Modern History*, p. 87
43 *SCMP*, 7 May 1917
44 See Mackenzie, *Propaganda and Empire*, pp. 148–58, for a survey of these societies
45 TNA, CO 129/444, Telegram of 10 November 1917; CO 129/447, Dispatch, 3 January 1918

46 Miners, *Hong Kong under Imperial Rule*, p. 8
47 Kwarteng, *Ghosts of Empire*, pp. 340–2
48 Lee, *Being Eurasian*, p. 29

Chapter 8: The Malaya Air Fleet Fund—the Straits Settlements and Malay states
1   TNA, CO 323/751, Memorandum, 'The Contributions of the Dominions and Colonies to the Common Cause', June 1916
2   Van der Vat, *The Last Corsair*, pp. 80–1
3   The *Malaya Tribune (MT)*, 28 June 1915
4   Ho Tak Ming, *Ipoh: When Tin Was King*, pp. 85–7
5   *Ibid*. p. 319
6   Chung Po-Yin, 'Migration and Enterprise: The Eu Yan Sang Firm'
7   Macdonald, *Imperial Patriot: Charles Alma Baker*, p. 54
8   Khoo and Lubis, *Kinta Valley*, pp. 117–19
9   Macdonald, *Imperial Patriot*, p. 36
10 Ernest Birch was the son of Perak's first Resident, J. W. W. Birch, who was murdered in 1875
11 *MT*, 10 March 1915
12 *PGSC*, 30 April 1915; 28 May 1915
13 *MT*, 22 September 1915
14 *MT*, 11 March 1915: Of the 34 people listed as attending the annual AGM of the FMS Chamber of Mines in 1915, there were 24 European names, 9 Chinese, and 1 Malay; of the 10 members elected to the Chamber's Perak Council, 7 were Europeans (including Alma Baker) and 3 Chinese (including Eu Tong Sen)
15 See Ho Tak Ming, *Ipoh*
16 Tregonning, *Straits Tin*, p. 31
17 Palmer and Joll, *Tin Mining in Malaya*, pp. 30–1; p. 34
18 Ho Tak Ming, *Ipoh*, p. 319
19 Macdonald, *Imperial Patriot*, p. 50
20 *MT*, 27 September 1915
21 Appeal of 1 August 1915, quoted in Alma Baker, *94 Gift Battle Planes*, p. 134
22 The *Times of Malaya and Planters' and Miners' Gazette (ToM)*, 22 April 1915
23 FMS Annual Report for 1916, quoted in Alma Baker, *94 Gift Battleplanes*
24 *ToM*, 29 April 1915
25 *SE*, 3 July 1915
26 *SE*, 21 October 1915; Wright, *Respected Citizens*, pp. 22–3; p. 68; pp. 76–7
27 Makepeace, 'Concerning Known Persons', p. 463
28 *MT*, 9 August 1915
29 *ToM*, 23 December 1915
30 *MT*, 27 April 1916
31 *MT*, 17 January 1916; *ToM*, 17 January 1916
32 *MT*, 12 September 1916
33 *PGSC*, 12 May 1916; *SE* 17 May 1916
34 *PGSC*, 2 June 1916
35 As listed in Alma Baker, *94 Battleplanes*

36 Dossett, *Who's Who In Malaya 1918*; Wong, *A Gallery of Chinese Kapitans*, pp. 24–5; Wright, *20th Century Impressions of British Malaya*, pp. 761–2; pp. 777–8
37 Alma Baker, *94 Battleplanes*
38 *Ibid.*
39 *MT*, 9 March 1916; TNA CO 273/445, Dispatch, 16 March 1916
40 TNA, AIR 1/14/15/1/52, List of RFC and RAF presentation machines—a 'Mrs. Hall' is identified as the collector
41 Wright, *Twentieth Century Impressions of British Malaya*, p. 891; Gullick, *Rulers and Residents*, p. vi
42 Cf. his entry, supplied or vetted by himself, in Dossett, *Who's Who in Malaya*
43 The number given for those executed by firing squad by the National Library of Singapore website; but other sources range from 31–47
44 Harper and Miller, *Singapore Mutiny*; Robertson, *The Battle of Penang*, p. 229
45 Cf. Shennan, *Out in the Midday Sun*, pp. 138–9, quoting Commander Shelley
46 Eyewitness letter in the *North-China Herald (NCH)*, 18 June 1915
47 Braddell, *The Lights of Singapore*, p.98
48 Vann and Waugh, 'Presentation Aircraft 1914–18' (Johore details to be found hidden in the India listing)
49 TNA, CO 715/1, Johore Annual Reports, 1916; 1917; 1918; 1919
50 *SE*, 29 August 1917; TNA, MUN 4/3945 has the correspondence about this
51 *ToM*, 8 August 1918, letter, Captain in the Tank Corps to his brother in the FMS
52 From www.clairegrey.co.uk/rd.grandchildren/archie/archie.html, a family history
53 Khoo and Lubis, *Kinta*, p. 204; p. 238
54 Lucas, *The Empire at War*, Vol. 2, pp. 392–409
55 *PGSC*, 15 February 1918

Chapter 9: West Africa, and most particularly Gold Coast, and Hugh Clifford
1 The *Lagos Weekly Record (LWR)*, 5–12 December 1914
2 See Grundlingh, 'The Impact of the First World War', pp. 64–5
3 The *Times of Nigeria (ToN)*, 29 December 1914
4 Darwin, *The Empire Project*, pp. 292–4
5 Webster, 'Political Activity in British West Africa, 1900–1940'
6 Conrad, *German Colonialism*, p. 47
7 The *Gold Coast Leader (GCL)*, 8 August 1914
8 The *Gold Coast Nation (GCN)*, 27 May 1915
9 Heartfield, *The Aborigines' Protection Society*, p. 40, p. 83
10 Wrench, *Struggle*, pp. 142–3
11 *ODM*, 16 October 1915
12 *The Times*, 25 May 1917; 6 June 1917
13 TNA, CO 616/51, Wrench to CO, 30 July 1915
14 The *Nigerian Pioneer (NP)*, 17 September 1915
15 Falola and Roberts, 'West Africa', p. 518
16 *NP*, 1 October 1915; 8 October 1915; 15 October 1915
17 *NP*, 1 October 1915; Frost, *Work and Community*, p. 20
18 TNA, CO 583/45, Dispatch, 17 March 1916

19 TNA, CO 583/58, Dispatch No. 553, 24 July 1917
20 TNA, CO 583/58, Internal CO minutes, 3 September 1917
21 Crowder, 'The 1914–1918 European war and West Africa'
22 Clifford's introduction to Claridge, *A History of the Gold Coast*, pp. xiv–xv
23 TNA, CO 96/550, Dispatch, 21 December 1914
24 Wrench, *Struggle*, p. 154, letter to his parents dated 27 February 1916
25 Boahen, *Ghana: Evolution and Change*, p. 32
26 Tidrick, *Empire and the English Character*, pp. 88–116
27 *Ibid*. pp. 116–8
28 Gailey, *Clifford: Imperial Proconsul*, p. 89
29 *Ibid*. p. 81
30 *Ethiopia Unbound* is discussed in Philip Holden, *Autobiography and Decolonization*, pp. 64–72; for Clifford's writings see Tidrick, *Empire*, pp. 93–109
31 *Writings of Ekra-Agiman (J. E. Casely Hayford)*, *Vol. 1*, pp. 90–1
32 See Mishra, *From the Ruins of Empire*
33 TNA, CO 583/32, Dispatch on Clifford's letters, 15 April 1915
34 The Anti-Slavery and Aborigines' Protection Society's *Annual Report for 1915*
35 TNA, CO 96/590, Dispatch No. 345, 17 June 1918
36 TNA, CO 96/569, Dispatch, 1 September 1916
37 TNA, CO 96/559, Acting Governor's Dispatch No. 699, 14 August 1915
38 TNA, CO 96/559, Acting Governor's Dispatch No. 713, 30 August 1915
39 As reported in the columns of *The Times*, various dates
40 Addo-Fening, *Akyem Abuakwa*, p. 170
41 Roger, 'Military Recruitment in the Gold Coast during the First World War'
42 TNA, CO 96/590, Dispatch No. 345, 17 June 1918 reports the gift; but it is absent from Vann and Waugh 'Presentation Aircraft' and from press reports
43 Gailey, *Clifford*, pp. 75–6
44 Tidrick, *Empire*, p. 115
45 TNA, CO 96/567, Clifford/CO, 26 May 1916
46 TNA, CO 96/571, Telegram Clifford/CO, 26 September 1916; CO/Clifford, 5 October 1916
47 TNA, CO 96/590, Dispatch No. 345, 17 June 1918
48 Hill, *The Marcus Garvey and Universal Negro Improvement Papers, Vol. 8*
49 Boahen, *Ghana: Evolution and Change*, pp. 119–34
50 Killingray, 'World War I in the Gold Coast', p. 42; p. 44
51 Addo-Fening, *Akyem Abuakwa*, p. 315
52 Acquah, *Cocoa Development in West Africa*, p. 41
53 Stockwell, 'Sir Hugh Clifford in Malaya, 1927–9', p. 25, *n.18*
54 Gailey, *Clifford*, p. 172
55 Stockwell, 'Sir Hugh Clifford in Malaya', p. 25
56 *ST*, 10 June 1927
57 *ST*, 22 March 1928; 29 March 1928
58 Tidrick, *Empire*, p. 88
59 Purcell, *The Memoirs of a Malayan Official*, pp. 274–5

Chapter 10: The Rhodesias—friends in high places, a Grey area?
1   BL, Add/MSS 59573
2   Southern Rhodesia became a self-governing Colony in 1923—a quasi-Dominion under effective internal white settler rule but with British residual rights (hardly at all exercised) over measures impacting on the African population, as well as foreign policy, the BSAC having no further role in government
3   Gann, *Central Africa: The Former British States*, p. 85
4   Ranger, *Revolt in Southern Rhodesia 1896-7*, pp. 46-7; pp. 88-9; p. 114
5   *Ibid.* p. 127
6   Palmer, *Land and Racial Domination in Rhodesia*, p. 42
7   Gann, *Central Africa*, p. 95
8   *BSAC Historical Catalogue and Souvenir of Rhodesia*
9   Stapleton, *No Insignificant Part*, p. 13
10 McLaughlin, *Ragtime Soldiers*, pp. 4-24
11 *Ibid.* pp. 73-9
12 *Ibid.* p. 5; p. 49; p.140
13 McLaughlin, 'The Legacy of Conquest', p. 121
14 *Ibid.* p. 84
15 RAFM, X005-0949, Nicholl, 'Journeys and Recollections', p. 10
16 *Ibid.* p. 20; pp. 31-2; p. 34
17 Gann, *A History of Southern Rhodesia*, p. 225
18 RAFM, X005-0949, Nicholl, 'Journeys and Recollections', p. 55
19 *Ibid.* pp. 56-7
20 www.rafweb.org/Biographies/Nicholl.htm; IWM documents no. 21698 contain Nicholl's notebook account of those rebuffs (later omitted from both manuscript and typescript versions of 'Journeys and Recollections') but makes no mention of Henderson's help to finally enlist
21 *Rhodesia Herald* (weekly edition) *(RH)*, 13 August 1915
22 McLaughlin, *Ragtime Soldiers*, p. 93
23 Steiner, 'The Foreign Office and the War'
24 Robbins, *Sir Edward Grey*, pp. 59-61; Raleigh Grey was also Albert Earl Grey's second cousin—Keppel-Jones, *Rhodes and Rhodesia*, p. 563
25 RAFM, X005-0949, Nicholl, 'Journeys and Recollections', pp. 29-30; p. 36; p. 46; another of the Grey brothers, Charles Grey, was killed by a wild buffalo in Tanganyika in 1928
26 Albert Earl Grey published a 'Memoir' of one: Hubert Hervey, who fought as a Volunteer in 1893, and in 1896 was killed in the second Matabeleland War
27 This author's emphases
28 The *Bulawayo Chronicle (BC)*, 2 July 1915
29 McLaughlin, *Ragtime Soldiers*, p. 3
30 Wills, *The Anglo-African who's who*, p. 157
31 Gann, *A History of Northern Rhodesia*, pp. 176-7
32 *BC*, 9 July 1915; 16 July 1915
33 TNA, CO 616/51, Wrench/CO, 30 July 1915
34 Full title as listed in Overseas Club pamphlet 'The Imperial Aircraft Flotilla'
35 *RH*, 31 March 1916; Gann, *A History of Northern Rhodesia*, pp. 176-7
36 See Long, *Drummond Chaplin*, pp. 212-17

37 BC, 21 January 1916
38 RH, 22 October 1915
39 RH, 11 February 1916
40 BC, 17 March 1916
41 BC, 26 January 1917
42 RAFM, X005-0949, Nicholl, 'Journeys and Recollections', pp. 58–63
43 Ibid. p. 67
44 McLaughlin, *Ragtime Soldiers*, p. 71
45 RH, 21 January 1916
46 BC, 7 January 1916
47 RH, 21 January 1916; McLaughlin, *Ragtime Soldiers*, p. 71 states that he was killed in *Gatooma No. 2*, but I have found no other mention of a second presentation aircraft from Gatooma
48 BC, 17 March 1916
49 Baring, *RFC HQ 1914–1918*, p. 176
50 Salt, *The Definitive History of the Rhodesian Air Force*, pp. 3–5
51 IWM Cat.no.3765, taped interview
52 Salt *The Definitive History*, pp. 3–5
53 TNA, CO 616/24, Dispatch, 31 May 1915
54 Coxhead, *The Native Tribes of North-Eastern Rhodesia*
55 Stapleton, *No Insignificant Part*, p. 7; p. 13; Barnes, *Politics in a Changing Society*, p. 110
56 Page, *The Chiwaya War*, p. 76; Rotberg, *The Rise of Nationalism in Central Africa*, p. 81
57 Morrow Jnr., *The Great War: An Imperial History*, pp. 97–8; pp. 144–5; p. 310
58 Carvalho, *A Guerra que Portugal quis esquecer*, p. 11; p. 20; p. 25
59 Isaacman, *The Tradition of Resistance in Mozambique*, pp. 156–77
60 Ribeiro de Menezes, 'The Portuguese Empire', p. 189
61 TNA, CO 616/25, Dispatch No. 486, 11 June 1915, forwarding Administrator's Dispatch of 31 May 1915 along with the letter etc.
62 Yorke, 'The Spectre of a Second Chilembwe'
63 TNA CO 616/24, Dispatch, 31 May 1915
64 TNA, CO 616/48, Manuscript minute by Lord Stamfordham, 6 July 1915
65 Yorke, 'The Spectre of a Second Chilembwe'

Chapter 11: The Basuto nation, the British sovereign, and 25 Sopwith Camels
1 Booth, 'Lord Selborne and the British Protectorates'
2 Address by the Earl of Selborne, 27 March 1914
3 Some would argue that it became, and remained, a Crown Colony with annexation in 1868
4 See Machobane, *Government and Change in Lesotho*, especially pp. 40–4
5 Lagden, *The Basutos: the Mountaineers and their Country*, Vol. 2, pp. 615–16
6 The *Bloemfontein Post (BP)*, 8 January 1910; Wills, *The Anglo-African who's who*, p. 336
7 Tylden, *The Rise of the Basuto*, p. 208
8 However Fiji's Great Council of Chiefs was more than fifty strong
9 See Machobane, *Government and Change in Lesotho*

10 Gluckmann, *The Tragedy of the Ababirwas*, p. 25
11 Marks, 'Southern Africa', p. 559
12 TNA, FCO 141/821, Secret and very secret papers on Defence, Basutoland
13 Basutoland Colonial Report 1915–16
14 *BP*, 10 January 1912.
15 Grundlingh, *Fighting Their Own War*, p. 6; pp. 12–13
16 *BP*, 10 November 1913; 19 January 1914
17 Tylden, *The Rise of the Basuto*, p. 216
18 TNA, CO 616/5, Sloley/Acting High Commissioner, 26 August 1914; CO 417/545, Dispatch, 23 September 1914
19 *BP*, 14 December 1914
20 TNA, CO 616/5, 26 October 1914 manuscript minute by the Secretary of State (in red), original emphases indicated by underlining; Griffith's letter of 23 June 1915 transmitting the cheque subsequently specified the British fund
21 Tylden, *The Rise of the Basuto*, pp. 202–3; Lagden, *The Basutos*, Vol. 2, p. 603; pp. 609–10
22 *BP*, 19 April 1915; 21 April 1915
23 TNA, CO 417/565, CO minutes, 1 June 1915, on Cape Town Dispatch No.336
24 TNA, CO 417/580, Dispatch, 12 September 1916; Basutoland Colonial Report 1915–16
25 TNA CO 417/580, CO/Buxton, 31 October 1916—*The Times* had miscopied it as a message on behalf of the 'Basuto Chiefs *and natives*' instead of 'Basuto Chiefs *and nation*'—a published slip that officials described as 'unfortunate'
26 *BP*, 14 January 1916
27 Youé, *Robert Thorne Coryndon*, pp. 111–12
28 TNA, CO 646/2, BNC Proceedings 1913–16, Address, 26 August 1916
29 Edgar, 'Lesotho and the First World War'
30 *BC*, 23 March 1917
31 *BC*, 10 August 1917; there is no indication whether, like Swaziland the following year, Basuto miners in South Africa were also expected to contribute—if so, collections there could also have been a reason for the delay
32 TNA, CO 616/75, Ministry of Munitions/CO, 1 January 1917
33 TNA, CO 616/73, Cubitt, WO/CO, 13 March 1917
34 TNA, CO 616/73, WO/CO, 29 March 1917
35 Heartfield, *The Aborigines' Protection Society*, p. 28; pp. 37–40; p. 259
36 Grant, *A Civilised Savagery*, p. 142
37 Anti-Slavery and Aborigines' Protection Society's *Annual Report for 1916*
38 Slolely, 'The African Native Labour Contingent'
39 TNA, CO 616/70, Batterbee, CO/Steel, 29 November 1917
40 Jingoes, *A Chief is a Chief by the People*, p. 90
41 TNA, CO 616/68, Telegram, Buxton/CO, 28 February 1917
42 RA PS/PSO/GV/PS/WAR/QQ9/05199, Leitrim, APS CO/Stamfordham, 10 March 1917; Stamfordham/Leitrim, 12 March 1917 (Quoted from the Royal Archive with the gracious permission of Her Majesty Queen Elizabeth II)
43 *The Times*, 17 March 1917
44 TNA, CO 616/69, Coryndon/CO, 20 April 1917
45 Vann and Waugh, 'Presentation Aircraft 1914–1918'

46 *The Times*, 28 September 1917; *Flight*, 4 October 1917
47 *BP*, 14 September 1911
48 *BP*, 4 June 1912; 3 January 1913; 7 February 1913; 19 August 1913; 9 September 1913 (it is not known if Weston employed Basuto on his farm)
49 The *Cape Times (CT)*, 27 November 1918
50 *CT*, 17 May 1919
51 TNA, CO 417/624
52 The *Rand Daily Mail (RDM)*, 6 June 1919
53 *CT*, 23 October 1919
54 *The Times*, 20 October 1919
55 *The Times*, 24 October 1919; 31 October 1919; 1 November 1919
56 *The Times*, 8 November 1919
57 See chapter 18, p. 293
58 TNA, CO 417/624, Text of BNC petition in draft, May 1919
59 *CT*, 8 January 1920
60 TNA, CO 417/645, Dispatch, 16 March 1920
61 The original gift was four ponies, but on arrival at Cape Town for shipment one was found to be suffering an equine disease, and was returned

Chapter 12: Swaziland, Major Miller, the Union of South Africa, and Jan Smuts
1 Hart, *Aces Falling*, p. 162
2 *RDM*, 10 April 1918
3 In (anon.) *Some Account of George Grey*
4 TNA, CO 616/77, Dispatch, 19 February 1918
5 *The Times*, 22 March 1918
6 TNA, CO 616/77, Telegram, Buxton/CO, 13 August 1918
7 *RDM*, 10 April 1918.
8 Grotpeter, *Historical Dictionary of Swaziland*, pp. 102–3; Jones, *A Biographical Register of Swaziland*, pp. 414–19
9 The newspaper commenced again in 1902 but was no longer publishing by the time of the Great War; it was revived in the 1930s
10 *CT*, 10 November 1916; 5 December 1916
11 *RDM*, 17 April 1918
12 Jones, 'The Lebombo Intelligence Scouts'
13 RAFM, Henderson papers, AC 71/4/1, has examples of such correspondence
14 Vann and Waugh 'Presentation Aircraft 1914–1918'
15 *CT*, 26 July 1917; 1 November 1917; 29 August 1917
16 *CT*, 29 October 1917; *RDM*, 5 December 1917; 8 December 1917
17 *CT*, 26 July 1917
18 *CT*, 1 May 1918
19 *RDM*, 8 December 1917
20 TNA, CO 616/70, Telegram Buxton to CO, 18 December 1917
21 The *Eastern Province Herald (EPH)*, 8 November 1917
22 *EPH*, 22 November 1917
23 *EPH*, 24 April 1918
24 Phillips, *Bush Horizons*, p. 17; p. 19
25 Tidy, 'They Mounted up as Eagles'

26 *CT*, 14 January 1915
27 *CT*, 16 August 1915
28 *CT*, 10 September 1915
29 TNA, CO 616/46, WO/CO, forwarding his Telegram for the South African High Commissioner in London, 30 August 1915
30 *CT*, 23 November 1915; TNA, CO 323/693, 9 November 1915, list
31 See Silberbauer, 'The Origins of South African Military Aviation'
32 Davenport and Saunders, *South Africa: A Modern History*, pp. 284–91
33 Anderson, *The Forgotten Front*, p. 180
34 TNA, CO 616/55, Telegrams Buxton/CO, 24 July and 19 August 1916; Buxton Dispatch No. 953, 22 August 1916, forwarding South Africa's conditions of employment; CO 616/57, Telegram Buxton/CO, 22 November 1916
35 Lloyd George, *War Memoirs,* Vol. 1, pp. 1032–4
36 Marks, 'Jan Smuts, race and the South African war'
37 Kennedy, *British Quakerism, 1860-1920*, p. 436
38 Marks, 'Jan Smuts, race and the South African war'
39 *BP*, 6 January 1916
40 Paice, *Tip and Run*, pp. 295–6
41 *BP*, 13 April 1912
42 Mahncke, 'Aircraft Operations in the German Colonies'; Silberbauer, 'The Origins of South African Military Aviation'
43 Australian Premier Billy Hughes was also invited, but declined—Millar, *Australia in Peace and War*, p. 111
44 Wrench, *Alfred Lord Milner*, p. 336
45 Grigg, *Lloyd George: War Leader*, pp. 246–52
46 *The Times*, 8 July 1918; *BC*, 30 August 1918
47 Samson, *1914-1918: The Union Comes of Age*, p. 180
48 Cmd. 8707, December 1952
49 Hyam and Henshaw, *The Lion and the Springbok*, p. 102; p. 107

Chapter 13: The Indian Empire: The sub-continent and Burma
1 Vann and Waugh, 'Presentation Aircraft 1914–1918', p. 50 and India list
2 *The Times*, 24 May 1919
3 Stevenson, *With Our Backs to the Wall*, p. 257
4 Henig 'Foreign Policy', pp. 204–30
5 Morrow Jnr., *The Great War*, p. 81
6 Das, 'Indians at home: Mesopotamia and France, 1914–1918'
7 Anon., *The Army in India and Its Evolution*, pp. 174–5
8 Hardinge, *My Indian Years, 1910-1916*, p. 103
9 Molkentin, *Australia and the War in the Air*, p. 77; p.80; p. 84
10 Quoted in *Gwalior's Part in the War*, pp. 48–9
11 Vann and Waugh 'Presentation Aircraft 1914–1918', India list
12 *The Army in India*, p. 175
13 The *Times of Ceylon (ToC)*, 16 July 1915; *Flight*, 30 July 1915; 13 January 1916
14 The *Statesman*, 24 June 1915; 9 July 1915; 16 July 1915; 17 September 1915; 26 November 1915
15 Das, 'Indians at home: Mesopotamia and France, 1914–1918'

16 *Flight*, 24 December 1915; 13 January 1916; 30 March 1916
17 *Times of India Illustrated Weekly*, 4 August 1915
18 Vann and Waugh, 'Presentation Aircraft 1914–1918'
19 Harper and Miller, *Singapore Mutiny*
20 Hardinge, *My Indian Years*, p. 102; pp. 127–8; Hopkirk, *On Secret Service East of Constantinople*, pp. 179–94; James, *The Eyes of the Navy*, p. 155; Pati, *India and the First World War*, pp. 98–135; Popplewell, *Intelligence and Imperial Defence*, pp. 235–6; p. 238
21 RAFM, X005-0949, Nicholl, 'Journeys and Recollections', pp. 75-7
22 It found its way eventually into the Royal Aircraft Museum, Hendon
23 Nicholl, 'Journeys and Recollections'
24 Karaka, *Fabulous Mogul*, p. 13
25 Bawa, *The Last Nizam*, pp. 71–4
26 Karaka, *Fabulous Mogul*, p. 67; Bawa, *The Last Nizam*, p. 74
27 www.raf.mod.uk/history/110squadron, accessed 2014
28 See Noorani, *The Destruction of Hyderabad*
29 Karaka, *Fabulous Mogul*, p. 66
30 See Kwarteng, *Ghosts of Empire*, Ch. 9
31 BL, V/10/520, 'Administration Report of the Government of India for 1916–17', Part I, p. iii
32 BL, V/10/520, 'Report on the Administration of Burma for the year 1916–17', p. 10; Scott, *Burma from the Earliest Times*, p. 355
33 Craddock, *Speeches by Sir Reginald Craddock*, p. 19
34 The *Weekly Rangoon Times and Overland Summary (RT)*, various dates in 1915
35 Myint-U, *The River of Lost Footsteps*, p. 189
36 *RT*, 24 July 1915
37 *RT*, 16 October 1915; 15 January 1916
38 *RT*, 2 September 1916
39 Myint-U, *The Making of Modern Burma*, pp. 216–7; pp. 234–5
40 *RT*, 20 November 1915; 26 August 1916
41 Hopkirk, *On Secret Service East of Constantinople*, pp. 179–94
42 See the *Bangkok Times Weekly Mail (BT)* 25 March–21 August 1916
43 BL, V/10/520, 'Administration Report of the Government of India for 1916–17', Part II, p.10
44 Thesiger, *Speeches by Lord Chelmsford*, pp. 154–5
45 TNA, AIR 1/14/15/1/52; AIR 1/14/15/1/56
46 *RT*, 23 September 1916
47 *RT*, 1 June 1918
48 TNA, AIR 76/523/146, his service record
49 *Flight*, 20 January 1921, p. 48
50 Hunt, *Dancing in the Sky*, p. 53
51 *Ibid.* p. 103; p. 106; p. 115
52 Winegard, *Indigenous Peoples of the British Dominions*, p. 202
53 TNA, AIR 76/360/88; AIR 76/479/34; AIR 76/336/166
54 Mentioned in Taylor, 'Naval Eight's First Ace'
55 Foley, *Pioneers of Aerial Combat*, p. 92; Martyn, *Swift to the Sky*, p. 48

56 TNA, AIR 76/438/159, his service record; Sapru, 'I. L. Roy of 40 Squadron'
57 Malik, *A Little Work, A Little Play*; TNA AIR 76/331/93, his service record
58 Paris, 'Air Power & Imperial Defence 1880–1919'
59 *The Army in India*, p. 176
60 Vann and O'Connor, 'Wings over Suez'; TNA, AIR 1/2423/305/18/24, A.4428 India Office, 28 September 1918
61 Renfrew, *Wings of Empire*, pp. 174–6
62 *Ibid.* p. 147; *The Army in India*, p. 176
63 James, *Churchill and Empire*, p. 165
64 See Renfrew, *Wings of Empire*

Chapter 14: Birds of Ceylon—a very strange campaign indeed

1 Ashton, 'Ceylon', pp. 455–6
2 Jones, ''Permanent Boarders': The British in Ceylon, 1815–1960'
3 *Oxford Dictionary of National Biography*
4 Eg. Chalmers, 'The King of Siam's Edition of the Pali Tipitaka'
5 Cf. Cambridge University Faculty of Asian and Middle Eastern Studies, The Rhys Davids family archive, RD J/6/6; RD J/21
6 Revell, *Brief glory: the life of Arthur Rhys Davids;*—an 'ace' was someone who had shot down more than 5 enemy aircraft
7 Van der Vat, *The Last Corsair*, p. 61; p. 64
8 Lucas, *The Empire at War*, Vol. 5, pp. 360–6
9 *Yearbook of the Planters' Association of Ceylon, 1917*, p. 28c
10 TNA CO 54/782, Dispatches, 31 May 1915; 1 June 1915; 7 June 1915
11 De Souza, *Hundred Days in Ceylon Under Martial Law*, p. 2
12 *RT*, 10 July 1915
13 TNA, FCO 141/2088: eg. Chalmer's Dispatch, 22 July 1915, appearing to draw on a 'statement of views' by the Inspector General of Police
14 TNA, CO 54/785, Dispatch, 14 October 1915
15 TNA, CO 54/784, Dispatch forwarding press accounts, 30 September 1915
16 Perera, 'Memorandum upon Recent Disturbances in Ceylon'
17 De Silva, 'The Reform and Nationalist Movements'
18 The *Ceylon Morning Leader (CML)*, 3 December 1915
19 TNA, CO 54/795, Dispatch, 27 June 1916
20 TNA, CO 54/804, Dispatch 26 May 1917, original emphases
21 *ToC*, 4 August 1915
22 *ToC*, 21 August 1915
23 Wrench, *Struggle*, p. 143
24 *Yearbook of the Planters' Association of Ceylon, 1916*
25 *ToC*, 16 October 1915; 14 October 1915; 27 October 1915; 9 November 1915
26 *ToC*, 2 November 1915; 15 November 1915; 29 November 1915
27 *ToC*, 22 February 1916
28 *CML*, 28 October 1915
29 *ToC*, 17 December 1915
30 *ToC*, 1 October 1915; 7 October 1915
31 *ToC*, 1 October 1915; 7 October 1915; 20 October 1915
32 *ToC*, 30 October 1915

33 *ToC*, 28 October 1915
34 *ToC*, 2 June 1916
35 *Reuters*, 28 July 1915
36 *Hansard*, Debates 28 September 1915, Vol. 74, col. 736
37 *ToC*, 16 October 1915
38 *ToC*, 9 October 1915
39 *ToC*, 9 September 1915
40 *ToC*, 22 February 1916
41 *ToC*, 18 October 1915
42 *ToC*, 12 October 1915
43 Perera, 'Memorandum upon Recent Disturbances in Ceylon'
44 *CML*, 2 September 1915; 4 September 1915; 20 September 1915
45 Lucas, *The Empire at War*, Vol. 5, p. 366; *ToC*, 13 September 1915
46 TNA CO 54/784, Dispatch of 10 September 1915 enclosing De Saram's letter
47 Vann and Waugh, "Presentation Aircraft, 1914–1918', Ceylon list
48 TNA, FCO 141/2089/2, Dispatch 12 June 1917 enclosing de Mel's letter; *CML*, 14 June 1917
49 *Ceylon Daily News (CDN)*, 16 March 1918
50 *The Year Book of the Ceylon Reform League 1917–1918*
51 *CML*, 13 June 1917
52 TNA, CO 54/805, Dispatch, 2 August 1917
53 *CDN*, 4 March 1918; *Ceylon: A General Survey*, pp. 53–8; MacMillan, *Seaports of India and Ceylon*, pp. 440–1
54 *CDN*, 16 March 1918; 21 March 1918
55 *CML*, 21 September 1915; 29 October 1915
56 TNA CO 54/784, papers CO/WO/Governor
57 *CML*, 22 June 1917
58 Reimann, *A History of Trinity College Kandy*, pp. 160–9
59 The Report along with Anderson's covering dispatch of 26 May 1917 was reprinted and published by the *CML*, whose editor was Armand de Souza
60 TNA, CO 54/805, Dispatch, 21 December 1917
61 *Yearbook of the Planters' Association of Ceylon, 1917*, p. 28m.
62 TNA, CO 54/805, Dispatch 31 December 1917
63 *CDN*, 24 March 1918
64 TNA, FCO 141/2089/4, Original bound copy with signatures
65 TNA, FCO 141/2089/3, Colonial Secretary's Office Colombo/Herbert Bois, Ceylon Chamber of Commerce and Planters' Association, 18 April 1918
66 *CDN*, 11 September 1918
67 De Silva, 'The Reform and Nationalist Movements'
68 Eg. Hulugalle, *British Governors of Ceylon*, Ch. xxi

Chapter 15: Furthest ripples of the Great War reach Abyssinia and Siam
1 Fedorowich, 'The British Empire on the Move'
2 Hyam, *Britain's Declining Empire*, p. 8
3 Marcus, *A History of Ethiopia*, pp. 104–5
4 Pankhurst, 'Addis Ababa, Capital of Ethiopia'
5 Bahru Zewde, *A History of Modern Ethiopia*, p. 127

6   TNA, FO 371/2593, Dispatch, 4 May 1916
7   TNA, FO 371/2594, Dodds, British Consul Harar/Thesiger, 21 July 1916; Dispatch No. 74 to FO, 3 August 1916
8   TNA, FO 371/2593-4, Dispatch No. 48, 7 May 1916; Dispatch No. 50, 11 May 1916; Dispatch No. 65, 22 June 1916; Dispatch No. 91, 20 September 1916
9   Bahru Zewde, *A History of Modern Ethiopia*, pp. 127–8
10 TNA, FO 371/2594, Dispatch No. 107, 31 October 1916
11 He was the eldest. The other three sons were Brian (b. 1911), Dermot (b. 1914), and Roderic (b. 1915)
12 Thesiger, *A Life of My Choice*, p. 26; p. 51
13 Black, *The Great War and the Making of the Modern World*, p. 123
14 The *Illustrated War News (IWN)*, 11 April 1917
15 *Flight*, 29 August 1918; *ODM*, 14 September 1918; *The Times*, 21 August 1918
16 Vann and Waugh, 'Presentation Aircraft 1914–1918'
17 The Italians had used aircraft to bomb Turkish positions near Tripoli in 1911–12 and they were used in reconnaissance and bombing in the French conquest of Morocco 1912–14; in 1916 the RFC flew in an operation against the Dervishes in Darfur, Sudan—Killingray, 'A Swift Agent of Government'
18 Dunckley, *Eight Years in Abyssinia*, pp. 51–2
19 Mockler, *Haile Selassie's War*, p. 11
20 Marcus, *A History of Ethiopia*, p. 129
21 Dunckley, *Eight Years in Abyssinia*, p. 52
22 *BT*, 12 January 1918, quoting Statistical Yearbook of Siam figures for 1915–16
23 Greene, *Absolute Dreams*, p. 104
24 Dossett, *Who's Who in Malaya 1918*
25 *BT*, 2 June 1916
26 *BT*, 8 October 1915; 9 February 1917
27 Vann and Waugh 'Presentation Aircraft 1914–1918'
28 Hamilton-Paterson, *Marked for Death*, p. 196
29 *BT*, 2 October 1915; 25 October 1915; 14 January 1916; 29 March 1916; 15 April 1916; Vann and Waugh 'Presentation Aircraft 1914–1918'
30 *BT*, 22 January 1916
31 *BT*, 21 February 1916; Wright, *Twentieth Century Impressions of Siam*, p. 287; p. 290
32 *BT*, 21 July 1916
33 *BT*, 15 September 1916
34 *The Times*, 14 March 1917
35 *BT*, 2 June 1916; 2 May 1917; 22 May 1918; 13 June 1918
36 Young, *Aerial Nationalism*, p. xxix
37 *BT*, 18 January 1911; 3 February 1911; 7 February 1911; 10 February 1911
38 *BT*, 6 February 1911
39 *BT*, 3 May 1913; Young, *Aerial Nationalism*, p. 3; p. 4
40 Lumholdt and Warren, *History of Aviation in Thailand*
41 *BT*, 14 January 1914; diary entry quoted in Vella, *Chaiyo!* pp. 85–6
42 Greene, *Absolute Dreams*, pp. 102–3
43 Vella, *Chaiyo!* p. 110

44 *Ibid.* p. 104; Greene argues in contrast that he simply took the first opportunity to do what he had long wanted, bring Siam into the war
45 Greene, *Absolute Dreams*, p.106; p.108
46 *Ibid.* p. 110
47 From the official communiqué—*BT*, 21 September 1917
48 Hart, 'A Note on the Military Participation of Siam in the First World War'
49 Young, *Aerial Nationalism*, pp. 10–11
50 Greene, *Absolute Dreams*, p. 104
51 *BT*, 21 August 1916—an editorial commented that 'India has reason for also acknowledging the services of the British Consulates in this country'
52 Young, *Aerial Nationalism*, p. 21
53 Vella, *Chaiyo!* pp. 85–6
54 *Ibid.* pp. 122–4
55 There was a Brazilian parallel with Siam: after the country declared war on the Central Powers in October 1917, Brazil concluded an agreement with Britain to give Brazilian pilots advanced instruction at British flying schools. They arrived in January–February 1918, but the Armistice put an end to their formal training and they returned home in 1919—Hart, 'Brazilians in Britain—1918'
56 TNA, FO 371/3127, Telegrams Rome/FO, 21 February 1918; FO/Rome, 11 March 1918

Chapter 16: Big and small donors: The Shanghai Race Club and Argentine Britons

1 Miners, *Hong Kong under Imperial Rule*, p.7
2 Khoo, *More Than Merchants*
3 Straits Settlements Colonial Report No. 862 for 1914
4 Bickers, 'Shanghailanders and Others', Table
5 Bickers, 'Shanghailanders', p. 270; p. 277
6 The *Shanghai Times (ShT)*, 10 February 1915
7 Feldwick, *Present Day Impressions of the Far East*, p. 382
8 *ShT*, 13 February 1915; 22 February 1915
9 *ShT*, 28 February 1915; 11 May 1915
10 The *North-China Herald (NCH)*, 6 November 1915
11 Patriotic League of Britons Overseas, *Second Annual Report*
12 *NCH*, 6 March 1915; 24 April 1915
13 *NCH*, 15 May 1915
14 Feldwick, *Present Day Impressions of the Far* East, p. 387; NCH, 26 June 1915
15 *NCH*, 22 May 1915
16 *NCH*, 4 September 1915
17 *ShT Christmas Supplement*, 1917
18 *NCH*, 3 April 1915
19 *NCH*, 12 June 1915
20 See Bujak, *Reckless Fellows*
21 *NCH*, 24 July 1915; Bickers, *Getting Stuck in for Shanghai*, pp. 30–1
22 *NCH*, 27 November 1915; TNA, AIR 76/493/118, his service record
23 *NCH*, 29 January 1916
24 Feldwick, *Present Day Impressions of the Far East*, p. 401; p. 554

25 Betta, 'From Orientals to Imagined Britons: Baghdadi Jews in Shanghai'
26 Bickers, *The Scramble for China*, p. 366; p. 368
27 Feldwick, *Present Day Impressions of the Far East*, p. 382
28 http://racingmemories.hk, accessed 2015
29 TNA, AIR 76/445/40, his service record
30 Paris, *Winged* Warfare, p. 86; Grace's *Guide to British Industrial History*, accessed 2015: www.gracesguide.co.uk/Ellice_Victor_Sassoon
31 The *Aeroplane*, 9 May 1912, p. 448, p. 450; and 27 June 1912, p. 628, p. 630
32 http://racingmemories.hk
33 Bickers, *Britain in China*, p. 132
34 Rose, Memorandum on 'German Trade in Shanghai', 12 February 1915, in Jarman, *Shanghai Political and Economic Reports*, Vol.12
35 *Asia*, Journal of the American Asiatic Assoc. November 1918, p. 984
36 Vann and Waugh, 'Presentation Aircraft 1914–1918', China list
37 As revealed in press lists of winners and runners-up at race meetings
38 *ShT*, 27 November 1917, has a full listing
39 *Buenos Aires Herald* (weekly edition) *(BAH)*, 13 April 1917
40 The *Magellan Times (MagT)*, 4 October 1917
41 Holder, *Activities of the British Community in Argentina*, p. 203; Albert, *South America and the First World War*, p.41; p.47; pp. 61–2
42 *BAH*, 9 March 1917; 18 May 1917; however, exports in general stagnated 1914–18—see Gravil, *The Anglo-Argentine Connection 1900–1939*, Ch. 5, pp. 111–50
43 *BAH*, 2 February 1918
44 The *Review of the River Plate (RRP)*, 1 December 1916
45 *RRP*, 19 March 1915
46 Rock, 'The British of Argentina'
47 Holder, *Activities of the British Community*, p. 13; pp. 210–11
48 *Ibid.* p. 300
49 Thompson, *The Empire Strikes Back? The Impact of Imperialism,* p. 113; p. 116; Mackenzie, *Propaganda and Empire*, pp. 155–6; pp. 231–4
50 *BAH*, 6 August 1915
51 *BAH*, 3 September 1915
52 *BAH*, 10 September 1915
53 *BAH*, 3 December 1915; 7 January 1916
54 Holder, *Activities of the British Community*, p. 15; p. 119; p. 257
55 *Ibid.* p. 117
56 Eg. *BAH*, 4 February 1916
57 *Hansard*, Vol. 110, cols. 3410–1 (20 November 1918)
58 Miller, 'The Second Regiment, King Edward's Horse'
59 Colville-Jones, *Your Ever Loving Son; BAH* (daily ed.), 8 January 1918
60 *BAH*, 22 January 1915
61 *BAH*, 28 January 1916
62 TNA, AIR 76/162/48, his service record
63 Rock, 'The British of Argentina'
64 *RRP*, 5 May 1916; *MagT*, 6 June 1918
65 Vann and Waugh, 'Presentation Aircraft 1914–1918'

66 *MagT*, 18 May 1916; 25 May 1916; 22 June 1916
67 *MagT*, 6 July 1916; 13 July 1916; 27 July 1916

Chapter 17: Charles Alma Baker and the Australian Air Squadrons Fund
1 *The Times*, 23 September 1915; 27 January 1916
2 Australian War Memorial figures—www.awm.gov.au
3 See Beckett, *The Making of the First World War*, Ch. 3 'The Making of a Nation'
4 Molkentin, *Fire in the Sky*, p. 337
5 Cutlack, *The Australian Flying Corps*, p. 64
6 Molkentin, *Australia and the War in the Air*, pp. 147–9; p. 156
7 As attested in journals and memoirs—Seward, *Wings over the Desert*; Hynes, *Lawrence of Arabia's Secret Air Force*
8 Keneally, *Australians: Eureka to the Diggers*, pp. 382–4; Molkentin, *Australia*, pp. 175–88
9 *Ibid.* p. 9; pp. 15–16; p. 29
10 Australian War Memorial, *An overview: The Australian Flying Corps*, accessed November 2013; the South Africans formed a small aviation corps early on that was dissolved and absorbed into the RFC
11 Molkentin, *Fire in the Sky*, p. 109; p. 116; *Australia*, p. 178
12 Vann and Waugh, 'Presentation Aircraft 1914–1918': Australia listing
13 Sutherland, *Aces and Kings*, p.20 – 2 other Bristol Fighters flown by 1 Squadron AFC shared the same serial number (C4623): *NSW Nos. 7 and 18.*
14 Molkentin, *Australia*, p. 29—confusingly, 1st Squadron AFC was No. 67 (Australian) Squadron RFC; and the 2nd, 3rd, and 4th Squadrons AFC were Nos. 69, 68, and 71 (Australian) Squadrons RFC respectively
15 Macdonald, *Imperial Patriot*, pp. 51–4
16 Alma Baker, *94 Battleplanes*
17 RAFM, Henderson papers, AC 71/4/1, no.25, Henderson/Birch, 25 June 1916
18 Alma Baker, *94 Battleplanes*
19 TNA, AIR 1/142/15/40/314
20 The *Austral Briton*, 16 September 1916, Special War Supplement
21 Quoted in *Austral-Briton* special supplement, 16 September 1916
22 *ToM*, 15 August 1917, quoting from 'The Soldier'
23 *Sydney Morning Herald (SMH)*, 3 October 1916
24 Quoted in Alma Baker, *94 Battleplanes*
25 *SMH*, 12 July 1917
26 Excepting Newfoundland where, lacking towns of any size, presentation aeroplanes other than *Reid-Newfoundland* were simply *Newfoundland Nos. 1–4*
27 Keneally, *Australians: Eureka to the Diggers*, p. 366
28 *SMH*, 25 September 1917—letter from 'a Soldier's Mother'
29 Alma Baker, *94 Battleplanes*
30 TNA, CO 881/14/1, Confidential Print Australian No. 217, August 1913
31 Ward, *The History of Australia*, pp. 104–5
32 Judging from the press photograph, this may well have been Mabel Strickland, the equally fearless editor of the *Times of Malta* during the Second World War
33 The *Sydney Mail (SM)*, 6 September 1916
34 Hayes, *Billy Stutt and the Richmond Flyboys*

35 *Ibid.* p. 20
36 TNA, CO 881/15/6, Australian No. 231, Section 4—Aviation Pilots 1916-1918
37 'Premier's Report—Mission to UK and France, July 1917' quoted in Hayes, *Billy Stutt*, p. 123
38 Molkentin, *Australia*, pp. 46-7
39 TNA, AIR 1/142/15/40/314, Annex 87/Aeroplanes/2155, Under Secretary of State CO/Secretary WO, 13 March 1917; but with this author's emphases
40 Alma Baker, *94 Battleplanes*
41 TNA, AIR 1/142/15/40/315, Griffiths/Secretary WO, 14 April 1917; WO/Griffiths, 24 April 1917
42 TNA, AIR 1/142/15/40/315, Various communications
43 Molkentin, *Australia*, p. 212
44 TNA, AIR 1/142/15/40/314, Flyer contained in 'Annex 87/Aeroplanes/1701'
45 TNA, AIR 1/678/21/13/2186, Memorandum by the Official Air Historian, J. C. Nerney, 'Design and Supply of Aircraft 1914-1918', 5 February 1935
46 Cooper, *The Birth of Independent Air Power*, pp. 85-6
47 TNA, AIR 1/142/15/40/314, 'Annex 87/Aeroplanes/1701', DADAE brief, 20 June 1917
48 Edgerton, *England and the Aeroplane*, pp. 11-12
49 See inset on p. 44
50 TNA, CO 448/14, Straits Settlements Dispatch, 9 March 1918, with enclosure
51 Eg. TNA, CO 448/14, 9 March 1918 letter, Government of South Australia/CO
52 TNA, CO 448/18, Governor Straits Settlements, telegram 9 January 1919
53 Dye, 'Biffy Borton's Bomber'
54 *Malaya No. 15*, a BE2e, was still on RAF charge in Egypt in January 1919, latterly at 3 School of Navigation and Bomb Dropping at Almaza/Helwan—Vann and Waugh, 'Presentation Aircraft 1914-18', p. 82; Davis, 'RFC/RAF Training Units in Egypt', p. 72
55 TNA, CO 616/81-2, CO internal minutes, January 1919, on his request for appreciative remarks for inclusion in souvenir *94 Battleplanes*
56 Macdonald, *Imperial Patriot*, Ch. 11 'Compost and Cosmic Forces'
57 *Ibid.* pp. 64-75
58 *Ibid.* Ch. 12 'In the Twilight of a Long and Full Life'

Chapter 18: New Zealand and Britain's aeroplane gifts to the Dominions
1 Beckett, *The Great War*, p. 92
2 Watson, *W. F. Massey*, p. 49; p. 58
3 Belich, *Paradise Reforged*, p. 96
4 Winegard, *Indigenous Peoples*, p. 80; p. 99; p. 103; p. 157
5 Cowan, *Maoris in the Great War*, p. 8
6 Belich, *Paradise Reforged*, pp. 44-6
7 *HKT*, 7 February 1913
8 Paris, *Winged Warfare*, p. 98
9 IAFC booklet, *The New Link and Spirit of the Empire*, p. 4
10 Pollock, *Kitchener*, pp. 445-6
11 Jones, *Peace and War*, p. 135
12 Brendon, *Eminent Edwardians*, p. 80

13 Davenport-Hines, *Ettie*, p. 143
14 *Ibid.* pp. 67–8; p. 78
15 Baring, *RFC HQ 1914–1918*; he was also a cousin of Caroline Rhys Davids, and in touch following the death in France of her son—Revell, *Brief Glory*, p. 204
16 See Collins, *Charmed Life*
17 Davenport-Hines, *Ettie*, p. 172–3; TNA, AIR 1/2423/305/18/23, IAFC leaflet May 1918
18 Paris, *Winged Warfare*, p. 97
19 Jones, *Peace and War*, pp. 144–5
20 *Flight*, 31 May 1913
21 www.teara.govt.nz/en/biographies
22 The *Aeroplane*, 12 June 1913, p. 685
23 *The New Link and Spirit of the Empire*, p. 6
24 Martyn, *Swift to the Sky*, p. 19
25 Paris, *Winged Warfare*, p. 98
26 TNA, AIR 1/755/204/4/84; Vann and Waugh, 'Presentation Aircraft', p. 66
27 *Flight*, 8 June 1916; 10 May 1917
28 *Flight*, 4 October 1917; 1 November 1917; 14 February 1918; 7 March 1918; 9 May 1918; 6 June 1918; 13 June 1918; Vann and Waugh 'Presentation Aircraft 1914–1918'
29 *The New Link and Spirit of the Empire*, p. 8
30 The *Manchester Guardian*, 4 March 1918
31 Sapru, 'Flying Sikh—Hardit Singh Malik'
32 Martyn, *Swift to the Sky*, p. 53
33 *MT*, 14 December 1915
34 Farland, *Farmer Bill*, p. 279
35 I am indebted to David Howlett for this observation
36 Ward, *The History of Australia*, p. 111
37 TNA, AIR 1/2423/305/18/23, IAFC leaflet May 1918
38 Sapru, 'Flying Sikh'; *The New Link and Spirit of the Empire*, p. 23
39 *Ibid.*
40 Letter quoted in Alma Baker, *94 Battleplanes*
41 *Ibid.*
42 Paris, 'Air Power and Imperial Defence'
43 Pirie, *Air Empire: British Imperial Civil Aviation*, pp. 17–18
44 *The Times*, 5 February 1919
45 Hunt, *Dancing in the Sky*, pp. 24–5
46 *Ibid.* pp. 107–8; pp. 304–5
47 *The Times*, 21 December 1918
48 TNA, AIR 76/279, his service record; Pollock, *Kitchener*, p. 363
49 *The Times*, 11 May 1918; 22 January 1919
50 Vann and Waugh, 'Presentation Aircraft 1914–1918', p. 93
51 TNA, AIR 1/14/15/1/50
52 *Overseas*, Vol. 4, March 1919
53 *Aeronautics*, 12 February 1919
54 *The Times*, 5 February 1919

55 TNA, AIR 1/14/15/1/50, HQ Overseas Military Forces of Canada London/ Director of Air Equipment, Air Ministry, 31 January 1919
56 Molkentin, *Australia*, p. 210
57 *The New Link and Spirit of the Empire*, p. 23; information on the original 'British Petroleum' from www.bp.com
58 *Flight*, 10 May 1917
59 www.saairforce.co.za, accessed 2013
60 *CT*, 22 March 1920
61 See Pirie, *Air Empire*, pp. 39–44
62 TNA, CO 448/21, 'Honours', Correspondence March–May 1920
63 *The New Link and Spirit of the Empire*
64 *The Times*, 16 April 1918
65 *The Times*, 14 May 1918
66 Vann and Waugh, 'Presentation Aircraft 1914–1918', p. 51
67 *Ibid.*—the papers are to be found on TNA, AIR 1/14/15/1/56
68 Martyn, *Swift to the Sky*, p. 48; p. 52
69 Ross, *Royal New Zealand Air Force*, Vol. 1, pp. 8–10; pp. 13–14
70 TNA, CO 752/6, referring to telegram Governor Liverpool/CO, 4 July 1916
71 Vann and Waugh, 'Presentation Aircraft 1914–1918'; *ODM*, various dates
72 Watson, *W. F. Massey*, p. 50
73 TNA, CO 209/300, Lord Liverpool/Milner, 5 June 1919, 66th quarterly secret report
74 Wrench, *Struggle*, pp. 207–15

Chapter 19: Cast list: minorities, colonials, 'subject peoples' and native rulers
1 *Pinang Gazette and Straits Chronicle* (daily edition), 16 November 1936
2 Oong Hak Ching, *Chinese Politics in Malaya*, p. 51
3 See Boot and Sturtivant, *Gifts of War*, which has detailed listings
4 *Ibid.* p. 16
5 Jackson, *The British Empire*, p. 260; p. 263
6 *NP*, 1 October 1915
7 TNA, CO 96/550, Dispatch, 21 December 1914
8 Arsan, *Interlopers of Empire*, pp. 39–40
9 Eg. in Jamaica—De Lisser, *Jamaica and the Great War*, pp. 106–7
10 Schatowski Schilcher, 'The Famine of 1915–1918 in Greater Syria'
11 *DG*, 6 November 1915
12 An expression loosely filched from Darwin, *The Empire Project*, as encapsulating the spirit of the enterprise
13 See Devine, *To the Ends of the Earth*
14 Devine, *Scotland's Empire*—Ch.13 'Warriors of Empire'
15 Devine, *The Scottish Nation*, p. 309
16 Olusoga, *The World's War*, p. 200
17 Of English West Country origin, Ridout had been trained at the Royal Military College of Canada, where his father was Captain of Cadets
18 *RDM*, 14 June 1916
19 *CT*, 25 September 1918
20 TNA, AIR 1/903/204/5/779

21 Morrow Jnr., 'The War in the Air', p. 158
22 *Ibid.* p. 162; p. 163
23 See Mathews, 'Reluctant Allies: Nigerian Responses to Military Recruitment', pp. 96–103, for the scale of forced carrier service in Nigeria and resistance to it
24 Killingray and Matthews, 'Beasts of burden', p. 9; pp. 21–2; Killingray, 'Military and Labour Policies in the Gold Coast'
25 Cf. Bayly, *The Birth of the Modern World*, pp. 204 ff on the neglected importance of war and conflict in explaining the emergence of nationalisms
26 Cf. Cannadine, *Ornamentalism*
27 Wrench, *Struggle*, p. 141
28 RAFM, Henderson papers, AC 71/4/1, no. 349, Wigram/Henderson, 16 October 1916; Henderson/Wigram, 17 October 1916

Chapter 20: The orchestration of support—the British Empire's last curtain call?
1 Written answer to arranged parliamentary question, 21 August 1917
2 Vann and Waugh, 'Presentation Aircraft 1914–1918'
3 TNA, AIR 1/14/15/1/52, Air Ministry minutes, 9 July 1919
4 Ferguson, *Empire: How Britain Made the Modern World*, p. 317
5 Morris, *Farewell the Trumpets: An Imperial Retreat*, pp. 207–11
6 Holland, 'The British Empire and the Great War', p. 136
7 Quoted in Butcher, *The British in Malaya*, p. 125
8 May, 'Founding Father'
9 *CDN*, 14 February 1918
10 Ban Kah Choon, *Absent History*; Popplewell, *Intelligence and Imperial Defence*
11 *MT*, 8 March 1915
12 *MT*, 21 April 1915
13 *MT*, 9 September 1915
14 Popplewell, *Intelligence and Imperial Defence*, pp. 263–4
15 *Ibid.* pp. 246–7.
16 There is a very entertaining account of the 'Christmas Day plot' and its nemesis in Hopkirk, *On Secret Service East of Constantinople*
17 TNA, FO 628/33/354
18 See Robertson, *The Battle of Penang*, pp. 63–4 etc.
19 TNA, WO 154/326, War Diary General Staff Branch, Straits Settlements
20 *BT*, 25 March 1916; 27 March 1916; 15 April 1916; 14 August 1916; 21 August 1916
21 *BT*, 21 August 1916
22 Popplewell, *Intelligence and Imperial Defence*, pp. 80–1; p. 265
23 See the Table on p. 240
24 Jones, *Peace and War*, p. 139
25 Palmer, *Letters from Mesopotamia*
26 Revell, *No. 56 Sqn. RFC/RAF*
27 *BT*, 14 May 1918—as reported by Herbert Sloley's cousin, Charles H. Ramsay, resident in Siam; Revell, *Brief Glory*, p. 200

Bibliography I—Primary Sources:

Newspapers and periodicals   **Key**

Aeronautics	
The Aeroplane	
Austral-Briton (Australia)	
Buenos Aires Herald*	BAH
Bulawayo Chronicle	BC
Bloemfontein Post	BP
Bangkok Times Weekly Mail	BT
Ceylon Daily News	CDN
Ceylon Morning Leader	CML
Cape Times	CT
Daily Argosy (British Guiana)	DA
Dominica Chronicle	DC
Dominica Guardian	
Daily Gleaner (Jamaica)	DG
Daily Mail Overseas Edition – see Overseas Daily Mail	
Daily News (Newfoundland)	DN
Eastern Province Herald (South Africa)	EPH
Evening Telegram (Newfoundland)	
Flight	
Gold Coast Leader	GCL
Gold Coast Nation	GCN
Hong Kong Telegraph	HKT
Illustrated London News	ILN
Illustrated War News	IWN
Lagos Weekly Record	LWR
Magellan Times (Chile)	MagT
Malaya Tribune	MT
Manchester Guardian	
Nigerian Pioneer	NP
North-China Herald	NCH
Overseas	
Overseas Daily Mail	ODM
Planters & Commercial Gazette (Maur.)	PCG
Pinang Gazette & Straits Chronicle*+	PGSC
Port of Spain Gazette	PoSG
Pall Mall Gazette	PMG

Rand Daily Mail	RDM
Rhodesia Herald*	RH
Review of the River Plate	RRP
Rangoon Times & Overland Summary	RT
South China Morning Post	SCMP
Straits Echo	SE
Singapore Free Press	SFP
Sydney Mail	SM
Sydney Morning Herald	SMH
Shanghai Times	ShT
Straits Times	ST
Statesman (Calcutta)*	
The Times	
Times of Ceylon	ToC
Times of India Illustrated Weekly	
Times of Malaya	ToM
Times of Nigeria	ToN
West India Committee Circular	WICC
* weekly edition	
+ mail edition	

Note: In the case of *The Times* news items are often sourced from the published index, and such references in this book are therefore to dates given therein

Other archived material

British Library, Northcliffe papers, Additional MS 62222, Wrench/Northcliffe letter, 25 June 1912; Additional MS 62223—Overseas Club Empire Day 1918 leaflet

British Library, Wrench papers, Additional MS 59,563-6; 59,570; 59, 572

British Library, India Office records, V/10/520

Cambridge University Faculty of Asian and Middle Eastern Studies, The Rhys Davids family archive, RD J/6/6; RD J/21

Imperial War Museum, IWM Cat.No.23153, Robin Hughes Chamberlain taped interview 1971; IWM Cat.No.3765, Arthur Harris taped interview 1978

Imperial War Museum, AVM Hazelton Robson Nicholl papers, IWM documents no. 21698, with manuscript 'Journeys and Recollections' and notebook

Royal Air Force Museum, X005-0949, AVM Hazelton Nicholl, 'Journeys and Recollections' typescript, with photographs (1950)

Royal Air Force Museum, Sir David Henderson Papers, AC 71/4/1

The National Archive Kew (TNA), Air Ministry Historical, AIR 1, series as detailed in the references
TNA, AIR 76 series, individual service records as detailed
TNA Cabinet Office: CAB 45/218; memoranda as detailed in the references
TNA, Colonial Office: in the series CO 54; CO 96; CO 129; CO 152; CO 209; CO 273; CO 323; CO 417; CO 448; CO 583; CO 616; CO 618; CO 646; CO 688; CO 715; CO 752; CO 881, as detailed
TNA, Foreign Office: in the series FO 84; FO 369; FO 371, as detailed
TNA, Foreign and Commonwealth Office 'migrated' files: FCO 141/821; 141/2088; 141/2089/1-4
TNA, Ministry of Munitions: MUN 4/3945
TNA, War Office: WO 154/326
The Royal Archive: RA PS/PSO/GV/PS/WAR/QQ9/05199 (Quoted from the Royal Archive with the gracious permission of Her Majesty Queen Elizabeth II)

Books, articles, reports and speeches

Alma Baker, Charles, *94 Gift Battle Planes which Fought in the Great War 1914–1918* (privately published London: 1920)
Anti-Slavery and Aborigines' Protection Society, *Annual Report for 1915* (London: 1916)
—*Annual Report for 1916* (London: 1917)
Baring, Maurice, *RFC HQ 1914–1918* (London: 1920)
Bell, Sir Henry Hesketh, *Glimpses of a Governor's Life, from diaries, letters and memoranda* (London: 1946)
—*Witches and Fishes* (London: 1948)
Braddell, Roland, *The Lights of Singapore* (London: 1934)
Casely Hayford, J. E., *Writings of Ekra-Agiman (J. E. Casely Hayford)*, Vol. 1, Introduction by Tom Lodge (Bristol and Tokyo: 2003)
Ceylon Morning Leader, 'Report of a Commission appointed by His Excellency the Governor to inquire into and report upon the circumstances connected with the shooting of L. Romanis Perera and nine others', reprinted by permission of the Government of Ceylon (Colombo: 1917)
Clifford, Sir Hugh, Introduction to W. Walton Claridge, *A History of the Gold Coast* (London: 1915) pp. xiv–xv
Colvill-Jones, Lorraine, *Your Ever Loving Son: the story of the first Argentine 'ace' of the First World War* (Buenos Aires: 2008)
Craddock, Sir Reginald, *Speeches by Sir Reginald Craddock, Burma, 1917–1922* (Rangoon: 1924)
Dafoe, John W., *The Imperial Press Conference: A Retrospect with Comment*, ('Reprinted for private circulation from The Manitoba Free Press', Winnipeg: 1909)
De Lisser, Herbert G., *Jamaica and the Great War* (Kingston: 1917)

De Souza, Armand, *Hundred Days in Ceylon Under Martial Law in 1915* (London: 1916)
Dunckley, Fan C., *Eight Years in Abyssinia* (London: 1935)
Gluckmann, Emanuel, *The Tragedy of the Ababirwas, and Some Reflections on Sir Herbert Slolely's Report*, Reprinted from the Rand Daily Mail (Johannesburg: 1922)
Hamelius, Paul, *The Siege of Liège* (London: 1914)
Hardinge, Charles, Baron Hardinge of Penshurst, *My Indian Years, 1910–1916: The reminiscences of Lord Hardinge of Penshurst* (London: 1948)
Holder, Arthur L. (ed.), *Activities of the British Community in Argentina during the Great War 1914–1919* (Buenos Aires: 1920)
IAFC booklet, *The New Link and Spirit of the Empire: 'Plane Pioneers of an Imperial Air Fleet* (London: 1920)
Ingrams, W. H., *Zanzibar: its History and its People* (London: 1931)
Jingoes, Stimela Jason, *A Chief is a Chief by the People: The Autobiography of Stimela Jason Jingoes*, recorded and compiled by John and Cassandra Perry (London: 1975)
Leclezio, Henri, 'People and Politics', in Allister Macmillan (ed.), *Mauritius Illustrated: Historical and Descriptive, Commercial and Industrial* (London: 1914), pp. 137–41
Lewis, Cecil, *Sagittarius Rising* (London: 1936)
Lloyd George, David, *War Memoirs of David Lloyd George* Vols. 1 and 2 (London: 1933–36)
Lugard, F. D., *The Dual Mandate in British Tropical Africa* (London: 1922)
Malik, H. S., *A Little Work, A Little Play: The Autobiography of H. S. Malik* (New Delhi: 2009)
Overseas Club booklet, 'The Imperial Aircraft Flotilla' (London: May 1916)
Palmer, Robert, *Letters from Mesopotamia in 1915 and January, 1916* (privately printed London: 1926)
Patriotic League of Britons Overseas, *Second Annual Report* (London: January 1917)
Pearce, Major F. B., *Zanzibar: The Island Metropolis of Eastern Africa* (London: 1920)
Perera, Edward W., *Memorandum upon Recent Disturbances in Ceylon* (London: 1915)
Planters' Association of Ceylon, *Yearbook 1916* (Colombo: 1917)
—*Yearbook 1917* (Colombo: 1918)
Purcell, Victor, *The Memoirs of a Malayan Official* (London: 1965)
Rafiullah, Mohammad (compiler), Gwalior Foreign Department, *Gwalior's Part in the War* (privately published London: 1920)
The Ceylon Reform League, *The Year Book of the Ceylon Reform League 1917–1918* (Colombo: 1918)

Rose, Archibald, 'Memorandum on German Trade in Shanghai' in Robert L. Jarman (ed.) *Shanghai Political and Economic Reports 1842-1943,* Vol.12, 1914-1920 (Slough: 2008)
Ruete, Emily Said, *Memoirs of an Arabian Princess of Oman and Zanzibar* (Berlin, 1886—reprint of the original 1907 English translation Coventry: 2008)
Selborne, Lord William Waldegrave Palmer, in Anon., *Some Account of George Grey and his Work in Africa (by men who knew him there)* (privately published, London: 1914), 78-9
—Address of 27 March 1914, *Journal of the African Society*, 13 (1913-14), 353-64
Slolely, H. C., 'The African Native Labour Contingent', *Journal of the Royal African Society*, 17:67 (1918), pp. 199-211
Sutherland, L. W, *Aces and Kings* (London: 1985 ed.—first published Sydney 1935)
Swettenham, Sir Frank, *British Malaya: An account of the origin and progress of British influence in Malaya* (London and New York: 1906)
—*Footprints in Malaya* (London, New York and Melbourne: 1942)
Thesiger, Frederic John Napier, *Speeches by Lord Chelmsford, Viceroy and Governor General of India* (Simla: 1919)
Thesiger, Wilfred, *A Life of My Choice* (London: 1987)
Urban, Frank, *Ned's Navy: The Private Letters of Edward Charlton from Cadet to Admiral* (Shrewsbury: 1998)
Wrench, John Evelyn, *Uphill: The First Stage in a Strenuous Life* (London: 1934)
—*Struggle, 1914-1920* (London: 1935)

Bibliography II—Secondary Sources:

Official UK publications

Lucas, Sir Charles, *The Empire at War*, Vols. 2 and 5 (Oxford: 1926)
Command Paper Cmd. 8707 'Basutoland, the Bechuanaland Protectorate and Swaziland: History of Discussions with the Union of South Africa 1909–1939' (HMSO: December 1952)
Basutoland Colonial Report 1915–1916
Straits Settlements Colonial Report No. 862 for 1914
Zanzibar *Blue Book* 1913

Reference works

BSAC Historical Catalogue and Souvenir of Rhodesia, Empire Exhibition (Johannesburg: 1936–37)
Ceylon: A General Survey (Colombo: 1924)
Dossett, J. W., *Who's Who In Malaya 1918* (Singapore: 1918)
Feldwick, W. (ed.), *Present Day Impressions of the Far East and Prominent and Progressive Chinese at Home and Abroad* (London: 1917)
Fisher, Julius S., *Who's Who in Malaya 1925* (Singapore: 1925)
Grace's Guide to British Industrial History
Grotpeter, John J., *Historical Dictionary of Swaziland* (Metuchen New Jersey: 1975)
MacMillan, Allister, *Seaports of India and Ceylon* (London: 1928)
The Oxford Dictionary of National Biography
Wills, Walter H. (ed.), *The Anglo-African who's who and biographical sketchbook 1907*, (London: 2006 reprint)
Wright, Arnold, (ed.), *Twentieth Century Impressions of British Malaya: Its History, People, Commerce, Industries, & Resources* (London: 1908)
—*Twentieth Century Impressions of Siam: Its History, People, Commerce, Industries, & Resources* (London: 1910)

Books and articles

Anon., *The Army in India and Its Evolution, including an account of the establishment of the Royal Air Force in India* (Delhi: 1985 reprint of government printing Calcutta, 1924)
Acquah, Benjamin, *Cocoa Development in West Africa: the early period with particular reference to Ghana* (Accra: 1999)
Addo-Fening, Robert, *Akyem Abuakwa 1700–1943* (Trondheim: 1997)
Albert, Bill, *South America and the First World War: the impact of the war on Brazil, Argentina, Peru and Chile* (Cambridge: 1988)

Anderson, Ross, *The Forgotten Front: The East African Campaign 1914-1918* (Stroud: 2014 edition)

Arsan, Andrew, *Interlopers of Empire: The Lebanese Diaspora in Colonial French West Africa* (London: 2014)

Ashton, S. R., Ch. 19 'Ceylon' in Brown and Louis *The Oxford History of the British Empire: The Twentieth Century*

Ban Kah Choon, *Absent History: The Untold Story of Special Branch Operations in Singapore, 1915-1942* (Singapore: 2001)

Barnes, J. A., *Politics in a Changing Society: A Political History of the Fort Jameson Ngoni* (London: 1954)

Bahru Zewde, *A History of Modern Ethiopia 1855-1974* (London, Athens Ohio and Addis Ababa: 1991)

Baughen, Greg, *Blueprint for Victory: Britain's First World War Blitzkrieg Air Force* (Stroud: 2014)

Bawa, V. K., *The Last Nizam: The Life and Times of Mir Osman Ali Khan* (New Delhi: 1992)

Bayly, C. A., *The Birth of the Modern World 1780-1914* (Oxford: 2004)

Beckett, Ian F. W., *The Great War 1914-1918* (Harlow: second edition, 2007)

—*The Making of the First World War* (New Haven and London: 2012)

Begbie, Harold, *Albert fourth Earl Grey: A Last Word* (London: 1917)

Belich, James, *Paradise Reforged: A History of the New Zealanders, From the 1880s to the Year 2000* (Auckland: 2001)

Betta, Chiara, 'From Orientals to Imagined Britons: Baghdadi Jews in Shanghai', *Modern Asian Studies,* 37:4 (2003), 999-1023

Bickers, Robert, *Britain in China: Community, Culture and Colonialism 1900-1949* (Manchester and New York: 1999)

—*Empire Made Me: An Englishman Adrift in Shanghai* (London: 2003)

— 'Shanghailanders and Others, 1843-1957: British Communities in China, 1843-1957' in Bickers (ed.) *Settlers and Expatriates: Britons over the Seas* (Oxford: 2010)

—*The Scramble for China: Foreign Devils in the Qing Empire 1832-1914* (London: 2011)

—*Getting Stuck in for Shanghai: The British at Shanghai and the Great War* (London: 2014)

Black, Jeremy, *The Great War and the Making of the Modern World* (London and New York: 2011)

Boahen, Adu, *Ghana: Evolution and Change in the Nineteenth and Twentieth Centuries* (London: 1975)

Boot, Henry and Ray Sturtivant, *Gifts of War: Presentation Aircraft in Two World Wars* (Tonbridge: 2005)

Booth, Alan R., 'Lord Selborne and the British Protectorates, 1908-1910', *Journal of African History,* 10:1 (1969), 133-48

Brendon, Piers, *Eminent Edwardians: Four figures who defined their age: Northcliffe, Balfour, Pankhurst, Baden-Powell* (London: 2003)

—*The Decline and Fall of the British Empire 1781–1997* (London: 2008)
Brown, Judith M. and Wm. Roger Louis, *The Oxford History of the British Empire: The Twentieth Century* (Oxford: 1999)
Bujak, Edward, *Reckless Fellows: The gentlemen of the Royal Flying Corps* (London and New York: 2015)
Butcher, John G, *The British in Malaya, 1880–1941: The Social History of a European Community in Colonial South-East Asia* (Oxford: 1979)
Cain, P.J and A. G. Hopkins, *British Imperialism: Innovation and Expansion 1688–1914* (London and New York: 1993)
Cannadine, David, *Ornamentalism: How the British saw their Empire* (London: 2002)
Carroll, John M., *Edge of Empires: Chinese Elites and British Colonialism in Hong Kong* (Cambridge Massachusetts and London: 2005)
Carvalho, Manuel, *A Guerra que Portugal quis esquecer: O desastre do exército português em Moçambique na Primeira Guerra Mundial* (Oporto: 2015)
Chalmers, Robert, 'The King of Siam's Edition of the Pali Tipitaka', *Journal of The Royal Asiatic Society* (1896), 1–10
Chung Po-Yin, Stephanie, 'Migration and Enterprise: The Eu Yan Sang Firm and the Eu Kong-pui Family in Foshan, Penang and Hong Kong' in Yeoh Seng Guan, Loh Wei Leng, Khoo Salma Nasution and Neil Khor (eds.), *Penang and Its Region: The Story of an Asian Entrepôt* (Singapore: 2009)
Collins, Damian, *Charmed Life: The Phenomenal World of Philip Sassoon* (London: 2016)
Conrad, Sebastian, *German Colonialism: A Short History* (Cambridge: 2012)
Cooksley, Peter G., *Royal Flying Corps Handbook 1914–1918* (Stroud: 2007)
Cooper, Malcolm, *The Birth of Independent Air Power: British Air Policy in the First World War* (London: 1986)
Cowan, James, *Maoris in the Great War: A History of the New Zealand Native Contingent and Pioneer Battalion, Gallipoli, 1915, France and Flanders, 1916–1918* (Auckland: 1926)
Coxhead, J. C. C., *The Native Tribes of North-Eastern Rhodesia: Their Laws and Customs*, Royal Anthropological Institute Occasional Paper No. 5 (London: 1914)
Crofton, R. H., *Zanzibar Affairs 1914–1933* (London: 1953)
Crowder, Michael, 'The 1914–1918 European war and West Africa' in J. F. Ade Ajayi and Michael Crowder (eds.), *History of West Africa*, Vol. 2 (London: 1974)
Cutlack, F. M., *The Australian Flying Corps in the Western and Eastern Theatres of War 1914–1918*, The Official History of Australia in the War of 1914–1918, Vol. 8 (Sydney: 1923)
Darwin, John, *The Empire Project: The Rise and Fall of the British World-System 1830–1970* (Cambridge: 2009)
—*Unfinished Empire: The Global Expansion of Britain* (London: 2012)

Das, Santanu, 'Indians at home: Mesopotamia and France, 1914–1918' in Santanu Das (ed.) ... *Race, Empire and First World War Writing* (Cambridge: 2011)

Davenport, Rodney and Christopher Saunders, *South Africa: a Modern History* (Basingstoke: fifth edition, 2000)

Davenport-Hines, Richard, *Ettie: The Intimate Life and Dauntless Spirit of Lady Desborough* (London: 2008)

Davis, Mick, 'RFC/RAF Training Units in Egypt', *Cross & Cockade International Journal*, 47:1 (2016)

Deal, Michael, 'Newfoundland's First Air War', *Newfoundland Quarterly*, 101:3 (2008)

De Silva, K.M, 'The Reform and Nationalist Movements in the early Twentieth Century' in K. M. de Silva (ed.), *History of Ceylon Vol. 3* (Colombo: 1973)

Devine, T. M., *Scotland's Empire: The Origins of the Global Diaspora* (London: 2003)

—*To the Ends of the Earth: Scotland's Global Diaspora, 1750–2010* (London: 2011)

—*The Scottish Nation: A Modern History* (London: 2012 edition)

Devine, T. M and John M. MacKenzie, 'Scots in the Imperial Economy' in MacKenzie and Devine (eds.) *Scotland and the British Empire* (Oxford: 2011)

Dickinson, Frederick R., *War and National Reinvention: Japan in the Great War, 1914–1919* (Cambridge Massachusetts and London: 1999)

—'The Japanese Empire' in Gerwarth and Manela (eds.), *Empires at War 1911–1923* (Oxford: 2014)

Dye, Peter 'Royal Naval Air Service Operations in German East Africa, 1914–1918: Part I', *Cross & Cockade International Journal*, 37:3 (2006)

—'Royal Naval Air Service Operations in German East Africa, 1914–1918: Part II', *Cross & Cockade International Journal*, 37:4 (2006)

—'Biffy Borton's Bomber', in *Lawrence of Arabia & Middle East Air Power* (Cross & Cockade International: 2016)

Edgar, Robert, 'Lesotho and the First World War: Recruiting, Resistance and the South African Native Labour Contingent', *Mohlomi, Journal of Southern African Historical Studies* (1981), 94–108

Edgerton, David, *England and the Aeroplane: Militarism, Modernity and Machines* (London: 1991)

Epstein, Katherine C., 'Imperial Airs: Leo Amery, Air Power and Empire, 1873–1945', *Journal of Imperial and Commonwealth History*, 38:4 (December 2010), 571–98

Falola, Toyin, and A. D. Roberts, Ch. 22 'West Africa', in Brown and Louis, *The Oxford History of the British Empire: The Twentieth Century*

Farland, Bruce, *Farmer Bill: William Ferguson Massey and the Reform Party* (Wellington: 2008)

Fedorowich, Kent, 'The British Empire on the Move, 1760–1914' in Sarah Stockwell (ed.), *The British Empire: Themes and Perspectives* (Oxford: 2008)
Ferguson, Niall, *The Pity of War 1914–1918* (London: 1998)
—*Empire: How Britain Made the Modern World* (London: 2004)
Finnegan, Terrence J., *Shooting the Front: Allied Aerial Reconnaissance in the First World War* (Stroud: 2011)
Foley, Michael, *Pioneers of Aerial Combat: Air Battles of the First World War* (Barnsley: 2013)
Frost, Diane, *Work and Community Among West African Migrant Workers Since the Nineteenth Century* (Liverpool: 1992)
Gailey, Harry A., *Clifford: Imperial Proconsul* (London: 1982)
Gann, L. H., *A History of Northern Rhodesia: Early Days to 1953* (London: 1964)
—*A History of Southern Rhodesia: Early Days to 1934* (London: 1965)
—*Central Africa: The Former British States* (New Jersey: 1971)
Gerwarth, Robert and Erez Manela (eds.), *Empires at War 1911–1923* (Oxford: 2014)
Gollin, Alfred, *The Impact of Air Power on the British People and their Government, 1909–14* (London: 1989)
Grant, Kevin, *A Civilised Savagery: Britain and the New Slaveries in Africa, 1884–1926* (New York and London: 2005)
Gratton, Robert F., *The Origins of Air War: The Development of Military Air Strategy in World War I* (London: 2009)
Gravil, Roger, *The Anglo-Argentine Connection 1900-1939* (Boulder, Colorado: 1985)
Greene, Stephen Lyon Wakeman, *Absolute Dreams: Thai Government Under Rama VI, 1910–1925* (Bangkok: 1999)
Grigg, John, *Lloyd George: War Leader, 1916–1918* (London: 2011)
Grundlingh, Albert, *Fighting Their Own War: South African Blacks and the First World War* (Johannesburg: 1987)
—'The Impact of the First World War on South African Blacks', in Page (ed.), *Africa and the First World War*
Gullick, J. M., *Rulers and Residents: Influence and Power in the Malay States 1870–1920* (Singapore: 1992)
Hamilton-Paterson, James, *Marked for Death: The First War in the Air* (London: 2015)
Harper, R. W. E., and Harry Miller, *Singapore Mutiny* (Oxford: 1984)
Hart, Keith, 'A Note on the Military Participation of Siam in the First World War', *Journal of the Siam Society*, 70 (1981)
—'Brazilians in Britain—1918', *Cross & Cockade GB Journal*, 16:2 (1985)
Hart, Peter, *Aces Falling: War Above the Trenches, 1918* (London: 2007)
Hayes, Neville F., *Billy Stutt and the Richmond Flyboys: The New South Wales State Aviation School 1915–1918 and Beyond* (Victoria: 2008)

Heartfield, James, *The Aborigines' Protection Society: Humanitarian Imperialism in Australia, New Zealand, Fiji, Canada, South Africa, and the Congo, 1836–1909* (London: 2011)

Henig, Ruth, 'Foreign Policy' in Stephen Constantine, Maurice W. Kirby and Mary B. Rose (eds.), *The First World War in British History* (London and New York: 1995)

Hernon, Ian, *Britain's Forgotten Wars: Colonial Campaigns of the Nineteenth Century* (Stroud: 2003)

Hill, Robert (ed.), *The Marcus Garvey and Universal Negro Improvement Association Papers Vol. VIII* (Berkeley California: 1995)

Ho Tak Ming, *Ipoh: When Tin Was King* (Ipoh: 2009)

Hodges, Geoffrey, Ch. 7 'Military Labour in East Africa and its Impact on Kenya' in Page (ed.), *Africa and the First World War*

Holden, Philip, *Autobiography and Decolonization: Modernity, Masculinity, and the Nation-state* (Madison Wisconsin: 2008)

Holland, Robert, 'The British Empire and the Great War, 1914–1918' in Brown and Louis, *The Oxford History of the British Empire: The Twentieth Century*

Honychurch, Lennox, *The Dominica Story: A History of the Island* (London and Basingstoke: 1995)

Hopkirk, Peter, *On Secret Service East of Constantinople: The Plot to Bring Down the British Empire* (Oxford: 2001)

Hough, Richard, *Dreadnought: A History of the Modern Battleship* (London: 1964)

Hulugalle, H. A. J., *British Governors of Ceylon* (Colombo: 1963)

Hume, Peter, 'Islands and Roads: Hesketh Bell, Jean Rhys, and Dominica's Imperial Road', *The Jean Rhys Review*, 11:2 (2000), 23–51

Hunt, C. W., *Dancing in the Sky: the Royal Flying Corps in Canada* (Toronto: 2009)

Hyam, Ronald, *Britain's Declining Empire: The Road to Decolonisation 1918–1968* (Cambridge: 2006)

—*Understanding the British Empire*, Cambridge: 2010

Hyam, Ronald, and Peter Henshaw, *The Lion and the Springbok: Britain and South Africa since the Boer War* (Cambridge: 2003)

Hynes, James Patrick, *Lawrence of Arabia's Secret Air Force: based on the diary of Flight Sergeant George Hynes* (Barnsley, South Yorkshire: 2010)

Isaacman, Allen F., *The Tradition of Resistance in Mozambique: Anti-Colonial Activity in the Zambesi Valley 1850–1921* (London: 1976)

Jackson, Ashley, *War and Empire in Mauritius and the Indian Ocean* (Basingstoke: 2001)

—*The British Empire and the Second World War* (London and New York: 2006)

James, Lawrence, *The Rise and Fall of the British Empire* (London: 1994)

—*Churchill and Empire: Portrait of an Imperialist* (London: 2013)

James, Admiral Sir William, *The Eyes of the Navy: A Biographical Study of Admiral Sir Reginald Hall* (London: 1955)

Jarrett, Philip, 'Ho Fook,' *Cross & Cockade GB Journal*, 6:3 (1975), pp. 133–135
Jefford, C. G., *Observers and Navigators and other non-pilot aircrew in the RFC, RNAS and RAF* (London: 2014)
Jones, H. A., 'Sir David Henderson, father of the Royal Air Force', *Journal of the Royal Air Force College*, 11:1 (1931), 6–12
Jones, Huw M., *A Biographical Register of Swaziland to 1902* (Pietermaritzburg: 1993)
—'The Lebombo Intelligence Scouts', *Military History Journal*, 12:6 (2003)
Jones, Margaret, "Permanent Boarders': The British in Ceylon, 1815–1960' in Bickers (ed.), *Settlers and Expatriates*
Jones, Nigel, *Peace and War: Britain in 1914* (London: 2014)
Judd, Dennis, *Radical Joe: A Life of Joseph Chamberlain* (Cardiff: 1993 edition)
—*Empire: The British Imperial Experience from 1765 to the Present* (London: 2012 edition)
Karaka, Dosabhai Framji, *Fabulous Mogul: Nizam VII of Hyderabad* (London: 1955)
Keegan, John, *The First World War* (London: 1998)
Keneally, Thomas, *Australians: Eureka to the Diggers* (Sydney: 2011)
Kennedy, Thomas C., *British Quakerism, 1860–1920: The Transformation of a Religious Community* (Oxford: 2001)
Keppel-Jones, Arthur, *Rhodes and Rhodesia: The White Conquest of Zimbabwe 1884–1902* (Pietermaritzburg: 1983)
Khoo Salma Nasution, *More Than Merchants: A History of the German-speaking Community in Penang, 1800s–1940s* (Penang: 2006)
Khoo Salma Nasution and Abdur-Razzaq Lubis, *Kinta Valley: Pioneering Malaysia's Modern Development* (Ipoh: 2005)
Killingray, David, 'World War I in the Gold Coast', *Journal of African History*, 9:1 (1978)
—'A Swift Agent of Government: Air Power in British Colonial Africa 1916-1939', *Journal of African History*, 25:4 (1984)
Killingray, David, and James Matthews, 'Beasts of burden: British West African carriers in the First World War', *Canadian Journal of African Studies*, 13:1/2 (1979)
Kimble, David, *A Political History of Ghana 1850–1928* (Oxford: 1963)
Kirk-Greene, Anthony, 'On Governorship and Governors in British Africa' in L. H. Gann and Peter Duigan (eds.), *African Proconsuls: European Governors in Africa* (New York: 1978)
Kwarteng, Kwasi, *Ghosts of Empire: Britain's Legacies in the Modern World* (London: 2011)
Lagden, Sir Godfrey, *The Basutos: the Mountaineers and their Country*, Vol. II, (London: 1909)
Layman, R. D., *Naval Aviation in the First World War* (London: 1996)
Lee, Vicky, *Being Eurasian: Memories Across Racial Divides* (Hong Kong: 2004)

Lee Thompson, J., *Politicians, The Press and Propaganda: Lord Northcliffe and the Great War, 1914–1919* (Kent Ohio and London: 1999)

—*Northcliffe: Press Baron in Politics 1865–1922* (London: 2000)

—'Selling the Mother Country to the Empire: The Imperial Press Conference of June 1909' in Julie F. Codell (ed.), *Imperial Co-Histories: National Identities and the British and Colonial Press* (New Jersey, London and Ontario: 2003)

Long, B. K., *Drummond Chaplin. His life and times in Africa* (London: 1941)

Lonsdale, John, Ch. 23, 'East Africa', in Brown and Louis *The Oxford History of the British Empire: The Twentieth Century*

Lumholdt, Neils, and William Warren, *History of Aviation in Thailand* (Hong Kong: 1987)

Macdonald, Barrie, *Imperial Patriot: Charles Alma Baker and the History of Limestone Downs* (Wellington: 1993)

—*Cinderellas of the Empire: Towards a history of Kiribati and Tuvalu* (Suva: 2001)

Machobane, L. B. B. J., *Government and Change in Lesotho, 1800–1966* (London: 1990)

Mackenzie, David, 'Eastern Approaches: Maritime Canada and Newfoundland' in Mackenzie (ed.), *Canada and the First World War: Essays in Honour of Robert Craig Brown* (Toronto: 2005)

—'Canada, the North Atlantic Triangle, and the Empire', Ch. 25 in Brown and Louis (ed.) *The Oxford History of the British Empire: The Twentieth Century*

Mackenzie, John M., *Propaganda and Empire: The Manipulation of British Public Opinion, 1880–1960* (Manchester: 1984)

McIntyre, W. David, Ch. 29 'Australia, New Zealand, and the Pacific Islands' in Brown and Louis (eds.), *The Oxford History of the British Empire: The Twentieth Century*

McLaughlin, Peter, *Ragtime Soldiers: The Rhodesian Experience in the First World War* (Bulawayo: 1980)

—Ch. 6 'The Legacy of Conquest: African Military Manpower in Southern Rhodesia During the First World War' in Page (ed.), *Africa and the First World War*

Magee, Gary B., and Andrew S. Thompson, *Empire and Globalisation: Networks of People, Goods and Capital in the British World, c.1850–1914* (Cambridge: 2010)

Mahncke, J. O. E. O., 'Aircraft Operations in the German Colonies: The South African Aviation Corps (SAAC)', *Military History Journal*, 12:3 (2002)

Makepeace, Walter, 'Concerning Known Persons' in Makepeace, Brooke and Braddell (eds.), *One Hundred Years of Singapore, Vol. 2* (London: 1921)

Manela, Erez, *The Wilsonian Moment: Self-Determination and the International Origins of Anti-colonial Nationalism* (Oxford: 2007)

Marcus, Harold G., *A History of Ethiopia* (Berkeley Los Angeles and London: 1994)

Marks, Shula, Ch. 24 'Southern Africa', in Brown and Louis, *The Oxford History of the British Empire: The Twentieth Century*
—'Before "the white man was master and all white men's values prevailed"? Jan Smuts, race and the South African war', text of lecture given at the Southern Africa Documentation and Cooperation Centre (SADOCC) and the University of Vienna, 24 October 2000
Marques, Ricardo, *Os Fantasmas do Rovuma: A epopeia dos soldados portugueses em África na I Guerra Mundial* (Alfragide: 2012)
Marshall, P. J. (ed.), *Cambridge Illustrated History of the British Empire* (Cambridge: 1996)
Martin, Ged, 'The idea of "Imperial Federation"', in Ronald Hyam and Ged Martin (eds.), *Reappraisals in British Imperial History* (London & Basingstoke: 1975), pp. 121–138
Martyn, Errol W., with the Air Force Museum of New Zealand, *Swift to the Sky: New Zealand's Military Aviation History* (Rosedale North Shore: 2010)
Massie, Robert K., *Dreadnought: Britain, Germany and the Coming of the Great War* (London: 2007)
Mathews, James K., Ch. 5 'Reluctant Allies: Nigerian Responses to Military Recruitment 1914–18' in Page (ed.), *Africa and the First World War*
May, Alex, 'Founding Father', *Overseas*, 3 (2010), 10–15
Millar, T. B., *Australia in Peace and War: External Relations 1788–1977* (London: 1978)
Miller, David, 'The Second Regiment, King Edward's Horse, 1914–17', *Journal of the Society for Army Historical Research*, 83:333 (2005), 1–10
Miners, Norman, *Hong Kong under Imperial Rule, 1912–1941* (Hong Kong, Oxford and New York: 1987)
Mishra, Pankaj, *From the Ruins of Empire: The Revolt Against the West and the Remaking of Asia* (London: 2012)
Mockler, Anthony, *Haile Selassie's War* (London: 1984)
Molkentin, Michael, *Fire in the Sky: The Australian Flying Corps in the First World War* (Crows Nest NSW: 2012 edition)
—*Australia and the War in the Air* (Melbourne: 2014)
Morris, Jan, *Farewell the Trumpets: An Imperial Retreat* (London: 1998 edition)
Morrow Jr., John H., *The Great War in the Air: Military Aviation from 1909 to 1921* (Washington and London: 1993)
—*The Great War: An Imperial History* (Abingdon and New York: 2004)
—'The War in the Air' in John Horn (ed.), *A Companion to World War I* (Oxford: 2012)
Mottram, Graham, 'The Early Days of the RNAS', *Cross & Cockade GB Journal*, 10:3 (1979), pp. 129–133
Murphy, Philip, 'Britain as a Global Power in the Twentieth Century' in Andrew Thompson (ed.), *Britain's Experience of Empire in the Twentieth Century* (Oxford: 2012)

Myint-U, Thant, *The Making of Modern Burma* (Cambridge: 2001)
—*The River of Lost Footsteps: a Personal History of Burma* (New York: 2007)
Nasson, Bill, *Britannia's Empire: Making a British World* (Stroud: 2004)
Noorani, A. G, *The Destruction of Hyderabad* (London: 2014)
O'Brien, Mike, 'Out of a Clear Sky: The Mobilization of the Newfoundland Regiment, 1914–1915', *Newfoundland and Labrador Studies*, 22:2 (2007)
Officer, Lawrence H. and Samuel H. Williamson, 'Purchasing Power of British Pounds from 1245 to Present', MeasuringWorth (2013)
Olusoga, David, *The World's War* (London: 2014)
Oong Hak Ching, *Chinese Politics in Malaya 1942–55: The Dynamics of British Policy* (Selangor: 2000)
Orwell, George, *Burmese Days* (London: 1986 edition)
Page, Melvin E., *The Chiwaya War: Malawians and the First World War* (Boulder Colorado: 2000)
—(ed.), *Africa and the First World War* (Basingstoke and London: 1987)
Paice, Edward, *Tip and Run: the Untold Tragedy of the Great War in Africa* (London: 2007)
Pakenham, Thomas, *The Scramble for Africa* (London: 1991)
Palmer, David, and Michael Joll, *Tin Mining in Malaya 1800–2000: The Osborne and Chappel Story* (Gopeng Perak: 2011)
Palmer, Robin, *Land and Racial Domination in Rhodesia* (London: 1977)
Paris, Michael, *Winged Warfare: The literature and theory of aerial warfare in Britain, 1859–1917* (Manchester and New York: 1992)
—'Air Power and Imperial Defence 1880–1919', *Journal of Contemporary History*, 4:2 (1989), 209–25
Pankhurst, Richard, 'Addis Ababa, Capital of Ethiopia' in Frederic A. Sharf (ed.), *Letters from Abyssinia: 1916 and 1917 by Major Hugh Drummond Pearson, R.E* (Hollywood California: 2004)
Pati, Budheswar, *India and the First World War* (New Delhi: 1996)
Penrose, Harald, *British Aviation: the Great War and Armistice 1915–1919* (London: 1969)
Phillips, Squadron Leader N. V., *Bush Horizons: The Story of Aviation in Southern Rhodesia 1896–1940* (Harare: 1998)
Pirie, Gordon, *Air Empire: British Imperial Civil Aviation, 1919–39* (Manchester and New York: 2009)
Pollock, John, *Kitchener comprising The Road to Omdurman and Saviour of the Nation* (London: 2001)
Popplewell, Richard James, *Intelligence and Imperial Defence: British Intelligence and the Defence of the Indian Empire, 1904–1924* (London: 1995)
Porter, Bernard, *The Lion's Share: A history of British imperialism 1850 to the present* (Harlow: fifth edition, 2012)
Potter, Simon, *News and the British World* (Oxford: 2003)
Ranger, T. O., *Revolt in Southern Rhodesia 1896–7: A Study in African Resistance* (London: 1967)

Reimann, Valesca L. O., *A History of Trinity College Kandy* (Madras: 1922)
Renfrew, Barry, *Wings of Empire: The Forgotten Wars of the Royal Air Force, 1919-1939* (Stroud: 2015)
Revell, Alex, *Brief Glory: the life of Arthur Rhys Davids, DSO, MC and Bar* (London: 1984)
—*No. 56 Sqn. RFC/RAF* (Oxford: 2009)
Ribeiro de Menezes, Filipe, 'The Portuguese Empire' in Gerwarth and Manela (eds.), *Empires at War 1911-1923*
Robbins, Keith, *Sir Edward Grey: a biography of Lord Grey of Fallodon* (London: 1971)
Robertson, J. R., *The Battle of Penang: 28th October 1914* (Kuala Lumpur: 2012)
Rock, David, 'The British of Argentina' in Bickers (ed.) *Settlers & Expatriates*
Rogan, Eugene, *The Fall of the Ottomans: The Great War in the Middle East, 1914-1920* (London: 2015)
Roger, Thomas, 'Military Recruitment in the Gold Coast during the First World War', *Cahiers d'études africaines*, 15:57 (1975), 57-83
Ross, Squadron Leader J. M. S., *Royal New Zealand Air Force*, Vol. 1 in the Official History of New Zealand in the Second World War 1939-45 (Wellington: 1955)
Rotberg, Robert I., *The Rise of Nationalism in Central Africa: the Making of Malawi and Zambia, 1873-1964* (Cambridge Massachusetts: 1972)
Salt, Beryl, assisted by Wing Cdr. Cooke and Group Capt. Sykes, *The Definitive History of the Rhodesian Air Force 1920-1980* (Johannesburg and London: 2001)
Samson, Anne, *1914-1918: The Union Comes of Age* (London and New York: 2006)
Sapru, Somnath, 'I. L. Roy of 40 Squadron,' *Cross & Cockade GB Journal* 5:1 (1974), pp. 13-14
Sayer, G. R., *Hong Kong 1862-1919* (Hong Kong: 1975)
Scarr, Deryck, *Ratu Sukuna: Soldier, Statesman, Man of Two Worlds* (Suva: 1980)
Schatowski Schilcher, L., 'The Famine of 1915-1918 in Greater Syria' in John P. Pagnolo (ed.), *Problems of the Modern Middle East in Historical Perspective* (Oxford: 1992)
Scott, Sir J. G., *Burma from the Earliest Times to the Present* (London: 1924)
Seward, Desmond, *Wings over the Desert: In action with an RFC pilot in Palestine 1916-18* (Yeovil, Somerset: 2009)
Shennan, Margaret, *Out in the Midday Sun: The British in Malaya 1880-1960* (Singapore: 2015)
Silberbauer, Dick, 'The Origins of South African Military Aviation: 1907-19, from South African Military Archives,' *Cross & Cockade GB Journal*, 7:4 (1976), pp. 174-80
Smith, Leonard V., 'Empires at the Paris Peace Conference' in Gerwarth and Manela, *Empires at War*

Smith, Richard, *Jamaican Volunteers in the First World War: Race, Masculinity and the Development of National Consciousness* (Manchester and New York: 2004)

—'"Heaven grant you strength to fight the battle for your race": nationalism, Pan-Africanism and the First World War in Jamaican memory' in Santanu Das (ed.), *Race, Empire and First World War Writing* (Cambridge: 2011)

Stapleton, Timothy J., *No Insignificant Part: the Rhodesia Native Regiment and the East Africa Campaign of the First World War* (Waterloo Ontario: 2006)

Steiner, Zara, 'The Foreign Office and the War' in F. H. Hinsley (ed.), *British Foreign Policy Under Sir Edward Grey* (Cambridge: 1977)

Stevenson, David, *1914 1918: The History of the First World War* (London: 2004)

—*With Our Backs to the Wall: Victory and Defeat in 1918* (London: 2011)

Stockwell, A. J., 'Sir Hugh Clifford in Malaya, 1927–9', *Journal of the Malaysian Branch of the Royal Asiatic Society*, 53:2 (1980), 21–44

Strachen, Hew, *The First World War* (London: 2003)

Sweetman, John, *Cavalry of the Clouds: Air War over Europe 1914–1918* (Stroud: 2010)

Taylor, A. J. P., *The First World War: An Illustrated History* (Harmondsworth: 1966)

Taylor, S. J., *The Great Outsiders, Northcliffe, Rothermere and the Daily Mail* (London: 1996)

Taylor, Stewart K., 'Naval Eight's First Ace, FSL Daniel Murray Galbraith DSC, French Croix de Guerre', *Cross & Cockade International Journal*, 41:4 (2010)

Thompson, Andrew, *The Empire Strikes Back? The Impact of Imperialism on Britain from the mid-Nineteenth Century* (Harlow: 2005)

Tidrick, Kathryn, *Empire and the English Character: The Illusion of Authority* (London: 2009)

Tidy, Major D. P., 'They Mounted up as Eagles (A brief tribute to the South African Air Force)', *Military History Journal*, 5:6 (1982)

Tooze, Adam, *The Deluge: The Great War and the Remaking of Global Order, 1916–1931* (London: 2014)

Tregonning, K. G., *Straits Tin: A brief account of the first seventy-five years of The Straits Trading Company Limited. 1887–1962* (Singapore: 1962)

Tsang, Steve, *A Modern History of Hong Kong* (London and New York: 2004)

Tylden, G., *The Rise of the Basuto* (Cape Town and Johannesburg: 1950)

Tyler, Paul, *Labour's Lost Leader: The Life and Politics of Will Crooks* (London and New York: 2007)

Van der Vat, Dan, *The Last Corsair: The story of the Emden* (Edinburgh: 2000)

Vann, Ray, and Mike O'Connor, 'Wings over Suez', *Cross & Cockade International Journal*, 47:1 (2016)

Vann, Raymond, and Colin Waugh, 'Presentation Aircraft 1914–1918', *Cross & Cockade GB Journal*, special issue, 14:2 (1983)

Vella, Walter F., *Chaiyo! King Vajiravudh and the Development of Thai Nationalism* (Honolulu: 1978)
Ward, Russel, *The History of Australia: The Twentieth Century 1901–1975* (London: 1978)
Watson, James, *W. F. Massey: New Zealand* (London: 2010)
Webster, J. B., 'Political Activity in British West Africa, 1900–1940', in J. F. Ade Ajayi and Michael Crowder (eds.), *History of West Africa*, Vol.2 (London: 1974)
West, Nigel (ed.), *MI5 in the Great War* (London: 2014)
White, Alan, *The King's Thunderbolts: No.44 (Rhodesia) Squadron Royal Air Force: An Operational Record and Roll of Honour 1917–1982* (Lincoln: 2007)
Williams, Stephanie, *Running the Show: Governors of the British Empire* (London: 2011)
Winegard, Timothy C., *Indigenous Peoples of the British Dominions and the First World War* (Cambridge: 2012)
Wong, C. S., *A Gallery of Chinese Kapitans* (Singapore: 1963)
Wrench, John Evelyn, *Alfred Lord Milner: The Man of No Illusions, 1854–1925* (London: 1958)
Wright, Nadia H., *Respected Citizens: The History of Armenians in Singapore and Malaysia* (Victoria: 2003)
Xu Guoqi, 'China and Empire' in Gerwarth and Manela, *Empires at War*
Yorke, Edmund, 'The Spectre of a Second Chilembwe: Government Missions, and Social Control in Wartime Northern Rhodesia, 1914–18', *The Journal of African History*, 31:3 (1990), 373–91
Youé, Christopher P., *Robert Thorne Coryndon: Proconsular Imperialism in Southern and Eastern Africa, 1897–1925* (Waterloo Ontario: 1986)
Young, Edward M., *Aerial Nationalism: A History of Aviation in Thailand* (Washington and London: 1995)
Zheng, Victor, *Chinese Family Business and the Equal Inheritance System: Unravelling the myth* (Abingdon: 2010)

Unpublished sources

Sadhu, Jagjit Singh, 'British Administration in the Federated Malay States, 1896–1920' (PhD thesis, University of London, January 1975)

Internet resources

www.awm.gov.au;
www.bp.com/en/global/corporate/about-bp/our-history/early-history;
www.clairegrey.co.uk/rd.grandchildren/archie/archie.html;
www.crossandcockade.com;
http://eresources.nlb.gov.sg/infopedia/articles/SIP_570_2005
www.gracesguide.co.uk/Ellice_Victor_Sassoon ;
www.measuringworth.com/ppoweruk;
http://racingmemories.hk;
www.rafweb.org/Biographies/Nicholl.htm;
www.raf.mod.uk/history/110squadron;
www.rhodesia.me.uk
www.saairforce.co.za;
www.teara.govt.nz/en/biographies;
www.25squadron.org.uk/History.htm

Index

A

A. A. Anthony & Co. 123
Abbott, Mac 266, 268
Abeokuta, Alake of 137
Aborigines' Protection Society 137, 142, 156, 181, 313
Aborigines' Rights Protection Society (ARPS) XIII, 137, 141, 142, 143, 144, 147, 148
Adansi, Omanhene of 146
Addison, Dr. 132
Aerial League of the British Empire 17
Aeronautical Society 17
Aftab Ahmed Khan, Sahibzada 292
Ala Bagh, Nawab of 204
Albert, Flt. Lt. Prince 299
Aldenham, Lord 11, 12, 13, 250, 334
Alexandra Aeroplane Fund 92, 307
Alexandra, Queen VII, 36, 37, 45, 92, 105, 162, 307, 315
Ali-bin-Hamoud, Sultan 71
Alma Baker, Charles
    In Malaya 38, 43, 44, 45, 117-26, 131, 133, 163, 232, 293, 309, 322, 324
    In Australia VI, 263, 265-6, 268-9, 270-1, 274, 275, 276, 277, 294, 312, 322, 324
    Post-war VIII, 278, 280, *281*, 296, 304
Amery, Leo 61
Amonoo V, Omanhene of Anamabu 146
Anderson, Sir John 218, 220, 226, 228, 334
Anglo-Persian Oil Co. 202
Angoni 166, 167, 168, 313
Arathoon, Hoseb S. 122, 124
Armenian Relief Fund 123

Army Council VII, 3, 23, 24, 30, 34, 35, 38, 39, 40, 41, 45, 147, 182, 275, 277, 313, 314, 320, 330
Arnhold Karberg & Co. 254
Arnhold, Harry E. 254, 317
Asfa Wossen 234
Ashenheim, Lewis 95
Ashworth Hope, H. 133
Association of British-Chinese Subjects 238
Australian Air Squadrons Fund 121, 263, 266, 267, 270, 271, 275, 276, 277, 279, 280, 310, 322
Australian Flying Corps (AFC) XIII, 264, 265, 274, 276, 279, 300, 310
Australian Light Horse 263, 285

B

Baden-Powell, Sir Robert 62, 332, 335
Baghdadi Jews 108, 123, 203, 252, 254, 306
Bagshaw, Maj. 190
Bahawalpur, Nawab of 204
Baird, Maj. J. E. 199
Baker, Henry D. 98
Baker, Pita Heretaunga 117, 285
Balfour, Arthur 13, 287, 334
Ban Seng Leong 119
Banerjee, Surendranath 60
Barghash, Sultan 69, 70, 71, 73
Baring, Maurice 287
Barker, Maj. Gen. Digby 103
Baroda, Gaekwar of 201
Barton, Charles 300
Barue Rebellion 167
Beaverbrook, Lord 63
Belfield, Sir Henry Conway 72, 74, 79

Bell, Sir (Henry) Hesketh VII, 19, 20, 21, 23, 28, 86, 88, 109
Beresford Melville, Lt. W. 260, 334
Bickford, Mrs. Harry 269
Bikanir, Maharajah of 201, 205
Billy Hughes 276, 293, 310
Bingham, Lt. Col. Sir A. E. 299
Birch, J. W. W. 9
Birch, Sir Ernest 38, 45, 117, 118, 120, 265, 278, 333
Blyden, Edward 148
Bonar Law, Andrew 38, 125, 223, 238, 307, 332
Borton, Brig. Gen. A. E. 264, 278, 279, 310
Botha, Louis 175, 176, 196, 197, 199, 200
Bourchier, Rev. 28
Bowring, Sir Edward 67
Brand, Flt. Lt. 298, 299
Brenon, Herbert 92, 93
British Guiana Aircraft Fund 99
British Military Aeroplane Fund 238
British Society 257, 258
British South Africa Co. (BSAC) XIII, 56, 153, 154, 155, 158, 162, 163, 165, 167, 168
British South Africa Police (BSAP) XIII, 153, 155
British West Indies Regiment (BWIR) XIII, 22, 89, 92, 93, 95, 96
Brittain, Sir Harry 60, 333
Broacha, Sir Shapurji 203
Brockman, Sir Edward L. 8, 122, 132
Brooke, Brig. Gen. Guy 337
Brown, A. S. 227
Brown, Emmanuel Joseph Peter 147
Bruce, John E. 148
Burma War Fund 209, 211
Burmah Oil Co. 207, 208
Burton, Henry 199

Butler, R. 117, 333
Buxton, Lord 155, 174, 177, 178, 179, 180, 182, 188, 192, 194, 196, 329, 332

C

Cain, William E. 18, 290
Calcutta Aeroplane Fund 203
Cargill, John Henry 96
Casely Hayford, Joseph Ephraim VIII, 137, 141, 142, *143*, 147, 148, 306, 312, 319, 322
Central War Fund 89
Ceylon Aeroplane Fund 216, 220, 222, 223, 225, 227, 322
Ceylon Reform League 226, 229
Chakrabongse, Prince 242
Chalmers, Sir Robert 215, 216, 217, 218, 225, 228, 229, 329
Chamberlain, Joseph 19, 20, 57
Chan Kai Ming 106, *107*, 108
Chaplin, Sir Drummond 162
Chapman, Arthur VII, *127*
Charles, Alfred Peter 29, 30
Charlton, Vice Adml. Edward 78, 79, 81
Charun, Prince 243
Chea Chee Seng 238
Chelmsford, Lord 210, 232
Chew Boon Juan 119
Chiang Kai-shek 303
Chilembwe, John 167, 168
China 5, 9, 10, 12, 13, 15, 16, 43, 102, 103, 104, 105, 107, 109, 110, 111, 112, 114, 115, 116, 117, 231, 237, 238, 248, 249, 250, 252, 253, 254, 255, 303, 305, 306, 317
Chinese Chambers of Commerce 122
Chinese Commercial Society of Kingston 307
Chow Kai 119
Churchill, Winston 6, 8, 11, 13, 207, 214, 287

Clark, Alice 197
Clark Gillett, Margaret 197
Clarke, Flt. Sgt. W. (Robbie) 90, 91, 179, 212
Clifford, Col. Henry VIII, *151*
Clifford, Lt. Hugh 149, *150*
Clifford, Sir Hugh Charles V, VIII, 135, 139, 140, 141, 142, 146, 147, 148, 149, *150*, *151*, 152, 225, 306, 313, 322, 329
Colombo Town Guard 216, 219, 220, 223
Colonial Office XII, XIII, 8, 14, 19, 20, 22, 23, 36, 38, 39, 47, 72, 84, 103, 111, 114, 125, 138, 142, 147, 155, 158, 162, 163, 173, 174, 176, 178, 181, 182, 185, 200, 217, 218, 225, 228, 231, 265, 271, 274, 275, 276, 278, 280, 296, 307, 328
Colquhoun-Symington, Lt. 251
Colvill-Jones, Capt. Thomas 32, 260
Committee for the Welfare of Africans in Europe 181
Congress of British West Africa 148, 319
Consolidated Goldfields of South Africa 160, 162
Coryndon, Robert T. 178, 179, 180, 183, 330
Crooks, Will 38, 332
Cull, Flt. Lt. J. J. 75, 76, 77, 78
Cullimore, Capt. 129
Curzon, Lord 56, 287, 334

D

Daily Mail VIII, 17, 29, 33, 55, 56, 58, 59, 60, 61, 62, 63, 189, 194, 242, 320
David Sassoon & Co. Ltd. 252
Davidson, Sir Walter E. 65, 66
Dering, Sir Herbert G. 237, 239, 242, 244, 327

Desborough, Lady Ettie 287, 288, *289*, 328
Desborough, Lord (William Grenfell) 160, 286, 287, 288, *289*, *291*, 292, 328
Douwes Dekker, E. F. E. 326
Drayton, Edward 21, 22, 23
Dreadnoughts 5, 6, 18
Driver, Bok 198
Du Bois, W. B. 148
Dyer, Gen. 205

E

East Africa campaign, African carriers in 74, 79, 167, 313
Eastern Smelting Co. 120
Elcho, Mary 287
Emden 109, 115, 216, 247, 326
Empire Day 29, 47, 62, 99, 104, 113, 115, 257
Empire Press Union 60
English-Speaking Union 302
Eu Tong Sen VII, 7, 38, 40, 110, 116, 117, *119*, 120, 124, 132, 133
Eu Yan Sang (EYS) 132
Eweka II, Oba of Benin 138
Ezra, Edward Isaac 249, 252

F

Faber, Capt. Walter 18
Faridkot, Rajah of 204
Fisher, Maj. Hubert F. 259, 260, 332
FMS Chamber of Mines 119, 120
Foreign Office XIII, 12, 13, 30, 38, 60, 72, 158, 231, 237, 248
Fox, William 92
Franco-Mauritians 86, 87
Fraser, Rev. A. G. 227
Fraser, Sir Everard 12, 248, 249, 250
Fund for the Relief of Polish Jews 95

G

Gan Ngoh Bee 119, 124, 126, *127*
Gandhi, Mohandas (Mahatma) 205, 320, 324
Garland, E. T. C. 133
Garraway, Col. 183
Garros, Roland 25
Garvey, Marcus 148
Gatooma and District Aeroplane Fund 163
George V, King XI, 13, 34, 60, 64, 71, 81, 89, 117, 120, 130, 157, 167, 168, 177, 178, 180, 182, 183, 185, 187, 188, 206, 243, 286, 299, 313, 315, 319, 324, 330
German aircraft mentioned
  Albatros 32
  Fokker E-type monoplane 26, 27, 63, 83, 105, 163
  Gotha bomber 165, 198
Ghadr 205, 210, 244, 324, 325, 326, 327
Gordon, Sqn. Ldr 75, 76
Governor General's Fund 176, 177, 195
Grahame-White, Claude 149, 288
Greenacre, Walter 199
Grenfell, Capt. Francis 328
Grenfell, Col. Harold Maxwell 160
Grenfell, Imogen 287
Grenfell, Julian 286, 287, 328
Grenfell, Monica 288
Grenfell, William (Lord Desborough) 286
Grey, Albert Earl VII, 11, 13, 56, 57, 58, *59*, 60, 61, 113, 153, 154, 159, 287, 329, 332
Grey, Charles G. 253
Grey, Sir Edward 11, 13, 56, 158, 159, 160, 188, 220, 231, 329
Grey, George 159, 188
Grey, Col. Sir Raleigh VIII, 158, 159, 160, *161*, 162, 163
Grey, Zane 280

Griffith Lerotholi, Paramount Chief VIII, 176, 177, 179, 181, *184*, 185, 319
Griffiths, Col. Thomas 275
Gugsa Wule 236
Gwalior, Maharajah Scindia of 202, 203

H

Hackwill, Capt. G. H. 165
Haggard, Sir Rider 270, 334
Haig, Field Marshal Sir Douglas 252, 287
Hamel, Gustav 13, 67, 253, 286, 287, 288, *289*
Harcourt Butler, Sir 209
Harcourt, Lewis 8, 23, 101, 111, 177, 209, 307, 332
Hardinge of Penshurst, Lord 38, 203, 332
Harris, Air Chief Marshal Arthur 165
Haydon, E. 268
Hayne, F. W. 10, 333, 334
Henderson, Lady 191
Henderson, Lt. Gen. Sir David VII, 17, 26, 34, 37, 39, 40, 41, 43, 45, 61, 64, 158, 165, 190, 191, 199, 213, 253, 265, 275, 278, 287, 290, 292, 299, 308, 310, 311, 315, 316, 329
Henderson, Ian 165
Hewett, Sir John 203
Hkun Hsan Gawn 210
HMS *Malaya* 5, 10, 38, 115, 128, 322
HMS *New Zealand* 6, 286
Ho Fook 106, *107*, 108, 112
Ho Kam Tong 106, *107*, 108, 110
Ho Tung, Robert 101, 106, *107*, 108, 110, 112, 114, 315
Hoare, Col. Cuthbert Gurney 296
Hobhouse, Emily 197
Holman, William 274, 275, 276

Horne, Air Mechanic Alfred 96, 309
Howe Browne, Lt. A. R. 164, *170*
Howick, Lord 56
Hudson, Maj. Frank 165
Hudson, Maj. Robert 165
Hughes Chamberlain, Robin 21, 22, 27
Hutton-Mills, Thomas 147
Hyderabad, Osman Ali Khan Nizam of 201, 206, 207, 304, 323

I

Ibrahim II, Sultan of Johore VII, 115, 128, 129, 130, *131*, 206, 314
Idris Shah, Sultan of Perak 7, 8, 9, 10
Immelmann, Max 83, 191
Imperial Air Fleet Committee (IAFC) VIII, XIII, 286, 287, 288, *289*, 290, *291*, 292, 293, 294, *295*, 297, 299, 301, 302, 328, 335
Imperial Aircraft Flotilla V, VII, 3, 17, 30, 32, 33, 34, 35, 36, 38, 39, 40, 41, 42, *48-51*, 55, 63, 64, 66, 67, 97, 99, 104, 113, 143, 148, 159, 162, 163, 166, 194, 196, 203, 211, 219, 224, 229, 232, 265, 299, 303, 304, 307, 310, 311, 313, 314, 316, 317, 320, 321, 322, 327, 329
Imperial federation 57, 68, 294, 321
Imperial Federation League 57
Imperial Maritime League 18
Imperial Patriotic Societies 113
Imperial Press Conference 59, 60
Imperial War Conference 184, 205, 293
Indian princes 8, 205, 206, 315
Indian Soldiers' Fund Committee 203

Irish Unity League 302
Islington, Lord 61, 290, 292, 332
Iyasu, Lij 233, 234, 235

J

Jacottet, Edouard 181
Jaffna Tamils 124, 312
Jamaica Aeroplane Fund 91
Jamaica Contingent Sufferers' Fund 95
Jamaican War Relief Fund 89
Jameson Raid VIII, 155, 159, 160, *161*
Jameson, Dr. Leander Starr VIII, 153, 154, 155, 159, 160, *161*, 166, 167, 168, 169, 332
Japan 110, 111, 112, 141, 264, 303, 317
Jardine Matheson 107, 108
Jayatillaka, D. B. 218, 226
Jayatilleke, Miss D. 222
Jind, Maharajah of 204

K

Kalat, Khan of 204
Kedah, Sultan of 124, 128, 133, 134, 314
Kellerman, Annette VII, 92, 93, 94, 95
Kemp, Sir Edward 297
Kenion, A. N. 133
Khoo Cheow Teong VII, 124, 126, 127
Kidman, Sidney 265, 266
King's African Rifles (KAR) XIII, 75, 167
2nd King Edward's Horse 258, 259, 309
King's Royal Rifle Corps (KRRC) XIII, 157
Kirk, Sir John 69, 70, 332
Kitchener, Field Marshal Lord H. H. 34, 36, 39, 70, 178, 190, 195, 242, 269, 286, 296, 299, 320

Königsberg 75, 77, 79
Kor, Fred de 95
Kraft, Vincent 325
Kru 138

L

Labotsibeni, Queen 187, 188
Lagden, Sir Godfrey 181
Lambert, Mrs. 137
Lane, Capt. Elton 223, 230, 309
Lau Chu Pak 106, *107*, 108, 110
Lawrence, T. E. 264
League of the Empire 257
Lebombo Intelligence Scouts
   (LIS) XIII, 190
Leclezio, Henri 86, 88
Lee Choon Guan 124
Leinst, Fred 280
Leong Eng Khean 119
Leong Sin 119
Lerotholi, Griffith 182, *184*
   see also under Griffith
   Lerotholi, Paramount Chief
Letsie II 175, 182
Lettow-Vorbeck, Lt. Col. von 74, 79, 156
Levy, Adolph 92
Lim Boon Keng, Dr. VII, 116, 122, *123*, 125, 126, 303, 318
Liverpool, Lord 18, 198, 290, 294, 297, 302, 332
Lloyd George, David 33, 39, 67, 197, 198, 215, 277, 293
Lloyd, W. F. 33, 39, 66, 67, 197, 198, 215, 277, 293
Lo Cheung Shiu 106, *107*, 108
Lobengula 153, 154
Loke Yew 110, 133
Londonderry, Lord 297
Long, Walter 179, 209, 228
Lou Htin Wah, Lt. 211
Lugard, Lord Frederick 9, 110, 137, 138, 139, 142, 313
Lukin, Gen. 183

M

Machine Gun Fund
   (Newfoundland) 66,
Machine Gun Fund (South
   Africa) 195, 199
Mackenzie, W. T. 288, 335
Madzimawe, Chief 168
Maguya, Chief 168
Malaya Air Fleet Fund V, 38, 42, 43, 45, 115, 119, 120, 121, 122, 124, 125, 126, 131, 133, 224, 229, 232, 238, 265, 277, 279, 280, 303, 305, 306, 307, 310, 322, 324, 326
Malcolm, Brig. Gen. 217, 229
Malik, Lt. Hardit Singh VIII, 212, 213, *292*
Manning, Sir William 89, 93
Maori 84, 117, 212, 285, 300, 301
Martin, Lt. Oliver Milton 212
Martin, Walter 29
Mary, Queen 13, 330
Massey, William F. 184, 293, 301, 332
Matabeleland Fund 163
Mate Kole, Konor of Manya Krobo 145
May, Sir (Francis) Henry VII, 101, 103, *104*, 105, 109, 110, 111, 112, 113, 114
Mbandzeni 187
McCorry, Capt. Edward 258
McCubbin, Lt. 83, 191
McIntosh, Flt. Sgt. Lancelot 90, 212
McIntyre, Cdr. Duncan C. 326
McMillan, T. R. 90
Meath, Lord 257, 258, 332
Mel, Henry Lawson de 225, 226, 227, 229
Menelik II, Emperor 232, 233
Meyer, Manasseh 123, 124, 306
Mikael, Negus of Wollo 234, 235

Miller, Maj. Allister Mackintosh V, VIII, 187, 188, 189, 190, 191, 192, 193, *194*, 195, 261, 308
Miller, Allister Mitchell (A. M. Miller senior) 188, 189, 190
Milner, Lord Alfred 56, 57, 185, 198, 334
Mix, Tom 280
Mohammed Ariff 122
Montagu of Beaulieu, Lord 18
Montagu, Edwin 205
Morris, Edward 66
Morris, Jan 318
Moses, Lt. James David 212
Moshesh 172, 173, 175, 182, 183, 185
Moshoeshoe 172, 182, 185
Mpeseni II 166, 167

N

Nabha, Maharajah of 204
National Aeronautical Defence Association 18
Navy League 248
New South Wales (NSW) VIII, XIII, 264, 265, 266, 268, 270, 271, 272, 273, 274, 275, 280, 323
Newfoundland Regiment 67, 68
Nicholl, Hazleton Robson 43, 44, 45, 157, 159, 163, 164, 165, 206, 309, 310, 329
Nicholls, Dr. 22
Nigeria Aeroplane Fund 137
Northcliffe, Lord 29, 33, 39, 55–6, 58, 59, 60, 61, 62, 63, 65, 113, 242, 316, 332
Northern Rhodesia Police (NRP) XIII, 166, 168

O

Ofori Atta, Omanhene of Akim Abuakwa VIII, 144, *145*, 146, 148
Oluma, E. S. D. 222

O'May, J. M. 128
Overseas Club VI, VII, 13, 15, 29, 32, 34, 35, 36, 38, 39, 40, 41, 45, 46, 47, 55, 58, 60, 61, 62, 63, 64, 65, 67, 70, 84, 91, 95, 97, 99, 101, 106, 109, 112, 113, 137, 139, 144, 146, 153, 158, 160, 162, 170, 191, 194, 196, 199, 203, 220, 224, 235, 242, 246, 249, 250, 251, 263, 265, 269, 297, 300, 309, 315, 318, 320, 332, 336, 337
Overseas Club Aircraft Fund 32, 46, 47, *48–51*, 65, 109, 113, 139, 195, 242, 250, 251
  Contribution in planes and cash 34, 40, 42–3, 46–7, 63, 113
Overseas Contingent Fund 158
Ovonramwen 138, 139

P

Pachee, K. 126
Pali Text Society (PTS) XIII, 215, 229
Parachatra, Prince 242
Pare, Victor B. 309
Paris Evangelical Mission Society (PEMS) XIII, 175, 181
Parliamentary Aerial Defence Committee 18
Passages Fund 227
Paterson, Compton 183, 195, 198, 309
Patriotic Association 66
Patriotic Committee 256, 257
Patriotic League of Britons Overseas V, VI, 3, 5, 10, 11, 12, 13, 14, 15, 16, 17, 30, 34, 38, 41, 47, 77, 158, 231, 235, 237, 242, 246, 248, 249, 250, 297, 300, 315, 320, 334
Pearce, Maj. F. B 72, 74, 79, 80, 323
Pearce, Senator G. F. 265, 274, 296
Pender, Lt. W. Gordon 164

Perera, E. W. 218, 226
Perez, Mrs. Mary 97, 98, *100*
Petrie, David 327
Presentation aircraft, models mentioned
 Blériot Experimental 2c – BE2c: VII, VIII, 18, 26, 27, 30, 34, 40, 42, 45, 46, 64, 67, 106, 112, 119, 122, 126, *127*, 137, 146, 165, 169, *170*, 190, *246*, 251, 258, 263, 277, 290, 312
 Blériot Experimental 2e – BE2e: VII, *100*, 190, 290
 Blériot monoplane (*Britannia*): 286, 288, *289*
 Bristol Fighter – F2b: VII, 32, 69, 80, *82*, 260, 264, 279, 297, 310
 Caudron biplane (Gaekwar of Baroda gift): 202
 De Havilland 4 – DH4: VIII, 290, *291*, 298
 De Havilland 5 – DH5: 27, 112, 301
 De Havilland 9A – DH9A: 206, 214
 Farman Experimental 2b – FE2b: VII, VIII, 40, 42, 64, 69, *82*, 83, 88, 99, 130, 222, 223, 230, *262*, 268
 Farman Experimental 2d – FE2d: VII, *100*, 268
 Gnome Vickers Gun biplane (Vickers Gunbus) – FB5: V, 17, 24, 26, 30, 34, 36, 40, 42, 45, 64, 67, 83, 251
 Martinsyde Elephant: 290
 Maurice Farman (Gaekwar of Baroda gift): 202
 Reconnaissance Experimental 7 – RE7: 209
 Reconnaissance Experimental 8 – RE8: 69, 112, 128, 137, 209, 211, 213, 290, 292, 299
 Scouting Experimental 5a – SE5a: VIII, 99, 133, 187, 235, *246*, 301
 Short 827 seaplane: VII, 13, 14, *16*, 77, *78*
 Sopwith 1½ Strutter: VII, *16*, 300
 Sopwith Camel: V, VIII, 27, 137, 171, 182, *186*, 213, 292, 309, 330
 Sopwith Pup: 99, 254
 Sopwith Triplane: 238
Presentation names

 As expression of identity 317
 Inscription and transfer 3, 36, 39, 40, 41, 44, 45, 80, 82, 104–5, 127, 299–300
Press Bureau 10, 24, 177, 316
Prince of Wales' Fund 3, 22, 84, 101, 135, 176, 177
Propaganda and counter-subversion 11, 17, 65, 72, 73, 137, 181, 205, 233, 234, 235, 257, 294, 313, 323–8
 See also under *Ghadr*
Punjab Armoured Aeroplane Fleet Fund 204
Purcell, Victor 152

Q

Quist, E. C. 142

R

Ramanathan, Solomon 128
Read, H. H. 250, 251
Red Cross 3, 67, 80, 95, 112, 213, 238, 303, 307, 308
Redemptorist Order 24
Reid, W. D. 46, 66, 67, 68, 250, 251, 332
Rewa, Maharajah of 85, 204
Reynolds, Mr. 268
Rhodes, Cecil 56, 57, 113, 153, 154, 160, 178, 189, 330, 332
Rhodesian Aeroplane Fund 158
Rhodesian Native Regiment (RNR) XIV, 156, 167
Rhys Davids, Arthur 215, 330
Rhys Davids, Thomas and Caroline 215
Rhys, Jean 21
Ridout, Brig. Gen. Dudley 129, 130, 308, 323, 324, 325, 326, 328
Riordan, L. J. 308
Roach, Trooper 309
Robinson, J. A. 66
Rolle, Mr. 22

Rose, Archibald 248, 250, 254
Rosling, Sir Edward 220, 333
Rothermere, Lord 63
Round Table 57
Roy, Indra Lal 213
Royal Air Force (RAF) XIII, 15, 27, 28, 40, 43, 63, 76, 99, 114, 165, 188, 198, 199, 206, 207, 211, 212, 213, 214, 235, 253, 260, 278, 280, 288, 296, 297, 298, 299, 300, 303, 304, 307, 309, 310, 311
Royal Aircraft Factory, Farnborough VII, 18, 26, 34, 36, 37, 162, 202, 258, 315
Royal Colonial Institute (RCI) XIII, 11, 13, 61, 113, 258
Royal Flying Corps (RFC) XIV, 15, 17, 18, 21, 22, 27, 28, 31, 34, 36, 38, 39, 40, 41, 42, 47, 64, 67, 70, 80, 83, 84, 85, 86, 88, 90, 92, 95, 98, 100, 104, 112, 124, 127, 130, 137, 147, 158, 182, 188, 198, 199, 201, 202, 203, 204, 206, 222, 225, 227, 238, 239, 276, 288, 299, 302, 317, 329, 330
  Argentine airmen in 32, 260
  Australian airmen in 263-4, 265, 274-5
  Canadian airmen in 65, 211-2, 290, 296
  'Colonials' in 164, 223, 240-1, 296, 307, 308-9, 311
  Colour bar on flying officer recruitment 90, 191, 211-2
  Fighter pilots as heroes, 'gallant' image 88, 190-1, 215, 251, 311-2
  Indian airmen in 212-4, 292
  New Zealand airmen in 212, 300, 301
  Reconnaissance role 25-6, 33
  Reports on presentation aircraft 43-7, 105-6
  Rhodesian airmen in 163, 164-5
  Rivalry with RNAS 23, 25, 63, 278, 291
  South African airmen in 76, 189-91, 192, 198, 199, 298, 308
  West Indian airmen in 90-1, 96
Royal Naval Air Service (RNAS) XIV, 13, 14, 23, 25, 30, 34, 41, 43, 69, 75, 76, 77, 78, 79, 80, 88, 137, 182, 186, 188, 198, 208, 212, 222, 225, 231, 238, 253, 261, 277, 300, 307, 311, 317, 330
Royal Over-Seas League (ROSL) XIV, 320
Ruete, Frau Emily 70
Russell, J. A. (Archie) 133
Ryneveld, Lt. Col. Pierre van 298, 299

S

Sakd, Maj. Luang 242
Salmond, Air Marshall Sir John 17, 288
Salmond, Brig. Gen. Geoffrey 213
Saram, Frederick John de 222, 225
Saram, Miss Amy de 222
Sarkies Brothers 123, 126
Sassoon, Sir David 203, 252, 306
Sassoon, Edward Elias 253
Sassoon, Sir Philip 252, 287
Sassoon, (Ellice) Victor 253
Sayiri, Chief 168
Schelfhaut, Bishop 24, 25
Scots 43, 65, 107, 120, 157, 189, 190, 208, 256, 260, 301, 307, 308, 327
Seely, Col. 18
Selborne, Lord 10, 11, 12, 13, 34, 38, 56, 158, 171, 172, 181, 187, 329, 332, 334
Self-government, trusteeship, self-determination 35, 57, 81, 148, 171, 183, 200, 215, 226, 318-9
Selous, Frederick 153, 165
Seow Keng Lin 238
Seyyid Khalid-bin-Barghash 71, 79

Seyyid Khalifa-bin-Harub, Sultan of Zanzibar V, VII, 69, 71, 72, 76, 77, 78, 79, 80, 81, 304, 314, 323
Seyyid Muhammed Abdullah Hassan 233, 236
Shackleton, Sir Ernest 261
Shand, Lt. Francis Brian Berkeley 30, 31
Shand, Mrs. Elfreda 31
Shanghai Race Club VI, 247, 250, 251, 252, 253, 254, 306
Shan states 209, 210, 211, 314
Shaw-Stewart, Patrick 328
Shepherd, Frederick 265
Short, Lt. 211
Siam British Subjects Aeroplane Fund 239, 327
Sim Cheng Mea 124
Simpson, Capt. A. M. 297
Singapore Chamber of Commerce 120, 122
Singh, Maj. Bhall 126
Singh, Rajkumar Hari 204
Sinha, Sir S. P. 205
Sloley, Sir Herbert 174, 179, 181, 330
Sloley, Lt. Robert 330
Smuts, Gen. Jan Christiaan V, VIII, 74, 171, 175, 187, 195, 196, 197, 198, 199, 200, 275, 290, 291, 293, 298, 299, 319, 329
Sobhuza II 187
South African Native Labour Contingent (SANLC) XIV, 180, 181, 184, 197, 330
South African Native National Congress (SANNC) XIV, 175
Spitfire Fund 303
Sri II, Fia of Awuna-Ga 146
Stacey, Lt. John Randolph 212
Stamfordham, Lord 34, 36
Stone, Lt. Stanley Standford 30, 31, 69, 76, 79

Straits Chinese British Association (SCBA) XIV, 116, 122, 125
Straits Trading Co. (STC) XIV, 120
Strickland, Gerald 271
Stromberg, Mr. & Mrs. H. P. 318
Stutt, Chief Instructor 271, 272, 273
Sudlow, F. N. 219
Sukuna, Ratu Sir Lala 85
Sutherland, Ernest Taniwha 300
Sutherland, L. W. 264
Swettenham, Sir Frank 9, 10, 117, 132
Syed Abubaker, K. M. 126
Sykes, Lt. Col. Frederick 296, 298
Syrian Christians 306

T

Tafari, Ras (Haile Selassie) 234, 235, 236, 245
Tai Yan Bank VII, 36, 104, 105, 106, 107, 108
Tan Jiak Kim 125
Tan Kim Wah 124
Tan Wi Yan 124
Tanganyika Concessions (Tanks) 159
Thesiger, Mrs. Kathleen 235
Thesiger, Wilfred 232, 233, 234
Thesiger, Wilfred (jnr.) 234
Thibaw, King 207
Thompson, J. F. 92
Tobacco Fund 29, 30, 34, 47, 63, 98, 158
Tower, Reginald 256
Trenchard, Maj. Gen. Sir Hugh 26, 206, 287
Trinidad Aeroplane Fund 98
Tsingtao 109, 111, 112, 114, 202, 247

Turkey 72, 73, 123, 202-3, 205, 206, 232, 233, 234, 235, 264, 306, 308, 323

U

United Gold Fields Rhodesia Co. 160

V

Vajiravudh, King 237, 242, 243, 244, 245, 319
Valat, Father 183
Vermeiren, Rev. Father 25
Verne, Jules 21
Victoria, Princess 36
Victoria, Queen 56, 85, 89, 173, 185
Visuvalingam, K. 227
Viswa, A. W. 227
Voeux, Lady Hylda des VII, 36, 37, 62
Volta-Bani War 167

W

Waller, Cpl. 83
Wambolt, Harry 212
War Office XIV, 17, 18, 21, 23, 26, 30, 36, 43, 45, 47, 67, 85, 104, 105, 113, 118, 121, 128, 158, 163, 169, 181, 195, 202, 208, 212, 213, 222, 225, 227, 242, 246, 258, 265, 266, 274, 275, 276, 277, 278, 280, 308, 315, 336, 337, 338
War Stamp League 95

Ward, Sir Joseph VIII, 286, 288, 289, 301, 335
Warneford, Lt. Reginald 208, 209, 261
Washington, Booker T. 148
Watkins, Flt. Lt. 75
Weir, Sir William 99
Wells, H. G. 17, 21
West India Committee 23, 24, 97
Weston, John 182, 183, 195
Wigram, Clive 315
Wilson, Woodrow 243, 319
Wong Fong 119
Wood, W. A. R. 199, 237
Wrench, (John) Evelyn VII, 12, 13, 15, 29, 30, 34, 35, 36, 37, 38, 39, 40, 41, 63, 64, 66, 95, 104, 105, 112, 113, 121, 137, 139, 153, 158, 162, 195, 219, 232, 266, 302, 315, 320, 328, 333
 And Albert Earl Grey 56, 57–9, 61, 153
 And Lord Northcliffe 33, 55–6, 58, 60, 61–2, 63, 242
Wrench, Winifrede 61, 153
Wright, Orvil and Wilbur 33

Y

Young, Sir Arthur 7, 8, 125, 278
Yrigoyen, Hipólito 255

Z

Zanzibar African Rifles (ZAR) XIV, 75, 78, 79
Zeppelin, Count 36
Zewditu, Empress 234, 235, 236

ibidem.eu